The European Social Charter: A Commentary

The European Social Charter: A Commentary

By

The Academic Network on the European Social Charter and Social Rights

Volume 4

Part II (Articles 20–31)

Edited by

Catarina de Oliveira Carvalho, Catarina Santos Botelho and Ana Teresa Ribeiro

BRILL | NIJHOFF

LEIDEN | BOSTON

The Library of Congress Cataloging-in-Publication Data is available online at https://catalog.loc.gov
LC record available at https://lccn.loc.gov/2022018237

Typeface for the Latin, Greek, and Cyrillic scripts: "Brill". See and download: brill.com/brill-typeface.

ISSN 2949-7876
ISBN 978-90-04-43408-0 (hardback)
ISBN 978-90-04-43415-8 (e-book)
DOI 10.1163/9789004434158

This book is printed on acid-free paper and produced in a sustainable manner.

Contents

Preliminary Remarks and Acknowledgments

Dear Reader,

We are pleased to present the fourth volume of an eight-part Commentary on the European Social Charter, prepared by the Academic Network on the European Social Charter and Social Rights (ANESC or the Network).[1]

As Giovanni Guiglia, former ANESC/RACSE's general coordinator, wrote in his preliminary remarks on the first volume: "Our Network aims to promote the European Social Charter and the other legal instruments for the protection of social rights, in law, policy-making and academic studies, across different countries and their academics, in Europe. To this end, the ANESC develops activities in the fields of education, training, research, and pro-bono legal practice. The Network is composed of nearly 200 members from 14 European countries (Belgium, Cyprus, France, Greece, Hungary, Ireland, Italy, Poland, Portugal, Romania, Slovenia, Switzerland, Turkey, and the United Kingdom). These are mainly academics who work in different legal fields, including social, constitutional, international and labour law, as well as few judges, lawyers and human rights consultants".

A few years ago, the ANESC's governing bodies decided that the Network would start the drafting of the first-ever-published Commentary on the European Social Charter System, and this volume is the fourth output of this process. We believe that, together with the other seven volumes, "this Commentary can become a particularly important reference document to navigate European social standards and procedures vis-à-vis the many socio-economic challenges of our times, and a useful companion for academics and human rights practitioners".[2]

The Commentary, which follows the numbering of the Revised Charter, is structured as follows: Volume 1 (Cross-cutting themes – published in May 2022); Volume 2 (Preamble, Part I, Articles 1 to 10 – published in February 2023); Volume 3 (Articles 11 to 19 – published in January 2024); Volume 4 (Articles 20 to 31); Volume 5 (Part III, Art A and B, Part IV, Art C); Volume 6 (Part IV, art D – Collective complaints); Volume 7 (Part V – Art E, F, G, H, I, J, Part VI – Art K, L, M, N, O and introduction of the Appendix); Volume 8 (Rules of the European Committee of Social Rights).

1 The network website is available at: https://www.racse-anesc.org/en/.

2 "Preliminary Remarks & Acknowledgments", in ANESC, Stefano Angeleri, and Carole Nivard (eds.), The European Social Charter: A Commentary. Volume 1, Cross-cutting Themes, Brill, 2022, p. X.

The first volume was edited by Stefano Angeleri and Carole Nivard (with the collaboration of the Secretaries of the ANESC, Brigitte Napiwocka and Danuta Wisniewska-Cazals). The following volumes were edited or are currently being edited as follows: French section (Volume 2), Belgian and Irish sections (Volume 3), Portuguese section (volume 4), Turkish section (volume 5), Greek section (Volume 6), Romanian section (Volume 7) and the Italian section (volume 8).

We wish to congratulate the authors of this volume for their valuable research (Anastasia Poulou, Johan Peeters and Filip Dorssemont, Ana Teresa Ribeiro and Filipe Venade, Luísa Andias Gonçalves and Maria Paula de Ribeiro Faria, Bruno Mestre, Murat Engin, Kübra Doğan-Yenisey, Güçlü Akyürek, Canan Ünal Adınır, Deniz Ugan Çatalkaya, Giovanni Calvellini, Septimiu Panainte, Giuseppe Recchia, Carole Nivard, and Silvio Troilo), as well as our peer-reviewers (Anna-Maria Konsta, Carole Nivard, Catarina de Oliveira Carvalho, Catarina Santos Botelho, Christina Deliyanni-Dimitrakou, Cristina Samboan, Despina Kiltidou, Evelien Timbermont, Fabrizio Proietti, Filip Dorssemont, Guido Van Limberghen, Konstantina Chatzilaou, Kübra Doğan-Yenisey, Lorenza Mola, Mouloud Boumghar, Murat Engin, Sébastien Van Drooghenbroeck, and Stefano Angeleri). Finally, we acknowledge the precious contribution of Isabel Ferreira, our proof-reader.

Special mentions go to Carole Nivard, Stefano Angeleri, Giovanni Guiglia, Brigitte Napiwocka, and Danuta Wisniewska-Cazals for their help in the administrative and coordination work and the preparation of the editorial guidelines.

We hope you enjoy reading this volume and that this project will contribute to the dissemination of knowledge and interest in the European Social Charter and the jurisprudence of the European Committee on Social Rights.

Catarina de Oliveira Carvalho, Catarina Santos Botelho and Ana Teresa Ribeiro
Porto, February 2024

Abbreviations

ACHR	American Convention on Human Rights
BetrVG	Betriebsverfassungsgesetz
BVerfG	Bundesverfassungsgericht
BvR	Aktenzeichen einer Verfassungsbeschwerde zum Bundesverfassungsgericht
CDDH/SCHR	Steering Committee for Human Rights
CEACR	Committee of Experts on the Application of Conventions and Recommendations
CEDAW	Convention on the Elimination of all Forms of Discrimination against Women
CEEP	European Centre of Employers and Enterprises providing Public Services
CFREU	Charter of Fundamental Rights of the European Union
CJEU	Court of Justice of the European Union
CM	Committee of Ministers of the Council of Europe
CoE	Council of Europe
CRC	Convention on the Rights of the Child
CRPD	Convention on the Rights of Persons with Disabilities
dec.	Decision
ECHR	European Convention on Human Rights
ECJ	European Court of Justice
ECmHR	European Commission of Human Rights
ECSR	European Committee of Social Rights (and, prior to 1998, the Committee of Independent Experts)
ECtHR	European Court of Human Rights
EEC	European Economic Community
ESC (rev)	European Social Charter (Revised)
ESC	European Social Charter
ETUC	European Trade Union Confederation
EU	European Union
EUCFR	EU Charter of Fundamental Rights
EWC	European Works Council(s)
ff	Following (pages)
IACHR	Inter-American Convention for the Protection of the Human Rights of Older Persons
IACmHR	Inter-American Commission of Human Rights
IACtHR	Inter-American Court of Human Rights

ICCPR	International Covenant on Civil and Political Rights
ICESCR	International Covenant on Economic, Social and Cultural Rights
ICJ	International Court of Justice
ICRMW	International Convention on the Protection of the Rights of all Migrant Workers and Members of their Families
ILJ	Industrial Law Journal
ILO	International Labour Office (BIT in French) / International Labour Organization (OIT in French)
ILR	International Labour Review
(I)NGO(s)	(International) Non-Governmental Organization(s)
KSchG	Kündigungsschutzgesetz
NGO	Non-governmental organization
OAS	Organization of American States
OECD	Organisation for Economic Co-operation and Development
OJ	Official Journal
PCIJ	Permanent Court of International Justice
RDT	Revue de Droit du Travail
SE	Societas Europaea
TEU	Treaty on European Union
TFEU	Treaty on the Functioning of the European Union
UDHR	Universal Declaration of Human Rights
UEAPME	European Association of Craft and SMEs
UN	United Nations Organization
WHO	World Health Organization

Table of Cases

European Committee of Social Rights

ECSR, *Associazione nazionale sindacato professionisti sanitari della funzione infermieristica – Nursing Up c. Italie*, complaint No. 169/2018, decision on the merits of 19 October 2022.

ECSR, *ATTAC ry, Globaali sosiaalityö ry and Maan ystävät ry v. Finland*, complaint No. 163/2018, decision on admissibility and immediate measures of 22 January 2022.

ECSR, *Central Union for Child Welfare (CUCW) v. Finland*, complaint No. 139/2016, decision on the merits of 11 September 2019.

ECSR, *Centre on Housing Rights and Evictions (COHRE) v. France*, complaint No. 63/2010, decision on the merits of 28 June 2011.

ECSR, *Centre on Housing Rights and Evictions (COHRE) v. Italy*, complaint No. 58/2009, decision on the merits of 25 June 2010.

ECSR, *Confédération Française de l'Encadrement (CFE-CGC) v. France*, complaint No. 9/2000, decision on the merits of 16 November 2001.

ECSR, *Confédération Française de l'Encadrement (CFE-CGC) v. France*, complaint No. 16/2003, decision on the merits of 12 October 2004.

ECSR, *Confédération Française de l'Encadrement (CFE-CGC) v. France*, complaint No. 56/2009, decision on the merits of 23 June 2010.

ECSR, *Confédération Générale du Travail Force Ouvrière (CGT-FO) v. France*, complaint No. 171/2018, decision on the merits of 26 September 2022.

ECSR, *Confédération Générale du Travail Force Ouvrière* (CGT-FO) v. France, complaint No. 171/2018, decision on the merits of 23 March 2022.

ECSR, *Confederazione Generale Italiana del Lavoro (CGIL) v. Italy*, complaint No. 158/2017, decision on the merits of 11 September 2019.

ECSR, *Confederazione Generale Italiana del Lavoro (CGIL) v. Italy*, complaint No. 158/2017, decision on the merits of 11 September 2019.

ECSR, *Confederazione Generale Sindacale (CGS) & Federazione Lavoratori Pubblici e Funzioni Pubbliche (FLP) v. Italy*, complaint No. 161/2018, decision on the merits of 19 October 2022.

ECSR, *Conference of European Churches (CEC) v. the Netherlands*, complaint No. 90/2013, decision on the merits of 1 July 2014.

ECSR, *Defence for Children International (DCI) and Others v. Spain*, complaint No. 206/2022, decision on admissibility and immediate measures of 19 October 2022.

ECSR, *Defence for Children International* (*DCI*) *v. Belgium*, complaint No. 69/2011, decision on the merits of 23 October 2012.

ECSR, *Defence for Children International* (*DCI*) *v. the Netherlands*, complaint No. 47/2008, decision on the merits of 20 October 2009.

ECSR, *European Committee for Home-Based Priority Action for the Child and the Family* (*EUROCEF*) *v. France*, complaint No. 82/2012, decision on admissibility and the merits of 19 March 2013.

ECSR, *European Committee for Home-Based Priority Action for the Child and the Family* (*EUROCEF*) *v. France*, complaint No. 114/2015, decision on the merits of 24 January 2018.

ECSR, *European Confederation of Police (EuroCOP) v. Ireland*, collective complaint No. 83/2012, decision on admissibility and the merits of 2 December 2013.

ECSR, *European Council of Police Trade Unions* (*CESP*) *v. Portugal*, collective complaint No. 40/2007, decision on admissibility of 21 May 2007.

ECSR, *European Council of Police Trade Unions* (*CESP*) *v. Portugal*, collective complaint No. 60/2010, decision on the merits of 17 October 2011.

ECSR, *European Federation of National Organisations working with the Homeless* (*FEANTSA*) *v. the Netherlands*, complaint No. 86/2012, decision on the merits of 2 July 2014.

ECSR, *European Federation of National Organisations Working with the Homeless* (*FEANTSA*) *v. France*, complaint No. 39/2006, decision on the merits of 7 December 2007.

ECSR, *European Federation of National Organisations Working with the Homeless* (*FEANTSA*) *v. Slovenia*, complaint No. 53/2008, decision on the merits of 8 September 2009.

ECSR, *European Roma and Travellers Forum* (*ERTF*) *v. France*, complaint No. 64/2011, decision on the merits of 24 January 2012.

ECSR, *European Roma Rights Centre* (*ERRC*) *v. Belgium*, complaint No. 195/2020, decision on admissibility and immediate measures of 29 June 2021.

ECSR, *European Roma Rights Centre* (*ERRC*) *v. Bulgaria*, complaint No. 31/2005, decision on the merits of 18 October 2006.

ECSR, *European Roma Rights Centre* (*ERRC*) *v. France*, complaint No. 51/2008, decision on the merits of 19 October 2009.

ECSR, *European Roma Rights Centre* (*ERRC*) *v. Greece*, complaint No. 15/2003, decision on the merits of 8 December 2004.

ECSR, *European Roma Rights Centre* (*ERRC*) *v. Ireland*, complaint No. 100/2013, decision on the merits of 1 December 2015.

ECSR, *European Roma Rights Centre* (*ERRC*) *v. Italy*, complaint No. 27/2004, decision on the merits of 7 December 2005.

ECSR, *European Roma Rights Centre (ERRC) v. Portugal*, complaint No. 61/2010, decision on the merits of 30 June 2011.

ECSR, *Federation of employed pensioners of Greece (IKA-ETAM) v. Greece*, complaint No. 76/2012, decision on the merits of 7 December 2012.

ECSR, *Finnish Society of Social Rights v. Finland*, complaint No. 106/2014, decision on admissibility and merits of 8 September 2016.

ECSR, *Frente Comum de Sindicatos de Administração Pública v. Portugal*, complaint No. 36/2006, decision on admissibility of 5 December 2006.

ECSR, *GENOP-DEI and ADEDY v. Greece*, complaint No. 65/2011, decision on the merits of 23 May 2012.

ECSR, *Greek General Confederation of Labour (GSEE) v. Greece*, complaint No. 111/2014, decision on the merits of 23 March 2017.

ECSR, *International Association Autism-Europe v. France*, complaint No. 13/2002, decision on the merits of 4 November 2003.

ECSR, *International Centre for the Legal Protection of Human Rights (INTERIGHTS) v. Greece*, complaint No. 49/2008, decision on the merits of 11 December 2009.

ECSR, *International Commission of Jurists (ICJ) and European Council for Refugees and Exiles (ECRE) v. Greece*, complaint No. 173/2018, decision on the merits of 26 January 2021.

ECSR, *International Commission of Jurists v. Portugal*, complaint No. 1/1999, decision on the merits of 9 September 1999.

ECSR, *International Federation for Human Rights (FIDH) v. Ireland*, complaint No. 110/2014, decision on the merits of 12 May 2017.

ECSR, *International Federation of associations of the Elderly (FIAPA) v. France*, complaint No. 145/2017, decision on the merits of 22 May 2019.

ECSR, *International Federation of associations of the Elderly (FIAPA) v. France*, complaint No. 162/2018, decision on the merits of 16 October 2018.

ECSR, *International Federation of Human Rights (FIDH) v. Belgium*, complaint No. 62/2010, decision on the merits of 21 March 2010.

ECSR, *International Federation of Human Rights (FIDH) v. Belgium*, complaint No. 75/2011, decision on the merits of 18 March 2013.

ECSR, International Federation of Human Rights (FIDH) v. France, complaint No. 14/2003, decision on the merits of 8 September 2004.

ECSR, *International Federation of Human Rights Leagues v. Ireland*, complaint No. 42/2007, decision on the merits of 3 June 2008.

ECSR, *International Movement ATD Fourth World v. France*, complaint No. 33/2006, decision on the merits of 5 December 2007.

ECSR, *Médecins du Monde – International v. France*, complaint No. 67/2011, decision on the merits of 11 September 2012.

ECSR, *Syndicat CFDT de la métallurgie de la Meuse v. France*, complaint No. 182/2019, decision on the merits of 19 October 2022.

ECSR, *Syndicat CFDT général des transports et de l'environnement de l'Aube v. France*, complaint No. 181/2019, decision on the merits of 19 October 2022.

ECSR, *Syndicat CGT FORD Blanquefort v. France*, complaint No. 184/2019, decision on admissibility of 13 May 2020.

ECSR, *Syndicat CGT YTO France v. France*, complaint No. 183/2019, decision on admissibility of 13 May 2020.

ECSR, *Syndicat de défense des fonctionnaires v. France*, complaint No. 73/2011, decision on the merits of 12 September 2012.

ECSR, *Syndicat national des Professions du tourisme v. France*, complaint No. 6/1999, decision on the merits of 10 October 2010.

ECSR, *The Central Association of Carers in Finland v. Finland*, complaint No. 70/2011, decision on the merits of 4 December 2012.

ECSR, *The Central Association of Carers in Finland v. Finland*, complaint No. 71/2011, decision on the merits of 4 December 2012.

ECSR, *Travail Affaires Sociales v. France*, complaint No. 24/2004, decision on the merits of 8 November 2005.

ECSR, *University Women of Europe (UWE) v. Belgium*, complaint No. 124/2016, decision on the merits of 6 December 2019.

ECSR, *UWE v. Belgium*, complaint No. 124/2016, decision on the merits of 6 December 2019.

ECSR, *UWE v. Bulgaria*, complaint No. 125/2016, decision on the merits of 6 December 2019.

ECSR, *UWE v. Croatia*, complaint No. 126/2016, decision on the merits of 5 December 2019.

ECSR, *UWE v. Cyprus*, complaint No. 127/2016, decision on the merits of 5 December 2019.

ECSR, *UWE v. Czech Republic*, complaint No. 128/2016, decision on the merits of 5 December 2019.

ECSR, *UWE v. Finland*, complaint No. 129/2016, decision on the merits of 5 December 2019.

ECSR, *UWE v. France*, complaint No. 130/2016, decision on the merits of 5 December 2019.

ECSR, *UWE v. Greece*, complaint No. 131/2016, decision on the merits of 5 December 2019.

ECSR, *UWE v. Ireland*, complaint No. 132/2016, decision on the merits of 5 December 2019.

ECSR, *UWE v. Italy*, complaint No. 133/2016, decision on the merits of 6 December 2019.

ECSR, *UWE v. Netherlands*, complaint No. 134/2016, decision on the merits of 6 December 2019.
ECSR, *UWE v. Norway*, complaint No. 135/2016, decision on the merits of 5 December 2019.
ECSR, *UWE v. Portugal*, complaint No. 136/2016, decision on the merits of 5 December 2019.
ECSR, *UWE v. Slovenia*, complaint No. 137/2016, decision on the merits of 5 December 2019.
ECSR, *UWE v. Sweden*, complaint No. 138/2016, decision on the merits of 6 December 2019.

European Court of Human Rights

ECtHR, 23 July 1968, *Case relating to certain aspects of the laws on the use of languages in education in Belgium v. Belgium*, Nos. 1474/62, 1677/62; 1691/62; 1769/63; 1994/63; 2126/64.
ECtHR, 13 June 1979, *Marckx v. Belgium*, No. 6833/74.
ECtHR, 28 November 1984, *Rassmunen v. Denmark*, No. 8777/79.
ECtHR, 29 May 1986, *Deumeland v. Germany*, No. 9384/81.
ECtHR, 9 December 1994, *López Ostra v. Spain*, No. 16798/90.
ECtHR, 2 September 1996, *Vogt vs. Germany*, No. 17851/91.
ECtHR, 16 September 1996, *Gaygusuz v. Austria*, No. 17371/90.
ECtHR, 29 September 1996, *Buckley v. the United Kingdom*, No. 20348/92.
ECtHR, 25 June 1997, *Halford v. UK*, No. 20605/92.
ECtHR, 19 February 1998, *Guerra and others v. Italy*, No. 14967/89.
ECtHR, 24 February 1998, *Botta v. Italy*, No. 36448/97.
ECtHR, 27 March 1998, *Petrovic v. Austria*, No. 2458/92.
ECtHR, 4 May 1999, *Marzari v. Italy*, No. 36448/97.
ECtHR, 6 April 2000, *Thlimmenos v. Greece*, No. 34369/97.
ECtHR, 13 May 2000, *Maggiolini v. Italy*, No. 35800/97.
ECtHR, 25 July 2000, *Lustig-Prean and Beckett v. United Kingdom*, Nos. 31417/96 and 32377/96.
ECtHR, 18 Jan 2001, *Chapman v. the United Kingdom*, No. 27238/95.
ECtHR, 27 March 2001, *Sutherland v. United Kingdom*, No. 25186/94.
ECtHR, 21 June 2001, *Sanchez Navajas v. Spain*, No. 57442/00.
ECtHR, 29 April 2002, *Pretty v. United Kingdom*, No. 2346/02.
ECtHR, 2 July 2002, *Wilson, National Union of Journalists and others v. The United Kingdom*, Nos. 30668/96, 30671/96 and 30678/96.
ECtHR, 7 November 2002 [dec.], *Madsen v. Denmark*, No. 58341/00.

ECtHR, 13 December 2002, *Florindo de Almeida Vasconcelos Gramaxo v. Portugal*, No. 26968/16.
ECtHR, 27 August 2004, *Connors v. the United Kingdom*, No. 66746/01.
ECtHR, 10 November 2004, *Surugiu v. Romania*, No. 48995/99.
ECtHR, 16 February 2005, *Moreno Gomez v. Spain*, No. 4143/02.
ECtHR, 30 November 2005, *Fadeyeva v. Russia*, No. 55723/00.
ECtHR, 7 February 2006, *Codona v. the United Kingdom*, No. 485/05.
ECtHR, 3 April 2007, *Copland v. the United Kingdom*, No. 62617/00.
ECtHR, 16 September 2008 7 novem,ber *Laurence Pay v. the United Kingdom*, No. 32792/05.
ECtHR, 31 March 2009, *Weller v. Hungary*, No. 44399/2005.
ECtHR, 21 April 2009, *Enerji Yapi-Yol Sen v. Turkey*, No. 68959/01.
ECtHR, 30 July 2009, *Danilenkov and others v. Russia*, No. 67336/01.
ECtHR, 23 September 2010, *Schüth v. Germany*, No. 1620/03.
ECtHR, 5 October 2010 [dec.], *Köpke v. Germany*, No. 40/07.
ECtHR, 10 October 2010, *Özpınar v. Turkey*, No. 20999/04.
ECtHR, 27 September 2011, *Şişman and others v. Turkey*, No. 1305/05.
ECtHR, 6 October 2011, *Vellutini and Michel v. France*, No. 32820/09.
ECtHR, 27 December 2011, *Bah v. the United Kingdom*, No. 56328/07.
ECtHR, 22 March 2012, *Markin v. Russia*, No. 30078/06.
ECtHR, 24 April 2012, *Jordanova and Others v. Bulgaria*, No. 25446/06.
ECtHR 25 September 2012, *Trade Union of the Police in the Slovak Republic and others v. Slovakia*, No. 11828/08.
ECtHR, 9 October 2012, *Szima v. Hungary*, No. 29723/11.
ECtHR, 27 April 2013, *Oleksandr Volkov v. Ukraine*, No. 21722/11.
ECtHR, 3 October 2013, *I.B v. Greece*, No. 552/10.
ECtHR, 17 October 2013, *Winterstein and Others v. France*, No. 27013/07.
ECtHR, 12 June 2014, *Fernández Martinez v. Spain*, No. 56030/07.
ECtHR, 2 December 2014, *Emel Boyraz v. Turkey*, No. 61960/08.
ECtHR, 2 February 2016, *Di Trizio v. Switzerland*, No. 7186/09.
ECtHR, 4 April 2017, *Tek Gıda İş Sendikası v. Turkey*, No. 35009/05.
ECtHR, 5 September 2017, *Bărbulescu v. Romania*, No. 61496/08.
ECtHR, 6 November 2017, *Garib v. the Netherlands*, No. 43494/09.
ECtHR, 25 September 2018, *Denisov v. Ukraine*, No. 76639/11.
ECtHR, 7 September 2020, *Hudorovič and Others v. Slovenia*, Nos. 24816/14 and 25140/14.
ECtHR, 6 July 2021, *Gruba and Others v. Russia*, Nos. 66180/09, 30771/11, 50089/11 and 22165/12.
ECtHR, 31 March 2022, *Faulkner v. Ireland and McDonagh v. Ireland*, Nos. 30391/18 and 30416/18.

Court of Justice of the European Union

CJEU, 8 April 1976, *Defrenne*, C-43/75.

CJEU, 13 May 1986, *Bilka-Kaufhaus GmbH v. Weber von Hartz*, C-170/84.

CJEU, 17 January 1996, *Rockfon A/S v. Specialarbejderforbundet I Danmark*, C-449/1993.

CJEU, 17 September 2002, *AG Lawrence v. Regent Office Care Ltd*, C-320/00.

CJEU, 13 January 2004, *Debra Allonby v. Rossendale College and Others*, C-256/01.

CJEU, 12 October 2004, *Commission v. Portugal*, C-55/02.

CJEU, 27 January 2005, *Irmtraud Junk v. Wolfgang Kühnel*, C-188/03.

CJEU, 5 January 2007, *Carol Marilyn Robins and Others v. Secretary of State for Work and Pensions*, C-278/05.

CJEU, 16 July 2009, *Mono Car Styling SA v. Dervis Odemis and Others*, C-12/08.

CJEU, 10 September 2009, *Akavan Erityisalojen Keskusliitto AEK ry and Others v. Fujitsu Siemens Computers Oy*, C-44/08.

CJEU, 10 December 2009, *Ovido Rodríguez Mayor and Others v. Herencia yacente de Rafael de las Heras Dávila and Others*, C-323/08.

CJEU, 24 April 2012, *Kamberaj v. Istituto per l'Edilizia Sociale della Provincia autonoma di Bolzano (IPES) and Others*, C-571/10.

CJEU, 18 April 2013, *Meliha Veli Mustafa v. Direktor na fond 'Garantirani vzemania na rabotnitsite i sluzhitelite' kam Natsionalnia osiguritelen institute*, C-247/12.

CJEU, 25 April 2013, *Thomas Hogan and Others v. Minister for Social and Family Affairs*, C-398/11.

CJEU, 15 January 2014, *Association de médiation sociale v. Union locale des syndicats CGI and others*, C-176/12.

CJEU, 13 February 2014, *Commission v. Italy*, C-596/12.

CJEU, 10 September 2014, *Monika Kušionová v. SMART Capital a.s.*, C-34/13.

CJEU, 30 April 2015, *USDAW and another v. WW Realisation 1 Ltd.*, C-80/14.

CJEU, 13 May 2015, *Cañas v. Nexea Gestión Documental SA and another*, C-392/13.

CJEU, 16 July 2015, *Maïstrellis v. Ypourgos Dikaiosynis, Diafaneias kai Anthropinon Dikaiomaton*, C-222/14.

CJEU, 11 November 2015, *Christian Pujante Rivera v. Gestora Clubs Dir SL and Fondo de Garantía Salarial*, C-422/14.

CJEU, 24 November 2016, *Webb-Sämann v. Christopher Seagon*, C-454/15.

CJEU, 21 December 2016, *AGET Iraklis*, C-201/15.

CJEU, 21 September 2017, *Małgorzata Ciupa and Others v. II Szpital Miejski im. L. Rydygiera w Łodzi obecnie Szpital Ginekologiczno-Położniczy im dr L. Rydygiera Sp. z o.o. w Łodzi*, C-429/16.

CJEU, 6 September 2018, *Greenville Hampshire v. The Board of the Pension Protection Fund*, C-17/17.

CJEU, 19 December 2019, *Pensions-Sicherungs-Verein VvaG v. Günther Bauer*, C-168/18.

CJEU, 4 June 2020, *Tj v. Srl Balga*, C-32/20.

CJEU, 10 June 2021, *Land Oberösterreich v. KV*, C-94/20.

Notes on Contributors

Canan Ünal Adınır
has a PhD in Labour and Social Security Law, and is an Associate Professor at Marmara University, Faculty of Law. She is a Member of the Academic Network on European Social Charter and Social Rights (ANESC), Member of the İstanbul Bar Association, and Member of the Turkish Labour and Social Security Law Association. She is a Mediator. She is the author of several books in Labour and Social Security Law, namely "Managing Executives in the Employment Law", "Age Discrimination in the Employment Law", and "Social Security Rights of the People with Disabilities and Suggestions in the Light of the New Approaches in the World", as well as the author of several articles in Labour and Social Security Law, such as "Can Employees Be Entitled to Discrimination Compensation in Case of the Breach of Equal Treatment in the Narrow Sense? (Decision Review)", *Sicil*, Vol. 2, No. 46, pp. 127–136; "Determination of the Objective Reason Condition in the Conclusion and Renewal of Fixed Term Employment Contracts", *İstanbul Hukuk Mecmuası*, Vol. 79, No. 3, pp. 797–835; and "The Effects of Covid-19 Vaccines on the Employment Relationships", *Marmara Üniversitesi Hukuk Fakültesi Hukuk Araştırmaları Dergisi*, Vol. 27, No. 1, pp. 693–715. Email: canan.unal@marmara.edu.tr.

Güçlü Akyürek
has a PhD in Criminal Law and is an Associate Professor at MEF University Faculty of Law. He is a Member of the Academic Network on European Social Charter and Social Rights (ANESC), Member of the İstanbul Bar Association, and Member of Turkish Penal Law Association. He is the author of several books in Criminal and Criminal Procedure Law, namely "Offence of violation of privacy", "Retrial", and "Criminal Labour Law: General Principles", and of several articles in Criminal and Criminal Procedure Law, such as "Crime of mobbing in the light of France Telecom Case", *Galatasaray University Law Faculty Review*, 2022/1, pp. 97–122; "Extraordinary African Chambers and the Case of Habré", *İnönü University Law Review*, Vol. 9, No. 2, 2018, pp. 415–440; and "The principle of legality in the consideration of ECHR's İmret-Turkey (2) Case", *Suç ve Ceza Review*, 2018/3, pp. 1–16. Email: akyurekg@mef.edu.tr.

Giovanni Calvellini
is a Researcher in Labour Law at the Department of Law of the University of Siena (Italy) and has been licenced for the function of Associate Professor in the same subject (Ph.D). His research interests include European social law,

work-life balance, working time, and anti-discrimination law. He has widely published in these areas, including the essay "Insufficienze e potenzialità della Carta sociale europea in tempo di crisi", *Diritti lavori mercati*, No. 1, 2018, pp. 89 ff., and the monograph *La funzione del* part-time*: tempi della persona e vincoli di sistema*, Napoli, ESI, 2020. Email: giovanni.calvellini@unisi.it.

Deniz Ugan Çatalkaya
has a PhD in Labour Law and Social Security Law, and is an Assistant Professor at Kadir Has University, Faculty of Law. She is a member of the Academic Network on European Social Charter and Social Rights (ANESC), and Member of the Turkish Labour and Social Security Law Association. She is the author of a book, namely "İş Hukukunda Ölçülülük İlkesi" (Principle of Proportionality in Labour Law), and of several articles on Labour Law and Social Security Law, such as "Droits et libertés fondamentaux du citoyen-salarié en droit du travail", *Annales de la Faculté de Droit d'Istanbul*, 71, 2022, pp. 221–263; "Demokratik ve Barışçıl Toplu Eylem Hakkının Kullanılması İş Sözleşmesini Fesih Nedeni Olabilir mi Sorusuna Yanıt Arayışı: Yargıtayın Zorlu Görevi" (Quest for an answer to the question of whether the democratic right to peaceful collective action can be a reason for termination of the employment contract: Court of Cassation's challenge), *Çalışma ve Toplum*, 78, 2023, pp. 2069–2120; "Labour relations under the influence of the globalization: Insights from Turkish collective labour law", in Adalberto Perulli (a cura di), *L'idea di diritto del lavoro, oggi, In ricordo di Giorgio Ghezzi*, Wolters Kluwer CEDAM, 2016, pp. 455–465. Email: deniz.ugan@khas.edu.tr.

Kübra Doğan-Yenisey
is a Professor of Labour Law and Social Security Law at İstanbul Bilgi University and the General Secretary of the Turkish Association of Labour and Social Security Law. Having graduated from the Faculty of Law, Ankara University, she received her doctorate degree from the University of Geneva. Her main interests are contract of employment, technology and its impacts on labour law, the principle of equality and gender discrimination, harmonization of Turkish law with *acquis communautaire*, collective labour rights, and migrant workers. She has authored and edited several books and numerous articles on individual and collective labour law. She is the founder director of the Comparative Labour and Social Security Law Research Centre at İstanbul Bilgi University. E-mail: kubra.dogan@bilgi.edu.tr.

Filip Dorssemont
is a full professor of Labour Law at the Faculty of Law of the Université Catholique de Louvain (in Louvain-La-Neuve). He is the President of the School of Labour Sciences (Uclouvain). He has been elected Co-President of the Association belge de droit du travail et de la sécurité sociale (2020–2023), after serving as President of this association (2014–2016). He is a member of the Transnational Trade Union Rights Expert Network (European Trade Union Institute). Dorssemont has read law (Antwerp University, Master in Law 1993), studied philosophy (bachelor Antwerp University 1990, and completed Complementary Studies in Philosophy at the Higher Institute of Philosophy, Leuven University, 1994). In 2001 he defended a PhD thesis in Law at Antwerp University. This research in the field of comparative labour law (B, NL, Fr, Germany) dealt with the legal status of trade unions in relation to the right to organize. He is also a Master Student in History of Art (UCLouvain). He was invited as guest lecturer in Strasbourg, Bordeaux, Università Statale di Milano, ULB, VUB, Université Saint-Louis de Bruxelles. Between 2002 and 2008, he worked as researcher and lecturer at Utrecht University. Email: filip.dorssemont@uclouvain.be.

Maria Paula Ribeiro de Faria
is an Associate Professor in Criminal Law at Porto Faculty of Law, Universidade Católica Portuguesa (currently teaching Criminal Law, Negligent Crimes and Omission (Undergraduate Programmes), Medical Law and Compensation and Crime (Master Programmes), and Crimes against the Elderly (PhD Programmes and Master's Programmes). She obtained her degree in Law from Universidade Católica Portuguesa, Master's in Criminal Law from the Faculty of Law of the University of Coimbra, and her Ph.D. in Criminal Law by the same Faculty of Law. She is a researcher at the Católica Research Centre for the Future of Law (CRCFL). Associate Professor with Aggregation since February of 2023. She is the author of *Os Crimes praticados contra idosos*, Porto, Edições Universidade Católica, 2019, 3ª ed., and "A proteção social das pessoas idosas na Carta Social Europeia Revista, no Código Europeu da Segurança Social e no Direito português", *Revista de los Derechos Sociales, Lex Social Monográfico,* No. 1, 2017, pp. 303 ff. Email: mfaria@ucp.pt.

Luísa Andias Gonçalves
is an Assistant Professor at the Faculty of Law of the University of Coimbra. She obtained her Degree in Law from the Faculty of Law of the University of Coimbra, her Master's in Legal and Business Sciences from the same institution, and her PhD in Labour and Social Labour from the Faculty of Law of the

University of Salamanca. She is the author of "A redução do valor das pensões à luz do artigo 1.º, do Protocolo n.º 1, da Convenção Europeia dos Direitos do Homem", *Lex Social*, vol. 7, 2017, pp. 141–156, and "Reflexões em torno da reforma das prestações sociais – das pensões em especial", in *Por Onde Vai o Estado Social em Portugal?*, Vida Económica, 2014, pp. 189–214. Email: luisa.andias@fd.uc.pt.

Bruno Mestre
is a Judge in the Portuguese Courts. He has a Degree in Law by the Porto Faculty of Law, Universidade Católica Portuguesa, a Master of Research, and a PhD in European and Comparative Labour Law by the European University Institute, Florence. He is a Member of ANESC (Academic Network on European Social Charter and Social Rights), APODIT (Portuguese Labour Law Association), and the author of several articles, book chapters and a book; he collaborates actively with Universities and the Portuguese School of Magistrates (CEJ) in several training sessions in Labour Law. Email: brunomestre@gmail.com.

Carole Nivard
is a Senior Lecturer in Public Law at Rouen University. As a member of the Centre Universitaire Rouennais d'Etudes juridiques CUREJ (EA 4703), she dedicates her research to the guarantee of fundamental social rights in national, European, and international law. She is the author of the book *La justiciabilité des droits sociaux. Etude de droit conventionnel européen*, published by Bruylant Editors in 2012. As a member of ANESC, she coordinates the French section, co-edited Volume I of the Commentary on the European Social Charter with Stefano Angeleri, and edited Volume II. Email: carole.nivard@univ-rouen.fr.

Septimiu Panainte
is the Director of the Department of Private Law and former Dean of the Law Faculty of Alexandru Ioan Cuza University, Iași, Romania, Associate Professor of Labour Law and Social Security Law, trainer and member of the Scientific Council of National Institute of Magistracy (Romania), and a lawyer. He is the author of *Individual Labour Law. University Course*, 2nd Edition, Bucharest, Hamangiu Publishing, 2021; *European Labour Law: Main Directives, CJEU jurisprudence, compliance of national legislation*, Bucharest, Hamangiu Publishing, 2017; *School of Organic Law*, Vol. I, Iaşi, Junimea Publishing, 2007; Vol. II, Bucharest, Hamangiu Publishing, 2019 (coord.); *Employment Contract – Jurisprudence*, Bucharest, Hamangiu Publishing, 2006. Email: septimiupanainte@yahoo.com.

Johan Peeters
obtained his PhD from UAntwerp in 2008 with a dissertation on employees' rights to information and consultation in case of company restructuring. He is currently a judge at the Antwerp Labour Court. In addition, he is a part-time senior lecturer at Hasselt University and a member of the editorial board of several Belgian legal journals (e.g. 'Rechtskundig Weekblad', 'Tijdschrift voor Sociaal Recht', 'ArbeidsrechtJournaal'). He has also been the secretary and treasurer of the Antwerp-based Employment Law Association since 2001. Before joining the judiciary, Johan Peeters was a lawyer at the bar for over 11 years, a job he combined with teaching assignments at, among others, the University of Antwerp, the University of Liège and the Free University of Brussels. Email: johan.peeters@uhasselt.be.

Anastasia Poulou
is currently a Judge at the Administrative Court of First Instance of Athens, Greece. Prior to this, she was a Senior Research Fellow at the Max Planck Institute for Social Law and Social Policy in Munich and a Max Weber Postdoctoral Fellow at the European University Institute in Florence. She conducted her undergraduate studies at the Aristotle University of Thessaloniki and at the Free University of Berlin, graduating with honours in 2011. She earned her PhD in Law from the University of Heidelberg in 2015. Her dissertation, titled 'Financial assistance conditionality and social rights: revisiting social rights protection in the EU in times of crisis', received the second prize in the humanities category of the German Thesis Award 2016. She also has a Master's in International Human Rights Law from the University of Oxford. Her research interests lie in the fields of European constitutional law and human rights. She is the author of a book on the Eurozone crisis and more specifically on the impact of financial assistance conditionality on social rights protection in the EU (Mohr Siebeck) and co-editor of a book on the European Welfare State Constitutions after the Financial Crisis (Oxford University Press). Email: anastasia.g.poulou@gmail.com.

Giuseppe Antonio Recchia
is an Associate Professor of Labour Law at the Department of Political Sciences of the University of Bari Aldo Moro. His main research areas are trade union law and industrial relations, anti-discrimination law, business transformation and employment relationship, and gig economy. He has widely published in this area, including the book *Studio sulla giustiziabilità degli interessi collettivi dei lavoratori* [*Study on the enforceability of workers' collective interests*], Bari, Cacucci, 2008, and has participated in national and international projects, the

most recent of which is the Italian Ministry of University and Research funded PRIN2020 on "Wage, Law and Collective Bargaining, in Italy and European Union" (2022–2024). Email: giuseppe.recchia@uniba.it.

Ana Teresa Ribeiro
is an Assistant Professor at the Porto Faculty of Law, Universidade Católica Portuguesa (PhD, Universidade Católica Portuguesa – Faculty of Law, 2020) and is affiliated with Católica Research Centre for the Future of Law. Her focus is on Labour Law, particularly collective bargaining and trade unionism. She has several articles on these issues and has participated in numerous conferences with interventions devoted to these matters. She is also a member of ANESC/RACSE and of the Transnational Trade Union Rights Expert Network (European Trade Union Institute). Email: aribeiro@ucp.pt.

Filipe Venade de Sousa
is an Invited Professor at the Faculty of Law, Lisbon School, Universidade Católica Portuguesa, and at the School of Education of the Polytechnic University of Porto (PhD, School of Law, University of Minho, 2018). He is a collaborating researcher at the Centre for Research in Justice and Governance of the School of Law of the University of Minho. His focus is on International Human Rights Law, particularly on the rights of persons with disabilities and language rights. He has several publications on these issues and has participated in numerous conferences with interventions dedicated to these matters. He is also a member of ANESC/RACSE. Email: filipe.sousa1@sapo.pt.

Silvio Troilo
is a Full Professor of Public Law at the Department of Law of the University of Bergamo (Italy). After graduating in Law, *cum laude*, from the University of Pavia, he was a Researcher at the University of Verona, then an Associate Professor and now a Full Professor at the University of Bergamo. Between 1997 and 2001 he was called upon to carry out research and consultancy at the Italian Constitutional Court – as an assistant to Vice-President Fernando Santosuosso – supporting the analysis of cases submitted to the Court. He is a member of the editorial board of scientific journals and of national and foreign research teams, as well as of various scientific societies, including the Academic Network on the European Social Charter and Social Rights, of which he is co-coordinator of the Italian section. He is the author of more than one hundred essays, both in the form of articles and of monographs, on issues relating to the functioning of governments, institutional reforms, regional

and local administration, the "constitutionalization" of the European Union, and fundamental rights and duties. His publications include, namely: the first Italian public law monograph on the right to education of pupils with disabilities: *Tutti per uno o uno contro tutti? Il diritto all'istruzione e all'integrazione scolastica dei disabili nella crisi dello Stato sociale*, Milano, Giuffrè, 2012, pp. 1–460; the first public law monographic essay on the right to a name in one's mother tongue of members of linguistic minorities: "Il diritto al nome nella propria madrelingua dei membri delle minoranze linguistiche", in Paolo Bonetti (ed.), *L'uso della lingua negli atti e nella comunicazione dei poteri pubblici italiani*, Torino, Giappichelli, 2016, pp. 277–403; and an examination of the principle of the rule of law in the European Union and its enforcement in Poland and Hungary: "La tutela dello Stato di diritto nell'Unione Europea post Covid-19", *Forum di Quaderni costituzionali – Rassegna*, Vol. 12, No. 4, 2021, pp. 74–93. Email: silvio.troilo@unibg.it.

ARTICLE 20

The Right to Equal Opportunities and Equal Treatment in Matters of Employment and Occupation without Discrimination on the Grounds of Sex

Anastasia Poulou

With a view to ensuring the effective exercise of the right to equal opportunities and equal treatment in matters of employment and occupation without discrimination on the grounds of sex, the Parties undertake to recognise that right and to take appropriate measures to ensure or promote its application in the following fields:

- a access to employment, protection against dismissal and occupational reintegration;
- b vocational guidance, training, retraining and rehabilitation;
- c terms of employment and working conditions, including remuneration;
- d career development, including promotion.

Introduction

The equal treatment between men and women in matters of employment was not included in the 1961 ESC as a distinct human rights principle. Yet, Article 1 § 2 of the 1961 ESC, which recognized the right to freely choose an occupation, prohibited discrimination on any grounds. Besides the inclusion of gender in the non-discrimination clause of the Preamble, the only explicit reference to gender equality was the obligation of states to recognize the right of men and women to equal pay for work of equal value under Article 4 § 3. The application of the principle of equal pay to for "work of equal value" reflected the guidance of the ILO Convention No. 100 on Equal Renumeration (1951). Moreover, this approach to equality was similar to the legal framework of the European Community of the time, which, while not including a general rule on gender equality, did recognize the principle of equal pay for male and

 | DOI:10.1163/9789004434158_002

female workers for work of equal value under Article 119 of the EEC Treaty (now Article 157 TFEU).

The right to equal opportunities and equal treatment in matters of employment and occupation without discrimination on the grounds of sex was originally added to the Charter by Article 1 § 1 of the first Additional Protocol to the ESC of 1988.[1] This provision was followed by three more paragraphs that aimed at defining the scope of the right to equal opportunities introduced. More precisely, Article 1 § 2 of the Additional Protocol stipulated that provisions concerning the protection of women, particularly as regards pregnancy, confinement and the post-natal period, shall not be deemed to be discriminatory, while § 3 underlined that the right to equal treatment shall not prevent the adoption of specific measures aimed at removing inequalities *de facto*. Moreover, Article 1 § 4 of the Additional Protocol specified that occupational activities which, by reason of their nature or the context in which they are carried out, can be entrusted only to persons of a particular sex may be excluded from the scope of this article or some of its provisions. According to the Appendix to the Additional Protocol, which forms an integral part of the Protocol,[2] Article 1 § 4 is not to be interpreted as requiring States Parties to embody in laws or regulations a list of occupations which, by reason of their nature or the context in which they are carried out, may be reserved to persons of a particular sex.[3] Furthermore, the Appendix to the Additional Protocol provides that social security matters, as well as other provisions relating to unemployment benefit, old age benefit and survivor's benefit, may be excluded from the scope of this article.

Overall, Article 1 of the first Additional Protocol to the ESC of 1988 was the outcome of a compromise. More precisely, the Member States of the Council of Europe proclaimed in the Declaration of Human Rights of 27 April 1978 their decision to explore "the possibility of extending the lists of rights of the individual, notably rights in the social, economic and cultural field", and to consider, whether there are any rights which might be suitable for inclusion in the ECHR.[4] Nevertheless, the realization of this declaration was influenced by

1 Council of Europe (1988), Additional Protocol to the European Social Charter (ETS No. 128), Strasbourg, 5 May 1988.

2 Article 13 of the Additional Protocol to the European Social Charter (ETS No. 128).

3 Council of Europe (1988), Additional Protocol to the European Social Charter (ETS No. 128), Appendix – Scope of the Protocol in terms of persons protected, Strasbourg, 5 May 1988.

4 Council of Europe (1978), Declaration on Human Rights adopted by the Ministers for Foreign Affairs of Member States of the Council of Europe assembled in the Committee of Ministers, on 27 April 1978 at its 62nd Session.

the lasting perception that civil and political rights were capable of government protection, since they required non-interference, whereas social and economic rights could only be gradually and progressively realized. As a result, instead of adding new social or economic rights to the ECHR, the rights under the Charter were extended by the adoption of the 1988 Protocol.

In 1996, the Additional Protocol of 1988 was incorporated, together with the subsequent Protocols as well as a new set of rights, to the revised Charter. To this end, Article 1 § 1 of the Additional Protocol of 1988 was incorporated as Article 20 of the ESC (rev), while §§ 2, 3 and 4 of the Additional Protocol, as well as the related provisions of the Appendix to the Additional Protocol, were moved to the Appendix of the ESC (rev), only for the purpose of harmonization and without any effect on the nature and scope of the legal obligations accepted under these provisions.[5] At the same time, in view of its particular importance, Article 20 was added to the very core of the ESC (rev), as determined by Article A § 1(b) of the ESC (rev).[6]

1 Other Relevant International Sources

Since the foundation of the ILO in 1919, ILO labour standards have promoted the principle of equality. More precisely, ILO Convention No. 100 on Equal Remuneration (1951) between women and men prohibits discrimination of women regarding pay, whereas ILO Discrimination Convention No. 111 (1958) and the Termination of Employment Convention No. 158 (1982) combat discrimination in employment on several grounds, including sex. Nevertheless, the most important UN instrument comprehensively protecting the right of women to be free from discrimination is the CEDAW, adopted in 1979. It provides a detailed framework that not only covers employment but also prohibits any distinction, exclusion or restriction impairing or nullifying the equal exercise by women of human rights and fundamental freedoms in the political, economic, social, cultural, civil or any other field. Furthermore, a distinct feature of the CEDAW is that, contrary to Article 20, it aims at the elimination of discrimination against women only and not of sex-based discrimination in general.

At the EU level, equality between women and men is set out in Article 2 TEU and equal pay is provided for in Articles 8 and 157 TFEU. Moreover, Article 23

5 Council of Europe (1996), Explanatory Report to the European Social Charter (revised), Strasbourg, May 1996, § 81.

6 Council of Europe (1996), Explanatory Report to the European Social Charter (revised), § 122.

CFREU prescribes gender equality "in all areas, including employment, work and pay", and allows for positive measures to reduce inequalities. Even more, the CJEU has established a wide range of case law on the issue. As early as 1976, the Court held that the principle of equal pay between men and women provided for by EU law has direct effect so that it may be relied upon by an individual against their employer.[7] Moreover, the Court held that the exclusion of part-time employees from an occupational pension scheme may constitute indirect discrimination against women, if that exclusion affects a far greater number of women than men and therefore could not be explained by objectively justified factors unrelated to any discrimination on grounds of sex.[8]

II Relation to Other Provisions of the Charter

Article 20 of the ESC (rev) is interconnected with a significant number of other articles of the Charter. First, Article 20 relates to the provisions that also explicitly target non-discrimination in the fields of employment and occupation. More precisely, Article 1 § 2 of the ESC (rev) guarantees the right of the worker to choose an occupation freely, thus without discrimination on any grounds, including sex. Hence, as the ECSR noted in the case *Syndicat de défense des fonctionnaires v. France*, Article 20 of the ESC (rev) can be viewed as *lex specialis* in relation to Article 1 § 2, since it protects equal treatment in employment matters only with regard to sex and not any discrimination in employment, regardless of the reason.[9] At the same time, however, Article 20 goes beyond the pure prohibition of discrimination, by promoting equal opportunities and *de facto* equality between women and men through positive measures. As a result, for states that have accepted both Article 1 § 2 and Article 20, issues concerning gender equality, including discrimination based on sex, are examined by the Committee under Article 20.[10]

Furthermore, Article 4 § 3 of the ESC (rev) recognizes the right of women and men workers to equal pay for work of equal value. Since Article 20 encompasses the right to equal pay without discrimination on the grounds of sex,

---

7 Cf. CJEU, 8 April 1976, *Defrenne*, C-43/75.

8 Cf. CJEU, 13 May 1986, *Bilka-Kaufhaus GmbH v. Weber von Hartz*, C-170/84.

9 Cf. ECSR, *Syndicat de défense des fonctionnaires v. France*, complaint No. 73/2011, decision on the merits of 12 September 2012, § 41.

10 Cf. ECSR, Conclusions 2002, Statement of interpretation on the link between Articles 1 § 2 and 20.

Article 4 § 3 is fully absorbed therein.[11] Hence, the notion of "equal pay" shall be interpreted uniformly under both provisions. Even more, as noted in the Explanatory Report to the Additional Protocol to the ESC, the principle of equal treatment recognised by Article 20 has a wider scope than the principle of "equal pay for work of equal value" under Article 4 § 3 of the ESC (rev). This is because, as will be shown below, Article 20 extends the concept of pay and requires progress in decreasing the gender pay gap.

Moreover, Article 20 of the ESC (rev) is considered *lex generalis* in relation to Article 8 of the ESC (rev), which guarantees the right of employed women to protection of maternity. Thus, any issues concerning discrimination against pregnant women, women who have recently given birth and women nursing their infants are examined by the Committee under Article 8. Similarly, Article 20 of the ESC (rev) is *lex generalis* in relation to Article 27 of the ESC (rev), which protects the right of workers with family responsibilities to equal opportunities and equal treatment.

Furthermore, although this is not evident at first glance, Article 20 of the ESC (rev) may overlap with several Charter provisions that protect workers' rights, if read in conjunction with the horizontal principle of non-discrimination, *inter alia*, on the grounds of sex, laid down by Article E of the ESC (rev). Those provisions include Article 1 § 4 on appropriate vocational, guidance, training and rehabilitation, Article 2 on the right to just conditions of work, Article 3 on the right to safe and healthy working conditions, Article 4 on the right to a fair remuneration, Article 9 on the right to vocational guidance, Article 10 on the right to vocational training, Article 24 on the right to protection in cases of termination of employment, Article 25 on the right of workers to the protection of their claims in the event of the insolvency of their employer, Article 26 on the right to dignity at work, as well as Article 27 on the right of workers with family responsibilities to equal opportunities and equal treatment. In this case, as it results from the related case law of the ECSR, such as the *Confédération française de l'Encadrement CFE-CGC v. France* case, the distinctive criterion that places a complaint within the scope of Article 20 is the allegation of discrimination in employment and occupation on the grounds of gender.[12]

---

11 Cf. Csilla Kollonay-Lehoczky, "The Right to Equal Opportunities and Equal Treatment in Matters of Employment and Occupation Without Discrimination on the Grounds of Sex", *in* Niklas Bruun, Klaus Lörcher, Isabelle Schömann, Stefan Clauwaert (eds.), *The European Social Charter and the Employment Relation*, Oxford, Hart Publishing, 2017, pp. 358–380, 364.

12 Cf. ECSR, *Confédération française de l'Encadrement CFE-CGC v. France*, complaint No. 56/2009, decision on the merits of 23 June 2010, § 82.

III Protective Scope

A *Personal Scope*

The personal scope of application of Article 20 of the ESC (rev) can be deducted from Part I of the Charter, which reads that "all workers" have the right to equal opportunities and equal treatment in matters of employment and occupation without discrimination on the grounds of sex. The concept of workers includes anyone working in the public sector or in the private sector, employees, but also independent contractors, self-employed persons, as well as anyone performing work for someone else.[13] Furthermore, according to the Explanatory Report to the Additional Protocol of 1988, the term "workers" shall be taken to include unemployed persons, persons seeking employment, those undergoing vocational training and all other potential workers.[14]

B *Material Scope*

1 Direct Discrimination

Under Article 20, the principle of equal treatment of women and men is, first of all, understood as the absence of any discrimination on the grounds of sex, whether direct or indirect.[15] Direct discrimination, as defined in the case law of the ECSR with regard to Article 1 § 2 of the ESC (rev), constitutes a difference in treatment between people in comparable situations that does not pursue a legitimate aim and is not based on objective and reasonable grounds.[16] Examples of direct discrimination found by the Committee in the employment legislation of States Parties include the prohibition of employment of women in underground or underwater work, night work or labour-intensive jobs, such as in the construction industry.[17]

13 Cf. Csilla Kollonay-Lehoczky, *cit.*, p. 365.

14 Council of Europe (1988), Explanatory Report to the Additional Protocol to the European Social Charter, Strasbourg, 3 May 1988, § 18.

15 Cf. ECSR, Conclusions XIII-5 (1997), Sweden – Article 1 of the Additional Protocol of 1988.

16 Cf. ECSR, *Syndicat national des Professions du tourisme v. France*, complaint No. 6/1999, decision on the merits of 10 October 2010, § 25.

17 Cf. ECSR, Conclusions 2012, Azerbaijan 2013 – Article 20, ECSR, Conclusions 2012, Bosnia and Herzegovina – Article 20 and ECSR, Conclusions 2012, Cyprus – Article 20, where the Committee found the situation in those states not in conformity with Article 20 of the ESC (rev) on the grounds that national legislation prohibited the employment of women in underground mining; ECSR, Conclusions 2012, Slovenia – Article 20, where the Committee found the situation not in conformity with Article 20 of the ESC (rev) on the grounds that national legislation prohibited the employment of women in underground mining, night work in industry and in the construction sector; ECSR, Conclusions 2012, Moldova – Article 20, where the Committee found the situation not in conformity

2 Indirect Discrimination

Indirect discrimination occurs, when a seemingly neutral provision affects women or men disproportionately, without legitimate reason. For example, given that in practice the majority of part-time workers are women, the ECSR has examined the framework applicable to part-time workers with a view to assessing whether women suffer indirect sex discrimination.[18] In this regard, the Committee found the situation in Sweden not to be in conformity with the Charter, because the social security legislation, which required a minimum of three workhours per day or 17 hours per week in order to be entitled to unemployment insurance, implied an indirect discrimination against women working part-time.[19]

3 Substantive Equality

Furthermore, building on the case law relating to the horizontal principle of non-discrimination, laid down by Article E of the ESC (rev), the ECSR has progressively broadened the concept of indirect discrimination in order to address the lack of measures ensuring that rights and collective advantages, which are open to all, are genuinely accessible by disadvantaged persons.[20] In other words, the Committee adopted a dynamic interpretation of equal treatment, according to which differences between individuals in a democratic society should be responded to with adequate steps and measures that ensure substantive equality. Against this background, the Committee has found States Parties to violate the principle of equal treatment enshrined in Article 20, when a high employment rate amongst women is not combated by active state measures[21] or when no particular steps are taken to promote women's access to employment.[22]

---

with Article 20 of the ESC (rev) on the grounds that national legislation prohibited the employment of women in heavy work and in underground work and ECSR, Conclusions 2012, Turkey – Article 20, where the Committee found the situation not in conformity with Article 20 of the ESC (rev) on the grounds that national legislation prohibited the employment of women in certain underground or underwater occupations.

18 Cf. ECSR, Conclusions XVII-2 (2005), Greece – Article 1 of the Additional Protocol of 1988.

19 Cf. ECSR, Conclusions 2004, Sweden – Article 20.

20 Cf. ECSR, *International Association Autism-Europe v. France*, complaint No. 13/2002, decision on the merits of 4 November 2003, § 52; ECSR, *European Roma Rights Centre (ERRC) v. Italy*, complaint No. 27/2004, decision on the merits of 7 December 2005, § 36.

21 Cf. ECSR, Conclusions 2012, Bosnia and Herzegovina – Article 20.

22 Cf. ECSR, Conclusions XX-1 (2013), Netherlands (Aruba) – Article 1 of the Additional Protocol of 1988.

4 Fields of Application

According to the wording of Article 20, its material scope of application encompasses four fields: a) access to employment, protection against dismissal and occupational reintegration, b) vocational guidance, training, retraining and rehabilitation, c) terms of employment and working conditions, including remuneration, and d) career development, including promotion.

a) *Access to Employment, Protection against Dismissal and Occupational Reintegration*

The protection of the right to equal access to employment without discrimination on the grounds of sex does not only prohibit the exclusion of women from access to certain types of jobs but also encompasses a non-discriminatory approach in the whole selection process, which prohibits the conduct of discriminatory tests and interviews or questions that relate to family burden.[23] Moreover, equal treatment of men and women must be guaranteed at each stage of employment, including dismissal. As the ECSR made clear, retaliatory dismissal in cases of pay discrimination must be forbidden.[24] Where a worker is dismissed on the grounds of having made a claim for equal pay, the worker should be able to file a complaint for dismissal without valid reason.[25] At the same time, the protective scope of Article 20 goes beyond protection against dismissal. More precisely, the Committee has stated that employees seeking to enforce their right to equality must be legally protected against any form of reprisal from their employers,[26] including not only dismissal, but also downgrading, and other negative changes to their working conditions. National legislation must provide for the same consequences where a worker is a victim of reprisal measures and offer the same protection in terms of a right to appeal and compensation.[27]

b) *Vocational Guidance, Training, Retraining and Rehabilitation*

The material scope of Article 20 involves the adoption of measures that help women to reinstate or upgrade their position in the labour market after situations of interruption, drop-out or involuntary stepping back from an achieved

---

23 Cf. Csilla Kollonay-Lehoczky, *cit.*, p. 366.

24 Cf. indicatively ECSR, *University Women of Europe* (UWE) *v. Belgium*, complaint No. 124/2016, decision on the merits of 6 December 2019, § 141.

25 *Ibid.*

26 Cf. ECSR, Conclusions XIII-5 (1997), Statement of interpretation of Article 1 of the Additional Protocol of 1988.

27 Cf. ECSR, Conclusions 2012, Italy – Article 20 of the ESC (rev).

position. As clarified in the Explanatory Report to the Additional Protocol to the ESC, the term "retraining" covers any supplementary training to enable workers to adapt their knowledge and skills to industrial, technological and scientific progress.[28] Possible measures that pursue the aforementioned aims include the possibility for employees returning to work after a period of parental leave to undertake training at the request of the employer, paid as working time,[29] in order to promote returning to the labour market by efficient vocational guidance and training or the provision of financial aid for companies that recruit women who have been victims of domestic violence so as to facilitate the professional reintegration of this category of employees.[30]

c) *Terms of Employment and Working Conditions, including Remuneration*

According to the Explanatory Report to the Additional Protocol of the ESC, the expression "terms of employment and working conditions" refers to all rights and situations associated with the specific position of the worker in his or her occupational relations and working environment.[31] Moreover, the same Explanatory Report notes that "Remuneration" shall mean "basic or minimum wages or salary plus all other benefits paid directly or indirectly in cash or kind by the employer to the worker by reason of the latter's employment".[32] Hence, since the wording of Article 20 explicitly includes remuneration, its protective scope encompasses the requirement for equal pay for work of equal value.[33] According to the ECSR, the principle of equal pay precludes unequal pay irrespective of the mechanism that produces such inequality, given that the source of discriminatory pay may be the law, collective agreements, individual employment contracts or internal laws of an employer.[34] Moreover,

28 Council of Europe (1988), Explanatory Report to the Additional Protocol to the European Social Charter, Strasbourg, 5 May 1988, § 21.

29 Cf. ECSR, Conclusions XV-2 (2001), Slovak Republic – Article 1 of the 1988 Additional Protocol.

30 Cf. ECSR, Conclusions XIX-1 (2008), Spain – Article 1 of the Additional Protocol of 1988.

31 Council of Europe (1988), Explanatory Report to the Additional Protocol to the European Social Charter, Strasbourg, 5 May 1988, § 22.

32 Council of Europe (1988), Explanatory Report to the Additional Protocol to the European Social Charter, Strasbourg, 5 May 1988, § 23. See also ECSR, *University Women of Europe* (*UWE*) *v. Belgium*, complaint No. 124/2016, decision on the merits of 6 December 2019, § 139.

33 As laid down also in Article 4 § 3 of the ESC (rev). On the relation between Article 4 § 3 and Article 20 of the ESC (rev), see Section II of the present analysis.

34 Cf. indicatively ECSR, *University Women of Europe* (*UWE*) *v. Belgium*, complaint No. 124/2016, decision on the merits of 6 December 2019, § 141.

the Committee considers that pay transparency is instrumental in the effective application of the principle of equal pay for work of equal value, since it contributes to identifying gender bias and discrimination and facilitates workers, employers, their organisations, as well as relevant authorities taking corrective action.[35] In this vein, the ECSR requests states to take measures in accordance with national conditions and traditions with a view to ensuring adequate pay transparency in practice, such as those highlighted in the European Commission Recommendation of 7 March 2014 on strengthening the principle of equal pay between men and women through transparency, notably the obligation for employers to regularly report on wages and produce disaggregated data by gender.[36] The Committee regards such measures as indicators of compliance with the Charter in this respect.

Furthermore, the Committee considers that the possibility of making job comparisons is essential to ensuring equal pay,[37] as lack of information on comparable jobs and pay levels could render it extremely difficult for a potential victim of pay discrimination to bring a case to court. Workers should be entitled to request and receive information on pay levels broken down by gender, including on complementary and/or variable components of the pay package. However, general statistical data on pay levels may not be sufficient to prove discrimination. Therefore, in the context of judicial proceedings, it should be possible to request and obtain information on the pay of a fellow worker, while duly respecting applicable rules on personal data protection and commercial and industrial secrecy.[38]

Moreover, the Committee clarified that the equal pay principle applies both to equal work and work of equal or comparable value.[39] In order to establish whether work performed is equal or of equal value, factors such as the nature of tasks, skills, educational and training requirements must be taken into account.[40] The Committee further observes that the notion of equal work or work of equal value has a qualitative dimension and may not always be satisfactorily defined, thus undermining legal certainty.[41] States should therefore seek to clarify this notion in domestic law as necessary, either through legislation or case law. In this respect, job classification and evaluation systems

35 *Ibid.*, § 154.
36 *Ibid.*, § 155.
37 *Ibid.*, § 157.
38 *Ibid.*
39 *Ibid.*, § 139.
40 *Ibid.*, § 156.
41 *Ibid.*

should be promoted and, where they are used, they must rely on criteria that are gender-neutral and do not result in indirect discrimination. Moreover, such systems must consider the features of the posts in question rather than the personal characteristics of the workers.[42] Hence, the comparability of work must be based on the objective characteristics of the job and not on the personal characteristics of the worker, such as her/his willingness to work overtime or her/his muscular strength.[43]

Comparison of wages is usually made between persons within the same enterprise. Nevertheless, already from its first assessments under the Additional Protocol of 1988, the ECSR expected States Parties to allow comparison of wages across enterprises, in order to apply the principle of equal pay on the basis of a larger scale of salaries.[44] In this regard, the Committee has recently reaffirmed that national law should not unduly restrict the scope of job comparisons, e.g. by limiting them strictly to the same company, but must make provision for comparisons of jobs and pay to extend outside the company concerned.[45] The Committee views pay comparisons across enterprises as an important means of ensuring that the equal pay principle is effective, in particular when the workforce is largely, or even exclusively, female or of one sex in general.[46] In 2012, the Committee further clarified the expected scope of equal pay comparison. Maintaining that meaningful comparison may require making pay comparisons across companies, it laid down that, at the very least, legislation should require pay comparisons across companies in one or more of the following situations: a) cases in which statutory rules apply to the working and pay conditions in more than one company, b) cases in which several companies are covered by a collective agreement or regulations governing the terms and conditions of employment, and c) cases in which the terms and conditions of employment are laid down centrally for more than one company within a holding (company) or conglomerate.[47] With regard to the latter, it is noteworthy that, in its subsequent conclusions, the ECSR established a direct

---

42 *Ibid.*

43 Cf. Csilla Kollonay-Lehoczky, *cit.*, p. 368.

44 Cf. ECSR, Conclusions XIII-3 (1995), Finland – Article 1 of the Additional Protocol of 1988.

45 Cf. ECSR, *University Women of Europe* (UWE) *v. Belgium*, complaint No. 124/2016, decision on the merits of 6 December 2019, § 158.

46 Cf. ECSR, Conclusions XIII-5 (1997), Statement of interpretation of Article 1 of the Additional Protocol of 1988. See also ECSR, *University Women of Europe* (UWE) *v. Belgium*, complaint No. 124/2016, decision on the merits of 6 December 2019, § 158.

47 Cf. ECSR, Conclusions 2012, Statement of interpretation of Article 20 of the ESC (rev). See also ECSR, *University Women of Europe* (UWE) *v. Belgium*, complaint No. 124/2016, decision on the merits of 6 December 2019, § 158.

link between its equal pay case law and the "single source" approach introduced by the CJEU in the *Lawrence* and *Allonby* cases.[48] More precisely, the Committee adopted the approach of the CJEU, according to which pay comparisons across companies can only be made, when the differences identified in pay conditions can be attributed to a "single source" and, thus, someone can be held responsible for such inequality.[49] Nevertheless, this approach rather limits than broadens the scope of comparison and may lead to a restrictive interpretation of Articles 20 and 4 § 3, if the existence of a "single source" is used as the main criterion for the assessment of whether States Parties respect the obligation to guarantee equal pay between women and men.

Moreover, other measures that States could adopt to reduce the gender pay gap and which the Committee regards as relevant indicators for assessing compliance with the obligations laid down by the Charter include the following: a) adoption and implementation of national action plans for employment which effectively ensure equality between women and men, including pay, b) requiring individual undertakings to draw up enterprise or company plans to secure equal pay, c) encouraging employers and workers to deal with equality issues in collective agreements, and d) raising awareness of the equal pay principle among employers, organisations and the public at large, including through the activities of equality bodies.[50]

d) *Career Development, including Promotion*

In its case law, the Committee has stated that Article 20, point d of the Charter imposes positive obligations on states to tackle vertical segregation in the labour market, by means of, *inter alia*, promoting the advancement of women in decision-making positions in private companies.[51] This obligation may entail the introduction of binding legislative measures to ensure equal access to management boards of companies. Measures designed to promote equal opportunities for women and men in the labour market must also include promoting an effective parity in the representation of women and men in decision-making positions in both the public and private sectors.[52]

---

48 Cf. ECSR, Conclusions 2012, Netherlands – Article 20 of the ESC (rev); Cf. ECSR, Conclusions 2014, Bulgaria – Article 4 § 3 of the Charter.

49 Cf. CJEU, 17 September 2002, AG *Lawrence v. Regent Office Care Ltd*, C-320/00; 13 January 2004, *Debra Allonby v. Rossendale College and Others*, C-256/01.

50 Cf. indicatively ECSR, *University Women of Europe* (UWE) *v. Belgium*, complaint No. 124/2016, decision on the merits of 6 December 2019, § 208.

51 *Ibid.*, § 218.

52 Cf. ECSR, Conclusions 2016, Portugal – Article 20.

5 Limits to the Material Scope

The Appendix to Article 20 of the ESC (rev) sets a limit to the material scope of the article. More precisely, social security matters, as well as other provisions relating to unemployment benefit, old age benefit and survivor's benefit may be excluded from the protective scope of Article 20. States Parties wishing to make use of this possibility would have had to indicate such exclusion explicitly either at the time of ratification of the Additional Protocol of 1988 or later, when accepting other articles.[53] So far, no State Party has opted for such an exclusion. Equal treatment with regard to social security implies the absence of any discrimination on the grounds of sex, particularly as far as the scope of schemes, conditions of access to schemes, the calculation of benefits and the length of entitlement to benefits are concerned.

IV State Obligations

The obligation of States Parties under Article 20 is to "ensure" or to "promote" the application of the right to equal treatment in respect of the full range of the fields that belong to its material scope. This obligation may be met by the Government, through the adoption of regulation, by employers and employees, through the conclusion of collective agreements, or by individuals, through the conclusion of contracts.[54] Moreover, the obligation to ensure equal treatment may be further met both by judicial processes and by other appropriate means that exist or may be instituted by each State Party.[55]

More specifically, as indicated by the Committee, Article 20 stipulates the following obligations for states: a) to promulgate the right of equal treatment between men and women in legislation, b) to take legal measures that ensure the effectiveness of the right, such as measures providing for the nullity of clauses in collective agreements and individual contracts that are contrary to the right, for adequate appeal procedures where the right has been violated and for the effective protection of workers against any retaliatory measures (dismissal or other measures) taken as a result of their demand to benefit from

53 Cf. ECSR, Conclusions XIII-3 (1995), Statement of interpretation of Article 1 Additional Protocol.

54 Cf. Council of Europe (1988), Explanatory Report to the Additional Protocol to the European Social Charter, Strasbourg, 3 May 1988, § 20.

55 *Ibid.*

the right, and c) to define an active policy, taking practical measures to implement the right.[56]

A Promulgation of the Right in Legislation

According to the Committee, the mere statement of the principle of equal treatment between men and women in the Constitution is not sufficient. States are thus obliged to enact legislation explicitly imposing equal treatment in all aspects.[57] This requirement has been explicitly stated in a series of ECSR cases on UWE v. Belgium, Bulgaria, Croatia, Cyprus, Czech Republic, Finland, France, Greece, Ireland, Italy, the Netherlands, Norway, Portugal, Slovenia and Sweden, respectively, with regard to the right of women and men to equal pay for work of equal value.[58] Even more, states have to enact clear and specific legal provisions on gender equality, since general provisions that prohibit discrimination *inter alia* on the grounds of sex are deemed insufficient.[59] Furthermore, any legislation, regulation or other administrative measure that fails to comply with the equality principle must be repealed or revoked. On the contrary, the non-application of discriminatory legislation is not sufficient for a situation to be considered by the Committee as compatible with the Charter.[60] In addition, the Committee considers it instrumental that a court or another competent authority be empowered to waive the application of a stipulation included in an individual employment contract or a collective agreement in case it infringes the principles of equality laid down by law.[61]

---

56 Cf. ECSR, Conclusions XIII-3 (1995), Statement of interpretation of Article 1 of the Additional Protocol of 1988.

57 ECSR, Conclusions XVII-2 (2005), Pays-Bas Aruba – Article 1 of the Additional Protocol of 1988.

58 Cf. indicatively ECSR, *University Women of Europe (UWE) v. Belgium*, complaint No. 124/2016, decision on the merits of 6 December 2019, § 138.

59 Cf. ECSR, Conclusions XV-2 (2001), Slovak Republic – Article 1 of the 1988 Additional Protocol, where the Committee concluded that the situation in Slovakia was not in conformity with Article 1 of the Additional Protocol as there were only general provisions on discrimination but no specific statutory guarantee of the right of women and men to equal pay for work of equal value; ECSR, Conclusions 2012, Bulgaria – Article 20, where the Committee asked for clarifications for the reluctancy of the Bulgarian government to enact a special law on gender equality.

60 Cf. ECSR, Conclusions XIII-3 (1995), Statement of interpretation of Article 1 of the Additional Protocol of 1988.

61 Cf. ECSR, Conclusions XIII-5 (1997), Statement of interpretation of Article 1 of the Additional Protocol of 1988.

B *Access to Effective Remedies*

In the event of violation of the principle of non-discrimination on the grounds of sex, national law must provide for appropriate and effective remedies.

1 Right of Appeal

Workers, who have suffered discrimination based on sex, must be able to take their case to an independent body, such as a court or a tribunal.[62] Therefore, according to the ECSR, proceedings should be affordable and timely.[63] By analogy with the case-law in relation to Article 1 § 2, the Committee underlines that, in order to make the right of appeal fully effective, a number of legal steps should be taken, such as setting up an independent body to provide legal assistance to victims or introducing a specific right for trade unions and other collective bodies to take legal action in employment discrimination cases, including the right to act as an intervener in individual litigation or to launch a class action on behalf of individuals.[64] In this regard, the Committee consistently asks for information on the forms of trade union involvement and on their roles in the prevention and correction of discrimination in the workplace.

2 Shifting of the Burden of Proof

According to the ECSR, Article 20 of the ESC (rev) implies an alleviation of the burden of proof in cases of alleged gender discrimination in favour of workers.[65] The shift in the burden of proof consists in ensuring that, where a person believes he or she has suffered discrimination on the grounds of sex and establishes facts which make it reasonable to suppose that discrimination has occurred, the onus is on the defendant to prove that there has been no infringement of the principle of equal treatment.[66] In the *SUD Travail Affaires Sociales v. France* case, the ECSR noted that, from the point of view of effective application of rules on protection against discrimination, the purpose of rules on alleviation of the burden of proof is to enable courts to deal with

62 Cf. ECSR, Conclusions XIII-3 (1995), Statement of interpretation of Article 1 of the Additional Protocol of 1988.

63 Cf. indicatively ECSR, *University Women of Europe (UWE) v. Belgium*, complaint No. 124/2016, decision on the merits of 6 December 2019, § 145.

64 Cf. ECSR, Conclusions XIII-5 (1997), Statement of interpretation of Article 1 of the Additional Protocol of 1988.

65 Cf. ECSR, Conclusions 2004, Romania – Article 20.

66 Cf. ECSR, Conclusions XIII-5 (1997), Statement of interpretation of Article 1 of the Additional Protocol of 1988. See also ECSR, *University Women of Europe (UWE) v. Belgium*, complaint No. 124/2016, decision on the merits of 6 December 2019, § 147.

discrimination in the light of the effects produced by a rule, act, or practice.[67] Therefore, the absence of a regulation as to the shift in the burden of proof in gender discrimination cases leads the Committee to the conclusion that the situation in the state concerned is not in conformity with Article 20.[68]

3 Adequate Compensation

Anyone who suffers discrimination on the grounds of sex must be entitled to adequate compensation, i.e., compensation that is proportionate to the loss suffered by the worker and sufficiently dissuasive for employers.[69] According to the ECSR, adequate compensation in the event of unlawful or unfair dismissal includes the reinstatement or the retention of the employee in the same or a similar post and, in case reinstatement is not possible or is not desired by the dismissed employee, the employer must pay compensation for any pecuniary and non-pecuniary damage suffered.[70] In the same vein, in all other cases, adequate compensation includes bringing the discrimination to an end and awarding compensation proportionate to the pecuniary and non-pecuniary damage suffered.[71] Moreover, the Committee notes that any ceiling on compensation that may preclude damages from compensating for the loss suffered and from being sufficiently dissuasive is contrary to the Charter.[72]

C *Equality Bodies and Other Institutions*

The ECSR has pointed out that measures to foster the full effectiveness of efforts to combat discrimination include setting up a specialised body to monitor and promote, independently, equal treatment, especially by providing discrimination victims with the support they need to take proceedings.[73] The status of such equality bodies in terms of their mandate, their independence and their

---

67 Cf. ECSR, *Travail Affaires Sociales v. France*, complaint No. 24/2004, decision on the merits of 8 November 2005, § 34.

68 Cf. ECSR, Conclusions 2004, Azerbaijan – Article 20.

69 Cf. ECSR, Conclusions XIII-5 (1997), Statement of interpretation of Article 1 of the Additional Protocol of 1988.

70 Cf. ECSR, Conclusions XIII-5 (1997), Statement of interpretation of Article 1 of the Additional Protocol of 1988; ECSR, *University Women of Europe* (UWE) *v. Belgium*, complaint No. 124/2016, decision on the merits of 6 December 2019, § 148.

71 Cf. ECSR, Conclusions XVII-2 (2005), Finland – Article 1 of the Additional Protocol of 1988. See also ECSR, *University Women of Europe* (UWE) *v. Belgium*, complaint No. 124/2016, decision on the merits of 6 December 2019, § 146.

72 Cf. ECSR, Conclusions 2012, Albania – Article 20.

73 Cf. ECSR, Conclusions XVI-1 (2003), Iceland – Article 1 § 2 of the ESC.

resources must be clearly defined.[74] As regards the mandate of equality bodies, the Committee considers that it should include provision for functions, such as the following: i) monitoring and promotion: in cooperation with labour inspectorates or other relevant bodies, monitor the situation regarding gender discrimination, including in respect of pay, and produce regular reports; conduct inquiries at their own initiative and make recommendations; raise awareness of the equal pay principle across society, b) decision-making: receive, examine and hear cases of discrimination; issue binding or authoritative decisions on complaints concerning alleged discrimination and ensure the implementation of such decisions, c) assistance to victims: provide personal and legal support to complainants; mediate settlements in cases of discrimination; represent victims in cases of discrimination; and monitor the implementation of decisions in such cases.[75] Moreover, the Committee has underlined that, in addition to having a clear and comprehensive mandate, these specialised equality bodies must be equipped with the necessary human and financial resources, as well as infrastructure to ensure that these bodies can effectively combat and eliminate pay discrimination.[76]

D *Gender Mainstreaming*

According to the ECSR, the obligation to take appropriate measures to promote equal opportunities entails gender mainstreaming, which is the internationally recognised strategy towards achieving gender equality.[77] This involves integrating a gender perspective into the preparation, design, implementation, monitoring and evaluation of policies, regulatory measures and spending programmes, with a view to promoting equality between women and men, in addition to combating discrimination. The Committee considers that gender mainstreaming should cover all aspects of the labour market, including pay, career development and occupational recognition, and gender mainstreaming should also extend to the education system.[78]

---

74 Cf. indicatively ECSR, *University Women of Europe* (UWE) *v. Belgium*, complaint No. 124/2016, decision on the merits of 6 December 2019, § 167. In this context, the Committee also has regard to the criteria for national human rights institutions set out in the so-called Paris Principles adopted in 1993 by the United Nations General Assembly.

75 *Ibid.*, § 168.

76 *Ibid.*, § 169.

77 *Ibid.*, § 206.

78 Cf. ECSR, Conclusions XVII-2 (2005), Greece – Article 1 of the Additional Protocol of 1988.

V Exceptions to the Principle of Non-discrimination

The Appendix to Article 20 of the ESC (rev), which goes back to Article 1 §§ 2, 3 and 4 of the Additional Protocol of 1988, lays down three possible exceptions to the principle of non-discrimination on the grounds of sex: (A.) provisions concerning the protection of women, particularly as regards pregnancy, confinement and the post-natal period, (B.) specific measures aimed at removing *de facto* inequalities, and (C.) occupational activities which, by reason of their nature or the context in which they are carried out, can be entrusted only to persons of a particular sex.

A *Protection Measures for Women*

As mentioned before, according to the Appendix to Article 20 of the ESC (rev), which goes back to Article 1 § 2 of the Additional Protocol of 1988, provisions concerning the protection of women shall not be deemed to be discriminatory. For this reason, the respective provisions must be objectively justified by needs that apply exclusively to women, such as those particularly related to maternity, pregnancy, childbirth and the post-natal period. As noted in the Explanatory Report to the Additional Protocol of 1988, the word "particularly" indicates that other kinds of protection, essential in other situations, are admissible.[79] Moreover, the Explanatory Report acknowledges that, in the particular context of gender equality, it will sometimes be difficult to establish which measure is the most favourable to women, as opinions may differ.[80] In this case, account will need to be taken of changing attitudes in this regard.[81] Against this background, the ECSR has consistently considered non-maternity related protections, such as banning night work and certain physically demanding jobs, as a violation of the prohibition of discrimination on the grounds of sex. More specifically, the Committee has underlined that prohibiting women from performing night work or underground mining, while authorising men to do so, is contrary to the principle of equal treatment, since those working conditions are just as detrimental to men as to women.[82]

79 Cf. Council of Europe (1988), Explanatory Report to the Additional Protocol to the European Social Charter, Strasbourg, 3 May 1988, § 24.

80 *Ibid.*, § 25.

81 *Ibid.*

82 Cf. ECSR, Conclusions XVII-2 (2005), Netherlands (Aruba) – Article 1 of the Additional Protocol of 1988; ECSR, Conclusions 2012, Bosnia and Herzegovina – Article 20.

B *Positive Measures Removing Inequalities*

According to the Appendix to Article 20 of the ESC (rev), which goes back to Article 1 § 3 of the Additional Protocol of 1988, measures aimed at removing *de facto* inequalities are not to be seen as discriminatory. Besides the fact that national legislation should not prevent the adoption of positive measures or positive action,[83] the ECSR emphasizes that States Parties are also required to adopt affirmative measures aimed at reducing the *de facto* inequalities between women and men workers.[84] Against this background, the Committee has interpreted Article 20 as placing positive obligations on States Parties to take measures that actively promote equal opportunities. Moreover, the positive measures allowed under this provision shall be transitional and repealed gradually once equality has been achieved.[85]

In its recent case law on Article 20, the ECSR underlined that among the measures that states could adopt in order to reduce gender inequality are the following: adopting and implementing national action plans on equal opportunities for women and men, requiring individual undertakings to draw up enterprise or company plans to secure greater equality between women and men, encouraging employers and workers to deal with equality issues in collective agreements, raising awareness on gender equality among employers, organisations and the public at large, including through the activities of equality bodies,[86] as well as integrating the issue of equality between women and men in national action plans for employment.[87]

Furthermore, another positive measure used to promote substantive equality is the application of quotas. In the area of employment and occupation, quotas have been introduced among States Parties for a balanced gender representation in professional bodies, such as boards of public and private companies, work councils and staff committees,[88] in the composition of selection bodies and tribunals in order to increase the employment of women in the public sector, or for positions of women in the armed forces.[89] It is noteworthy

---

83 Cf. ECSR, Conclusions XIII-5 (1997), Statement of interpretation of Article 1 of the Additional Protocol of 1988.

84 Cf. ECSR, Conclusions 2002, Romania – Article 20; ECSR, *University Women of Europe* (*UWE*) *v. Belgium*, complaint No. 124/2016, decision on the merits of 6 December 2019, § 204.

85 Cf. Council of Europe (1988), Explanatory Report to the Additional Protocol to the European Social Charter, Strasbourg, 3 May 1988, § 26.

86 Cf. ECSR, *University Women of Europe* (*UWE*) *v. Belgium*, complaint No. 124/2016, decision on the merits of 6 December 2019, § 208.

87 Cf. ECSR, Conclusions XVII-2 (2005), Greece – Article 1 of the Additional Protocol of 1988.

88 Cf. ECSR, Conclusions 2008, France – Article 20.

89 Cf. ECSR, Conclusions XIX-1 (2008), Spain – Article 1 of the Additional Protocol of 1988.

that the ECSR follows the existence of quotas with increased attention, even if they go beyond the area of employment, for example, in the fields of education[90] or political representation.[91]

C *Occupational Activities Restricted to Persons of a Particular Sex*

Moreover, as mentioned before, according to the Appendix to Article 20 that goes back to Article 1 § 4 of the Additional Protocol of 1988 and its Appendix, exceptionally and subject to strict interpretation, certain occupational activities may be limited to persons of one sex, due to the nature of such activities or the context and conditions in which they are carried out. As stated in the Explanatory Report to the Additional Protocol of 1988, States Parties are allowed to exclude certain occupational activities for persons of one sex without having to adopt a list thereof in laws or regulations. Nevertheless, States Parties have to specify in the reports that they submit which occupational activities are reserved to persons of a particular sex, as well as the reasons and the criteria governing such reservation.[92] More specifically, such limitations can only be in conformity with the Charter in respect of professions where gender constitutes a genuine occupational requirement. In determining whether sex constitutes a decisive factor, States Parties may take account of public order or national security-related requirements, provided that they are prescribed by law, pursue a legitimate aim and are necessary in a democratic society.[93] In practice, such differentiations of access based on sex are often encountered in religious communities[94] or with regard to positions in the police or the army. Given, however, that the respective exceptions must be interpreted restrictively and not go beyond the legitimately pursued aim, the ECSR found restrictions on the admission of women to the police college and the corresponding exclusion of women from 85 % of police duties to be not in conformity with Article 20.[95] In any case, and given the danger of a proliferation of provisions that exclude persons of one sex from certain occupational activities, states should gradually reduce, if not abolish, the number of excluded activities.[96]

---

90 Cf. ECSR, Conclusions XV-2 (2001), Norway – Article 1 of the Additional Protocol of 1988.

91 Cf. ECSR, Conclusions 2006, Italy – Article 20.

92 Cf. Council of Europe (1988), Explanatory Report to the Additional Protocol to the European Social Charter, Strasbourg, 3 May 1988, § 27.

93 Those criteria are laid down in Article G of the ESC (rev).

94 Cf. ECSR, Conclusions 2012, Norway – Article 20.

95 Cf. ECSR, Conclusions XVI-2 (2004), Greece – Article 1 of the Additional Protocol of 1988.

96 Cf. Council of Europe (1988), Explanatory Report to the Additional Protocol to the European Social Charter, Strasbourg, 3 May 1988, § 27, which includes the soft warning,

VI Related Case Law

Initially, Article 20 of the ESC (rev) and the respective Article 1 of the Additional Protocol of 1988 to the 1961 ESC were mainly interpretated by the ECSR either through statements of interpretation or in the framework of the reporting system, rather than through its case law. This was due to the fact that, even though Article 20 was invoked by complainants in collective complaints, it was found by the Committee to be not applicable. The first relevant case was *Confédération française de l'Encadrement* CFE-CGC *v. France.*[97] In this case, the complainant trade union Confédération française de l'Encadrement CFE-CGC alleged that the annual working time scheme, and in particular the annual working days system, as prescribed in National Act No. 2008–789 of 20 August 2008, infringed the right to equal treatment in matters of employment and occupation without discrimination on the grounds of sex provided by Article 20, the right of workers with family responsibilities to equal treatment provided by Article 27 and the right not to be discriminated against in the enjoyment of the rights protected by the Revised Charter provided by Article E, in that the annual working days system applied only to certain employees and violated their rights to reasonable working hours and to fair remuneration.[98] The complainant union's reasoning was entirely based on a general allegation of discrimination against employees coming under the annual working days system insofar as both the reasonableness of their working time and their right to fair remuneration, in particular for overtime work, were at stake. In assessing this claim, the Committee responded that the complainant union did not put forward any argument that would establish the existence of discrimination under Articles 20 and 27.[99] Moreover, the complainant union's arguments, which were based on the alleged discrimination faced by workers under the annual working days system in terms of reasonable working time and fair remuneration, were dealt with under Articles 2 § 1 and 4 § 2, which had been raised separately in the complaint. Against this background, the Committee did not consider it necessary to re-examine the arguments put forward by the CFE-CGC and held that the claim under Article E taken in conjunction with Articles 20 and 27 regarding the impact of the working time and overtime

---

that States Parties should bear in mind that the intention is to gradually reduce the number of excluded activities to a strict minimum.

97 Cf. ECSR, *Confédération française de l'Encadrement* CFE-CGC *v. France*, complaint No. 56/2009, decision on the merits of 23 June 2010.

98 *Ibid.*, § 7.

99 *Ibid.*, § 82.

work of employees coming under the annual working days systems was not substantiated.[100]

The second case in which Article 20 was invoked is *Syndicat de défense des fonctionnaires v. France*.[101] In this case, the complainant trade union Syndicat de défense des fonctionnaires alleged that the so-called redeployed civil servants employed by France Telecom and La Poste did not enjoy several of the rights provided for in the Charter, among which the right to non-discrimination in one's career based on Article 20, read alone or in conjunction with Article E, given that they were subject to discrimination with regard to promotion. In its assessment of this complaint, the Committee recalled that Article 20 can be viewed as a *lex specialis* in relation to Article 1 § 2 of the Charter, which prohibits any discrimination in employment, regardless of the reason.[102] Hence, in view of the fact that the complainant organization did not provide any indication or evidence of discrimination on the grounds of sex, the Committee held that the complaints relating to the discriminatory arrangements for the management of careers, including the promotion of civil servants who remained in the redeployed corps, fell neither within the scope of Article 20 nor, consequently, within that of Article E read in conjunction with Article 20.[103] At the same time, however, the ECSR concluded that the above complaints should be reclassified so that they could be examined under Article 1 § 2 of the Charter.[104]

Nonetheless, in its recent case law, in the context of the collective complaint procedure, the ECSR further developed the relevant States Parties' obligations under Article 20. More precisely, in 2019, the ECSR adopted a series of decisions on equal pay and equal opportunities between women and men in the workplace.[105] Following the collective complaints lodged by the non-governmental

---

100 *Ibid.*, §§ 83–84.

101 Cf. ECSR, *Syndicat de défense des fonctionnaires v. France*, complaint No. 73/2011, decision on the merits of 12 September 2012.

102 *Ibid.*, § 41.

103 *Ibid.*, §§ 41 and 46.

104 *Ibid.*, § 45.

105 Cf. ECSR, *UWE v. Belgium*, complaint No. 124/2016, decision on the merits of 6 December 2019; *UWE v. Bulgaria*, complaint No. 125/2016, decision on the merits of 6 December 2019; *UWE v. Croatia*, complaint No. 126/2016, decision on the merits of 5 December c 2019; *UWE v. Cyprus*, complaint No. 127/2016, decision on the merits of 5 December 2019; *UWE v. Czech Republic*, complaint No. 128/2016, decision on the merits of 5 December 2019; *UWE v. Finland*, complaint No. 129/2016, decision on the merits of 5 December 2019; *UWE v. France*, complaint No. 130/2016, decision on the merits of 5 December 2019; *UWE v. Greece*, complaint No. 131/2016, decision on the merits of 5 December 2019; *UWE v. Ireland*, complaint No. 132/2016, decision on the merits of 5 December 2019; *UWE v. Italy*, complaint No. 133/2016, decision on the merits of 6 December 2019; *UWE v. Netherlands*, complaint No. 134/2016, decision on the merits of 6 December 2019; *UWE v. Norway*, complaint No. 135/

international organization University Women of Europe (UWE), the Committee assessed the compliance with these standards to the ESC of all the fifteen States Parties that have ratified or acceded to the Additional Protocol, which provides for a system of collective complaints, namely Belgium, Bulgaria, Croatia, Cyprus, the Czech Republic, Finland, France, Greece, Ireland, Italy, the Netherlands, Norway, Portugal, Slovenia and Sweden. The complainant organization based the alleged violation of the ESC on two main arguments. The first argument addressed the failure of the states to implement the principle of equal pay between men and women, as a gender pay gap still exists despite the existent national and international legal framework. The second argument addressed the under-representation of women in decision-making positions in the private sector, in particular in private companies. These two main arguments were specified for each of the states under assessment in the respective complaints.

The ECSR examined the first argument, namely the alleged violation of the principle of equal pay due to the existence of a gender pay gap, under Article 4 § 3 in combination with Article 20(c) of the ESC (rev), and, for States Parties that have not ratified it, under the respective Article 1(c) of the Additional Protocol of 1988 to the 1961 ESC. The obligations deriving from the above provisions, according to the ECSR's interpretation, may be divided into, first, the obligation to recognise and enforce the right to equal pay and, second, the obligation to actively promote the right to equal pay. In order to assess whether the first obligation was satisfied, the ECSR assessed four subsequent elements, referring to both the substantive and the procedural aspect of the right. The first element is the explicit protection of the right to equal pay in the national legal order, which goes beyond constitutional protection of gender equality. Secondly, the ECSR examined the availability of effective remedies for victims of pay discrimination, such as their access to affordable and

---

2016, decision on the merits of 5 December 2019; *UWE v. Portugal*, complaint No. 136/2016, decision on the merits of 5 December 2019; *UWE v. Slovenia*, complaint No. 137/2016, decision on the merits of 5 December 2019; *UWE v. Sweden*, complaint No. 138/2016, decision on the merits of 6 December 2019. For a detailed analysis of these cases, cf. Maria Kotsoni, "Placing Gender Equality in the Workplace at the Forefront of Social Rights in Europe: Equal Pay and Equal Opportunities under the Scrutiny of the European Committee of Social Rights", *Strasbourg Observers*, 5 October 2020, available at https://strasbourgobservers.com/2020/10/05/placing-gender-equality-in-the-workplace-at-the-forefront-of-social-rights-in-europe-equal-pay-and-equal-opportunities-under-the-scrutiny-of-the-european-committee-of-social-rights; Barbara Kresal, "Gender Pay Gap and Under-Representation of Women in Decision-Making Positions: UWE Decisions of the European Committee of Social Rights", *ERA Forum*, No. 22, 2021, pp. 311–325.

timely proceedings, their entitlement to adequate compensation, as well as the shifting of the burden of proof from the claimant to the respondent. The third element concerned whether pay transparency was ensured in practice and whether the national legal framework allowed for job comparisons and access to relevant data on the part of victims of alleged pay discrimination. Fourthly, the ECSR examined the effectiveness of independent equality bodies or other similar institutions in monitoring and promoting equal treatment focused on equal pay. In its assessment regarding the second obligation to promote equal pay, the ECSR considered data available from Eurostat on the gender pay gap for every State Party alone, as well as in comparison to the EU average. Additionally, it determined the obligation on the part of states to adopt positive action measures suggesting gender mainstreaming as a suitable – yet not the only – strategy. Based on the collection and analysis of statistical data, States Parties are obliged to adopt policies promoting equal pay, as well as to assess the effectiveness of such policies. In reviewing whether the measures presented by the states under review had been effective, the ECSR relied upon the trends in the gender pay gap, as illustrated in statistical data.

The ECSR's compliance review regarding equal pay revealed that, with the exception of Sweden, the situation in all other fourteen States Parties was not in conformity with the ESC. Despite the fact that, in all the States Parties under review, legislation explicitly protects equal pay, the failure to ensure pay transparency and job comparisons led to the findings of non-conformity. Apart from France, Portugal and Finland, the situation in all other States Parties was found to be in violation of the ESC on these grounds. Another reoccurring basis for non-conformity was the failure to actively promote equal pay. All states, apart from Belgium and Sweden, were in violation of the ESC on these grounds. In some cases, it was also the obstacles to accessing effective remedies and the failure to establish independent equality bodies that monitor and promote equal pay that were combined to bring about the findings of non-conformity with the right to equal pay.

Furthermore, the ECSR examined the second argument, namely the alleged violation of the right to equal opportunities in the workplace due to the underrepresentation of women in decision-making positions in the private sector, under Article 20(d) of the ESC (rev) and, for States Parties that have not ratified it, under the respective Article 1(d) of the Additional Protocol of 1988 to the 1961 ESC. The ECSR subsequently elaborated on the obligation of states to actively address vertical segregation in the workplace by means of, but not exclusively, legislation. It held that the introduction of legislation that ensures equal representation in decision-making positions is a measure that promotes equality of opportunity in the workplace. However, as in the promotion of equal pay, the reference to potential strategies was non-exhaustive. Therefore, available statistical data and trends were considered, as well as the promotion of equal representation through other non-legislative or non-binding measures, such as action plans or codes of corporate governance. As for the participation of women in company management boards, the ECSR referred to the 40% quota proposed by the Parliamentary Assembly of the Council of Europe (PACE) in its Resolution 1715 (2010).

The ECSR's compliance review regarding the representation of women in decision-making positions in the private sector revealed that the recommended quota of 40% was only reached in two countries, namely Sweden and Norway. However, the majority of states were found to be in conformity with the ESC on this point. The ECSR relied on states' efforts to enhance equal gender representation in decision-making positions, as reflected in the relevant trends in the statistical data from 2010 to 2019. Therefore, it was the progress that was assessed rather than whether states reached the recommended threshold of 40%. Where measures had been adopted resulting in a gradual increase in the proportion of women in decision-making positions over time, the situation in States Parties was found to be in conformity with the ESC. This was the case for Belgium, Finland, France, Italy, the Netherlands, and Slovenia, where the rate of participation of women in management boards was not much lower than the recommended threshold. The same applies for Portugal and Slovenia, where, even though the rate was not close to the recommended one, the ECSR considered the progress shown by statistical trends as satisfactory.

Concluding Remarks

Article 20 is one of the core provisions of the ESC (rev), since the observance of one main element of its protective scope, i.e., equal pay, is reviewed every 2 years by the ESCR both under Article 4 § 3 and under Article 20. Moreover, with the ESC being the counterpart of the ECHR in the field of social rights, the recent case-law of the ECSR complements the case-law of the ECtHR on gender equality, especially in terms of that which is concerned with gender equality in the field of employment and social policy. In addition, the use of statistical data by the ECSR as proof of the existence of discrimination – an approach that was adopted also by the ECtHR in *di Trizio v. Switzerland*[106] – indicates methodological convergence among these two bodies, when it comes

106 ECtHR, 2 February 2016, *di Trizio v. Switzerland*, No. 7186/09, § 88.

to the examination of gender discrimination cases. Finally, the ECtHR itself, in *Emel Boyraz v. Turkey*,[107] referred to the ESC as a legal source, when adjudicating on matters related to gender discrimination in employment.

Overall, through its statements of interpretation, its conclusions in the framework of the reporting system and its recent case law, the ECSR has set comprehensive and timely standards on equal opportunities and equal treatment between women and men in matters of employment and occupation. At the same time though, the Committee's recent findings of non-conformity for fourteen of the fifteen States Parties to the ESC that are subject to review under the collective complaints procedure, with regard to the right to equal pay and/or the right to equal opportunities in the workplace, suggest that the failure on the part of states to eliminate gender pay gap and gender segregation in the field of employment is a persistent and structural problem shared among numerous European countries.

107 ECtHR, 2 December 2014, *Emel Boyraz v. Turkey*, No. 61960/08, § 29.

ARTICLE 21

The Right of Employees to Information and Consultation in the Company

Filip Dorssemont and Johan Peeters

With a view to ensuring the effective exercise of the right of workers to be informed and consulted within the undertaking, the Parties undertake to adopt or encourage measures enabling workers or their representatives, in accordance with national legislation and practice:

a to be informed regularly or at the appropriate time and in a comprehensible way about the economic and financial situation of the undertaking employing them, on the understanding that the disclosure of certain information which could be prejudicial to the undertaking may be refused or subject to confidentiality; and

b to be consulted in good time on proposed decisions which could substantially affect the interests of workers, particularly on those decisions which could have an important impact on the employment situation in the undertaking.

•••

Appendix to the European Social Charter (Revised)
Articles 21 and 22

1. For the purpose of the application of these articles, the term "workers' representatives" means persons who are recognised as such under national legislation or practice.
2. The terms "national legislation" and "practice" embrace as the case may be, in addition to laws and regulations, collective agreements, other agreements between employers and workers' representatives, customs as well as relevant case law.
3. For the purpose of the application of these articles, the term "undertaking" is understood as referring to a set of tangible and intangible components, with or without legal personality, formed to produce goods or provide services for financial gain and with power to determine its own market policy.
4. It is understood that religious communities and their institutions may be excluded from the application of these articles, even if these

 DOI:10.1163/9789004434158_003

institutions are "undertakings" within the meaning of paragraph 3. Establishments pursuing activities which are inspired by certain ideals or guided by certain moral concepts, ideals and concepts which are protected by national legislation, may be excluded from the application of these articles to such an extent as is necessary to protect the orientation of the undertaking.

5. It is understood that where in a state the rights set out in these articles are exercised in the various establishments of the undertaking, the Party concerned is to be considered as fulfilling the obligations deriving from these provisions.
6. The Parties may exclude from the field of application of these articles, those undertakings employing less than a certain number of workers, to be determined by national legislation or practice.

ETS 163 – European Social Charter (Revised), 03.V.1996

∴

Introduction

Article 21 ESC (rev) has so far been the subject of a limited number of complaints. Since three complaints were declared inadmissible and another complaint that was declared admissible was not pursued, these complaints are not useful for an analysis of the scope of Article 21 ESC (rev).[1] Two complaints have been declared admissible, and decisions on the merits were adopted on 19th October 2022.[2]

The explanation in the *Appendix* to Article 21 ESC (rev) is essentially more developed than the analysis given in the *Digest* of the ESC (rev), and it also must be noted that the appendix is an integral part of the ESC (rev), making

1 ECSR, *European Confederation of Police (EuroCOP) v. Ireland*, complaint No. 83/2012, decision on admissibility and the merits of 2 December 2013; ECSR, *European Council of Police Trade Unions (CESP) v. Portugal*, complaint No. 40/2007, decision on admissibility of 21 May 2007; ECSR, *Frente Comum de Sindicatos de Administração Pública v. Portugal*, complaint No. 36/2006, decision on admissibility of 5 December 2006; ECSR, *ATTAC ry, Globaali sosiaalityö ry* and *Maan ystävät ry v. Finland*, complaint No. 163/2018, decision on admissibility and immediate measures of 22 January 2022.

2 ECSR, *Associazione nazionale sindacato professionisti sanitari della funzione infermieristica – Nursing Up* c. Italie, complaint No. 169/2018, decision on the merits; ECSR, *Confederazione Generale Sindacale (CGS) & Federazione Lavoratori Pubblici e Funzioni Pubbliche (FLP) v. Italy*, complaint No. 161/2018, decision on the merits of 19 October 2022.

it still the most authoritative part for examining the scope of this article. To date, only 16 Conclusions of non-conformity have been found by the ECSR. These conclusions of non-conformity were mainly motivated by the consideration that a number of States had not demonstrated that the vast majority of employees had a right to information and consultation.[3] This criticism is relevant but is limited to the issue of the personal scope of national provisions or practices in this area and so these conclusions are not useful for a more substantive analysis of the scope of Article 21 ESC (rev). A recent negative conclusion related to France indicates that people who are considered workers under French law cannot be excluded for the sake of thresholds.[4] A recent negative conclusion related to Turkey expresses dissatisfaction with the absence of economic and financial information as such.[5] For this reason, this contribution opts for an analysis of the right to information and consultation, which shows intertextuality. A reading of this article can gain in intelligibility by reading Article 21 ESC (rev) in the light of secondary EU law.

1 The Right to Information and "Consultation" in the ESC (rev)

The right to information and consultation was not included in the original version of the European Social Charter (1961). It was introduced by Article 2 of the Additional Protocol (1988). In 1996, this text was integrated into the Revised European Social Charter. The Additional Protocol was a pivotal moment for recognising the right to worker involvement. Prior to this Protocol, the term "consultation" only appeared in Article 6 § 1 ESC (rev). Article 6 ESC (rev) was, and still is, dominated by the right to collective bargaining. *Prima facie*, such a subsumption of consultation under the category of negotiation seems odd. As a rule, consultation and negotiation are distinguished as forms of social dialogue. This distinction relates to the actors and to the outcome of the process. Collective bargaining takes place in a classical approach between individual employers and trade unions or between employers' organisations and trade unions. It is precisely these actors that are explicitly mentioned in Article 6 § 2 ESC (rev), which deals with the promotion of procedures "for voluntary

3 See Andrzej Swiatkowski, *The Charter of Social Rights of the Council of Europe*, Alphen aan den Rijn, Kluwer, 2007, 247. Karin Lukas states that the provision states the highest conformity rate of all the provisions of the ESC (rev) (Karin Lukas, *The revised European Social Charter*, Cheltenham, Edward Elgar, 2021, p. 247).

4 ECSR, Conclusions 2022, France.

5 ECSR, Conclusions, Turkey.

bargaining between employers or employers' and workers' organisations with a view to determining pay and working conditions by means of collective agreements". Article 6 § 1 concerns the promotion of "joint consultation between workers and employers". In the authentic French version, the term *consultation paritaire* is used. The authentic English version refers to "joint consultation". It does not indicate which actors have a mandate to represent those workers and employers. Nor is it indicated that the outcome of these consultations would be collective agreements. Contrary to Article 6 § 2, nor is the subject of consultation indicated.

The term "collective bargaining" in the *rubric* and in the opening words of Article 6 ESC (rev) may be referred to as a *genus*, as opposed to the term referred to in Article 6 § 2. In the English version, a distinction is made between "bargaining" (in the introduction) and "negotiations" in Article 6, § 2 ESC (rev). It would likely have been preferable to conceive "negotiations" as the broadest category and "bargaining" as the specific category related to collective agreements.

The added value of Article 6 § 2 ESC (rev) lies in the possibility of identifying actors of collective negotiations *other* than those traditionally reserved for collective bargaining. It seems obvious to us that the use of the terms 'employees' and 'employers' in that provision cannot indicate a 'direct' form of consultation by the employer in the undertaking. Such an atomising model of employee involvement runs counter to the idea of representation and cannot be reconciled with the idea that consultation should be *joint*. After all, joint consultation presupposes that the employees' side is represented. It is apparent that the word *parity* should not be interpreted in an overly numerical or mathematical sense.

The ESC (rev) also offers the possibility of guaranteeing a form of collective consultation for parts of the *public sector* in which there is no collective bargaining.[6] Since Article 21 ESC (rev) does not apply to the public sector, this issue is important.[7] In the absence of collective bargaining in the public sector,

---

6 See the recent conclusion of non-conformity against Bulgaria for not providing joint consultation in the public sector: ECSR, Conclusions, XX-3, Bulgaria, and also ECSR, Conclusions, XX-3, former Yugoslav Republic of Macedonia.

7 As recently confirmed in *Confederazione Generale Sindacale* (CGS) *and Federazione dei Lavoratori Pubblici e Funzioni Pubbliche* (FLP) *v. Italy*, Complaint No. 161/2018, decision on the merits of 19 October 2022, § 46; *Associazione Nazionale Sindacato Professionisti Sanitari della Funzione Infermieristica – Nursing Up v. Italy*, Complaint No. 169/2018, decision on the merits of 19 October 2022, § 42.

Article 6 § 1 may offer some relief.[8] It might also be a fallback scenario for those states not having accepted Article 21 ESC (rev).

In such a situation, the role of the state as facilitator of consultation and that of the employer may coincide. In one case, the question arose to what extent and to which state power this obligation to promote collective bargaining should be addressed. In Complaint No. 25/2004, a trade union in the public sector invoked the infringement of Article 6 § 1 ESC (rev). Under Belgian law, the government is obliged to submit draft laws on the regulation of working conditions to specialised joint negotiating committees for advice. However, a breach of this obligation shall not be subject to jurisdictional sanctions. Nor is there an obligation to submit legislative proposals or amendments by the government for its opinion. The ECSR considered that the Belgian situation was not contrary to Article 6 § 1 ESC (rev). The Committee considered that the restriction on the right to joint consultation was legitimate because of the need not to paralyse legislative work.[9]

The so-called joint consultation can also be broader than the consultation on terms of employment *sensu stricto*. The *Digest*[10] refers to "matters of mutual interest, and particularly: productivity, efficiency, industrial health, safety and welfare, and other occupational issues (working conditions, vocational training, etc.), economic problems and social matters (social insurance, social welfare, etc.)". This clarification is in line with an explanation (statement of interpretation) of 1969.[11] The use of the ideologically coloured term "mutual interest" clarifies that consultation takes place in an atmosphere other than collective bargaining.[12] In ILO Recommendation No. 94 concerning Consultation and Cooperation between Employers and Workers at the Level of the Undertaking (1952), the concept of "mutual concern" appears. The

8 See also Filip Dorssemont and Marco Rocca, "Article 6 ESC: The Right to Bargain Collectively", in Niklas Bruun, Klaus Loercher, Isabelle Schoemann and Stefan Clauwaert, *The European Social Charter and the Employment Relation,* Oxford, Hart Publishing, 2017, pp. 255–256.

9 For a critique of the position adopted by the ECSR in this decision, see Jean Jacqmain, "La Négociation Collective dans les Services Publics et la Charte Sociale Européenne", *Chron. D. S.* 2006, No. 7, pp. 369–370.

10 See *Digest of the case law of the European Committee of Social Rights,* Council of Europe, 2022, p. 87.

11 ECSR, Conclusions I, 31 May 1969.

12 *Contra* Csilla Kollonay Lehoczky, "The Fundamental Right of Workers to Information and Consultation Under the European Social Charter", in Filip Dorssemont and Thomas Blanke (eds.), *The Recast of the European Works Council Directive,* Antwerpen, Intersentia, 2010, p. 7.

Committee has indicated that the subject matter of joint consultations covers a wide range of subjects.[13]

II Situations Requiring Information and Consultation

Article 2 of the aforementioned Additional Protocol (1988) cannot be seen in isolation from a major development in labour law in the European Union between 1961 and 1988. In the years 1975 to 1977, a number of directives were adopted which apply to specific scenarios of restructuring, in particular collective redundancies and transfers of undertaking. If the employer is contemplating collective redundancies, he shall be obliged to consult the workers' representatives in good time with a view to reaching an agreement. In the case of a transfer of undertaking, there is an obligation on the transferor and transferee to inform their employees of the transfer. If the transferor or transferee envisages measures in relation to his own employees, he shall consult the representatives of his employees in good time on such measures with a view to reaching an agreement.

In 1988, Article 2 of the Additional Protocol represented a twofold added value in the light of this *acquis communautaire*. First of all, a principle was induced which was exemplified in both directives. Employees have the right "to be consulted in good time on proposed decisions likely to have a significant effect on employees' interests and, in particular, on decisions which could have a significant effect on employment within the undertaking". Secondly, a right to information was assumed to be more recurrent by nature (regular or timely). It does not relate to a specific restructuring scenario, but to the generic economic and financial situation of the undertaking. It is noteworthy that no obligation has been encapsulated to provide information on the social situation of the undertaking.

Article 2 of the Additional Protocol was taken over unaltered in the revised European Social Charter, thus prefiguring a later development of European labour law. Indeed, it was not until the adoption of EWC Directive 94/45 that this principle of a generic right to information and consultation in the event of restructuring scenarios[14] and before a right to recurrent information on

13 ECSC, Conclusions XIX, Croatia. ECSR, Conclusions, 22 October 2010, Bulgaria. ECSR, Conclusions, 22 October 2010, Moldova.

14 The subsidiary requirements of EWC Directive 94/45 stipulated that where special circumstances arise which have a significant impact on employees' interests, particularly in the

the development of the undertaking's activities was generally recognised for employees in groups or undertakings with a EU dimension.[15] This approach was followed in the Framework Directive 2002/14 on Information and Consultation. This Directive relates to information and consultation within the boundaries of a Member State at the undertaking level or at the level of an establishment. In accordance with Article 4 of this Directive, the information to be provided must relate to the recent and probable development of activities and the economic situation of the undertaking or establishment. Employees (representatives) must also be informed and consulted, on the one hand, as to the situation, structure, and probable development of employment within the undertaking or establishment and, on the other hand, as to any anticipatory measures envisaged, particularly in the event of a threat to employment and, where appropriate, on decisions likely to lead to substantial changes in work organisation or in contractual relations.

The revision of the European Social Charter in 1996 subsequently led to a treaty provision specifically dealing with the restructuring scenario of collective redundancies. Article 29 ESC (rev) now requires employers to inform and consult workers' representatives in good time prior to such collective redundancies on ways and means of avoiding collective redundancies or limiting their occurrence and mitigating their consequences, for example by recourse to accompanying social measures aimed, in particular, at aid for the redeployment or retraining of the workers concerned. This provision fundamentalises the core provision of the aforementioned European Directive on collective redundancies.

---

event of relocation, closure of undertakings or establishments, or collective redundancies, the selected committee or, failing that, the EWC shall have the right to be informed. It shall have the right to convene, at its request, a meeting with the central management or any other more appropriate level of management with its own powers of decision within the Community-scale undertaking or Community-scale group of undertakings in order to be informed and consulted on measures significantly affecting employees' interests. The same provision is now included in Article 3 of the subsidiary requirements in the EWC Recast Directive 2009/38.

15 According to the subsidiary requirements of EWC Directive 94/45, this information must relate in particular to "the structure of the undertaking or group, its financial and economic situation, the probable development of its activities, production and marketing, the employment situation and trend, investments, substantial changes in its organisation, the introduction of new working methods or manufacturing processes, the transfer of production, mergers, the reduction or closure of undertakings, establishments or significant parts thereof and collective redundancies". The same provision is now included in Article 1(a) of the subsidiary requirements in the EWC Recast Directive 2009/38.

The revision of the European Social Charter also gave rise to the inclusion of a provision requiring a stronger form of worker participation. Article 22 ESC (rev) refers to a right of workers to take part in the determination and improvement of working conditions and working environment in the undertaking, which is qualified as a right to "participate" in health and safety policy. Once again, this is a fundamentalisation of an approach previously elaborated in the European Framework Directive 89/391. Article 11 of this Directive refers to the right of workers or their representatives to "participate" in a balanced way in the safety policy developed by the Directive. This form of employee participation goes beyond mere information and consultation. It allows employees' representatives to work out proposals themselves proactively, rather than being informed if an employer is considering a decision.

III Information and Consultation, Test of Definition

One shortcoming of Article 21 concerns the finding that the European Social Charter does not define two key concepts of this provision. It neither defines information nor consultation. Nor is there any definition in the "case law" of the supervisory ECSR. This observation is not specific. There are no definitions of the fundamental rights proclaimed in the ESC (rev) or in its appendix.

It seems to us that, in a spirit of intertextuality, inspiration can be drawn from the definitions provided by European Union law in this area. The right to information implies an obligation on the part of the employer to communicate certain information in such a way as to enable the recipients, in particular the employees (representatives), to acquire knowledge of the socioeconomic situation of the undertaking or of the consequences of a particular decision. In this sense, the concept of information was defined by the EU legislator in the SE Directive (Article 2(i)),[16] in the Framework Directive (Article 2(f))[17] and finally in the EWC Recast Directive (Article 2(1)(f)).[18] It follows from these definitions that the information provided is intended to serve a specific purpose. The information provided must enable recipients to obtain an adequate view

16 Council Directive 2001/86/EC of 8 October 2001 supplementing the Statute for a European company with regard to the involvement of employees, *OJ L* 283, 27.10.2001. *L.* 10 November 2001, exp. 294.

17 Directive 2002/14/EC of the European Parliament and of the Council 11 March 2002 establishing a general framework for informing and consulting employees in the European Community.

18 Directive 2009/38/EC of the European Parliament and of the Council 6 May 2009 on the establishment of a European Works Council or a procedure in Community-scale

of the undertaking by processing these data and drawing conclusions from them. The information provided also constitutes the basis for the consultation procedure and collective bargaining.[19] In other words, the right to information plays a pivotal role in the implementation of the other fundamental social rights relating to worker involvement. In view of this dual objective, the mere transmission of a set of incoherent data, of partial knowledge or of mere opinions relating to certain facts is insufficient. The right to information implies that the information provided is structured, complete, objective, and truthful, so that the recipient can gain insight with the help of this information.

The way in which the information is to be provided is by no means uniformly regulated in the various sources of law. Although only a limited part of the legal instruments explicitly stipulates the written nature of the obligation to provide information,[20] the provision of written information is often recommended for reasons of proof. The subjects on which the employees (representatives) must be informed are varied and differ in the various schemes. In general, a distinction can be made between the right to information on the general situation of the undertaking and the right to information on specific entrepreneurial decisions. Taken together, the various relevant sources of law on the right to information cover virtually the entire spectrum of business events. In any case, the right to information only implies that certain objectively correct data are made available to employees. However, the mere knowledge of information cannot influence the decision-making process. Influence can only be exerted if the information obtained is used in a targeted manner within the framework of a consultation procedure. Viewed in isolation, the right to information is not such that it may affect the employer's decision-making power (the so-called "managerial prerogative").

As in the case of the right to information, it was once again the EU regulator who defined the notion of consultation in the SE Directive (Article 2(j)), the Framework Directive (Article 2(g)) and the EWC Recast Directive (Article 2(1)(g)).

---

undertakings and Community-scale groups of undertakings for the purposes of informing and consulting employees.

19 As can be seen, for example, from the definition of "information" in Article 2(i) of the SE Directive. In a similar sense, Article 7 of ILO Recommendation No. 163 states that the employer is obliged to disclose all information on the economic and social situation of the undertaking, or part thereof, which is necessary for the conduct of collective bargaining.

20 See, for example, the collective redundancy scheme or Articles 5 and 6 of Collective Labour Agreement No. 9, which deals with the obligation to provide information in the event of changes in the structure of the company, and does not, on the other hand, pronounce on the oral or written nature of the information provided, nor do most other legal norms.

It is clear from these definitions that the right to consultation implies an exchange of views and the establishment of a dialogue between the employees' representatives and the employer. It is also stressed that establishing a meaningful exchange of views and dialogue presupposes, first and foremost, sufficient and correct information. The difference between the provision and receipt of information lies in the fact that consultation relates to an evaluation of the data communicated and the formation of an opinion on these data. In addition, consultation is about communicating the opinion formed within the framework of a dialogue established for that purpose. The establishment of a dialogue and an exchange of views necessary for consultation is thus opposed to a passive attitude on the part of the employer. After all, it is difficult to see how ideas can be exchanged and dialogue established when the employer would only be obliged to collect the opinions and suggestions of the employees without communicating his own insights. Finally, effective consultation presupposes a certain procedural framework, with the minimum requirement that the parties to the consultation process be allowed sufficient time to examine each other's proposals and comments and to take a position on them.

The areas to be covered by the consultation, as well as the persons that are to be informed, cannot be understood in general terms. Part of the legal instruments that guarantee the right to consultation involves a broad, general interpretation of the subject matter of the right.[21] However, other sources of law provide a more specific consultation obligation in well-defined cases, such as collective redundancies, transfers of undertakings or other types of restructuring. In any case, it is inherent to the right to consultation that, as in the case of the right to information, the final decision-making power of the employer is, in principle, not affected. The *managerial prerogative* is, at most, subject to procedural restrictions but by no means substantially curtailed.

IV Timeliness of Information and Consultation

The ESC (rev) stresses the importance of the timeliness of information and consultation. Information is said to be communicated on a regular and timely basis ("at the appropriate *time*"). This turn of phrase is somewhat unfortunate. Recurrent information on the general economic and financial situation of the

---

21 See, for example, some ILO standards (Article 57 ILO Tripartite Declaration for Multinational Enterprises, Article 1 ILO Recommendation No. 94) and the OECD Guidelines for Multinational Enterprises (Articles IV, 2, c and IV, 8), which guarantee the right to consultation in *matters of mutual concern*.

company should be provided on a regular basis, while information in the context of restructuring should be given on a timely basis. The timeliness of the information is particularly relevant for the purposes of the consultation procedure referred to in Article 21(b) ESC (rev). Such consultation presupposes timely information. In this respect, there is obviously no choice between regularity *or* timeliness.

The moment at which employees (representatives) are involved in the decision-making process is a crucial factor for the effectiveness of the right to information and consultation. The aim of these rights can only be optimally reached if this moment is situated in such a way that the employees (representatives) not only have insight into the decisions taken by the management but also have the opportunity to influence the decisions to be taken. This presupposes anteriority of the information and consultation of employees (representatives) not only with regard to the consequences of a decision, but also with regard to the decision itself. In other words, against the background of the protective and emancipatory purpose of the right to information and consultation of employees (representatives), it is difficult to argue for anything other than timely information and consultation procedures prior to taking the decision. Otherwise, any right to information and consultation would be deprived of its *effet utile.*

Nevertheless, it is important to underline that neither in the EU legal order nor in the national legal systems do information and consultation procedures fundamentally affect the (economic) freedom of decision of the economic operator. Information and consultation procedures are, at most, such as to modulate the managerial prerogative solely from a procedural point of view. The development of labour law did generate, to some extent, some kind of security, but only acts to a minor extent to the detriment of economic freedom. The introduction of information and consultation obligations, capable of suspending the exercise of the economic decision-making process, has been an important element in that process. This idea was at the heart of a number of EU legal instruments, such as, for example, the EWC Recast Directive. According to the 14th recital in the preamble to this Directive, the arrangements for informing and consulting employees must be defined and implemented in such a way as to ensure their effectiveness with regard to the provisions of the Directive. To this end, the information and consultation of the EWC should make it possible to deliver an opinion to the undertaking in a timely fashion without calling into question the ability of undertakings to adapt.

There is a logical link not only between the aim of the right to information and consultation but also with the moment at which employees' representatives must be involved in the decision-making process. The subject of the information and consultation obligation also largely determines this point in time. It goes without saying that this point in time will be different when employees' representatives are informed and consulted solely on the consequences of a decision than when they are involved in the actual decision-making process itself. Furthermore, in international groups of undertakings there is often an additional cross-border element. A decision with (potentially) significant consequences for the employees is rarely taken at the same level as that at which the decision is implemented. Important decisions (e.g., to reorganise the company) are, in many cases, taken by an entity in a country other than that in which the employees are linked to their employer by a contract of employment and, thus, in a country with a different legal system compared to that from which the employees derive their right to information and consultation. It is precisely because of these differences resulting from the application of the principle of territoriality that may otherwise lead to unequal treatment of the employees concerned that the EU regulator in particular has considered it useful and necessary to devise a system ensuring that employees of undertakings or groups of undertakings operating in different (Member) States are informed and consulted in an equivalent manner on decisions which, directly or indirectly, affect their interests. The fact that the legislator's main focus was on (cross-border) restructuring decisions is shown, *inter alia*, by the preliminary recitals to the original EWC Directive 94/45/EC and the Recast Directive 2009/38/EC. It noted that the functioning of the internal market involves a process of concentrations of undertakings, cross-border mergers, takeovers and cooperation agreements between undertakings, and that the harmonious development of the economic activities of undertakings or groups of undertakings operating in different Member States requires that employees be informed and consulted (equally). As can also be seen from the other preliminary considerations, the European legislator seemed to consider that, in the case of cross-border restructuring in undertakings or groups of undertakings with a transnational structure, a purely local information and consultation procedure was not sufficient to ensure that the right to information and consultation was properly implemented.

V The Level of the Undertaking

Whereas the EU regulator – in particular in the EWC Directives – has paid attention to linking the levels at which information and consultation should take place, Article 21 ESC (rev) (only) stresses that information and consultation should take place at the level of the undertaking. This is also explicitly provided for in the first part of the ESC (rev), in which fundamental rights are listed.

The concept of undertaking is a multi-faceted concept. In the Appendix to the Additional Protocol, this concept was defined in the following terms: "a set of tangible and intangible components, with or without legal personality, intended for the production of goods or the provision of services, for profit and with the power to determine its own market policy". In our view, this economic concept of enterprise is in line with the economic and financial approach to the subject matter of the information. This is without prejudice to the fact that, according to the Appendix, the rights to information and consultation can also be exercised at the level of the establishments. Yet, the Appendix does not further define the concept of establishment. It may be assumed that it concerns a part of a company that does not manifest itself on the market and so one can think of the company in a more social-law sense of a working community.

The Appendix does not leave room for the reverse movement where the rights are exercised at group level. The ESC (rev) clearly allows for this, but it does not relieve Member States of the duty to guarantee the right to information and consultation also at a lower level. It seems obvious that this distinction between the level of the undertaking and the level of the establishment is at the basis of the option developed in the Framework Directive 2002/14. Just as many other European directives relating to employee involvement implicitly or explicitly stipulate an employment threshold, the Framework Directive also stipulates that the minimum information and consultation requirements must at least be complied with by undertakings employing a certain number of employees. In particular, Member States were given the option of imposing these minimum requirements either in undertakings employing at least 50 employees or in establishments employing at least 20 employees (Article 3(1) of the Framework Directive). Both the notion of undertaking and the notion of establishment were defined in the Framework Directive, albeit in a rather ambiguous way. In particular, the undertaking "means a public or private undertaking carrying out an economic activity, whether or not operating for gain, which is located within the territory of the Member States" (Article 2(a)). An establishment within the meaning of the Framework Directive "means a unit of business defined in accordance with national law and practice, and located within the territory of a Member State, where an economic activity is carried out on an ongoing basis with human and material resources" (Article 2(b)).

The Appendix considers some of the privileges granted to "Establishments pursuing activities which are inspired by certain ideals or guided by certain moral concepts, ideals and concepts" in a number of legal orders. The most prominent example of such a privilege is exemplified by the German Works

Constitution Act. The Provision of the BetrVG stipulates that the "provisions of this Act shall not apply to enterprises and establishments which directly and predominantly serve political, coalition, confessional, charitable, educational, scientific or artistic purposes or purposes of reporting or expression of opinion to which Article 5 para. 1 sentence 2 of the Basic Law applies, insofar as the specific nature of the enterprise or establishment precludes this".

The Appendix states that religious communities and their institutions may be excluded from the application of these Articles even where these institutions are undertakings within the meaning of paragraph 3. Institutions which pursue activities inspired by certain ideals and beliefs protected by national law may be excluded from the application of these Articles in so far as this is necessary to protect the purpose of that undertaking.

Both formulas are so close to each other that the ECSR has so far never noticed that the German exception would be wider than the European one. This German exception was also neatly paraphrased in the Framework Directive.[22]

The Appendix allows another exception that can affect *all* employees in a company. According to the Appendix, undertakings whose staff numbers are under the limit set by national law or practice may be excluded from the application of these Articles. The way to calculate the number of workers is not beyond scrutiny. Hence, the French state has recently been confronted with a negative conclusion because "certain employees are excluded from the calculation of the undertaking's workforce which is carried out for the determination of the minimum thresholds for the establishment of employee representative institutions which ensure the information and consultation of employees".[23]

A second limit to the restrictions has been elaborated in case law. The ECSR shall closely monitor that the right to information and consultation of the vast majority of employees remains guaranteed. States unable to do so will face criticism.

---

22 See Article 3(2): "Member States may, in compliance with the principles and objectives laid down in this Directive, lay down specific provisions for undertakings or establishments pursuing political, professional, religious, charitable, educational, scientific or artistic aims, or aims involving information or the expression of opinions, or serving professional organisations, provided that such specific provisions already exist in national law on the date of entry into force of this Directive".

23 ECSR, Conclusions 2014, France.

VI Restrictions: Confidential and Secret Information

Few fundamental rights are absolute. However, the ESC (rev) limits these potential restrictions. As is the case for the right to collective action, a distinction must be made between the internal restrictions that arise from the phrasing of the article proclaiming the right and those which stem from the horizontal provision of Article G. Article 21 ESC (rev) contains a single provision setting an internal limit to the right to information and consultation. The right to information and consultation may, in particular, be restricted where the disclosure of certain information could harm the undertaking. Article 21 ESC (rev) offers possibilities both to refuse disclosure and to demand confidentiality.

The possibility of restricting the right to information by classifying certain information as secret or confidential is not trivial. Labour relations are pre-eminently power relations, and the acquisition of knowledge is a crucial element in the acquisition of power. But even more than ordinary knowledge (information), the acquisition of hidden knowledge (secret information) or of knowledge one prefers to keep hidden as much as possible (confidential information) implies the acquisition of power. In other words, a proper understanding of the scope of the right to information requires an understanding of the limits of the obligation to provide information, in particular the possibility for the party responsible for providing information to keep certain information secret or confidential.

Various sources of law relating to the right to information and consultation provide for the possibility for corporate management to classify information as secret or confidential. In addition to the provision of Article 21(a) ESC (rev), provisions relating to confidential information are included in the EWC Directive, the SE Directive and the Framework Directive.[24] Like Article 21(a) ESC (rev), these provisions also provide for the possibility of derogating from the obligation to communicate certain information (secret information). Under the conditions laid down by law, information may also be classified as confidential.

However, under no circumstances will the management of a business with a duty to provide information be able to determine *ad libitum* which information is confidential, and which is not. Accountability by the head of the enterprise in the interest of the enterprise is always required. The criterion of corporate interest also applies when classifying information as secret information. An essential difference, however, is that classified information relates

24 Art. 8 EWC Directive (Recast); Art. 8 SE Directive; Art. 6 Framework Directive.

only to the points listed in the aforementioned legislative provisions, whereas confidential information can, in principle, relate to any information. Moreover, contrary to secrecy, the confidentiality of information should in principle not be subject to prior authorisation. The degree of prejudice, whether serious or minor, is manifestly irrelevant in the light of Article 21(a) ESC (rev).

Concluding Remarks

It is not easy to draw an unambiguous conclusion from the elements analysed above. One perspective could be the question of the added value of Article 21 ESC (rev). First, there is the question of the added value of this provision compared to other provisions in fundamental rights instruments. Although a comparison between the libelling of Article 21 of the ESC and the libelling of Article 27 of the CFREU[25] is not the subject of this study, it is to be regretted that the Charter cannot match the standard of the ESC (rev) nor that of secondary EU law. The most problematic element is the total absence of a description of the object of information and consultation. In the context of the TFEU, the conditioning by EU and national law of the right to information and consultation might lead to a downgrading of the right to information and consultation to a mere principle. In the AMS case, the Court of Justice deprived this "fundamental right" of the limited justiciability that principles enjoy.[26] The Court reduced it to a provision deprived of direct effect. The only added value of the Charter seems to us to be the idea that information and consultation should take place at the appropriate level. This idea opens up the prospect of developing information and consultation at a multi-layered company level that embraces the European level.

The added value of the ESC (rev) in relation to secondary EU law is of a different order. *Prima facie*, this article in the charter seems to be a fine reproduction of the extensive *acquis*. Placing the development of Union law in a historical perspective, Article 21 ESC (rev) announces a programme for the

25 "Workers and their representatives must, in the cases and under the conditions provided for by Union law and national laws and practices, be guaranteed timely information and consultation at appropriate levels".

26 CJEU, 15 January 2014, C-176/12; see also in this respect: Filip Dorssemont, "The Right to Information and Consultation in Article 27 of the Charter of Fundamental Rights of the European Union: Less Than a Right and Less Than a Principle, Just an Ordinary Provision Lacking Direct Effect?", *Maastricht Journal of European and Comparative Law*, 2014, pp. 704–722.

future development of labour law in another European legal order. At the time the Additional Protocol was signed, directives protecting participation law had not yet developed in this way. In fact, the Additional Protocol is older than the Community Charter for Workers of the European Union. In the meantime, EU labour law has evolved. Hence, the added value of this provision might be more evident for those countries of the Council of Europe that are not members of the European Union.

The libelling of Article 21 ESC (rev) seems to us to be primarily indebted to existing practices in the Member States of the European Union. It can be seen as a fundamentalisation of those practices in the European Union, just as the recognition of the right to information and consultation used to be a consecration and consolidation of an existing legislative and conventional practice.

In undertakings without consultative bodies and without a trade union delegation, recurring information and consultation will be non-existent. The granting of this fundamental right only to a large majority, as permitted by the Additional Protocol, is sufficient to overcome this loophole. If the development of the business world is such that only a minority of employees are entitled to such a right, another provision in the appendix may still help. The explanatory memorandum to Article 21 ESC (rev) states that undertakings may be excluded if their staff numbers do not reach the threshold set by national law or practice.

ARTICLE 22

The Right to Take Part in the Determination and Improvement of the Working Conditions and Working Environment

Ana Teresa Ribeiro and Filipe Venade de Sousa

With a view to ensuring the effective exercise of the right of workers to take part in the determination and improvement of the working conditions and working environment in the undertaking, the Parties undertake to adopt or encourage measures enabling workers or their representatives, in accordance with national legislation and practice, to contribute:

a to the determination and the improvement of the working conditions, work organisation and working environment;
b to the protection of health and safety within the undertaking;
c to the organisation of social and socio-cultural services and facilities within the undertaking;
d to the supervision of the observance of regulations on these matters.

Introduction

Article 22 of the ESC (rev) was a new provision, included in Part II of the 1996 Charter, despite the fact that its material content had already been included in Article 3 of the Additional Protocol to the European Social Charter of 1988[1]

1 This means that there are some States that have ratified the Additional Protocol and which are bound to this provision, even though they have not ratified the ESC (rev) – Niklas Bruun, "Article 22 The Right to Take Part in the Determination and Improvement of the Working Conditions and Working Environment", in Niklas Bruun, Klaus Lörcher, Isabelle Schömann and Stefan Clauwaert (eds.), *The European Social Charter and the Employment Relation*, Bloomsbury, London, 2017, p. 405; Teun Jaspers, "Article 22 The Right to Take Part in the Determination and Improvement of the Working Conditions and Working Environment", in Edoardo Ales, Mark Bell, Olaf Deinert and Sophie Robin-Olivier (eds.), *International and*

 | DOI:10.1163/9789004434158_004

(a document approved with the intent of extending the protection of the social and economic rights guaranteed by the original Charter of 1961).[2] This provision is closely linked to Article 21, and several of its key concepts, such as "workers", "workers' representatives", and "undertakings", shall be applied in the same way as under Article 21.[3]

This norm guarantees the right of workers, by themselves or through their representatives, to participate in the shaping and improvement of their working environment.[4] Therefore, given its scope, it is not only closely connected to Article 3, on occupational health and safety (which is the more operational and technical counterpart of Article 22),[5] but also to Articles 2 and 4 of the Charter,[6] on the right to just conditions of work and the right to fair remuneration, respectively, since it applies to working conditions and work organisation.[7] Finally, it is also linked to other provisions of the Charter that deal with different aspects of workers' participation, namely Articles 21, 28, and 29, on the right to information and consultation, the right to workers' representatives to protection in the undertaking and facilities to be accorded to them, and the right to information and consultation in collective redundancy procedures, respectively.[8]

European Labour Law. Article-by-Article Commentary, Nomos/Beck/Hart, Baden-Baden/München/Oxford, 2018, p. 331.

2 See Preamble, Additional Protocol to the European Social Charter, Strasbourg, 5.V.1988; Niklas Bruun, *cit.*, p. 405.

3 See *idem, ibidem*, p. 405.

4 Karin Lukas, *The Revised European Social Charter. An Article-By-Article Commentary*, Edward Elgar Publishing, Cheltenham/Northampton, 2021, p. 275.

5 Since these Articles partly overlap for States Parties that have accepted them both, the ECSR assesses these matters under Article 22 – *idem, ibidem*, p. 277. Niklas Bruun (*cit.*, p. 405) adds that Article 22 contains procedural guarantees that are necessary to ensure the effectiveness of Article 3 of the Charter, such as the involvement of workers' representatives. Similarly, Teun Jaspers (*cit.*, p. 331) states that Article 22 not only complements Article 3 by providing the involvement of workers and their representatives in determining and improving the working conditions, work-organization, and working environment, but also by empowering these actors to contribute to the protection of health and safety within the company. Therefore, it strengthens the right enshrined in Article 3.

6 Karin Lukas, *cit.*, p. 275.

7 Niklas Bruun, *cit.*, p. 406.

8 *Idem, ibidem*, p. 406.

1 General Considerations

A *Contextualization of Sources*

Aside from Article 22 of the ESC (rev), there are other relevant international sources which also state the workers' right to take part in the determination of their working conditions and environment. Namely, at the UN level, ILO Conventions No. 155 (on occupational health and safety)[9] and No. 187[10] (on the promotional framework for occupational health and safety), which allude to the participation of workers in these domains.

In turn, within the EU, Directive 89/391/EEC, on the introduction of measures to encourage improvements in the safety and health of workers at work (wherein Article 11 enshrines the consultation and information of workers regarding occupational health and safety) should be stressed, as well as Directive 2002/14/EC, on information and consultation. In addition, Article 27 of the CFREU enshrines the workers' right to information and consultation within the undertaking – even though this is not mentioned in its explanations, the interpretation of this should also take into account the contents of Article 22 ESC (rev)[11] –, while Articles 17, 18, and 19 of the Community Charter of the Fundamental Social Rights of Workers also delve on the right of workers and their representatives to information, consultation and participation (namely regarding health and safety).

B *Scope of Application*

The personal scope of application of Article 22 (which is to be interpreted in the light of Articles 18 and 19) includes foreigners only insofar as they are nationals of other States Parties, lawfully residing or working regularly within the territory of the Party concerned.[12]

For the purpose of this Article, the term "undertaking" is understood as referring to a set of tangible and intangible components, with or without legal personality, formed to produce or provide services for financial gain and with

9 Approved in 1981, this convention had a clear impact on the content and wording of Article 22 – see *idem, ibidem*, p. 405.

10 According to Teun Jaspers (*cit.*, p. 332), this instrument was partially inspired by Article 22.

11 Niklas Bruun, *cit.*, p. 411.

12 This interpretation does not prejudice the extension of similar facilities to other persons by any of the States Parties – see Appendix (to the Additional Protocol to the European Social Charter) – Scope of the Protocol in terms of persons protected, Strasbourg, 5.V.1988.

power to determine its own market policy.[13] This provision also applies to all companies, public or private,[14] but not to public administration.[15]

However, and according to Article 3 § 2 of the Additional Protocol to the European Social Charter, States Parties may exclude from the field of application of this provision those undertakings employing fewer than a certain number of workers to be determined by national legislation or practice.[16] Furthermore, the Committee has already considered to be compatible with the Charter to exclude, from this provision, undertakings employing fewer than 10 people, when employees are in direct contact with the employer.[17] The Committee has also deemed it compatible with the Charter that, in companies with more than 50 workers, consultation and participation takes place in specific bodies, while, in companies with fewer than 50 workers, their opinions are expressed in the framework of negotiations.[18]

Furthermore, even if encompassed by this notion of undertaking, religious communities and their institutions may be excluded from the application of these articles. Similarly, establishments pursuing activities which are inspired

---

13 Furthermore, when these rights are exercised in the various establishments of the undertaking, the State Party will be considered as fulfilling the obligations deriving from these provisions – See Appendix (to the Additional Protocol to the European Social Charter) – Scope of the Protocol in terms of persons protected, Strasbourg, 5.V.1988.

14 ECSR, Conclusions 2007, Norway, Conclusions 2010, Portugal, and Conclusions 2014, Hungary.

15 See Niklas Bruun, *cit.*, p. 409 (to whom the Committee seems to adhere to a very restricted and formal interpretation of the word "undertaking") and ECSR, *Council of Police Trade Unions v. Portugal*, Complaint No. 40/2007, decision on the merits of 23 September 2008, § 42, and ECSR, *European Council of Police Trade Unions v. Portugal*, Complaint No. 60/2010, decision on the merits of 17 October 2011, § 36. This interpretation was recently confirmed in ECSR, *Confederazione Generale Sindacale* (CGS) *and Federazione dei Lavoratori Pubblici e Funzioni pubbliche* (FLP) *v. Italy*, Complaint No. 161/2018, decision on the merits of 19 October 2022, §§ 44–45.

16 ECSR, Conclusions 2014, Hungary. In addition, these rights may be exercised by delegation – see Explanatory Report to the Additional Protocol to the European Social Charter, Strasbourg, 5.V.1988, pt. 17. However, and as stressed by Antonio Márquez Prieto ("Derecho a Participar en la Determinación y en la Mejora de las Condiciones de Trabajo y del Entorno de Trabajo. Artículo 22 de la Carta Social Europea", in Cristina Monereo Atienza and José Luis Monereo Pérez (coord.), *La Garantía Multinivel de los Derechos Fundamentales en el Consejo de Europa:* El Convenio Europeo de Derechos Humanos y la Carta Social Europea, 2017, p. 813), it should be noted that since this possibility – to exclude companies under a certain threshold – is merely mentioned in Article 3 § 2 of the Additional Protocol, but not in Article 22 of the ESC (rev), it will only apply to the States Parties who have ratified the former, but not the latter.

17 ECSR, Conclusions 2005, Estonia.

18 ECSR, Conclusions 2014, Turkey.

by certain ideals or guided by certain moral concepts, ideals, and concepts which are protected by national legislation may be exempted from the application of Article 22 to the extent necessary to protect the orientation of the undertaking.[19]

Finally, the reference to the workers' representatives alludes to the persons who are recognised as such under national legislation or practice,[20] "trade unions, worker's delegates, health and safety representatives, works councils".[21] It has also been noted that the conjunction "or" used in the expression "workers or their representatives" is not exclusive. It merely means that the rights afforded by these two provisions may be exercised by workers, by their representatives, or by both, and the fact that they are conferred upon one group does not mean that they cannot be conferred upon the other, as stipulated in the Articles themselves.[22]

II The Contents of Article 22

A *General Normative Framework of Article 22*

According to Article 22, workers or their representatives are entitled to participate in the determination and improvement of their working conditions and working environment through the company's internal informative and consultive mechanisms. Such issues will, however, be ultimately decided by the company, since workers or their representatives are not given a veto right or a joint-decision power.[23] It is also noted that these rights to participate in the determination and improvement of working conditions and working

19 See Appendix (to the Additional Protocol to the European Social Charter) – Scope of the Protocol in terms of persons protected, Strasbourg, 5.V.1988; ECSR, Conclusions 2014, Hungary.

20 See Appendix (to the Additional Protocol to the European Social Charter) – Scope of the Protocol in terms of persons protected, Strasbourg, 5.V.1988. As stated by the Explanatory Report to the Additional Protocol to the European Social Charter (Strasbourg, 5.V.1988, pt. 31), this definition draws from Convention No. 135 of the ILO, so as to harmonize the definitions contained in the various international instruments.

21 See ECSR, *Greek General Confederation of Labour* (*GSEE*) *v. Greece*, Complaint No. 111/2014, decision on the merits of 23 March 2017, § 243.

22 See Explanatory Report to the Additional Protocol to the European Social Charter, Strasbourg, 5.V.1988, pt. 29.

23 See Explanatory Report to the Additional Protocol to the European Social Charter, Strasbourg, 5.V.1988, pt. 50.

environment through informative and consultive mechanisms in no way hinder the right to collective bargaining.[24]

Workers or their representatives are nevertheless entitled to take part in the decision-making process, which requires them to have full access to adequate information[25] in a timely manner.[26] This means that such participation has to take place before the implementation of measures, in order to ensure that workers and their representatives can have an effective influence on the decisions.[27]

In addition, since Article 22 enshrines a right to (effective) representation and consultation in the decision-making process and to supervision of the observance of regulations in all matters referred to in this provision, the Committee has indicated the need to look beyond the law to ensure participation in fact.[28]

To that effect, national laws must provide workers with legal remedies when these rights are not observed and establish sanctions for employers who do not fulfil their obligations under this provision.[29] The Committee will assess the severity of penalties, which should effectively act as a deterrent in respect to the violation of this Article.[30]

The term "national legislation and practice" encompasses, in addition to laws and regulations, collective agreements, other agreements between employers and workers' representatives, customs, as well as relevant case law.[31] Moreover,

---

24 See Explanatory Report to the Additional Protocol to the European Social Charter, Strasbourg, 5.V.1988, pt. 49.

25 Unless considerations on secrecy apply – see Teun Jaspers, *cit.*, p. 332.

26 Particularly since, especially regarding the working environment, this intervention will take place in a preventive fashion and, therefore, occur before the adoption of other measures – see Niklas Bruun, *cit.*, p. 408.

27 Teun Jaspers, *cit.*, p. 333.

28 David Harris and John Darcy, *The European Social Charter*, Transnational Publishers Inc., Ardsley/New York, 2001, 2nd edition, p. 249 and ECSR, Conclusions XIII-3, Finland and Conclusions 2007, Italy.

29 ECSR, Conclusions 2003, Bulgaria and Conclusions 2003, Slovenia. The effectiveness of this right requires workers to be able to lodge a complaint in the case of infringement. The right of appeal to a labour court is compatible with this Requirement – see Niklas Bruun, *cit.*, p. 408.

30 Teun Jaspers, *cit.*, p. 335.

31 See Appendix (to the Additional Protocol to the European Social Charter) – Scope of the Protocol in terms of persons protected, Strasbourg, 5.V.1988 and Explanatory Report to the Additional Protocol to the European Social Charter, Strasbourg, 5.V.1988, pt. 35. Given how this national legislation and practice is defined, encompassing collective agreements, among other sources, Niklas Bruun (*cit.*, p. 410) finds it slightly surprising that the Committee has found (on ECSR, *GENOP-DEI and ADEDY v. Greece*, Complaint No. 65/2011, decision on the merits of 23 May 2012, § 39) that this right, particularly § 1a, does not

it covers both the adoption and the encouragement of the measures envisaged to ensure the exercising of these rights, as well as the designation of the workers' representatives to whom such exercise may, then, be entrusted.[32] The States Parties may allow management and labour to decide the level at which workers or their representatives are normally informed and consulted and take part (undertaking, production unit, sector or branch, or even local, regional or national level).[33] However, when the definition of the measures necessary for the implementation of this provision is left to collective bargaining or other forms of voluntary negotiation, it must prove to be effective and adequate.[34]

B *The Right to Contribute to the Determination and Improvement of the Working Conditions, Work Organisation and Working Environment*

The compliance of national orders with this provision is evaluated taking into consideration the system of participation regarding the establishment of working conditions. When there are collective agreements, the extent of coverage of workers by these instruments is crucial. If the number of workers encompassed is low, the ECSR tends to conclude negatively in terms of compliance with Article 22 § 1(a), unless other forms of participation have been installed and operate in practice.[35]

Furthermore, according to Niklas Bruun, the material scope of this subparagraph goes further than the existing case-law, since the term "working conditions" should be understood in a broad sense, likely covering the whole area of at least individual labour law, in particular the rights to just conditions of work, to safe and healthy working conditions, to a fair remuneration, to protection in case of termination of employment, to dignity at work, and to equal opportunities and equal treatment, concerning workers with family responsibilities, thus requiring consultation on those issues.[36]

It should also be noted that, even though Article 22 provides great focus to the protection of workers' health and safety,[37] the Committee also attaches

concern the right to collective bargaining (a view that was, more recently, confirmed in ECSR, *Greek General Confederation of Labour* (GSEE) *v. Greece*, cit., § 243).

32 See Explanatory Report to the Additional Protocol to the European Social Charter, Strasbourg, 5.V.1988, pt. 30.

33 See Explanatory Report to the Additional Protocol to the European Social Charter, Strasbourg, 5.V.1988, pt. 33.

34 See Explanatory Report to the Additional Protocol to the European Social Charter, Strasbourg, 5.V.1988, pt. 32.

35 Teun Jaspers, *cit.*, p. 333 and ECSR, Conclusions 2010, Estonia.

36 Niklas Bruun, *cit.*, p. 407.

37 As stated by Niklas Bruun (*cit.*, p. 406), most of the Committee's practices have concerned subparagraph b, on health and safety.

importance to the other elements present in the text (working conditions, work organisation, and working environment). Therefore, it has criticized States Parties and asked for further information when, concerning this heading, reports merely convey the protection of health and safety, missing these other features.[38]

In its recent 2022 conclusions, the Committee asked for information on specific measures taken during the pandemic to ensure the respect of the right to take part in the determination and improvement of working conditions and the working environment. It "requested, in particular, specific reference to the situation and arrangements in the sectors of activity hit worst by the crisis whether as a result of the impossibility to continue their activity or the need for a broad shift to distance or telework, or as a result of their frontline nature, such as health care, law enforcement, transport, food sector, essential retail and other essential services". Additionally, it considered States Parties to be in conformity with this provision when no specific measures were taken, as long as the right to take part in the determination and improvement of the working conditions and working environment was already guaranteed by previous legislation.[39]

In fact, during the pandemic, the ECSR released a statement where it recalled the new dimensions social dialogue had taken and its new importance during the COVID-19 crisis.[40] To this end, "Trade unions and employers' organisations should be consulted at all levels on both employment-related measures focused on fighting and containing COVID-19 in the short term and efforts directed towards recovery from the economically disruptive effects of the pandemic in the longer term. Agreements to this effect, whether tripartite or bipartite, should be concluded where appropriate. This is called for at all levels, including the industry/sectoral level and the company level where new health and safety requirements, new forms of work organisation (teleworking, work-sharing, etc.) and workforce reallocation, all impose obligations with regard to consultation and information of workers' representatives in terms of Articles 21 and 22 of the Charter".[41]

38 *Idem, ibidem*, p. 406 and ECSR, Conclusions 2014, Bulgaria and Conclusions 2014, France.

39 See ECSR, Conclusions 2022, Estonia, Conclusions 2022, Finland, and Conclusions 2022, Portugal.

40 ECSR, Statement on COVID-19 and social rights, adopted on 24 March 2021, available at https://rm.coe.int/statement-of-the-ecsr-on-covid-19-and-social-rights/1680a230ca (accessed on 10 April 2023).

41 *Idem, ibidem*, pp. 5–6.

C *The Right to Contribute to the Protection of Health and Safety within the Undertaking*

This provision complements Article 3 of the Charter and, according to the Appendix, it affects neither the powers and obligations of States as regards the adoption of health and safety regulations for workplaces, nor the powers and responsibilities of the bodies in charge of monitoring their application.[42]

As stressed by Teun Jaspers, the Committee requires some form of workers' representation in this matter, accepting all kinds of representation if they involve workers in the policy of an enterprise, be it involvement in the decision-making by the employer, or information and consultation of a representing body.[43] Furthermore, when such a body does not exist, the employer must provide for the workers' participation, either by themselves or by external specialists.[44]

This norm can be complied with by providing for the representation of workers on a safety committee within the company.[45]

D *The Right to Contribute to the Organisation of Social and Socio-cultural Services and Facilities within the Undertaking*

The term "social and socio-cultural services and facilities" refers to social and/or cultural facilities provided for workers by some undertakings, such as welfare assistance, sports fields, rooms for nursing mothers, libraries, children's holiday camps, etc.[46] According to the Committee, this provision does not require employers to offer such social and socio-cultural services and facilities to their employees. It merely requires that workers be granted the right to participate in their organisation when the aforementioned services and facilities have already been established.[47]

---

42 Appendix (to the Additional Protocol to the European Social Charter) – Scope of the Protocol in terms of persons protected, Strasbourg, 5.V.1988.

43 Teun Jaspers, *cit.*, pp. 333–334 and ECSR, Conclusions 2005, Estonia, Conclusions 2014, Bosnia and Herzegovina and Conclusions XX-3, Denmark.

44 *Idem, ibidem*, p. 334.

45 David Harris and John Darcy, *cit.*, p. 250.

46 See Appendix (to the Additional Protocol to the European Social Charter) – Scope of the Protocol in terms of persons protected, Strasbourg, 5.V.1988. See ECSR, Conclusions 2014, Hungary, Conclusions 2014, Serbia.

47 ECSR, Conclusions 2007, Italy, Conclusions 2007, Armenia, Conclusions 2014, Serbia, Conclusions 2014, Russian Federation, Conclusions 2014, Ireland, and Conclusions 2014, Hungary. And, adds Karin Lukas, *cit.*, p. 279, where these services and facilities have already been planned.

E *The Right to Contribute to the Supervision of the Observance of Regulations on These Matters*

The contribution of workers or their representatives to the supervision of the observance of health and safety regulations shall be materialized taking into account the rules in force in each country and subject to the jurisdiction and the responsibilities of the bodies and authorities vested with such power.[48] However, their intervention does not replace the role of public authorities who possess legally conferred powers to supervise compliance with regulations in accordance with national legislation.[49] The role of workers or their representatives is, rather, to ensure that supervision is as effective as possible, complementing the national system.[50]

As stressed by Niklas Brunn, supervision cannot be exercised without rights to information and access to enforcement mechanisms, courts, and labour inspections.[51] Therefore, States Parties should allow for the presentation of complaints and the revision of decisions regarding complaints and should also enshrine sanctions and economic compensations in the case of violation of this right.[52]

Concluding Remarks

This provision contributes to one of the cornerstones of industrial democracy, the participation of workers and the taking in of their views within the undertaking. It allows workers and their representatives to be heard on issues pertaining to the working conditions in the company, to take part in the organisation of social and socio-cultural services and facilities within the undertaking, and to take action when such conditions are not in accordance with national legislation.

Nevertheless, this Article resorts to ample and ambiguous terms,[53] whose meaning could benefit from further development from the Committee's

48 Niklas Bruun, *cit.*, p. 408.

49 See Explanatory Report to the Additional Protocol to the European Social Charter, Strasbourg, 5.V.1988, pt. 51.

50 Teun Jaspers, *cit.*, p. 334.

51 Niklas Bruun, *cit.*, p. 408.

52 ECSR, Conclusions 2003, Slovenia, Conclusions 2003, Bulgaria, Conclusions 2014, Cyprus, Conclusions 2014, Lithuania, Conclusions 2014, Serbia, Conclusions 2014, Russian Federation, Conclusions 2014, the Netherlands, Conclusions 2014, Portugal.

53 Antonio Márquez Prieto, cit., p. 809. According to the Author, even its four main areas are unable to sufficiently identify the general meaning of this norm. Conversely, Karin Lukas

jurisprudence, such as the exact meaning of the reference made to working conditions,[54] the terms and procedures in which the workers' contribution is supposed to take place,[55] or the State's duties regarding the right of workers to contribute to the supervision of the observance of regulations on these matters.[56]

(*cit.*, p. 278) believes this provision to be clearly defined and that, in addition, it does not require much legislative and administrative effort. Therefore, it is not surprising that, in the latest reporting cycle (2018), it scored the second highest conformity rate of 84.4 per cent.

54 Antonio Márquez Prieto (*cit.*, p. 811) criticizes the wording of Article 22 (a), since, if it really aims to encompass all working conditions, then it partially overlaps with the following subparagraphs.

55 Antonio Márquez Prieto, *cit.*, p. 810.

56 As noted by Teun Jaspers (*cit.*, p. 334), even though it is not clear, from the ECSR's case law, what is required in order to conclude that a State Party's situation is in conformity with this particular provision, the effective involvement of workers' representatives in supervision must be ensured. It is clear, however, that the access to courts must be guaranteed – see ECSR, Conclusions 2003, Bulgaria and Conclusions 2010, Italy.

ARTICLE 23

The Right of Elderly Persons to Social Protection

Maria Paula Ribeiro de Faria and Luísa Andias Gonçalves

With a view to ensuring the effective exercise of the right of elderly persons to social protection, the Parties undertake to adopt or encourage, directly or in co-operation with public or private organisations, appropriate measures designed in particular:

- to enable elderly persons to remain full members of society for as long as possible, by means of:
  a) adequate resources enabling them to lead a decent life and play an active part in public, social and cultural life;
  b) provision of information about services and facilities available for elderly persons and their opportunities to make use of them;
- to enable elderly persons to choose their lifestyle freely and to lead independent lives in their familiar surroundings for as long as they wish and are able, by means of:
  a) provision of housing suited to their needs and their state of health or of adequate support for adapting their housing;
  b) the health care and the services necessitated by their state;
- to guarantee elderly persons living in institutions appropriate support, while respecting their privacy, and participation in decisions concerning living conditions in the institution.

Introduction

1 *Generalities*

The ageing population and the protection of their human rights is one of the most pressing issues on the agenda of Europe today.[1] This concern has become increasingly relevant in recent years (unlike women's rights and ethnic

1 Benny Spanier, Israel Doron and Faina Milman-Sivan, "Older Persons' Use of the European Court of Human Rights", *J Cross Cult Gerontol*, No. 28, 2013, pp. 407 ff., p. 407.

 | DOI:10.1163/9789004434158_005

minorities' rights, which have been receiving special attention for decades). One possible explanation for the relative paucity of decisions and studies on the elderly's rights is the difficulty to define what an "old person" is, hand in hand with the difficulty to recognize the violations of these rights, and the absence of the elderly's rights in some of the most relevant international conventions.[2]

The right of elderly persons to protection (including social protection) is very important. Age discrimination, as a "behaviour in which a person is disadvantaged as a result of their age",[3] has a great impact on older people and is believed to affect more than 164 million seniors living in Europe, which means that a significant proportion of Europeans is exposed to ageism.[4] Ageism is becoming of common concern in European forums, including the Council of Europe.

According to Article 1 of the Statute of the Council of Europe, one of the major aims of this Council is to "achieve a greater unit between its members for the purpose of safeguarding and realizing the ideals and principles (through) discussion of questions of common concern and by agreements and common action in (…) the maintenance and further realization of human rights and fundamental freedoms". According to Barbara Mikolajczyc,[5] "the substantial legal output of the Council of Europe bodies and the establishment of mechanisms controlling and monitoring the fulfilment of obligations arising from human rights treaties makes it possible to speak of a Council of Europe's 'mega-system' of human rights protection", covering over 820 million people in Europe, including older persons. For this reason, the Council of Europe appears to be a legitimate forum to take on the issues of ageing, the status of older persons and, finally, ageism, because, as social challenges, they fully match the goals of this organization.

The rights of older persons and their protection is increasingly becoming a subject of interest to various Council of Europe institutions, in particular to the Parliamentary Assembly, the Committee of Ministers and the Commissioner for Human Rights. During his 2006–2012 mandate, the Commissioner recalled

2 Diego Rodriguez-Pinzon and Claudia Martin, "The International Human Rights Status of Elderly Persons", *American University International Law Review*, No. 18, 2003, pp. 915–1008.

3 Jonathan Herring, *Older People in Law and Society*, OUP Oxford, 2009, p. 12. The term ageism was used for the first time by Robert Butler, *Why Survive? Being Old in America*, New York, Harper and Row, 1975, p. 35.

4 Barbara Mikolajczyc, "The Council of Europe's Approach Towards Ageism", in *Contemporary Perspectives on Ageing*, Ayalon, Liat/Tesch Römer, Clemens, Springer Verlag, 2013, Vol. 19, pp. 321 ff., p. 321.

5 Barbara Mikolajczyc, *op. cit.*, p. 321 (own translation).

several times in his country reports and human rights comments on the situation of older persons and the need to adopt better legislation to protect the elderly against ageism and abuses. He also praised the initiatives of the States that successfully contributed to fighting negative stereotypes against older adults, reinforcing the European awareness as to the rights of older people and the threats of ageism.[6]

II *Age as a Prohibited Ground for Discrimination*

Age is nowadays generally recognized as a prohibited ground for discrimination. The principle of equal treatment does not allow a person to be arbitrarily treated differently on the basis of age.

Outside the European context, the IACHR, approved on 15 June 2015, aims to promote, protect and ensure the recognition and the full and equal enjoyment and exercise of all human rights and fundamental freedoms of older persons, in order to contribute to their full inclusion, integration and participation in society. The Convention also enables individuals to submit complaints to the IACHR as to alleged violations of the human rights of older persons recognized in this instrument. In particular, Articles 5 (right to equality and non-discrimination for reasons of age), 6 (right to life and dignity), 7 (right to independence and autonomy) and 8 (right to participation and community integration) present remarkable similarities to Article 23 and E of the Charter, as they also intend to eliminate discrimination for reasons of age and to guarantee elderly people a full, independent, and autonomous life, health, safety, integration, and active participation in the economic, social, cultural and political spheres of society. At the soft law level, reference must be made to the Madrid International Plan on Ageing, adopted in 2002, with the purpose of building a society for all ages, and to the UN Principles for Older Persons, adopted by Resolution 46/91 of 16 December 1991.

The Convention on Social Security (Minimum Standards) of 1952 (No. 102) of the ILO establishes minimum standards for all branches of social security, including old-age benefits. In the labour field, it is important to remember Convention No. 128 on Invalidity, Old-Age and Survivors' Benefits of 1967, Recommendation No. 131 on Invalidity, Old-Age and Survivors' Benefits of 1967, and Recommendation No. 162 on Older Workers of 1980.

Nonetheless, a comprehensive Convention protecting the rights of elderly persons is still lacking at the international level.[7]

---

6 Barbara Mikolajczyc, *op. cit.*, p. 321, p. 323.

7 On the relevance of a UN Convention on elder's rights, see, for example, "Strengthening Older People's Rights: Towards a UN Convention", a resource for promoting dialogue on creating a new UN Convention on the rights of older persons presented by various

The protection of Human rights within the Council of Europe results from the convergence between the ECHR, which consecrates civil and political rights, and the ESC, which guarantees fundamental economic and social rights. The ESC has had less application than the ECHR, which is justified by the different nature of social rights and the institutional monitoring of the state of implementation of the ESC in the framework of the reporting system and the collective complaints procedure.

Yet, according to the ECSR, the ESC's rights must be interpreted as being as concrete and effective as the ECHR, in line with the case law of the ECtHR[8] (cf. ECSR, *International Federation of the Elderly Associations v. France*, complaint No. 145/2017, decision on the merits of 22 May 2019, § 56).

The ECSR considers that the function of Article E, Part VI, of the ESC is similar to that of Article 14 of the ECHR.[9] Therefore, Article E has no independent application and must be combined with the ESC's substantive provisions, which naturally includes Article 23.[10, 11]

entities, such as the INPEA, the IFA, the HelpAge International, the ILC-US, the IAHSA, the AARP International, the Age UK, the Global ageing and the IAGG, https://social.un.org/ageing-working-group/documents/Coalition%20to%20Strengthen%20the%20Rights%20of%20Older%20People.pdf (last consulted on 28 January 2020). See also Paula Ribeiro de Faria, *Os Crimes Praticados Contra Idosos*, 3rd edition, Porto, Edições Universidade Católica, 2019, p. 31.

8 Régis Brillat, "La Carta Sociale Europea e il Sistema di Tutela dei Diritti Sociali nelle Fonti Europee", *in La Carta Sociale Europea e la Tutela dei Diritti Sociali, Atti del Convegno del 18 Gennaio 2013 Università degli Studi di Milano*, Edizione Scientifiche Italiane, 2013, pp. 22–23.

9 Digest of the Case Law of the European Committee of Social Rights 2018, p. 43. Marilisa d'Amico, "La Carta Sociale Europea e la Tutela dei Diritti Sociali", in *La Carta Sociale Europea e la Tutela dei Diritti Sociali, Atti del Convegno del 18 Gennaio 2013, Università degli studi di Milano*, Napoli, Edizioni Scientifiche Italiane, 2013, p. 11.

10 Digest of the Case Law of the European Committee of Social Rights 2018, p. 43. ECtHR, 23 July 1968, "*Case related to certain aspects of the laws on the use of languages in education in Belgium" v. Belgium*, Procs. No. 1474/62, 1677/62; 1691/62; 1769/63; 1994/63; 2126/64, and ECtHR, 28 November 1984, *Rassmunen v. Denmark*, No. 8777/79. See also ECtHR, 16 September 1996, *Gaygusuz v. Austria*, No. 17371/90, Reports of Judgments and Decisions, 1996-IV, § 36.

11 Moreover, the ECSR takes into account the decisions of the ECHR regarding the application of Article 14 in order to define the significance of Article E (Régis Brillat, *op. cit.*, p. 23. ECtHR, 28 November 1984, *Rassmunen v. Denmark*, No. 8777/79, and ECtHR, 13 June 1979, *Marckx v. Bélgica*, No. 6833/74), therefore considering that a difference in treatment is discriminatory "when States treat differently persons in analogous situations without providing an objective and reasonable justification" (ECtHR, 29 April 2002, *Pretty v. United Kingdom*, No. 2346/02, § 32, and ECtHR, 6 April 2000, *Thlimmenos v. Greece*, No. 34369/97), that is, without the existence of a legitimate aim or a reasonable relationship of proportionality between the means employed and the aim sought to be realized. It adds that, being certain that States Parties enjoy a certain "margin of appreciation" in

The ECHR does not refer to the rights of older persons as such, but older persons have resorted to the ECtHR to demand protection of their rights.[12] For instance, in the case of *Schwizgebel v. Switzerland*,[13] the Court considered that there was no discriminatory treatment when the State refused to authorize the adoption of a Vietnamese child mainly because of the applicant's age (Article 14 and Article 8 ECHR). The Court has not yet applied Article 14 to the social rights which are not included in the Convention but has nonetheless accepted that the proceedings involving social security payments require "particular diligence" in the case *Deumeland v. Germany*[14] (the complainant was an elderly woman who suffered several damages with the delay in the payment of pensions).

The grounds for prohibited discrimination foreseen in Article E are the same as those listed in Article 14 of the ECHR, with two exceptions: health, which is included among the factors of discrimination provided for by the Charter, but was not considered by the ECHR, and wealth, which was not contemplated by the Charter, because it was considered that the different treatment of people based on their assets and wealth and the different financial effort they have to make to access certain services may be justified in the context of the protection of social rights. The latter was deemed important because the unequal treatment of persons on the basis of wealth and the effort required of them in order to benefit from a certain kind of services can be justified in the field of social rights.

Both articles (Article 14 ECHR & Article E ESC (rev)) do not include disability or age among the list of prohibited grounds of discrimination, although, in the course of time, both have become accredited grounds of discrimination.[15] Like Article 14, Article E consecrates an open listing of prohibited grounds of differentiation as it starts with the phrase "such as" and ends with the phrase

defining which differences between similar cases justify different treatment by the law, it is ultimately for the ECSR to decide what consists a discriminatory treatment. The ECSR also refers to the decisions of the ECtHR where it is held that there is no discrimination within the meaning of Article 14 when States Parties do not apply different treatment to persons in different situations (ECtHR, 29 April 2002, *Pretty v. United Kingdom*, No. 2346/02, § 32). Furthermore, it considers that Article E includes both direct discrimination and indirect discrimination, which may arise by failing to take due and positive account of all relevant differences, or by failing to take adequate steps to ensure that the rights and collective advantages that are open to all are genuinely accessible by and to all (Régis Brillat, *op. cit.*, p. 24).

12 For further analysis of the number of cases brought to the ECHR between the years of 2001 and 2010, see Benny Spanier, Israel Doron and Faina Milman-Sivan, *op. cit.*, p. 407.

13 ECtHR, 15 June 2010, *Schwizgebel v. Switzerland*, No. 25762/07.

14 ECtHR, 29 May 1986, *Deumeland v. Germany*, No. 9384/81.

15 ECtHR, 27 March 2001, *Sutherland v. United Kingdom*, No. 25186/94.

"or other status", which has been emphasized many times by the Court when deciding cases related to age discrimination in a wide range of fields, and also by the ECSR (ECSR, *International Federation of Human Rights Leagues v. Ireland,* complaint No. 42/2007, decision on the merits of 3 June 2008, declaration of vote of Jean-Michel Belorgey: "as Article E on non-discrimination includes an 'other status' category as well as those it lists expressly, it can be interpreted as prohibiting discrimination against nationals not residing permanently in their country"; however, the ECSR considered that the concrete situation did not constitute a hypothesis of discrimination).

The Explanatory Report to the revised ESC on Article E indirectly indicates that age may be a potential ground of prohibited discrimination and Article 23 includes, among the duties of the States Parties, the obligation to lay down the explicit prohibition of discrimination regarding old age.[16] From Conclusions 2003 onwards, States are asked about the existence of non-discrimination legislation specifically concerning elderly persons. Protection against age discrimination also encompasses the employment field, excluding old age as a possible valid reason for termination of employment at the initiative of the employer (in *GENOP-DEI and ADEDY v. Greece*, complaint No. 66/2007, § 62, the ECSR considered that discrimination on grounds of age can constitute a violation of Article 4 § 1).

In 2009, the Treaty of Lisbon gave binding force to the Charter of Fundamental Rights of the EU (CFREU), which includes age among the prohibited grounds for discrimination consecrated in Article 21 and dedicates Article 25 to the rights of elderly persons, stating that the Union recognizes and respects the rights of the elderly to lead a life with dignity and independence and to participate in social and cultural life. The CFREU sets out a whole range of civil, political, economic and social rights relevant for older people, such as the right to social security, health care and education, and the CJEU, overseeing the interpretation and implementation of the Charter in the EU legal framework, and has built a body of case law regarding the rights of elder people.[17]

EU law contains many references to the ESC, although coordination between the two sets of norms has not yet been fully achieved. The ECSR adopts a different position on the relationship between the ESC and EU legislation from the

16 The explicit recognition of age as an autonomous ground for discrimination surrounds itself with several difficulties, as discrimination may arise in relation to a later age as it may comprise younger people. Moreover, age discrimination is prohibited not only in the labour and employment field but also in all the areas of State intervention.

17 Israel Doron, "Older Europeans and the European Court of Justice", *Age and Ageing,* Vol. 42, No. 5, September 2013, pp. 604 ff.

ECtHR on the same issue concerning the ECHR. While the ECtHR has already found that there may be a presumption of conformity of European Union Law with the ECHR, the ECSR considers that neither the situation of social rights in the European Union nor the process of elaboration of secondary legislation can justify a similar presumption of conformity of the legal texts of the European Union with the ESC. At the same time, the European Union has shown little political will to provide the same level of access to the rights consecrated in the ECHR and in the ESC,[18] which is incompatible with the principles solemnly recalled during the Conference on Human Rights, in Vienna, in 1993: "all human rights are universal, indivisible and interdependent and interrelated". On the other hand, in times of crisis, the ESC has a fundamental role to play in ensuring that the human rights of the citizens in Europe are adequately protected. Therefore, the ECSR examines, on a case-by-case basis, the respect for the rights guaranteed by the ESC by domestic law.

In the context of the universal protection of the human rights system, Article 26 of the ICCPR also enshrines the principle of equality and the prohibition of discrimination before the law and establishes an "open" enumeration of prohibited factors of discrimination but admitting that, in addition to the factors provided for, discrimination may result from other "conditions". In the *Brooks v. Netherlands case*, in which Mrs Brooks complained that she had been refused certain social benefits on the basis of gender and marital status, the Human Rights Committee (the treaty body overseeing the implementation of the International Covenant on Civil and Political Rights) held that Article 26 of the ICCPR includes all differences in legal treatment in any area of State intervention applying the principle of equality to civil and political rights as well as to social, economic and cultural rights, including the right to social security. This decision led to the presentation of several complaints to the Committee related to the violation of elderly rights to social protection without discrimination,[19] but the scope of application of Article 26 is restricted to the ICCPR, not including the ECHR or other instruments and conventions of international and European rights.

The Council of Europe's report "Human rights of older persons and their comprehensive care" was produced by the Committee on Social Affairs, Health and Sustainable Development, aiming to promote the human rights of older persons. This report highlights that older people continue to suffer from negative stereotypes that lead to their discrimination, isolation and exclusion.

---

18 For more information on this subject, you may consult the relative Chapter in Vol. 1 of the Commentary.

19 Diego Rodríguez-Pinzón and Claudia Martin, *op. cit.*, p. 9.

It also notes that abuse remains a major problem and should be efficiently tackled, starting by raising public awareness on the issue, data collection and monitoring of long-term care institutions by an independent body. It also calls on the Committee of Ministers to consider a legally binding instrument. The report was adopted by the Parliamentary Assembly of the Council of Europe on 30 May 2017.

Since 2000, European legislation protects everyone living in the EU from discrimination at work on grounds of age thanks to Council Directive 2000/78/EC of 27 November 2000, establishing a general framework for equal treatment in employment and occupation. In 2008, the European Commission proposed a new draft Directive to protect everyone living in the EU against discrimination based on age, disability, sexual orientation and religion or belief beyond the workplace (in access to goods and services).

III *The Protection of Elderly Persons in the European Social Charter*

The original version of the European Social Charter did not provide for an autonomous right of elderly persons to social protection, ensuring this protection in general terms through the right to protection of health (Article 11), the right to social security (Article 12), the right to social and medical assistance (Article 13), the right to benefit from social welfare services (Article 14), and the right of physically or mentally disabled persons to vocational training, rehabilitation and social resettlement (Article 15).

However, the revision process of the Charter system[20] led the Committee of Ministers of the Council of Europe to adopt the 1988 Additional Protocol to the Charter,[21] which contains the right of elderly persons to social protection in Article 4 [then incorporated in Article 23 of the ESC (rev)].[22] It was the first human rights treaty provision specifically protecting the rights of the elderly and this "point[ed] towards a new and progressive notion of what life should be for elderly persons, obliging the [States] Parties to devise and carry out coherent actions in the different areas covered".[23]

---

20 See Stefano Angeleri and Carole Nivard (eds.), *The European Social Charter: A Commentary.* Volume 1 – *Cross-Cutting Themes*, Leiden, Brill, 2022, chapter 2.

21 Explanatory report to the revised European Social Charter https://rm.coe.int/CoERMPublicCommonSearchServices/DisplayDCTMContent?documentId=090000168048b059 (consulted last time on 28 January 2020).

22 On the evolution of the European Social Charter from 1961 until today, see David Harris and John Darcy, *The European Social Charter*, New York, Transnational Publishers 2001, 2nd edition, pp. 1 ff. cross reference to ch. 2 Vol. 1 commentary.

23 ECSR, Conclusions XIII-3 (1995), Statement of Interpretation on Article 23, Digest 2018 (Appendix), No. 1198, p. 270.

In 2015, Article 23 of the ESC (rev) was accepted by Andorra, Bosnia and Herzegovina, Finland, France, Ireland, Italy, Malta, Montenegro, the Netherlands, Norway, Portugal, Serbia, the Slovak Republic, Slovenia, Sweden, Turkey and Ukraine.[24]

To date, no systematic study has been performed on the work of the ECSR regarding the rights of elderly people or on its construction of ageism. However, there are some decisions and evaluations of the ECSR in regard to the state of implementation of elderly rights in the various signature States. Until 2005, the large majority of decisions were deferred because of a lack of data in the States' reports.[25]

In 2009, the ECSR changed its mode of delivering conclusions. Half of its conclusions declared that the States were not in conformity with the requirements, whereas six conclusions were deferred, and only three conformed with Article 23. In 2013, the ECSR consolidated its norms in Article 23. In the same year, all 21 signature States to Article 23 submitted reports, and 71% of the States (15 States) did not conform to the norm established by the ECSR. The ECSR deferred its conclusions regarding issues to five States, and only one State was in conformity with the Article. In relation to the reports presented in 2017, the ECSR examined seven categories derived from what is written in the norm: 1. Legislative frameworks; 2. Adequate resources; 3. Elder abuse; 4. Services and facilities; 5. Housing; 6. Health care; and 7. Institutional care.[26]

Developments

I Enable Elderly Persons to Remain Full Members of Society for as Long as Possible

A *Defining Terms*

1 Elderly Person: An Undefined Right Holder

One of the primary aims of Article 23 is to enable elderly persons to remain "full members of society for as long as possible". There is much dispute over how to define an elderly person. Traditionally it is accepted that an elderly

24 European Social Charter – Collected texts (7th Edition – updated to 1 January 2015) – Council of Europe, p. 75.

25 Benny Spanier, Israel Doron, "The European Social Charter and the Rights of Older Persons", in *Ageing, Ageism, and the Law: European Perspectives on the Rights of Older Persons*, Cheltenham, Edward Elgar Publishing, 2018, pp. 146 ff., p. 154.

26 Benny Spanier, Israel Doron, *op. cit.*, p. 155.

person is someone who has reached a certain age,[27] but there is another perspective, which considers that an elderly person is someone who is entitled to receive a retirement pension.[28] The latter approach offers a clear definition of the category and links the definition of old age to the state of pensioner, which may be associated with social problems such as poverty, exclusion and vulnerability. However, this definition seems to be somewhat outdated, as it is becoming increasingly rare to identify a particular point of life when a person completely stops working and starts retirement. Another definition of old age is adopted by the Employment Equality (age) Regulation of the United Kingdom (2010), which protects people from being discriminated for being part of a particular age group or for sharing a protected characteristic of the persons of the same age group (apparent age). The ESC does not provide for a definition of elderly persons, thus depending on the States Parties and their legislation. The most common definition of elderly people lies in the 65-year-old criterion,[29] although it is possible to divide elderly people into several subgroups: the early elders (approximately 65–74), the middle-old elders (ages 75–84) and the late elders (over age 85), who usually depend on the help of others in their everyday life.[30] The WHO refers to the need to establish a multifunctional definition of an elderly person, but this task has proved to be very difficult.[31]

27 Bonnie Brandl, Tess Meuer, "Domestic Abuse in Later Life", *Elder Law Journal*, No. 8, 2001, p. 298.

28 Paul Kowal and J. Edward Dowd, *Definition of an Older Person. Proposed Working Definition of an Older Person in Africa for the MDS Project*, World Health Organization, 2001, pp. 1–2.

29 The Organization for Economic Co-operation and Development (OECD) defines elderly population as people aged 65 and over – https://data.oecd.org/pop/elderly-population.htm (consulted last time on 19 October 2022).

30 Hajime Orimo *et al.*, "Reviewing the Definition of 'Elderly'", *Geriatrics and Gerontology International*, Vol. 6, No. 3, February 2005, pp. 149 ff., suggest the updating of these ages as a reference point in order to be considered an elderly person. On p. 157, we can read the following: "We would like to recommend that to realize a vigorous aging society, we should change the definition of elderly to those over 75 years of age instead of the current 65 years". In turn, the WHO proposes 50 years of age as a reference age to be considered old in developing countries https://www.who.int/healthinfo/survey/ageingdefnolder/en/ (consulted last time on 22 January 2020), which seems to indicate some openness to consider the definition of an elderly person dependent of social, functional, and chronologic factors.

31 https://www.who.int/healthinfo/survey/ageingdefnolder/en/ (last consulted on 22 January 2020).

2 The Meaning of "Remain Full Members of the Society" and "for as Long as Possible"

Article 23 aims to enable elderly persons to remain full members of society. The expression *full members* means that elderly persons must suffer no ostracism because of their age.[32] Therefore, the right to take part in society's various fields of activity should be ensured to "everyone active or retired, living in an institution or not".[33]

The Appendix of the Charter clarifies that the term "for as long as possible" refers to the elderly person's physical, psychological and intellectual capacities.[34]

B *Legal Regime*

1 Non-discrimination Legislation

With the view to guaranteeing that elderly persons remain full members of society, it is fundamental that States Parties adopt non-discrimination legislation on grounds of age.[35] As we have already pointed out, the expression "full members" means that elderly persons must suffer no ostracism on account of their age, for they should have the right to participate in all areas of social activity: "the right to take part in the various fields of social activity should be granted to everyone active or retired, living in an institution or not".[36]

> The ECSR underlines that the focus of Article 23 is the protection of elderly persons outside the employment field, whereas non-discrimination in employment and the protection in cases of termination of employment are regulated by Articles 1 § 2 and 24, respectively.[37]

Article 23 aims to protect elderly persons against discrimination in areas such as access to goods, facilities and services, healthcare, education, services such as insurance and banking products, participation in policy-making/civil dialogue, and allocation of resources and facilities.[38] The ECSR considers that there is still much age discrimination in Europe,[39] and therefore "invites the

32 Digest of the Case Law of the European Committee of Social Rights 2018, Article 23, p. 199.
33 ECSR, Conclusions 2021, Montenegro, Serbia, Sweden, Netherlands, Norway, Turkey, Ukraine, Slovak Republic, Slovenia, Malta and Bosnia and Herzegovina.
34 https://rm.coe.int/168007cde4 (consulted last time on 19th October 2022).
35 ECSR, Conclusions 2017, Andorra, Bosnia and Herzegovina and Slovak Republic.
36 Digest of the Case Law of the European Committee of Social Rights, 2018, p. 199.
37 Digest of the Case Law of the European Committee of Social Rights, 2018, pp. 199–200.
38 ECSR, Conclusions 2009, Andorra; Digest 2018 (Appendix), No. 1199, p. 270.
39 ECSR, Conclusions 2009, Andorra.

States Parties to introduce appropriate legal measures to combat age-related discrimination outside the employment field".[40]

When analysing the Countries' reports on the state of implementation of Article 23, the ECSR requests States Parties to provide information on:

1) whether there is legislation against age discrimination; on this matter, in the Conclusions of 2017, the ECSR noted that Andorran, Bosnian, Italian, Portuguese and Ukrainian national laws, despite not having specific legislation on this subject, establish the principle of equal treatment, or/and the prohibition of discrimination in general terms, including age.[41] In its 2021 Conclusions, the ECSR declared that Malta, the Netherlands and Norway are not in conformity with Article 23 of the ESC on the ground that there is no legal framework prohibiting discrimination on grounds of age outside of employment;[42]
2) which measures are being taken to ensure its applicability; for instance, in the Conclusions of 2017 concerning Italy, the ECSR found that regions and municipalities have a wide measure of discretion in the social domain and asked to be informed about the legal provisions or administrative measures adopted to combat age-related discrimination. As far as Montenegro is concerned, the Conclusions of 2017 and 2021 noted that despite the existence of a legislative framework prohibiting discrimination, discrimination on the ground of age was still very widespread in various domains and asked what practical measures Montenegro was taking to counter this type of discrimination outside the employment field;[43]
3) whether any relevant case law and available statistics on the number of complaints registered or cases dealt with in relation to age discrimination exist. In the Conclusions of 2017, regarding the country reports of Ukraine, Portugal, Andorra and Italy, the ECSR found that the existent legislation was too generic and asked whether there was a case law on age discrimination outside the employment field. Ukraine reported that there is no case law of the Supreme Court, so

40 ECSR, Conclusions 2009 Andorra; Digest 2018 (Appendix), No. 1199, p. 270. Also, ECSR, Conclusions 2017, Italy.

41 ECSR, Conclusions 2017, Andorra, Bosnia and Herzegovina, Italy, Portugal, and Ukraine.

42 ECSR, Conclusions 2021, Malta, the Netherlands, and Norway.

43 ECSR, Conclusions 2017 and 2021, Montenegro.

in its 2021 Conclusions the ECSR asks whether there is any case law from any courts or the Commissioner for Human Rights.[44]

Regarding the situation in Finland, in the Conclusions of 2017, the ECSR asked the next report to provide more information on the experiences of discrimination by elderly minority members and all other projects and initiatives in this field, including the results and measures envisaged to address them.

In the decision on the admissibility of the case *International Federation of Associations of the Elderly* (*FIAPA*) *against France*, the ECSR had to address the issue of the violation of Articles 5, 23, E and G of the ESC.[45] *FIAPA* alleged that a provision of the French Public Health Code, setting an age limit of 71 years for candidates to elections as members of boards of healthcare professionals' Orders or as assessors of a Disciplinary Chamber is discriminatory and a sign of ageism. According to *FIAPA*, Articles E (non-discrimination) and G (restrictions) must be read in combination with the substantial rules of Articles 5 and 23 of the Charter. This resulted in the ECSR rejecting Article G as grounds for the complaint and in the ECSR stating that the violation of Article G cannot be invoked autonomously, although it can "be taken into account for the interpretation of the substantive provisions of the Charter which are at stake in a given complaint".[46]

2 Assisted Decision-Making

Domestic laws must ensure that elderly persons are not arbitrarily deprived of the right to take their own decisions even in case of limited capacity. Therefore, the law should provide for procedures of assisted decision-making and ensure that the representatives of elderly persons interfere as little as possible in their rights and wishes.[47]

Elderly persons cannot be assumed incapable of making their own decisions when they suffer from a particular medical condition or disability or lack legal capacity.[48] The capacity to make a particular decision "should be

44 ECSR, Conclusions 2021, Ukraine.

45 ECSR, *International Federation of Associations of the Elderly* (*FIAPA*) *v. France*, complaint No. 162/2018, decision on the admissibility, of 16 October 2018.

46 ECSR, *International Federation of Associations of the Elderly* (*FIAPA*) *v. France*, complaint No. 162/2018, decision on the admissibility, of 16 October 2018, § 8.

47 ECSR, Conclusions 2013, Statement of Interpretation, Article 23; Digest 2018 (Appendix) No. 1200, p. 270; ECSR, Conclusions 2017, Andorra, Bosnia and Herzegovina and Slovak Republic.

48 This means that even if the elderly person has been declared legally incapable, the legal representative must make space for autonomous decision-making, which should not be

established in relation to the nature of the decision, its purpose and the state of health of the elderly person at the time of making it. Elderly persons may need assistance in expressing their will and preferences, therefore all possible ways of communicating, including words, pictures and signs, should be used before concluding that they cannot make a decision on their own".[49]

In this context, it is useful to recall Recommendation 99 (4) of 23 February 1999 of the Council of Europe on the protection of incapable adults, which consecrates the main principles applicable in this area: the respect for human rights and the dignity of the incapable adult, the flexibility of the protection measures to enable a suitable legal response to different degrees of incapacity in different situations, the maximum preservation of capacity, the publicity of the measures of protection in accordance with the necessity protecting the adult concerned or third parties, the necessity and subsidiarity of the measures, the proportionality, the procedural justice and efficiency, the paramount nature of the interests and welfare of the person concerned, the respect for the wishes and feelings of the person concerned, and the consultation to the extent reasonable and practicable for the persons having a close interest in the welfare of the adult concerned.[50]

When analysing individual legislation, the ECSR looks for safeguards to prevent the arbitrary deprivation of autonomous decision-making. The person acting on behalf of elderly persons should interfere to the least possible extent. Furthermore, the ECSR considers it important to know how the designation of the person responsible for assisting an elderly person who has been declared incapable is made by Court, what their duties are and whether they can be dismissed, and if there is a mechanism that allows an elderly person to appoint a trusted third party of their own choice to assist with their decisions.[51] Among the countries which were considered to be in conformity with Article 23 in this respect are Italy, Finland and France. Italy has a scheme of judicial protection allowing any person with limited legal capacity to be assisted, but not replaced, by a special representative appointed by a guardianship judge and a scheme of disqualification and incapacity for the cases in which judicial protection is no longer appropriate.[52] Finland requires that the elderly person be notified and

---

disregarded (similarly to the exceptions to the legal incapacity of minors consecrated in Article 127 of the Portuguese Civil Code).

49 Digest of the Case Law of the European Committee of Social Rights, 2018, p. 200.

50 Recommendation No. R (99) 4 of the Committee of Ministers to Member States on Principles concerning the legal protection of incapable adults (adopted by the Committee of Ministers on 23 February 1999).

51 ECSR, Conclusions 2017, Italy, Finland, France, and Serbia.

52 ECSR, Conclusions 2017, Italy.

give consent before any measure is taken, whether this is a medical treatment or a social service, and distinguishes between the intervention of a legal representative and a trusted person.[53] France has several schemes which make it possible to protect the elderly from persons with bad intentions or to potentially protect them from themselves, such as *power of attorney*, mandates for future protection, judicial protection, supervision and guardianship, as well as personalized (Masp) or judicial (Maj) social support measures and *family authorization*. Law No. 2015–1776, of 28 December 2015, on the Adaptation of Society to Ageing, introduced new guarantees to the process of admission to retirement homes by enabling elderly persons to nominate a person of trust in case they encounter difficulties in ascertaining and understanding their rights.[54] In a general way, thus, the majority of countries consecrate a double system on this matter: on the one hand, the possibility of assistance of elderly persons in their decision-making processes and, on the other hand, their replacement by a legal representative when they are no longer able to make their own decisions.

In the Conclusions of 2017, the ECSR reports that Serbia had declared that the beneficiaries of social security have the right to free and informed consent and to its corollary, the right to information, as well as the right to the respect for their private life, which was considered insufficient by the ECSR in terms of this subject.[55] In this matter, the 2021 Conclusions note that Serbia recognized that the existing legislation on deprivation of legal capacity requires amendments. The ECSR asks that the next report provide information on those

53 ECSR, Conclusions 2017, Finland.

54 ECSR, Conclusions 2017, France.

55 ECSR, Conclusions 2017, Serbia. The same applied to Malta, which only referred to the existence of the Commissioner for Older Persons Act, which the ECSR considered insufficient, as well as to Ireland and Bosnia, whose reports provided no information with regard to assisted decision-making for elderly persons – ECSR, Conclusions 2017, Malta, Ireland, and Bosnia. Malta already reported that existing legislation will be amended, based on the concept of legal equality and introducing supported decision-making and co-decision-making procedures – ECSR, Conclusions 2021, Malta. Concerning Bosnia, it was reported that in the Republika Srpska legislation provides for the complete or partial deprivation of legal capacity and only a court can decide on deprivation of capacity. The Brcko District of Bosnia and Herzegovinian 2007 Family Law contains provisions related to assisted decision-making and protective measures to prevent arbitrary deprivation of legal capacity. However, no information was provided on the situation in the Federation of Bosnia and Herzegovina. Consequently, the ECSR asks for the next report to provide information on assisted decision-making procedures in all entities – ECSR, Conclusions 2021, Bosnia and Herzegovina.

changes.[56] The Portuguese report[57] stated that a person who is not able to safeguard their interests can only be declared incapable by a court decision. The report added that residential structures for the elderly and other support facilities ensure compliance with the principle of participation and joint responsibility between residents, or their legal representative and their families. The ECSR took note of the information provided in the report and asked whether the introduction of procedures related to assisted decision-making for the elderly who are not placed in institutions had been considered.[58]

Finally, as another point of example, the ECSR considered Turkey was not in conformity with the Charter since assisted decision-making procedures for elderly persons had not been established.[59]

3 Measures against Elder Abuse

To accomplish the goals of Article 23, States Parties must also take appropriate measures against elder abuse, which is described by the WHO and by the International Network for the Prevention of Elder Abuse as a "significant global problem" affecting hundreds of thousands of older people in Europe every year. According to the ECSR, "the victims are pressed to change their will, their bank account is plundered, they are pinched or beaten, called names, threatened and insulted and sometimes they are raped or sexually abused otherwise".[60] It is very difficult to identify, as its signs are easily confused with age pathologies, and it is frequently not denounced while having terrible consequences

56 ECSR, Conclusions 2021, Serbia.

57 ECSR, Conclusions 2017, Portugal.

58 Law No. 49/2018, of 14th August, established the legal system of the adult accompanied, eliminating legal institutes of interdiction and incapacitation, and instituted a new judicial process that allows for considering the circumstances of the case in the definition of the incapacity and the form of substitution by the judge. The accompanier is designated by the accompanied, although it is the judge who makes their appointment. It is also the judge who specifies in the decision which acts are subject to the authorization of the accompanier. In more severe situations of incapacity, the judge may appoint a legal guardian. In the field of health, Law No. 5/2012, of 16 July, applies, which institutes the legal scheme of the Vital Will and the designation of a health care proxy. Regarding the Portuguese context, see António Pinto Monteiro, "Das incapacidades ao maior acompanhado – Breve apresentação da Lei n.º 49/2018", in *O Novo Regime do Maior Acompanhado*, Lisboa, Centro de Estudos Judiciários, 2019, Mafalda Miranda Barbosa, *Maiores Acompanhados – Primeiras Notas Depois da Aprovação da Lei no. 49/2018*, Lisboa, Gestlegal, 2018, e Paula Ribeiro de Faria, *Os Crimes Praticados Contra Idosos*, *op. cit.*

59 ECSR, Conclusions 2017 and 2021, Turkey.

60 ECSR, Conclusions 2010, Slovak Republic.

on the self-esteem and the fundamental values of the victim,[61] thus requiring the development and the use of effective tools of prevention, investigation, reaction and treatment.

The ECSR is guided by the definition of abuse contained in the Toronto Declaration on the Global Prevention of Elder Abuse (2002), which describes it "as a single or repeated act or lack of appropriate action occurring within any relationship where there is an expectation of trust which causes harm or distress to an older person".[62] Elder abuse can take many forms, such as physical, psychological, emotional, or sexual abuse, financial abuse, or as the expression of negligence (whether intentional or non-intentional).[63] It is important to stress that there is no coincidence between this definition and the types of crime recognized by Criminal law, which considers negligence as a form of perpetrating the crime and not as an autonomous form of abuse. Elder abuse may arise as an individual abuse, an institutional abuse, or a collective abuse.[64]

Given the seriousness and the dimension of the problem, which compromises the full realization of the elderly's abilities and well-being and the accomplishment of the goals aimed by Article 23, States Parties must take measures in order "to evaluate the extent of the problem, to raise awareness on the need to eradicate elder abuse and neglect, and adopt legislative or other measures",[65] such as training programmes that allow health professionals and volunteers to detect signs and situations of abuse, prevent and react to these situations,[66] free telephone helplines for elderly people exposed to violence,[67] publication of guides and instructions to raise awareness among the elderly

61 Paula Ribeiro de Faria, "A Proteção Social das Pessoas Idosas na Carta Social Europeia Revista, no Código Europeu da Segurança Social e no Direito português", *Revista de los Derechos Sociales, Lex Social Monográfico*, No. 1, 2017, p. 303 ff., p. 319, and also *Os Crimes Praticados Contra Idosos, op. cit.*, pp. 95 ff.

62 Digest 2018 (Appendix), No. 1201, p. 270. Conclusions 2017, Andorra, Bosnia, and Herzegovina.

63 Brian Payne, *Crime & Elder Abuse, an Integrated Perspective*, Illinois, Charles C. Thomas Publisher Ltd, 2011, 3rd edition, p. 13, refers to another form of abuse: abandonment, which consists in the desertion of an elder by someone who has the duty to guard him or has assumed the responsibility of taking care of him.

64 Brian Payne, *op. cit.*, p. 6, identifies collective abuse with the situations in which society as a whole undertakes activities that result in the harm or victimization of elderly people (politics or legislation). See Paula Ribeiro de Faria, *Os Crimes Praticados Contra Idosos, op. cit.*, pp. 102 ff.

65 Digest of the Case Law of the European Committee of Social Rights, 2018, p. 200.

66 ECSR, Conclusions 2017, Finland, Malta, Turkey, and Ukraine.

67 ECSR, Conclusions 2017, Norway, and France.

and the general public as to the types of violence committed against elderly persons,[68] and studies on the relationship between ageing and abuse[69] or on active ageing.[70] In Ireland, the Health Service Executive published a new policy on the safeguard of vulnerable persons at risk of abuse, including the elderly (Strategic Plan 2017–2020). This policy provided for the establishment of a National Safeguarding Committee. Afterwards, the Department of Health established a partnership with the Health Service Executive and an organization named Healthy and Positive Ageing Initiative to monitor progress in the implementation of the National Positive Ageing Strategy.[71]

In the decision of 22 May 2019, on the merits of complaint No. 145/2017 lodged by the International Federation of associations of the elderly (FIAPA) against France, the ECSR stressed that "in order to fully guarantee the rights under Article 23, national criminal legislations should include provisions making it an offence to abuse an individual's position of weakness and provide effective remedies before national courts".[72] In the present case, the question was whether advanced age should be considered sufficient to characterize a state of particular vulnerability, or if the article of the French Criminal Code making the existence of a state of particular vulnerability and the realization of the crime dependent on the evaluation of the circumstances of the case and the weakness or ignorance of the victim caused by age violates the requisites of Article 23 of the Charter. According to the ECSR,[73] "in order to protect elderly persons' independence, age can not suffice to characterize a state of particular vulnerability". Therefore, the ECSR "considers that the national legislation criminalizing the abuse of weakness of the elderly provides an adequate framework for the implementation of Article 23 of the Charter" and does not violate it.[74]

In its 2021 Conclusions, the ECSR declared that Bosnia and Herzegovina is not in conformity with Article 23 of the ESC on the grounds that adequate measures to combat the abuse of older persons are lacking.[75]

---

68 ECSR, Conclusions 2017, Finland.

69 ECSR, Conclusions 2017, Portugal.

70 ECSR, Conclusions 2017, Slovak Republic.

71 ECSR, Conclusions 2017, Ireland.

72 ECSR, *International Federation of associations of the elderly* (FIAPA) *against France*, complaint No. 145/2017, decision on the merits of 22 May 2019, § 48.

73 ECSR, *International Federation of associations of the elderly* (FIAPA) *against France*, complaint No. 145/2017, decision on the merits of 22 May 2019, §§ 48, 58 and 59.

74 ECSR, *International Federation of associations of the elderly* (FIAPA) *against France*, complaint No. 145/2017, decision on the merits of 22 May 2019.

75 ECSR, Conclusions 2021, Bosnia and Herzegovina.

4 Adequate Resources

The maintenance of elderly persons as full members of society for as long as possible demands that they have sufficient income to lead a decent life and to participate actively in social, cultural and political life.[76] On the adequacy of personal resources to achieve the above-indicated desirable living standards, the ECSR takes into account, for its assessment, all the contributory and non-contributory pensions and other State benefits awarded to elderly persons. Furthermore, it considers all the social protection measures ensured to elderly persons and other eventual cash benefits at their disposal.[77] In the Conclusions of 2000 regarding Denmark, the ECSR considered that the general policy regarding the elderly "should stimulate the use of own resources".[78]

The total amount of available resources is then compared with the median equalised income in the country concerned.[79] Therefore, "the Committee considers the level of pensions and social assistance to be adequate when the monthly benefit – basic and/or additional – paid to single persons is not manifestly below the poverty level, set at 40–50% of median equalised disposable income".[80]

The ECSR recalls that its task is to assess not only the law, but also the compliance of practice with the obligations arising from the Charter.[81] For this purpose, the ECSR considers it important to take into consideration relevant indicators relating to at-risk-of-poverty rates for persons aged 65 and over.[82]

For instance, in its 2017 Conclusions, relating to Ireland, the ECSR considered that in this country, the levels of the full old-age pensions – both contributory and non-contributory – were above the poverty line and a number of supplements were available, therefore the level of those benefits was considered adequate. Nevertheless, the rate of persons aged 65 and over receiving income falling below 40% of the median equalised income had increased, remaining higher than the average level in the EU (respectively, 3.0% and 2.9%

---

76 The income guarantee for elderly people is also relevant to Article 13 § 1. Therefore, the level of the non-contributory pension paid to a single elderly person without resources is examined from the standpoint of Article 23 for those States that accepted this provision, and under Article 13 § 1 as regards States Parties that have not accepted Article 23 – Digest of the Case Law of the European Committee of Social Rights, 2018, p. 145.

77 Digest of the Case Law of the European Committee of Social Rights, 2018, pp. 200 and 201. ECSR, Conclusions 2017, Ireland.

78 ECSR, Conclusions 2000, Denmark.

79 ECSR, Conclusions 2017, Malta.

80 ECSR, Conclusions 2017, Italy.

81 ECSR, Conclusions 2013, Statement of interpretation on Article 23.

82 ECSR, Conclusions, 2017, Slovak Republic.

in 2014 and 2015), which led the ECSR to hold its position on conformity/not conformity with Article 23 depending on information on why such a high percentage of persons aged 65 and over were receiving income falling below 40% of the median equalised income and what specific measures were being taken to address their situation.[83] The same happened regarding Sweden, in the 2013 Conclusions, where the ECSR similarly considered that the level of resources, plus supplements, together with the low costs of health care, conformed to the requirements of the Charter. However, as 2.1% of persons aged 65 and over received an income falling below 40% of the median equalised income, the ECSR decided to reserve its position, asking for explanations as to why this group of persons did not qualify for the minimum guarantees established in law and whether (and which) measures were being taken to reverse that situation.[84] Sweden reported that the Swedish Government had instructed the Swedish Pensions agency to analyse the problem and find methods to reach those individuals and informed the ECSR about increasing the guaranteed pension. However, in its 2021 Conclusions, the ECSR declared that it was still lacking information to assess the situation, asking that the next report provide up-to-date information on benefits and assistance to older persons in receipt of the guaranteed pension and maintenance support.[85] With regard to Italy, the ECSR concluded in the 2017 Conclusions that the situation was not in conformity with Article 23 of the Charter, since the minimum level of retirement pensions (both contributory and non-contributory) paid to elderly persons was manifestly inadequate for a significant proportion of the elderly population, as it was below the poverty level.[86] Also Montenegro national law was declared as non-conformant with the Charter in this matter, on the grounds that the amount of the minimum old-age pension fell below the national absolute poverty threshold (it lacked information on the at-risk-of-poverty threshold, defined as 50% of the median equalised income).[87] Serbian national law was also considered in non-conformity with the Charter. Despite the minimum pension being above 50% of the median equalised income (40% for farmers), 19.7% of people aged 65 and over lived on the at-risk-of-poverty threshold, and 5% of the population aged 65 years and over had no pension.[88] Ukraine and

83 ECSR, Conclusions 2017, Ireland.

84 ECSR, Conclusions 2013, Sweden.

85 ECSR, Conclusions 2021, Sweden.

86 ECSR, Conclusions 2017, Italy.

87 ECSR, Conclusion 2017, Montenegro. The non-conformity was maintained in ECSR 2021 Conclusions.

88 ECSR, Conclusions 2017, Serbia. The non-conformity was maintained in ECSR 2021 Conclusions.

Bosnia Herzegovina were sanctioned with a non-conformity sentence, too: it has not been established that the minimum pension levels are adequate.[89]

5 Provision of Information about Services of Information and Facilities Available for Elderly Persons and Their Opportunities to Make Use of Them

a *The Right to Services and Facilities*

The reading of Article 23 makes it appear that the right concerned is only the right for elderly persons to be informed about available services and facilities and ways of using them. Nevertheless, the ECSR is of the opinion that the right to information (analysed above, in point *c.*) implies the existence of another right: the right to certain services and facilities.[90]

Accordingly, when examining domestic laws, the ECSR evaluates not only the provision of information on services and facilities but also the services and facilities themselves. In particular, the ECSR wants to know about "the existence, extent and cost of home help services, community-based services, specialised day care provision for persons with dementia and related illnesses and services such as information, training and respite care for families caring for elderly persons, in particular, highly dependent persons, as well as cultural, leisure and educational facilities available to elderly persons".[91] The ECSR asks which services are available, who the services providers are and what efforts are being made towards their implementation and modernization.[92]

Among the services and facilities available for elderly persons, we can find social assistance, home help (home care provision, home helplines, host families, household services involving meals, personal hygiene, transport, clothing and *emergency calls*), day care (day care centres and old people's centres, providing elderly persons with daytime accommodation, meals, medical supervision and recreational activities), support services (guardianship services, personal services, support for family carers, adapted transport services), specialised service to assess situations of dependence, social welfare benefits,

89 ECSR, Conclusions 2017 and 2021, Ukraine and Bosnia Herzegovina.

90 ECSR, Conclusions 2003, France: "Although Article 23 only refers to the provision of information about services and facilities, the Committee considers that Article 23, 1b presupposes the existence of services and facilities and that elderly persons have the right to certain services and facilities. Therefore, the Committee decided to analyse not only information relating to the provision of information about these services and facilities but also the services and facilities themselves".

91 Digest of the Case Law of the European Committee of Social Rights, 2018, p. 201.

92 ECSR, Conclusions 2017, Slovak Republic.

cultural, leisure and educational facilities, programmes to enable elderly persons to engage in physical, social and wellness activities, discounts on the cost of medicine, transport, and even exemptions from some costs for the most disadvantaged elderly persons, personal assistance (counselling, management and guidance, in order to enable individuals to develop, retain and improve their social skills), parking badges for parking places for disabled, improvement of accessibility in public transport, reimbursed taxi or shared-taxi fares, or mobility scooters.[93] Elderly persons suffering from dementia or Alzheimer's disease should benefit from specific services.[94]

In the Conclusions of 2017 regarding Serbia, the ECSR asked for information on any possible services or facilities which families caring for elderly persons, in particular highly dependent persons, could request, as well as on any particular services for those suffering from dementia or Alzheimer's disease. It also enquired about the existence of cultural, leisure and educational facilities available to elderly persons. In Conclusions 2013 relating to the situation in Finland, the ECSR asked to be updated on any evaluation of the effectiveness of the system of individual service needs assessment for persons over 80 years of age. The 2017 report states that the Act on Services for Older Persons came into force on 1 July 2013, and it places a whole series of obligations on the municipal decision-making bodies responsible for social protection, particularly in terms of supervision, organization, accessibility, transparency and financing. According to section 15 of the Act, an elderly person's need for services must be assessed in their presence or, where necessary, in the presence of their family members or any other person that is close to them. The report also states that a survey on the capacity of municipalities to assess the needs of the elderly was carried out in 2014. The ECSR asks for information on this survey and its results in the following report.[95]

The ECSR considers it important for the supply of home help services for the elderly to match demand. For example, in the Conclusions of 2017 concerning Ukraine, the ECSR noted that the number of social service centres had been steadily decreasing since its initial conclusion (Conclusions 2009) and asked for the next report to explain why there had been this decrease and what impact it had had on the elderly. It also asked about the proportion of the elderly in the Ukrainian population. The persons who are unable to care for themselves because of their old age, their state of health or their disability,

93 ECSR, Conclusions 2017, Andorra, Malta, and Serbia, and Conclusions 2013, Slovenia and Netherlands.

94 ECSR, Conclusions 2017, Bosnia and Herzegovina, Montenegro, Portugal, and Serbia.

95 ECSR, Conclusions 2017, Finland.

have free access to the social services under the Law of 2003 on the social services, but a fee may, however, be charged. The ECSR asked for information on the number of elderly people who benefit from these services and, among these, what proportion must pay for them. It also asked how the quality of services was monitored. Finally, it asked how the participation of elderly persons in cultural and leisure facilities was ensured and encouraged. Despite the information provided by Ukraine in response to those questions, in its 2021 Conclusions the ECSR "asks the next report to provide updated information on the range of services and facilities available to older persons, including long-term care, in particular those enabling them to remain active members of their community and to remain in their home. It also asks for information on the costs of such services, whether there is an adequate supply of care services, including long-term care services and whether there are waiting lists for services".[96] In the 2017 Conclusions, the ECSR considered that the Slovak Republic did not provide enough information about whether the supply of services to the elderly matched demand.[97] Despite information provided in response by the Slovak Republic on occupancy and waiting times for admission to care homes, no data was reported as to waiting times for other services, therefore the ECSR repeats its request for this information in the Conclusions of 2021.[98]

In the decision that resolved the case of *The Central Association of Carers in Finland v. Finland*,[99] the ECSR had to look at the unequal distribution (in different parts of the country) of informal carers looking after elderly persons, as well as at the unequal treatment (also in different parts of the country) of their funding, which was negatively affecting access to informal care to a segment of elderly persons. Since the Act on informal care support established only basic guidelines on informal care, every municipality sets their own criteria on how the law is applied. For this reason, the type and amount of informal care provided under the minimum remuneration fixed by law can vary considerably across municipalities, which undermines elderly people's access to informal care allowances. In its analysis, the ECSR recalled the general principle of international law according to which, "in terms of the international responsibility of states, the conduct of any state organs, including local authorities, is deemed to be an act of State".[100] Consequently, if States Parties delegate powers to local

---

96 ECSR, Conclusions 2021, Ukraine.

97 Similarly in ECSR, Conclusions, 2017, Turkey.

98 ECSR, Conclusions 2021, the Slovak Republic.

99 ECSR, *The Central Association of Carers in Finland v. Finland*, complaint No. 70/2011, decision on the merits of 4 December of 2012.

100 ECSR, *International Federation of Human Rights (FIDH) v. Belgium*, complaint No. 62/2010, § 54; see, mutatis mutandis, ECtHR, Case Assanidze v. Georgia, Judgment of

authorities or social partners, they do not get relieved from the obligations under international agreements[101] such as the ESC. Additionally, although the Charter does not require the same level of protection across the entire country, the ECSR considered that a reasonable uniformity of treatment is required, therefore having concluded unanimously on the violation of Article 23 of the ESC, on the grounds that the law allows for practices leading to some of the elderly population being denied access to informal care allowances or other alternative support. Nevertheless, the ECSR was of the opinion that the lack of uniformity in the services provided for elderly persons throughout Finland, resulting from the lack of uniformity in the funding of such services by municipalities, does not as such violate Article 23 of the ESC.

b *Services and Facilities' Standards*

The ECSR considers that the existence of the services is not enough. It is also necessary for States Parties to have a system for monitoring the quality of those services, as well as a procedure for complaining about services' standards (for example, through the *Ombudsman* in Ireland,[102] the *County Governor* in Norway,[103] or the supervisory services of governmental departments, in Malta).[104]

With a view to guarantee the quality of the services, States Parties may require their licencing, entrust an entity to inspectorate them, ask for users' feedback and suggestions, license social workers and service providers themselves, perform accredited training programmes, among other adequate measures.[105]

Reports by States Parties should inform the ECSR about details of the main steps in the complaint procedure, "the penalties that may be applied to the providers of social services if they fail to fulfil their obligations or violate the legislation, and whether it is possible for a service user to dispute the authorities' decision before an impartial and independent court".[106]

08.04.2004" – ECSR, *The Central Association of Carers in Finland v. Finland*, complaint No. 70/2011, decision on the merits of 4 December of 2012, § 55.

101 ECSR, Conclusions 2006, General Introduction, § 10.

102 ECSR, Conclusions 2017, Ireland.

103 ECSR, Conclusions 2017, Norway.

104 ECSR, Conclusions 2017 and 2021, Malta.

105 ECSR, Conclusions 2017, Montenegro, Turkey, Portugal, and Serbia; ECSR, Conclusions 2013, the Slovak Republic.

106 ECSR, Conclusions 2017, the Slovak Republic.

c *The Right to Information*

The ECSR believes that the right to information covers the existence, extent and cost of home help services, community-based services, specialized day care provision for persons with dementia and related illnesses, and services.[107] The right to information also includes the existence of financial support for people caring for elderly persons.[108]

The right to information can be concretized in various ways, such as websites (Andorra set up a website which proposes an interface to elderly people's needs[109] and Serbia set up the *Penzin* portal, aimed at informing elderly persons of their rights and the services available at the national and local level),[110] good practice guides, visits paid to elderly people to assess their needs for services and inform them about the services and facilities at their disposal,[111] leaflets,[112] one-stop shops,[113] and information centres.[114] The ECSR concluded in the decision of *The Central Association of Carers in Finland against Finland* case that the Charter does not require the same level of protection across the country, but a reasonable uniformity of treatment must be ensured by the States Parties,[115] having the duty to take measures to ensure that elderly persons living in rural areas are as well informed of their rights as others.[116]

It has to be taken into account that elderly people's difficulty in accessing certain information may stem from limited mobility or difficulties in the use of the internet.[117] Indeed, in the Conclusions of 2017 with regard to Finland, the ECSR noted that the visits paid to elderly people when assessing their needs for services is also a means of informing them about the services and facilities placed at their disposal by the municipality. In the 2000 Conclusions,

---

107 Such as information, training and respite care for families caring for elderly persons, in particular, highly dependent persons, as well as cultural, leisure and educational facilities available to elderly persons. See ECSR, Conclusions 2013, Statement of interpretation on Article 23.

108 ECSR, Conclusions 2003, France.

109 ECSR, Conclusions 2017, Andorra and Bosnia and Herzegovina; ECSR, Conclusions XIII-3, Finland.

110 ECSR, Conclusions 2017, Serbia.

111 ECSR, Conclusions 2017, Finland.

112 ECSR, Conclusions 2017, Ireland.

113 ECSR, Conclusions 2017, Italy.

114 ECSR, Conclusions 2017, Serbia.

115 ECSR, *The Central Association of Carers in Finland v. Finland*, complaint No. 70/2011, decision on the merits of 4 December of 2012, § 58.

116 ECSR, Conclusions 2017, Serbia.

117 Paula Ribeiro de Faria, "A Proteção Social dos Idosos na Carta Social Europeia Revista ..., *op. cit.*, p. 310. See also ECSR, Conclusions 2021, Sweden, Malta, and Turkey.

concerning Denmark, and according to Act No. 1117/1995 on Preventive Home Visits, the ECSR observed that everyone who has reached 75 years of age has the right to an offer of two annual preventive home visits where the municipal authority provides information about their services for the elderly.

Insufficient regulation of fees for services may amount to a violation of Article 23 as well.[118] In the decision on *The Central Association of Carers in Finland v. Finland* case, the ECSR considered that insufficient regulation of fees for service housing and service housing with 24-hour assistance, combined with the fact that the demand for these services exceeds supply, constitutes a violation of Article 23. In fact, it constitutes a violation of the right to "the provision of information about services and facilities available for elderly persons and their opportunities to make use of them" as guaranteed by Article 23 of the ESC, "as [they] create legal uncertainties to elderly persons in need of care due to diverse and complex fee policies" and "constitute an obstacle to the right to 'the provision of information about services and facilities available for elderly persons and their opportunities to make use of them as guaranteed by Article 23(b) of the Charter'".[119]

11 Enable Elderly Persons to Choose Their Lifestyle Freely and to Lead Independent Lives in Their Familiar Surroundings for as Long as They Wish and Are Able

Elderly people have the right to choose their lifestyle freely and to lead independent lives in their family surroundings for as long as they wish and can. The ECSR noted, in the Conclusions of 2000 with regard to Denmark, that traditional nursing homes are in the process of being replaced by elderly housing, and in the 2005 Conclusions, reporting to Slovenia, the ECSR points out their replacement by sheltered homes funded by public-private partnership ventures and some entirely by private investors. However, the majority of elderly people in Slovenia live in (mostly owner-occupied) private dwellings, so financial instruments are being developed in order to enable the elderly to obtain loans and grants to adapt their dwellings to their needs.[120] In the 2001 Conclusions, it is noted that Finland reported that 86% of people aged

118 Digest of the Case Law of the European Committee of Social Rights, 2018, p. 201.

119 ECSR, *The Central Association of Carers in Finland v. Finland*, complaint No. 71/2011, decision on the merits of 4 December of 2012, § 53.

120 ECSR, Conclusions 2005, Slovenia.

seventy-five or over lived in their own homes (in the Conclusions of 2017 this percentage increased to 90.5%). Italy also declared in 2001 that nearly 70% of old people owned their homes and were among the beneficiaries of a housing policy geared toward building new residential accommodation and enhancing the conversion of old housing.[121] For a few years, the policy has been to encourage people to remain in familiar surroundings, while taking the measures necessary to enable them to do so by developing housing service and reducing intake capacity in old people's homes.[122]

A *Provision of Housing Suited to Their Needs and Their State of Health or of Adequate Support for Adapting Their Housing*

According to the ECSR's monitoring, the needs of elderly persons must be taken into account by housing law and national and local housing policies.[123] The supply of adequate housing for elderly persons must be sufficient.[124] The ECSR asks what type of housing elderly persons have access to,[125] how many older people live in their own dwellings, and how the right to suitable social accommodation for the elderly is implemented. The ECSR also wants to know whether elderly persons are treated on equal footing as regards access to social housing and whether there are any compensation mechanisms for the elderly to meet the costs of private rental housing.[126] Malta stated that when it comes to allocating small apartments at ground floor level, the Housing Authority gives priority to elderly persons. It also gives them grants to have their houses adapted to their needs. The Housing Authority undertakes to ensure that any new apartments that are built in the near future will have small-sized apartments accessible by lifts.[127] Regarding Italy's housing policy, the ECSR asked to be informed on the regulations and practice for evicting old people.[128] In Denmark, according to the Act on Social Housing, social housing for the elderly can take the form of an independent dwelling, assisted living accommodation or shared housing arrangements. The dwelling must be especially suited for elderly and disabled persons, including being suited for wheelchairs

121 ECSR, Conclusions XV-2, Italy.

122 ECSR, Conclusions 2017, Italy.

123 ECSR, Conclusions 2017, Ukraine; ECSR, Conclusions 2017 Serbia and Malta. ECSR, Conclusions 2017, Finland. In the Conclusions of 2017, referring to Ukraine, the ECSR asked about the proportion of elderly living in their own homes.

124 ECSR, Conclusions XVII, Spain.

125 ECSR, Conclusions 2017, Malta.

126 ECSR, Conclusions 2017, Malta.

127 ECSR, Conclusions 2017, Malta.

128 ECSR, Conclusions XV-2, Italy.

and having a layout/access adapted to walking-impaired persons. It must also have a private toilet and shower.[129] Serbia ensures that vulnerable persons living in social housing may be granted a discount on their electricity, gas and heating bills.[130]

The ECSR expresses a preference for the maintenance of elderly people in their own homes.[131] Policies should help elderly persons to remain in their own homes for as long as possible through the provision of sheltered/supported housing and assistance in the adaptation of homes.[132] In relation to the report presented by Greece in 2013, the ECSR reminded that "the improvement of housing conditions by moving elsewhere is often not a viable option in that it uproots the elderly person from his 'natural' environment".[133] The housing provided to the elderly must be suited to their particular needs.[134] Funding must be made available to assure that the elderly may remain in their own homes, adapting them to their needs.

It is very important to stress the relationship between housing conditions and the mental and physical health of elderly persons with resultant costs in the national health services and social care. For older people, living in a cold home may cause chronic diseases and lead to reduced mobility, because people stay in the warmest parts of the house and do not move around, while it sometimes also leads to depression.[135] The problem is exacerbated by the fact that older people spend more time at home and may be living on a low income in homes that are harder to heat. The consequences of falls and accidents at home caused by often trivial hazards can be catastrophic, precipitating a serious decline in older people's physical and mental health.[136]

The ECSR, taking note of the measures taken during the reference period to improve elderly people's housing (renovation works, mainly installing bathrooms), wants to know who bears the costs of such work, the percentage of

129 ECSR, Conclusions XIX-2, Denmark.
130 ECSR, Conclusions 2017, Serbia.
131 ECSR, Conclusions 2009, Netherlands: "The Committee finds that this type of measure can contribute to the objective of maintaining people in their own homes for as long as possible, in line with the Charter requirements".
132 Digest of the Case Law of the European Committee of Social Rights 2018, §§ 1206 and 1207, p. 201.
133 ECSR, Conclusions XX-2, Greece.
134 ECSR, Conclusions 2017, Finland.
135 https://publications.parliament.uk/pa/cm201719/cmselect/cmcomloc/370/37006.htm (last visit on 14 July 2022).
136 https://publications.parliament.uk/pa/cm201719/cmselect/cmcomloc/370/37006.htm (last visit on 14 July 2022).

people over 65 living in poorly equipped housing, given that well-equipped housing is defined as having electric or central heating, a proper sewage system, piped water, hot water, washing facilities and a flush toilet, if new housing suited to old people's needs is being built with State Housing Fund loans, and to what extent such efforts have improved housing conditions for persons over 65 years of age.[137]

The ECSR also wants to know if there is financial assistance to adapt or renovate elderly persons' private dwellings.[138] For instance, in the 2013 Conclusions, the ECSR asked Portugal to provide extensive and accurate information on social housing and financial assistance to cover housing costs and the necessary work to adapt homes. Moreover, the ECSR noted that Serbia intends to develop a plan for reconstructing at least 90 buildings in its 30 least developed municipalities to make them more accessible.[139] Turkey declared that people over 65 who live in old, neglected or substandard houses are entitled to financial support from the Social Assistance and Solidarity Fund to refurbish their homes or build new ones.[140]

The ECSR asks for full information about services such as home help and specialized social and health services. The ECSR also wishes to know who runs these services, what their capacity is in relation to the existing demand, and what public funding is allocated to them.[141]

In the Conclusions of 2005 concerning Slovenia, the ECSR asked to be informed about the minimum standards for the services and care provided by *sheltered homes* and whether the observation of these standards is subject to control by an independent inspection mechanism.[142]

Older people's housing should be within easy reach of local services, amenities and public transport in order to prevent isolation and depression.[143]

B *The Health Care and the Services Necessitated by Their State*

In the context of elderly persons' right to adequate health care, Article 23 requires health care programmes and services (in particular primary health care services, including domiciliary nursing care) specifically aimed at the

137 ECSR, Conclusions XV-2, Finland, Additional Protocol, reference period 1996–1998.

138 ECSR, Conclusions 2017, Serbia.

139 ECSR, Conclusions 2017, Serbia.

140 ECSR, Conclusions 2017, Turkey.

141 ECSR, Conclusions XX-2, Italy.

142 ECSR, Conclusions 2005, Slovenia.

143 https://publications.parliament.uk/pa/cm201719/cmselect/cmcomloc/370/37012.htm (last visit on 14 July 2022).

elderly.[144] For example, in its Conclusions of 2017 regarding Ireland, the ECSR asked to be informed about the progress of the Draft Act on Supporting the Functional Capability of the Ageing Population and on Social and Health Services for Older Persons. In relation to Ukraine, the ECSR wanted to know whether specialized centres were sufficient to meet the needs of elderly persons in all regions of the country, taking into account their capacity and geographical location, and if the reduction in hospitals in activity during a specific period impacted the health of elderly persons. It also considered it relevant to know about the possibility of receiving primary health care services at home, including domiciliary nursing services. The ECSR wanted to know more about the health policies aimed at the elderly and their practical effect.[145]

Regarding the Turkey Healthy Ageing Action Plan and Implementation Programme 2015–2020, aimed, among other things, at the development of health services geared to the needs of elderly persons, the ECSR showed some concern about the coordination of health care services, the rules and measures imposed by the existent protocols on local authorities and their monitoring. In its 2017 Conclusions, the ECSR asked Serbia for information on any new measures taken to improve the co-ordination of social and healthcare services in respect of the elderly. Andorra, for example, set up an Interministerial Commission on Medical Social Services, whose main task is to provide advice, help with medical-social activities and set up systems to co-ordinate social and medical-social services. The ECSR supports the existence of guidelines on healthcare for elderly persons.[146]

In addition, there should be mental health programmes for the elderly's psychosocial problems.[147] Regarding Ukraine, the ECSR asked whether the offer of psychiatric hospitals with geriatric departments for elderly people suffering from cognitive diseases covered the entire country. In the Conclusions of 2017, the ECSR asked the Slovak Republic to provide, in the next report, comprehensive information on mental health programmes for persons with dementia and related illnesses. Ireland, for instance, launched the National Dementia Strategy (2014–2019), with the aim to develop a national Alzheimer's and other dementia strategy to increase awareness, ensure early diagnosis and intervention and

144 ECSR, Conclusions 2003, France. Digest 2018 (Appendix), No. 1208, p. 272.

145 ECSR, Conclusions 2017, Ukraine.

146 ECSR, Conclusions 2003, France. Digest 2018 (Appendix) No. 1208, p. 272. Conclusions 2017, the Slovak Republic.

147 ECSR, Conclusions 2003, France. Digest 2018 (Appendix) No. 1208, p. 272. Conclusions 2017, Malta. Conclusions 2017, the Slovak Republic.

develop enhanced community-based services.[148] France also developed an Alzheimer's Plan (2008–2012) which made it possible to adopt consistent measures and suitable communication to help sufferers and their families. One of the measures in this Alzheimer's plan was the provision of training for non-professional carers. The French report also stated that a Neurodegenerative Diseases Plan 2014–2019 was implemented in 2014. The Plan was aimed at all sufferers of Alzheimer's disease, Parkinson's disease and multiple sclerosis and extended to all neurodegenerative diseases. It guaranteed that elderly persons who were beneficiaries of assistance and social action arrangements could choose freely between staying at home and receiving suitable assistance and living in an institution. France also has specialist Alzheimer's teams.

The ECSR addresses specific attention to palliative care.[149] Ireland refers to the launch of a national policy on Palliative Care, to the existence of several specialist palliative care beds distributed countrywide and Community Specialist Palliative Home Care Teams.[150] These services are most frequently provided by hospitals and specialized wards inside the hospitals, but some States Parties have palliative home care units.

The ECSR is also concerned about the costs of health care for elderly persons. In its Conclusions of 2017 concerning Portugal, the ECSR asked for information on these costs. In the same Conclusions, but with regard to Bosnia, the ECSR requested that the next report provide details on the programmes and health care which are specific to elderly persons and on their financial contribution to the health care and medication included in the health package.

The ECSR asks frequently if there is any special training for individuals caring for older persons.[151] Andorra, for instance, states that training courses are offered: one intended for non-professional carers and another intended for professionals wishing to improve the quality of the services provided in specialized establishments.

148 ECSR, Conclusions 2017, Ireland.
149 Digest 2018 (Appendix), No. 1208, p. 272. ECSR, Conclusions 2017, Italy.
150 ECSR, Conclusions 2017, Ireland.
151 ECSR, Conclusions Italy, Ireland, and Andorra.

III Ensure that Older People Living in Institutions Receive Adequate Support, Respecting Their Private Lives, and that They Are Involved in Determining the Living Conditions of the Institutions

The final part of Article 23 deals with the rights of elderly persons living in institutions. In this context, it provides that the following rights must be guaranteed: the right to appropriate care and adequate services, the right to privacy, the right to personal dignity, the right to participate in decisions concerning the living conditions in the institution, the protection of property, the right to maintain personal contact with persons close to the elderly person and the right to complain about treatment and care in institutions.[152] There should be a sufficient supply of institutional facilities for elderly persons (public or private), care in such institutions should be affordable and assistance must be available to cover the cost. All institutions should be licensed and subject to an independent inspection regime. Moreover, emphasis is put on the importance of a truly independent inspection body.[153] Issues such as the requirements regarding staff qualifications, staff training and the staff wage levels, compulsory placement, social and cultural amenities and the use of physical restraints are also examined under this provision.[154]

The ECSR, in its Conclusions 2017 regarding Finland,[155] asked whether the supply of institutional facilities and alternative services for elderly persons was sufficient,[156] whether the costs of such facilities were affordable (and, if not, whether financial aid was available), and how the quality of such services was ensured.[157] In accordance with its report, Finland disclosed it had intended to limit institutional-type care, giving preference to home help, informal care and outpatient services (and housing services). To achieve this, Finland adopted Act No. 980/2012 on Services for the Elderly and a structural policy programme,

152 Digest of the Case Law of the European Committee of Social Rights, 2018, p. 202.

153 Digest 2018 (Appendix), §§ 1209 and 1211.

154 Digest of the Case Law of the European Committee of Social Rights, 2018, p. 202.

155 ECSR, Conclusions 2017, Finland.

156 The ECSR concluded that the situation in the Slovak Republic was not in conformity with Article 23 of the Charter because it has not been established that the existing capacities in residential care were sufficient to match the demand of elderly people – Conclusions 2017, the Slovak Republic. However, in the 2021 Conclusions, the analysis of the reported data was able to remove that non-conformity – ECSR, Conclusions 2021, the Slovak Republic.

157 In the Conclusions of 2013, the ECSR asked Ukraine what kind of services were offered in both large boarding facilities and smaller residential homes, and if there were enough places for elderly persons in institutional facilities and whether they were affordable.

which it subsequently fleshed out with an elderly housing programme for 2013–2017, a government project to improve home help for the elderly and support informal carers (or nurses), and a series of legislative reforms.

In relation to Italy, the ECSR requested updated information on the effects of the social policies designed to reduce the number of persons placed in institutions. The ECSR had already requested this information in 2013 but considered that, in 2017, the information was still insufficient to assess the impact of recent policies on the reduction of the number of persons in institutional care.

The ECSR asks repeatedly for information on the licensing of residential facilities and applicable quality standards. For example, the ECSR wanted to know, regarding Ukraine,[158] whether these facilities are licensed. As for Portugal, the ECSR showed some concern in regard to the requirements of staff qualifications, training and wage levels, as well as the guidelines on the social and cultural amenities to be provided in institutions.[159] In the 2017 Conclusions, Montenegro was considered not to be in conformity with the ESC because it did not have the legal means to verify the compliance of services provided with quality standards or to ensure appropriate staff qualifications.[160] However, in its 2021 Conclusions, the ECSR analysed the information reported by Montenegro and that non-conformity had disappeared.[161] Malta includes among the National Minimum Standards for Care Homes the guarantee that retirement and care homes promote a *culture* of active ageing while providing care for the elderly. All the standards set out minimum requirements for the establishment of a care home, as well as the knowledge, skills and competencies needed by both management and staff.[162]

In order to ensure the quality standards of the services, the ECSR asks for information on the existence of a monitoring and inspection system, which must be independent. The ECSR asked Ukraine whether these facilities were licensed and inspected and whether there were procedures to complain about the standard of care and services or about ill treatment in this type of institutions.[163] According to the Conclusions of 2017, Ukraine adopted a number of measures to monitor respect for residents' rights. A telephone helpline was set up together with bodies charged with supervising the activities of residential

158 ECSR, Conclusions 2009 and 2013, Ukraine.
159 ECSR, Conclusions 2017, Portugal. See also ECSR, Conclusions 2009 and 2013, Ukraine.
160 ECSR, Conclusions 2017, Montenegro.
161 ECSR, Conclusions 2021, Montenegro.
162 ECSR, Conclusions 2017, Malta.
163 ECSR, Conclusions 2009 and 2013, Ukraine.

institutions. Representatives of the Commissioner for Human Rights also carry out inspection visits. The ECSR asked whether reports or records were published following these visits. It also asked how many breaches of the legislation were recorded by these supervisory bodies every year and what powers and/or resources they had to remedy them. The Finland report stated that the Regional State Administrative Agencies guided and monitored municipal and private social welfare and health care services and their staff's skills. It also assessed the availability and quality of municipal services. The ECSR asked for further information on this point. Serbia stated that quality control of services, including placement in institutions, was carried out by social welfare inspectors. The ECSR asked that the following report provide more information on this subject, in particular whether these inspectors were part of an independent body. Serbia has an accreditation system for service providers, developed standards and monitoring mechanisms, while social work centres and residential care facilities are bound by law to report annually to the competent minister on their work. In its Conclusions of 2017, with regard to Turkey, the ECSR asked to know the status of the inspectors and officials responsible for auditing public and private institutions (private institutions are inspected once a year by inspectors from the Ministry of Family and Social Policy, who may order the closure of the institutions if neglect, exploitation, violence or breaches of legislation or moral rules are determined), and whether procedures existed for complaining about the standard of care or services or about ill-treatment in this type of institution.

In the 2017 Conclusions, the ECSR noted that a comprehensive database on service providers and care provided should be established in Serbia. It asked that the following report indicate whether the establishment of such a database was still planned and, if so, on what timescale.

Also in the Conclusions of 2017, the ECSR reminded Portugal that, in accordance with Article 23, States Parties were required to ensure that elderly persons living in care facilities enjoyed the right to appropriate care and services, the right to privacy, the right to personal dignity, the right to participate in decisions concerning the living conditions in the institution, the right to the protection of property, the right to maintain personal contact with persons close to them, and the right to complain about treatment and care in institutions. In this regard, the ECSR asked whether measures had either been taken or were envisaged to implement such rights. As far as Turkey is concerned, the ECSR considered in its 2017 Conclusions that the information on this subject was insufficient. With respect to Malta,[164] in 2017 the ECSR noted that

164 ECSR, Conclusions 2017, Malta.

the report provided no information concerning the privacy of elderly persons in residential facilities and asked the next report to clarify how the rights of the elderly were safeguarded in residential facilities. Malta reported that *Social Care Standards Authority* (SCTA) was established as an independent body to regulate social welfare services, including services for older persons. It licenses and inspects residential facilities, and ensures that the Regulations for Residential Homes for Older Persons are implemented. Given this information, in its 2021 Conclusions, the ECSR asked if those regulations are National Minimum Standards for Care Homes now on a legislative basis and whether the SCTA also licenses and inspects private residential facilities.[165]

The ECSR asked Portugal, in the Conclusions of 2017, whether compulsory placement in such institutions was allowed and, if so, under which conditions, and if there were guidelines on the use of physical restraints in institutions. It revealed some concern in regard to the use of physical restraints in institutions in the Ukraine,[166] and asked Italy for information about this subject.[167]

In its 2000 Conclusions referring to Denmark, the ECSR considered that "the elderly in nursing homes should have influence on their own daily life and economy".

The ECSR expressed its concern with the information disclosed by the *Auser report* on the nursing homes in Italy, indicating that significant shortcomings and/or offences had been reported in retirement homes, including, most frequently, absence of accreditation, inadequate facilities, admission of more elderly persons than the authorized capacity, health and safety deficiencies, and improper nursing care. The ECSR asked whether measures had been taken or planned to remedy this situation.[168]

Concluding Remarks

The rights of older persons and their protection are increasingly becoming a subject of interest for various institutions, including the Council of Europe. The ESC (rev) was the first human rights treaty provision specifically protecting the rights of the elderly.

Elderly persons must suffer no ostracism because of their age and cannot be subject to abuse. These goals are yet not completely achieved in Europe.

165 ECSR, Conclusions 2021, Malta.
166 ECSR, Conclusions 2009 and 2013, Ukraine.
167 ECSR, Conclusions 2017, Italy.
168 ECSR, Conclusions 2017, Italy.

Therefore, it is vital that States Parties adopt non-discrimination legislation on grounds of age, as well as take appropriate measures against elder abuse, and implement means that guarantee their applicability.

Even in case of limited capacity, elderly persons should not be arbitrarily deprived of the right to make their own decisions. Domestic laws should provide procedures for assisted decision-making and ensure that the representatives of elderly persons interfere as little as possible in their rights and wishes.

In order to maintain elderly persons as full members of society, States Parties should guarantee that they have sufficient income to lead a decent life and to participate actively in social, cultural, and political life. It is also important to ensure that elderly persons have the right to certain services and facilities (such as home help services, as well as cultural, leisure and educational facilities) and are properly informed on the ways of using them, having in mind that elderly persons should remain in their own homes for as long as possible, while ensuring a sufficient supply of institutional facilities for when necessary. It is also necessary for States Parties to have a system for monitoring the quality of those services, as well as a procedure for complaining about services' standards.

Health care programmes and (affordable) services specifically targeted to elderly persons (including mental health programmes) are also a concern, with specific attention to palliative care.

ARTICLE 24

The Right to Protection in Cases of Termination of Employment

Bruno Mestre

With a view to ensuring the effective exercise of the right of workers to protection in cases of termination of employment, the Parties undertake to recognise:

a the right of all workers not to have their employment terminated without valid reasons for such termination connected with their capacity or conduct or based on the operational requirements of the undertaking, establishment or service;

b the right of workers whose employment is terminated without a valid reason to adequate compensation or other appropriate relief.

To this end the Parties undertake to ensure that a worker who considers that his employment has been terminated without a valid reason shall have the right to appeal to an impartial body.

•••

Appendix

1. It is understood that for the purposes of this article the terms "termination of employment" and "terminated" mean termination of employment at the initiative of the employer.
2. It is understood that this article covers all workers but that a Party may exclude from some or all of its protection the following categories of employed persons:
   a. workers engaged under a contract of employment for a specified period of time or a specified task;
   b. workers undergoing a period of probation or a qualifying period of employment, provided that this is determined in advance and is of a reasonable duration;
   c. workers engaged on a casual basis for a short period.

 | DOI:10.1163/9789004434158_006

3. For the purpose of this article the following, in particular, shall not constitute valid reasons for termination of employment:
   a. trade union membership or participation in union activities outside working hours, or, with the consent of the employer, within working hours;
   b. seeking office as, acting or having acted in the capacity of a workers' representative;
   c. the filing of a complaint or the participation in proceedings against an employer involving alleged violation of laws or regulations or recourse to competent administrative authorities;
   d. race, colour, sex, marital status, family responsibilities, pregnancy, religion, political opinion, national extraction or social origin;
   e. maternity or parental leave;
   f. temporary absence from work due to illness or injury.
4. It is understood that compensation or other appropriate relief in case of termination of employment without valid reasons shall be determined by national laws or regulations, collective agreements or other means appropriate to national conditions.

Introduction

The protection of the employee against unilateral termination of the employment contract by the employer is, together with coverage provided by Labour Law (the "law of employees" v. the "law of workers"), one of the most intensely debated topics in Labour Law. As a preliminary word, one of the established Principles of European Contract Law is the possibility for either party of a contract for an indefinite period of time to end it simply by giving notice of reasonable length to the other (Article 6:109);[1] each of the parties to the contract does not need to have a valid reason to terminate it, and the position of the other party is secured with the provision of a fair period of previous notice. The two major exceptions to this rule in nearly all national regulations are

1 https://www.trans-lex.org/400200.

tenancy contracts and employment contracts. This article of the Charter deals with the latter.

Art 24 of the ESC neither formed part of the original version of 1961 nor of its revision of 1988; instead, it was a new provision inserted by the revised European Social Charter in 1996. It was inspired by international developments in Labour Law and Social Policies since the Charter was adopted in 1961. The Explanatory Report mentioned that this provision had to be accepted in its entirety and that it laid out two fundamental principles: (a) the right not to be dismissed unless there are valid grounds and (b) the right to adequate compensation or other relief in cases of unfair dismissal; it further establishes a right to appeal to an impartial body in the event an employee feels that he/she has been denied rights provided for in this article. Article 24 was inspired by ILO Convention 158 (termination of employment) of 1982. As to the nature of the "impartial body", it makes an express mention to Article 8 of the ILO Convention; therefore, the two provisions (Article 24 of the ESC and Article 8 of ILO Convention No. 158 of 1982) should be read together.

The purpose of this annotation is to attempt to expose the content of the rights enshrined in this article. Firstly, we will begin with a short explanation of the rationale for protection against unilateral termination of the employment contract by the employer under the doctrine of Law and Economics; secondly, we will attempt to analyse the substance of the article, namely which grounds are recognised as valid and the rights of the employee in cases of unilateral termination of the employment contract by the employer; thirdly, we will attempt to consider the express exemptions and limitations to the right; fourthly, we will make a brief exposition of other international legal sources providing for similar protection; finally, we will end with a short exposition of the case law of the ECSR in regard to Article 24 in the "compensation cap" cases, in which it summed up its understanding of the substance of this provision. Lastly, we present our concluding remarks.

1 The Rationale for the Protection against Termination of Employment

Nearly – if not all – European States have some kind of statutory protection against the unilateral termination of the employment contract by the employer. In Germany, we find the famous and influential *Kündigungsschutzgesetz* (KSchG); in France, it is regulated in Title III of the *Code du Travail* (Articles L1231–1 to L1238–5); in Italy, it is provided for in Article 2218 of the *Codice Civile*, Article 18 of the Statuto dei Lavoratori and various other statutes; in Spain, by

Section 4 (Articles 49–56) of the *Estatuto de los Trabajadores*; in Portugal, by Title II, Chapter VII (Articles 338–403) of the *Código do Trabalho* (Portuguese Labour Code); in the UK, by Part X of the Employment Relations Act (1996).

This protection has been heavily debated for years in political, economic, and legal terms. Its advocates have put forward several defences for it: some claim that it is justified by the generally recognised Private Law principle of the protection of the weaker party; since it is easier for an employer to replace an employee than for an employee to find another job, the latter should be protected against unilateral termination of employment. In a logical sequence, others claim that it is a form of compensation for the subjugation of the employee to the will of the employer. Since EU Law and most European States qualify the employment relationship by means of the concept of legal subordination, which is nothing but the subjection of one party to the will of the other, it is considered fair that this subjection should be rewarded by means of a protection against unilateral termination by the strongest party, subjecting it to the existence of a valid reason. Alternatively, its opponents claim that protection does more harm than good to employees: it creates incentives for atypical employment relationships and false independent work, thus creating a dual labour market, discouraging employers from creating new jobs because employment contracts have higher tax burdens, the termination is procedurally burdensome and monetarily expensive and that all of this stunts' occupational levels.[2]

Protection against unilateral termination by the employer in the employment contract has been the subject of an extremely sophisticated analysis by the apostles of the Law and Economics movement. The most widely shared justification lies in the compensation of information asymmetries and the distribution of risk in the performance of the contract. When both parties engage in an employment contract, there is an inevitable element of uncertainty about future events liable to affect both parties which naturally forms part of the employment relationship: the employer does not know beforehand whether the employee is going to perform the job to the best of his/her abilities, whether the employee is going to relate well to his fellow employees and the company's stakeholders, whether the employee is going to perform well, despite his/her best efforts, whether the employee is able to adapt to technological and organizational changes, whether the employee is going to abide

2 Peter Auer and Bernard Grazier, *The Future of Work, Employment and Social Protection. The Dynamics of Change and the Protection of the Workers*, ILO, 2002; Ulrich Mückenberger and Hans-Henning Lühr, "Dokumentation zum Rationalisierungsschutz", *Kritische Justiz*, No. 13, 1980, pp. 84–102.

by company rules and behave consistently in the job; on the other hand, the employee does not know which future events might affect his employer's activity and eventually make his/her job redundant (such as the loss of an important customer or some technological transformation), whether the employer or other employees are going to treat him/her respectfully or whether he/she will suffer harassment (whatever the motive) in the workplace.

In the absence of transaction costs, both parties to the contract could balance those risks by negotiating a compensation for the risks he or she faces: if the employer knew in advance that the employee is not going to relate well to the company's stakeholders, adapt to organizational changes or progressively reduce his/her commitment to the job, he/she may negotiate a lower wage to compensate for future losses or even automatic termination of the contract after a period of time; if the employee knew in advance that a reduction in demand was inevitably going to make his/her job redundant or that he/she was going to suffer harassment, he/she could negotiate adequate protection against those risks.

Since neither party can know in advance the contingencies which are going to affect the job, the legislator introduced a default distribution of risk: since the major risks affecting the employment relationship are connected to operational requirements as well as the capacity or conduct of the employee, the employer is protected against those risks by the explicit admission of validity of these reasons for terminating the employment contract; on the other hand, the employee knows beforehand that those are the only reasons recognised as legitimate for terminating an employment contract and that the employee is protected against all other reasons. Additionally, if he/she is dismissed without a valid reason, the employee will be entitled to compensation or other relief which must be of a sufficient amount or nature so as to effectively deter the employer from invoking invalid reasons or engaging in behaviour that the employee could not have reasonably foreseen, thus taking adequate measures to protect him/herself therefrom.[3]

Neither perspective can properly explain the adaptation of this principle. It is better to conceive them as different worldviews converging to the justification of this principle. From a Private Law perspective, it is easy to justify this rule by the principle of the protection of the weakest party since the employment relationship is generally characterized by the subordination of one party to the other; from a Law and Economics perspective, it is justifiable as a default

3 Pietro Ichino, *Lezioni di Diritto el Lavoro. Un Approccio di Labour Law and Economics*, Padova, Cedam 2008.

distribution of risk affecting both parties to the employment relationship by expressly admitting the validity of the termination of the contract on those specific grounds and by providing the employee with some form of sufficient compensation if the employer does not comply with that set of default rules.[4]

II The Substance of the Article

As to the substance of the article, the grounds which are recognised as valid reasons for the termination of employment contracts will be examined, as well as those which are not. Furthermore, the rights of workers whose employment is terminated without a valid reason will be analysed as well.

A *Valid Grounds for the Termination of the Contract*

The grounds recognized as valid for the termination of the employment contract may be classified into three distinct categories: objective, subjective, and a third intermediate, which may be regarded as subjective-objective.

The objective grounds are those connected with the operational requirements of the undertaking, establishment, or service. These are external factors unrelated to the will of the parties to the contract, normally of an economic, organisational, or technological nature, that justify ending the employment relationship. The Signatories to the Charter have a wide margin of discretion in that matter, and States' regulations and the national courts' case law vary widely as to the densification of these grounds in the event there are others recognised as valid and to the extent that courts can assess their validity. Some jurisdictions are more inclined to protect the employer's freedom to conduct business, others to protect the employee's interests in maintaining his/her position; some jurisdictions also provide for some sort of administrative control by the Labour Authorities, especially when the dismissals involve a large number of employees.

---

4 Ibid; Ann-Sophie Vandenberghe, "Employment Contracts", *Labor and Employment Law and Economics*, Elgar 2009, pp. 61–95; Simon Deakin and Frank Wilkinson, "Labour Law and Economic Theory: A Reappraisal", Centre for Business Research – University of Cambridge, 1998, p. 92; Antonio Viscomi, "Labour, Law and Economics", *Hungarian Labour Law E-Journal* 67, pp. 67–82, 2015; Stewart Schwab, "Law-and-Economics Approaches to Labour and Employment Law", *International Journal of Comparative Labour Law and Industrial Relations*, Vol. 33, Issue 1, 2017, p. 115; Pietro Ichino, "I Giuslavoristi e La Scienza Economica Istruzioni per l'Uso", CSDLE "Massimo D'Antona" 2005, p. 40; Ewan McGaughey, "Behavioural Economics and Labour Law", King's College, 2015, p. 4.

The ECSR has ruled that economic reasons for dismissal must be reasons based on the operational requirements of the undertaking, establishment or service, and that the assessment of the existence of those reasons is delegated to domestic courts: courts must have the competence to review a case on the economic facts underlying the reasons for dismissal and not just on issues of law; Article 24 of the Charter requires a balance to be struck between an employer's right to direct/run their enterprise as they see fit and the need to protect the rights of the employees; in cases of collective dismissals due to a reduction or change in the company's activities caused by the Covid 19 crisis, the ECSR decided that due respect had to be accorded to the Charter requirement that workers' representatives be informed and consulted in good time before redundancies and that the purpose of such consultations be respected in redundancy procedures, namely that the workers be made aware of reasons and scale of planned redundancies and that the position of the workers be taken into account when their employer is planning collective redundancies.[5]

The subjective grounds are those related to the conduct of the employee; these are situations in which the employee breaks obligations towards his/her employer arising either from the law or from the contract, thus making it unreasonable to oblige the employer to maintain the employment contract. It is also called "disciplinary dismissal" or termination of contract for disciplinary reasons. Similarly to the objective grounds, national jurisdictions vary widely as to what extent certain employee behaviours justify termination of the contract by the employer; some are more protective of the entrepreneurial initiative, others of the employee's interests. As an example: in its ruling of 2 of November 2020 (1 BvR 2727/19),[6] the German Constitutional Court (BverfG) decided that national courts had not violated the fundamental right to freedom of speech when they considered the dismissal of an employee who had turned to a fellow dark-skinned co-worker and uttered the words "Ugah, Ugah!" valid; the German Constitutional Court considered that freedom of speech did not protect racial slurs and that national courts had not breached the Constitution when they considered that behaviour as a break of the employees' duties of respect and non-discrimination arising from the contract and the law. In its ruling of 3 of March 2016 (20/14.7T8VRL.G1),[7] the Court

5 Conclusions 2016, Latvia; Conclusions 2021, Turkey; Statement on Covid-19 and Social Rights Adopted on 24 March 2021 – see ECSR Digest (2019), p. 183.

6 Available at: https://www.bundesverfassungsgericht.de/SharedDocs/Entscheidungen/DE/2020/11/rk20201102_1bvr272719.html (22/01/2024).

7 Available at http://www.dgsi.pt/jtrg.nsf/86c25a698e4e7cb7802579ec004d3832/302fdd824b16519780257f85004f8071?OpenDocument.

of Appeal of Guimarães considered that an employer could use GPS tracking installed in a vehicle to control the veracity of the claims of distance travelled by an employee for reimbursement purposes (later the ECtHR considered in its ruling of 13 December 2002, Florindo de Almeida Vasconcelos Gramaxo c. Portugal, No. 26968/16 that there had been no violation of the ECHR). In contrast, in the "Baby Loup" cases (*Cour de Cassation,* ruling of 19 March 2013, case No. 11–28845 and ruling of 25 June 2014, case No. 13–28369), the highest French court considered that an employee had been validly dismissed for refusing to remove her headscarf to comply with an internal rule of the undertaking of religious neutrality. The court considered that she had broken her duties as an employee because religious neutrality was part of the educational project of the undertaking and that the restriction on her fundamental rights was legitimate and proportionate.

The ECSR has ruled that a prison sentence delivered in court can be a valid ground for termination of an employment contract if such sentence is delivered for employment-related offences; this is not the case with prison sentences for offences unrelated to the person's employment, which cannot be considered valid reasons unless the length of the custodial sentence prevents the person from carrying out their work.[8]

The subjective-objective grounds are related to the capacity of the employee; they are considered as the recognition of the employee's inaptitude to perform the job as a valid reason to terminate the employment contract. The "inaptitude" may be regarded as the inability of the employee to perform his/her job adequately through no fault of his/her own. Consequently, they are both objective and subjective grounds.[9]

B *Invalid Grounds for Termination of the Contract*

Firstly, according to § 3 of the appendix, the following reasons do not constitute valid reasons for termination of employment: (a) participation in trade union or worker representation activities; (b) having filed a complaint against the employer in judicial or administrative authorities; (c) certain grounds

8 Conclusions 2008, Lithuania – see ECSR Digest (2019), p. 183.

9 Júlio Vieira Gomes, *Direito do Trabalho – Relações Individuais*, Coimbra, Coimbra Editora, 2007, p. 997. Karin Lucas, *The Revised European Social Charter: An Article-by-Article Commentary*, Elgar 2021, pp.; J. Kenner, "Protection in the Event of Unjustified Dismissal", in S. Peers and others (eds.), *The EU Charter of Fundamental Rights: a commentary,* Hart Publishing, 2021, annotation to Article 24; M. Schmitt, "The Right to Protection in Cases of Termination of Employment", in Niklas Bruun *et al.* (eds.), *The European Social Charter and the Employment Relationship*, Oxford and Portland, Hart Publishing, 2017.

for discrimination (race, colour, sex, marital status, family responsibilities, pregnancy, religion, political opinion, national extraction or social origin); (d) maternal or paternal leave; and (e) temporary absence from work due to illness or injury. The reasons for these exemptions are easy to explain: to begin with, since all but three of them correspond to rights provided for in the Charter, it would be illogical for the Charter to provide those rights and allow the employer to terminate the employment contract for exercising them. These are the cases of (a) discrimination (Article 1 §§ 2 and Article 4, § 3, and Article 20); (b) trade union activities (Article 5); (c) participation in strikes (Article 6 § 4); (d) maternity (Article 8 § 2); (e) disability (Article 15); (f) family responsibilities (Article 27); and (g) worker representation (Article 28).

Furthermore, the appendix expressly provides for three specific exemptions, which are easily justifiable on social grounds:

(h) the filing of a complaint or the participation in proceedings against an employer involving alleged violation of laws or regulations or recourse to competent administrative authorities; this is known in Discrimination Law as "victimization" and is a corollary of the right of access to Justice; a person should not be hindered from or suffer consequences for recurring to Courts.

(i) temporary absence from work due to illness or injury; although this may be considered a logical derivation of the right to safe and healthy working conditions (Article 3), it is nonetheless expressly provided for as an exception; in Conclusions 2012 (Ukraine), the ECSR decided that a time limit could be placed on protection against dismissal in such cases; in the Digest (2019),[10] the ECSR considered that absence due to illness or injury could constitute a valid reason for dismissal only if it severely disrupted the smooth running of the undertaking and a genuine, permanent replacement was provided for the absent employee. As regards dismissal without notice in the event of permanent invalidity, the ECSR considered that the following factors had to be taken into consideration for the assessment of the conformity of the national provision with the Charter: (1) if dismissal without notice for reasons of permanent invalidity was permitted regardless of the origin of the invalidity – in particular, may this occur in cases of workplace injuries or occupational diseases; (2) if employers were required to pay compensation for termination in such cases?; (3) if, despite permanent invalidity, the worker

10 P. 184.

could still carry out light work, was the employer required to offer a different placement? (4) if the employer was unable to meet this requirement, which alternatives were available?

(j) dismissal of the employee at the initiative of the employer on grounds of age; although age is not expressly provided for as a prohibited discrimination ground in Article E of the Charter, dismissal on grounds of it is recognised as such in the Appendix. In the Digest (2019),[11] the ECSR considered dismissal solely on grounds of age when the person became entitled to a pension contrary to the Charter unless the termination is properly justified in conjunction with reference to one of the valid grounds expressly established by this provision of the Charter. This means that age in itself is not a valid reason for dismissal, but it may be considered as such when combined with other accepted grounds for termination of the contract.

C *The Employees' Rights*

In the event that the employer terminates the employee's contract without a valid reason, Article 24 provides the employee with the right to adequate compensation or other appropriate relief and a right to appeal.

1 The Right to Adequate Compensation or Other Appropriate Relief

Firstly, it is important to note that this provision places upon States the obligation to provide employees who have been dismissed without a valid reason with a form of monetary compensation, which must be deemed as adequate to the damage incurred or another kind of remedy for his/her situation. § 4 of the Appendix delegates the task of determining the form and amount of this compensation to national laws or regulations, collective agreements or other means appropriate to national conditions. On the other hand, this provision does not oblige States to provide employees who have been dismissed for a valid reason with some form of monetary compensation. This is important especially on dismissals for objective grounds such as those of an economic or technological nature; although many States have opted to provide employees with some form of compensation when their employment relationship is terminated on those grounds, due to no fault or inaptitude of their own, this is a choice of the State and is not commanded by the article.

The ECSR has decided that this provision only applies to termination of employment on the initiative of the employer; a situation where a mandatory

11 Pp. 183–184.

retirement age is set by law which results in automatic termination of the employment relationship does not fall within the scope of this provision; however, the ECSR has ruled that it is unjustified for an employer to terminate the employment relationship solely on the grounds of having reached a pensionable age without being expressly mandated by law.[12]

Secondly, according to the ECSR Digest (2019),[13] compensation systems can only be considered appropriate if they include the following provisions: (a) reimbursement of financial losses incurred between the date of dismissal and the decision of the appeal body and (b) the possibility of reinstatement and/or compensation of a high enough level to dissuade the employer and make good the damage suffered by the employee. This principle deserves a few words of clarification.

As regards the financial losses incurred between the date of the dismissal and the decision of the appeal body, this provision essentially determines the reimbursement of the wages lost because of the dismissal. This is qualified as pecuniary damage *per se*, which must be compensated autonomously.[14]

Furthermore, reinstatement can be either cumulative or alternative to the compensation for the termination of the contract deprived of a valid reason, at the choice of the signatory State, on condition that this compensation amount performs both a compensatory and a deterrent function. The compensation awarded to the employee must necessarily cover both pecuniary and moral damages and be proportional to the loss incurred. The ECSR summed up its understanding of this article in § 153 of complaint No. 171/2018 (*Confédération Générale du Travail Force Ouvrière* (*CGT-FO*) *v. France*), published on 26/09/2022 in the following terms:

> A compensation system is deemed to be in conformity with the Charter if it provides […] an indemnity of an amount high enough to deter the employer and repair the harm suffered by the victim (Finnish Society of Social Rights v. Finland, complaint No. 106/2014, decision on admissibility and merits of September 8, 2016, para. 45; Confederazione Generale Italiana del Lavoro (CGIL) v. Italy, complaint No. 158/2017, decision on the merits of 11 September 2019, par. 87). Compensation for unfair dismissal should be both proportional to the harm suffered by the victim and sufficiently dissuasive for the employer (see Conclusions 2016, North

12 See Conclusions 2012, Statement of Interpretation on Article 24; Conclusions 2020, Malta; Conclusions 2003, Italy; ESCR Digest (2019), pp. 182.

13 P. 185.

14 Ales, Bell and Robin-Olivier (n 5); Schmitt (n 5); Lucas (n 5); Kenner (n 5).

> Macedonia, section 24). Any cap which would have the effect that the indemnities granted are not related to the harm suffered and are not sufficiently deterrents violates section 24 of the Charter (Finnish Society of Social Rights v. Finland, cit.). In the event of a ceiling on the indemnities granted in compensation for material damage, the victim must be able to request compensation for non-pecuniary damage suffered by other legal means, and jurisdictions competent to award compensation for the damage material and moral suffered must decide within a reasonable time.
>
> Findings 2012, Slovenia; Findings 2012, Finland

Thirdly, this article has spawned three highly discussed decisions from the ECSR on the so-called "compensation cap cases" for unfair dismissals introduced in jurisdictions such as France, Italy and Finland, which were considered contrary to the provisions of the Charter (complaints No. 106/2014 (*Finnish Society of Social Rights v. Finland*), published on 31/01/2017, No. 158/2107 (*Confederazione Generale Italiana del Lavoro (CGIL) v. Italy*), published on 11/02/2020 and No. 171/2018 (*Confédération Générale du Travail Force Ouvrière (CGT-FO) v. France*) published on 26/09/2022). In these cases, national jurisdictions had implemented pecuniary caps of various amounts and configurations, for pecuniary and moral losses, on compensations for illegitimate terminations of employment contracts. The idea was to combat unemployment by creating incentives for the hiring of persons, by providing a maximum amount of compensation in cases of illegitimate dismissal. The employer knew beforehand that he/she would not have to pay more than a certain amount in material and moral damages if he/she wished to end the contract outside the situations expressly admitted by law. These measures were meant to foster employment and combat false independent work. In particular, employees could not claim more damages than those provided for by law.

The ECSR expressly prohibited any ceiling on compensation that could preclude damages from being commensurate with the loss suffered and sufficiently dissuasive. This deserves further clarification: firstly, the ECSR distinguished between pecuniary and non-pecuniary damages. The ECSR did not expressly prohibit the existence of caps on pecuniary damages for unfair dismissals; it simply placed upon the State the burden of demonstrating that the amount awarded by law was sufficient to cover the losses incurred by the employee and deterrent of unlawful dismissals by the employer. As regards non-pecuniary damages, in the event of the existence of such a ceiling on compensation for pecuniary damage, the ECSR further stated that the victim had to be able to seek compensation for non-pecuniary damage through other legal avenues (e.g. anti-discrimination legislation) and the courts competent for awarding compensation for pecuniary and non-pecuniary damage had an obligation to decide within a reasonable time (Conclusions 2012, Slovenia; Conclusions 2012, Finland; Finnish Society of Social Rights v. Finland, decision on the merits of 08 September 2016; CGIL v. Italy, decision on the merits of 11/02/2020; CGT-FO v. France, decision on the merits of 26 September 2022).[15]

2 The Right to Appeal

The Charter also ensures employees whose employment contract has been terminated by their employer the right to appeal to an impartial body. This is nothing but a specific recognition of the right of access to Justice in employment matters. The configuration of this body varies widely across national jurisdictions: some provide for a collective court with representatives of employers' organisations and trade unions with a professional judge presiding (like the French *Conseil de Preud'hommes*); others trust a single professional judge (like the Portuguese Labour Courts, or the German *Arbeitsgericht*, which is a separate jurisdiction in Germany).

IV Possible Limitations to the Right

The appendix to the Charter provides for certain limitations to the employees' rights.

Firstly, § 2 of the appendix provides that three categories of employees may be excluded from this protection: (a) fixed-term workers, covering both workers who are engaged for a certain period of time or for a certain task; since the reason for their employment is transitory by nature, it is logical that they do not benefit from the protection referred to above; (b) occasional workers, meaning workers who are hired for a short period on a casual basis (very common in agriculture or to substitute an employee who has unexpectedly fallen ill); (c) workers in a probationary period; like we saw above, since neither

15 Simone D'Ascola, "Anche il Comitato Europeo dei Diritti Sociali Boccia le Tutele Crescenti", LABOR – Il lavoro nel diritto, 06/03/2020; Francesco Perrone, "La Forza Vincolante delle Decisioni del Comitato Europeo dei Diritti Sociali: Riflessioni Critiche alla Luce della Decisione CGIL c. Italia dell'11 Febbraio 2020 sul Jobs Act Sulle Tutele Crescenti", *Lavoro Diritti Europa* 1, 2020, pp. 1–12; Cármen Salcedo Beltrán, "Las Indemnizaciones por despido Injustificado y el Articulo 24 de la Carta Social Europea Revisada: No Hay dos Condenas (Finlandia e Italia) Sin Tres (Francia)", *Lex Social,* Vol. 12, No. 1, 2022, pp. 625 ss.; Emilia Straziuso, "La Carta Sociale del Consiglio d'Europa e l'Organo di Controllo: Il Comitato Europeo dei Diritti Sociali. Nuovi Sviluppi e Prospettive di Tutela", Gruppo di Pisa, 2012, available at: http://www.gruppodipisa.it/wp-content/uploads/2012/09/StraziusoDEF.pdf.

party to the contract knows beforehand how the other is going to perform, the admission of a probationary period in which the employee has the duty to demonstrate that the employer has made the right choice and that he/she is fit for the job is recognised as an express exception to the protection against unjustified dismissal.

Secondly, like all Fundamental Rights, this right can also be limited under the conditions set out in Article G, which essentially lays out the common preconditions also recognised in Comparative Constitutional Law and the ECHR for the restriction of fundamental rights: legality, necessity in a democratic society for the protection of the rights and freedoms of others or for the protection of public interest, national security, public health, or morals; they must also not go beyond the purpose for which they have been prescribed (proportionality).

V International Sources Providing for Similar Protection

There are also other international sources providing for similar protection against the unilateral termination of the employment contract.

First and foremost, we have ILO Convention No. 158/1982 of 26/06; this legal instrument drew on the standards laid out in the Termination of Employment Recommendation of 1963 and developed them, laying down minimum standards for termination of the employment contract at the initiative of the employer. The standards laid down are fairly equivalent to those we have been analysing above in relation to Article 24 of the ESC (rev) and its appendix: it covers all employed persons in all branches of economic activity albeit allowing for exemptions to be made with respect to certain categories of employees due to the transitory nature of their contracts or when working in a period of probation. The Convention delegates the implementation of its standards to the uses and traditions of national jurisdictions (Articles 1 to 3). The convention further prohibits termination of the employment contract without a valid reason: the motives recognised as valid are the same as those we have seen above (the capacity or conduct of the worker, or the operational requirements of the undertaking, establishment or service), with the addition of a list of forbidden grounds for dismissal, all connected with reasons of a social nature (Articles 4 to 6). The Convention also provides for the right to appeal against wrongful termination of the employment contract (Articles 7 to 10).

The Convention differs from Article 24 of the ESC (rev) because it provided employees with a greater degree of protection in several matters. It begins by providing the employee with a right to a period of notice or compensation in lieu thereof before the termination of the contract (Article 11). In addition, it commands signatory States to guarantee a form of severance allowance, unemployment insurance, or a combination of both in all cases of termination of the employment contract, unless the employee engages in serious misconduct, in which case the State may provide for the loss of those benefits (this possibility, however, is left at the discretion of the State (Article 12)). This is considerably more protective than Article 24 of the ESC (rev) because the latter only provides compensation to employees who have been dismissed without a valid reason.[16]

Finally, it also provides the right to information and consultation to employee representatives and ensures the employers' duty to notify the administrative authorities competent for employment matters in situations of termination for objective reasons (in the terms laid out above); this is a form of industrial democracy which goes considerably further than the article in analysis (Articles 13 and 14).

Secondly, Article 30 of the Charter of Fundamental Rights of the European Union (CFREU) also provides for protection against unilateral termination of the employment contract in the context of Chapter IV (Solidarity). The provision is quite sparse, however, because it limits itself to providing the employee with the right to protection against unjustified dismissal and delegating EU Law and national jurisdictions the implementation of that right. In the Explanations relating to the Charter of Fundamental Rights (OJ C 303, 14.12.2007), the text mentioned that this article drew on Article 24 of the ESC (rev), Directive 2001/23/EC on the safeguarding of employees' rights in the event of transfers of undertakings (whose Article 4 expressly prohibits the invocation of the transfer of undertaking as a valid reason for terminating the employment contract), and Directive 80/987/EEC on the protection of employees in the event of the insolvency of their employer, as amended by Directive 2002/74/EC (whose Article 3 commands Member States to ensure that guarantee institutions insure the payment of employees' outstanding claims resulting from contracts of employment or employment relationships, including, where provided for by national law, severance pay on termination of employment relationships).[17]

16 Niamh Casey, "The European Social Charter and the Revised European Social Charter", *Fundamental Social Rights. Current European Legal Protection and the Challenge of the EU Charter on Fundamental Rights*, European Commission, 2000, pp. 55–77.

17 Ibid; Olivier de Schutter, "The European Social Charter in the Context of Implementation of the EU Charter of Fundamental Rights" (2016), Directorate-General for Internal Policies, Policy Department C, PE 536.488, available in https://www.europarl.europa.eu/RegData/etudes/STUD/2016/536488/IPOL_STU(2016)536488_EN.pdf (22/01/2024)

Article 30 CFREU has been applied directly by the CJEU in the case *Anonymi Geniki Etairia Tsimenton Iraklis* (AGET Iraklis) v. *Ypourgos Ergasias, Koinonikis Asfalisis kai Koinonikis Allilengyis* (C-201/15) concerning the conformity with the freedom of establishment guaranteed in Article 49 TFEU of a national rule providing administrative authorities with considerable power in situations of dismissal for economic reasons. The Court considered that the freedom of establishment (Article 49 TFEU) and the fundamental right to conduct business (Article 16 CFREU) had to be balanced with the right to protection against unilateral termination of the employment contract (Article 30 TFEU) and decided that the national authorities had not exceeded their margin of appreciation in this matter (§§ 83–90).

Since the Preamble of the CFREU determines that the rights enshrined in the Charter should be interpreted in accordance with the case law of the ECHR, we believe that the case law mentioned below must be considered in the interpretation of the article.

Hugh Collins believes that the ECtHR has been interpreting Article 8 ECHR in such a way as to construct a right to protection against termination of the contract of employment based on the adverse consequences on ordinary private life caused by an unjustified dismissal. The author considers that instead of requiring the employer's reason for the dismissal to be connected to an aspect of an employee's private and family life, in order to engage Article 8 ECHR, the ECtHR's new, broader approach focuses on major adverse effects or consequences caused by dismissals on an employee's family life, personal and professional relationships, his/her self-respect, and his/her chosen way of life and career; this consequence-based approach allows the application of Article 8 regardless of the reason the employer puts forward for the dismissal. He drew on the cases ECtHR, 02 September 1996, *Vogt v. Germany,* No. 17851/91, in which the Court found a violation of freedom of expression in Article 10 for the dismissal of a schoolteacher for her political views expressed outside work; in ECtHR, 25 June 1997, *Halford v. UK,* No. 20605/92, ECtHR, 3 April 2007, *Copland v. the United Kingdom,* No. 62617/00 and ECtHR, 5 September 2017, *Bărbulescu v. Romania,* No. 61496/08, it applied to dismissals or disciplinary actions that involved unjustified interception of communications and correspondence; it applied to control over the information that is known about him or her as in the case of drug testing in ECtHR, dec., 7 November 2002, *Madsen v. Denmark,* No. 58341/00 or the use of CCTV cameras in the workplace ECtHR, dec., 5 October 2010, *Köpke v. Germany,* No. 40/07; it was also used in ECtHR, 25 July 2000, *Lustig-Prean and Beckett v. United Kingdom,* No. 31417/96 and 32377/96, ECtHR, dec., 16 September 2008, Laurence Pay v. the United Kingdom, No. 32792/05, ECtHR, 10 October 2010, *Özpınar v. Turkey,* No. 20999/04, ECtHR, 27

April 2013, *Oleksandr Volkov v. Ukraine*, No. 21722/11, ECtHR, 2 December 2014, *Emel Boyraz v. Turkey*, No. 61960/08, ECtHR 12 June 2014, *Fernández Martinez v. Spain*, No. 56030/07, ECtHR, 23 September 2010, *Schüth v. Germany*, No. 1620/03, ECtHR, 03 October 2013, *I.B v. Greece*, No. 552/10, to protect those aspects of privacy that concern the peaceful enjoyment of family relations, living in one's home without disturbance by others, and the privacy of sexual and intimate relations.

The most important ruling so far in this matter is found in ECtHR, 25 September 2018, *Denisov v. Ukraine*, No. 76639/11, in which the Grand Chamber unanimously confirmed that where a dismissal or other disciplinary action by an employer has severe consequences on a person's ordinary private life, in order to comply with the right to respect for private life, national law had to require the employer to justify the dismissal under a test of proportionality in accordance with Article 8 § 2 ECHR. Under the positive duties placed on contracting States by the Convention, national laws must be adjusted to conform to Article 8 ECHR by providing the worker with an adequate legal remedy against the unjustified dismissal.[18]

Concluding Remarks

The protection of the employee against unilateral termination of the contract by the employer is an exception to the generally recognised principle that each party to a contract of indefinite duration has a right to terminate it simply by giving notice of reasonable length to the other party. The rationale for this limitation consists of a default distribution of risk: since neither party to the contract can anticipate the future contingencies that may affect the employment relationship, the law reduces the transaction costs by recognizing the validity of certain grounds to terminate the contract.

Several international sources provide for this right, although it is not a generally recognised human right. The most important ones are ILO Convention No. 158 (1982), Article 24 ESC (rev), and Article 30 CFREU. Some authors also believe that the ECtHR is also jurisprudentially constructing a right to protection against unilateral termination of the employment contract by considering the invocation of certain grounds for dismissal as a violation of the right to privacy, provided for in Article 8 ECHR, due to the adverse effects or consequences

18 Hugh Collins, "An Emerging Human Right to Protection against Unjustified Dismissal", *Industrial Law Journal*, Vol. 50, Issue 1, March 2021 36, 2021, p. 36.

caused by dismissals to an employee's family life, personal and professional relationships, his/her self-respect, and his/her chosen way of life and career.

The grounds recognised as valid can be of an objective, subjective or objective-subjective nature. The extension of the densification of these grounds varies considerably across jurisdictions, depending on the legislators' options and the courts' interpretations. Not all workers benefit from this protection, though: generally, they are workers under a probation period or whose contracts are transitory by nature, such as fixed-term work or occasional work contracts. On the other hand, the employer is also prevented from invoking some specific grounds corresponding to the exercise of other rights expressly recognised in the ESC (rev) or because of their social nature.

If the employer dismisses the employee without a valid ground, the article provides the latter with a right to adequate compensation. The ECSR has issued several decisions on the so-called "compensation caps" for unfair dismissals introduced in jurisdictions such as France, Italy and Spain, ruling that the compensation must perform both a compensatory and a deterrent function. Unlike ILO Convention No. 158 (1982), Article 24 contains no provision for compensation when the dismissal is due to valid grounds, especially those of an objective nature, which are not due to a fault of the employee.

The article also provides for the right of the employee to have access to justice and to appeal to an impartial body for evaluating the validity of his/her dismissal.

ARTICLE 25

The Right of Workers to the Protection of Their Claims in the Event of the Insolvency of Their Employer

Kübra Doğan-Yenisey

With a view to ensuring the effective exercise of the right of workers to the protection of their claims in the event of the insolvency of their employer, the Parties undertake to provide that workers' claims arising from contracts of employment or employment relationships be guaranteed by a guarantee institution or by any other effective form of protection.

•••

Appendix: Article 25

1 It is understood that the competent national authority may, by way of exemption and after consulting organisations of employers and workers, exclude certain categories of workers from the protection provided in this provision by reason of the special nature of their employment relationship.

2 It is understood that the definition of the term "insolvency" must be determined by national law and practice.

3 The workers' claims covered by this provision shall include at least:

   a the workers' claims for wages relating to a prescribed period, which shall not be less than three months under a privilege system and eight weeks under a guarantee system, prior to the insolvency or to the termination of employment;

   b the workers' claims for holiday pay due as a result of work performed during the year in which the insolvency or the termination of employment occurred;

   c the workers' claims for amounts due in respect of other types of paid absence relating to a prescribed period, which shall not be less than three months under a privilege system and eight weeks under a guarantee system, prior to the insolvency or the termination of the employment.

 | DOI:10.1163/9789004434158_007

4 National laws or regulations may limit the protection of workers' claims to a prescribed amount, which shall be of a socially acceptable level.

∴

Introduction

Article 25 of the revised European Social Charter sets out principles to protect workers' claims in the event that their employer experiences financial difficulties. The right of workers to protection of their outstanding claims is among the new rights introduced by the revised Charter. The ILO Convention No. 173 on the Protection of Workers' Claims (Employer's Insolvency) of 1992 and the European Community Directive 80/987/CEE of 20 October 1980 on the approximation of the laws of the Member States relating to the protection of employees in the event of the insolvency of their employer were two previous instruments which served as a source of inspiration to the revised Charter.[1]

Since remuneration is of major importance for the livelihood of workers and their families, reinforced legal protection compared to other monetary claims was provided by international instruments. The ILO Convention No. 95 on the Protection of Wages of 1949, inspired by a significant number of national laws, lays down the main principles to protect wages.[2] Article 11 of the Convention states that workers shall be treated as privileged creditors in terms of their wages in the event of bankruptcy or judicial liquidation of an undertaking. Thus, wages are ranked among the privileged debts and shall be paid in full before ordinary creditors may establish any claim to shares of assets. It is left to national regulations to establish the relative priority of wages that constitute privileged debts compared to other privileged debts (Article 11(2) and (3) of Convention No. 95). Nevertheless, Article 11 of Convention No. 95 has drawn criticism for a number of reasons, including the possibility that it may have

1 Explanatory Report to the European Social Charter (Revised), Strasbourg 3. V. 1996 no. 91.

2 For ILO standard-setting activities relating to the protection of wages cf. ILC, 91st Session 2003, Report III (Part I B), General Survey of the reports concerning the Protection of Wages Convention (No. 95) and the Protection of Wages Recommendation (No. 85), 1949, Report of the Committee of Experts on the Application of Conventions and Recommendations (Articles 19, 22 and 35 of the Constitution), §§ 2–11.

little practical application when the bankrupt estate lacks sufficient realizable assets. Second, the privilege system grants workers' claims a relative priority but does not guarantee a minimum rank for such claims. Additionally, Article 11 acknowledges the potential for capping the privilege without prescribing a minimal threshold for socially acceptable protection. Since insolvency does not necessarily result in the closure of the business, it does not resolve the issue of salary claims for work performed after the insolvency.[3]

The economic crisis of 1971 and the growing number of bankruptcies during that period revealed shortcomings of the preferential treatment to workers' claims.[4] If the individual enforcement of workers' claims has, in principle, no particularity, treating workers' claims in equal terms to other creditors' claims in collective procedures results in the non-satisfaction of workers' outstanding claims. Therefore, the unbalanced nature of employment relationships requires special protection of workers' outstanding claims in the case of collective procedures. Such protection should also remedy the adverse effect resulting from the fact that workers are entitled to wages after they have performed their services.[5]

Thus, Convention No. 173 on the Protection of Workers' Claims, referring to (among others) the "significant developments"[6] which had taken place in the law of many Member States, was adopted in 1992. The European Council Directive 80/987/CEE of 20 October 1980 is surely among the "significant developments", besides extending wage guarantee funds in Europe.[7] The European Community Directive 80/987/CEE, which was substantially amended several times and repealed by Directive 2008/94/EC of 22 October 2008 on the protection of employees in the event of the insolvency of their employers, aims to guarantee payment of outstanding worker claims while seeking balanced

3 ILC, *cit.*, § 331.

4 Cf. Arturo S. Bronstein, "The Protection of Workers' Claims in the Event of the Insolvency of Their Employer", *ILR*, Vol. 126, No. 6, November-December 1987, pp. 722–724; for a comparative analysis of preferential systems at the time of the preparatory work of the Convention cf. Arturo S. Bronstein, "Comparative Study", in Edward Yemin and Arturo S. Bronstein (dir)., *The Protection of Workers' Claims in the Event of Employer's Insolvency*, Geneva, International Labour Office, 1991 (Labour-Management Relations Series No. 76), pp. 13–32.

5 Bronstein, "The Protection of Workers' Claims", *cit.*, pp. 715–716.

6 Preamble of Convention No. 173.

7 Wage guarantee funds, which had their origins in Europe, started to be established as of 1967. Belgium (1967), the Netherlands (1968), Sweden (1970), Denmark (1972), Finland, Norway and France (1973), the Federal Republic of Germany (1974), the United Kingdom (1975), Spain (1976), Austria (1977), Greece (1981), Switzerland (1982), Ireland (1984), and Portugal (1985) are the first countries to provide protection of outstanding wages of workers. Cf. Bronstein, "The Protection of Workers' Claims", *cit.*, p. 725; Bronstein, "Comparative Study", *cit.*, pp. 35–36.

economic and social development. Guarantee institutions protect outstanding worker claims in the event of insolvency of their employers. Therefore, these new legal instruments have strengthened protections by introducing new concepts, such as wage guarantee schemes designed to offer better protection than the conventional privilege system.[8] A model based on the contractual responsibility of the employer has been replaced by a model based on social security principles.[9]

During the discussions of the revised Charter, even though certain delegations doubted the need for such protection, others argued for strengthening the protection of workers' claims in the event of insolvency considering the rapid industrial change in progress. Finally, the importance of providing workers with a guarantee mechanism which is not restricted to the assets of the employer was recognized. Therefore, a new right was introduced by Article 25, in line with Directive 80/987/CEE and ILO's Convention No. 173 on Employers' Insolvency.[10]

Under Article A of the revised Charter, a State Party must accept at least six out of nine so-called "hard core provisions": Articles 1, 5, 6, 7, 12, 13, 16, 19 and 20.[11] Thus, Article 25 is not among the hard-core provisions of the revised Charter. As of July 2022, the revised Charter was ratified by 35 States and signed but not ratified by 9 States.[12] Andorra, Armenia, Azerbaijan, Bosnia and Herzegovina, Georgia, Hungary, Italy, Montenegro, North Macedonia, the Republic of Moldova, the Russian Federation and Ukraine did not make a declaration to be considered bound by Article 25.[13]

1 Personal Field of Protection

The revised Charter affords protection to all workers. Nevertheless, the Appendix to the revised Charter states that "the competent national authority may, by way of exemption and after consulting organizations of employers and

8 ILC, *cit.*, §§ 298, 335.

9 Bronstein, "The Protection of Workers' Claims", *cit.*, pp. 724–725, 729.

10 François Vandamme, "The Revision of the European Social Charter", *ILR*, 1994, Vol. 133, No. 5–6, p. 646; Karin Lukas, *The Revised European Social Charter, An Article-By-Article Commentary*, Camberley, Edward Elgar Publishing, 2021, § 25.04.

11 Cf. Karin Lukas, *cit.*, § 5.

12 Cf. https://www.coe.int/en/web/conventions/full-list?module=signatures-by-treaty&treatynum=163.

13 Edoardo Ales *et al.*, *International and European Labour Law, Article-by-Article Commentary*, Baden-Baden, Nomos/Beck/Hart, 2018, p. 341, note 1.

workers, exclude certain categories of workers from the protection provided in this provision by reason of the special nature of their employment relationship" (Article 25(1) of Appendix, ESC (rev)). The structure is very similar to that of Convention No. 173.

In that respect, Article 4 of Convention No. 173 enables States, after consulting the most representative organizations of employers and workers, to exclude specific categories of workers, in particular, public employees, because of the particular nature of their employment relationship, provided that other types of guarantee exist. In a case where workers recruited in state-owned enterprises were excluded from protection, the Committee of Experts requested the concerned government "to clarify how workers' claims are protected in the case of state-owned enterprises" under the framework of Convention No. 173.[14]

The original Directive 80/987/EEC also had the same pattern with regard to the exclusion of some workers from the scope of protection. Member States had the power to exclude some categories of workers by virtue of the special nature of employment relationship. This provision, however, was removed. The codified version, Directive 2008/94/EC, states that domestic servants employed by a natural person and share-fishermen may continue to be excluded from the scope of protection (Article 1(3)(a)(b) of Directive 2008/94/EC). Member States have the sole discretionary power to exclude certain groups of workers by virtue of the existence of other forms of guarantee (Article 1(2) of Directive 2008/94/EC).[15]

The European Committee of Social Rights (ECSR) recognizes that States have the power of discretion to determine the personal field of guarantee systems. Therefore, it is possible to leave some groups out of the cover of protection after consulting organizations of employers and workers as long as they are provided adequate and effective protection by other systems. It is up to the Committee to assess how effective these guarantee mechanisms are.[16] The conformity of such exclusions is examined on a case-by-case basis.[17]

The Committee underlines the principle that all workers, regardless of the nature of their employment contracts and their seniority, should benefit from protection for their claims. Thus, an entitlement requirement that workers are to have worked at least for one year for the same employer was held to not be

---

14 CEACR, Observation, adopted 2019, 109th ILC session (2020), Ukraine.

15 Cf. Malcolm Sargeant, "Protecting employees with insolvent employers", *ILJ*, Vol. 32, No. 1, March 2003, pp. 56–57.

16 ECSR, Conclusions 2008, Belgium.

17 Karin Lukas, *cit.*, § 25.07.

in conformity with Article 25.[18] Any seniority requirement to have access to protection conflicts with the minimum standards.

The same line of reasoning applies to the types of employment contracts. The worker may be recruited on a different contractual basis, such as an employment contract for a definite or indefinite period, a part-time or full-time contract, an on-call contract, or a temporary employment contract. However, the type of employment contract does not justify exclusion from protection.[19] Therefore, there are no legitimate grounds for excluding part-time workers, those recruited with fixed-term contracts, or temporary employees.[20] Similarly, leaving casual workers, homeworkers, or agricultural workers out of the scope of this protection is hardly consistent with the Charter.[21]

Nevertheless, the special nature of an employment relationship may justify the exclusion of certain workers. The public employees and the managerial staff in small undertakings are given as an example in the Explanatory Report to the Social Charter.[22] The Committee held in conformity the exclusion that "employees who either individually or together with a close relative, owned a substantial part of the business less than six months before the bankruptcy petition was filed and had considerable influence on the running of it. The same applies when the holding was owned by a close relative of the employee".[23] The wording of the conclusion reveals that not only having ownership but also actual power of management on the business is required. Workers holding 20% or more in a company may be excluded from the protection if they are considered responsible for the bankruptcy.[24] In order to prevent abuses, the ECSR established that workers who have considerable managerial powers, thus sharing the responsibility for the insolvency, fall out of the scope of protection. In addition, partners and board members of insolvent undertakings, as well as their spouses and close families, are left out of this protection.[25] Therefore, the nature of the employment relationship warrants the exclusion of certain workers, such as the staff of bodies financed by the state budget

---

18 ECSR, Conclusions 2012, Turkey.

19 Karin Lukas, *cit.*, § 25.07; Edoardo Ales *et al.*, *cit.*, Art. 25 § 4.

20 ECSR, Conclusions 2008, Statement of interpretation on Article 25; ECSR Conclusions 2008, Netherlands; ECSR, Conclusions 2008, Portugal.

21 Similarly, the Committee of Experts noted with concern that leaving large number of workers unprotected was not consistent with Article 2 § 2 of Convention No. 95, ILC, *cit.*, § 64.

22 Explanatory Report, No. 93.

23 ECSR, Conclusions 2003, Sweden.

24 ECSR, Conclusions 2008, Norway.

25 ECSR, Conclusions 2008, Belgium; ECSR, Conclusions 2008, Bulgaria.

or municipal budgets, civil servants, domestic staff, share-fishermen and wage earners who, on their own or with a close relative, owned all or part of the undertaking. Meanwhile, to provide an effective exercise of workers' claims, the Committee scrutinizes the number of protected workers by the guarantee fund and whether there is any other form of effective protection for those who are excluded.[26]

II Material Scope of Protection

A *Claims*

1 The Nature of Claims

Article 25 grants protection to workers' claims arising from the contract of employment or employment relationship in harmony with Directive 2008/94/EC. The minimum protection scope of the Charter is basically modelled on Convention No. 173. The only difference consists of Convention No. 173 additionally providing protection to severance pay upon termination of employment (Article 6(d) of Convention No. 173).

The Charter makes no distinction regarding the source of the claims in the sense that it makes no difference whether it is a contract of employment or employment relationship. The term "claims" covers all kinds of monetary rights arising from the employment relationship. Nevertheless, the Appendix restricts the minimum scope of protection to wages. National legal systems may give a legal definition of wages, which risks leaving aside the payments which are not the monetary counterpart of the work performed. Therefore, the Appendix states that claims refer not only to wages but also to holiday pay and other types of paid absence.[27] Whether it is called a "wage" or not, all payments due "as a result of work performed" or "due in respect of other types of paid absence" fall in the scope of minimum protection of the Charter.

Indemnities are another group of monetary claims arising from the employment contract. The Charter provides protection to all kinds of indemnities arising from termination of the employment contract,[28] i.e., indemnities in lieu of notice, severance payments, and indemnities for dismissal. Nevertheless, the Appendix stating what claims should include "at least" sets out that indemnities do not fall under the cover of the compulsory scope of the protection.

---

26 ECSR, Conclusions 2008, Lithuania; ECSR, Conclusions 2008, Malta.

27 ECSR, Conclusions 2003, Bulgaria.

28 ECSR, Conclusions 2007, Belgium.

In respect to social security contributions, the Appendix to the Charter makes no explicit reference to pension contributions while determining the minimum scope of protected claims. Therefore, the question is whether an employer's outstanding pension contributions are covered by the minimum protection of the revised Charter. Within the framework of Convention No. 173, the Committee of Experts noted that contributions payable by the employer in terms of social security were not included in the "workers' claims".[29]

Directive 2008/94/EC grants protection to non-paid contributions through two different types of ways, which are complementary:[30] Article 3 and Article 8 of that Directive. Article 3 of the Directive obliges Member States to ensure that concerned institutions guarantee payment of employees' outstanding claims. Furthermore, Article 6 recognizes the discretionary powers of Member States to preclude, both in terms of length and amount, contributions due under national statutory social security schemes or supplementary occupational or inter-occupational pension schemes.[31] Thus, such a provision implies that these contributions fall, in principle, under the cover of Article 3.[32] Nevertheless, Article 8 of the Directive is concerned with the protection of pension claims, referring to the protection of long-term interests of employees as pension beneficiaries who can continue to enjoy old-age or survivors' benefits under supplementary pension schemes. Nevertheless, Member States have considerable discretion in determining both the means and the level of protection, and Article 8 cannot therefore be interpreted as requiring a complete guarantee of the rights in question.[33] The European Court of Justice held in its previous interpretations of Article 8 that, in order to ensure a minimum degree of protection in the event of insolvency of the employer, an employee is to receive at least half of the old-age benefits arising out of the accrued pension rights for which he has paid contributions under a supplementary occupational pension scheme.[34] Nevertheless, the Court stated that this does not preclude the possibility that, in certain situations, the losses suffered by an employee or former employee may also be regarded as being manifestly

29 CEACR, Report III, Part 1A, ILC, 87th session 1999.

30 ECJ, 24 November 2016, *Webb-Sämann v. Christopher Seagon*, 454–15, §§ 25 ff.

31 ECJ, 24 November 2016, *Webb-Sämann*, § 26.

32 ECJ, 24 November 2016, *Webb-Sämann*, § 22.

33 ECJ, 6 September 2018, *Greenville Hampshire v. The Board of the Pension Protection Fund*, 17/17, § 41; ECJ, 19 December 2019, *Pensions-Sicherungs-Verein VvaG v. Günther Bauer*, 168/18, § 38.

34 ECJ, 5 January 2007, *Carol Marilyn Robins and Others v. Secretary of State for Work and Pensions*, 278/05, § 57; ECJ, 25 April 2013, *Thomas Hogan and Others v. Minister for Social and Family Affairs*, 398/11, § 51.

disproportionate in light of the obligation mentioned in Article 8.[35] The Court held that a reduction in the amount of occupational old-age benefits must be regarded as being manifestly disproportionate if the former employee receives at least half of the benefits deriving from his or her acquired rights and, as a result of the reduction, is already living, or would have to live, below the at-risk-of-poverty threshold determined.[36]

In terms of the wording of the Appendix, outstanding social security contributions are not covered by the terms 'claims for wages', 'claims for holiday pay', or 'claims for amounts due in respect of other types of paid absence'. Since the Appendix is based on the model of the ILO Convention No. 173, non-paid social security contributions do not fall within the minimum scope of protection. Nevertheless, States have all the power to improve this minimum protection level.

2 The Scope of Claims

Article 25 enables States to guarantee all kinds of workers' claims arising from the employment relationship. Nevertheless, the Appendix to the revised Charter descopes the amount and nature of claims, since providing a full range of guarantees to all claims requires a considerable financial burden on funds. In addition, it seems necessary to take measures to prevent possible abuses. Therefore, it is a common feature of guarantee mechanisms to provide limited protection. Funds are, in general, responsible for paying benefits up to a limit determined in connection with a reference wage, described as enough for "subsistence".[37] Thus, the ECSR admits of the power of States to put a ceiling on the guaranteed amounts.[38]

Furthermore, the prescribed period determines the limits of all kinds of outstanding claims. Those who have not made the necessary effort to collect their claims within the prescribed period are not entitled to apply to guarantee institutions.

In addition, the Appendix makes a systematic distinction in regard to the nature of claims: wages, holiday pay due as a result of work performed, and other types of paid absence. We can infer from the third paragraph related to Article 25 that claims in return for work performed are protected by subsection a; claims due as a result of work performed, mainly paid leave, are under subsection b, and claims for amounts due for paid absence under subsection c.

35 ECJ, 24 November 2016, *Webb-Sämann*, § 35; ECJ, 6 September 2018, *Hampshire*, § 50.
36 ECJ, 19 December 2019, *Pensions-Sicherungs-Verein VvaG*, §§ 43–46.
37 Bronstein, "Comparative Study", *cit.*, p. 45.
38 ECSR, Conclusions 2005, Estonia; ECSR, Conclusions 2007, Lithuania.

Subsection a, the third paragraph related to Article 25, protects wages. The term wages *stricto sensu* covers the amount of money to be paid in return for work performed. According to Article 1 of the ILO Convention No. 95, the term "wages" means remuneration or earnings capable of being expressed in terms of money and payable to an employed person for work done or to be done or for services rendered or to be rendered. Besides basic wage, overtime, commission, and gratifications may all be considered under the cover of subsection a. If there is a privilege system which provides preferential treatment of wage claims over other creditors, the guaranteed amount shall not be less than three months. If there is a guarantee institution, the guaranteed amount shall not be less than eight weeks.

Wages paid for weekly rest, as well as public holidays, also fall within the scope of subsection a, even though one may argue for the applicability of subsection c. In any case, considering paid weekly rest, as well as paid public holidays, which are among the long-standing standards of labour law, these payments are to be protected.

Claims for holiday pay due as a result of work performed during the year in which the insolvency or the termination of employment occurred are protected under subsection b. Every worker who has completed a minimum length of service, generally one year, is entitled to an annual paid holiday. If a worker has outstanding holiday pay claims relating to services performed during the year in which the insolvency or the termination of employment occurred, he/she benefits from protection. The question is whether workers may enjoy this protection if they have accumulated leaves, meaning they have not taken any or some vacation leave in prior years. A negative response seems proper, as only holiday pay due as a result of work performed during the year in which the insolvency occurred falls within the scope of core protection.

Depending on the legal system, the employer may continue to remunerate workers despite their absences due to sickness, maternity, or other reasons. Such claims for the amount due in respect of paid absence relating to a prescribed period are protected under subsection c. Regardless of whether these payments may be qualified as "wages" or not, if there is a privilege system, the guaranteed amount shall not be less than three months and, under a guarantee system, not less than eight weeks.

3 Due Date of Claims

The insolvency procedure comprises different legal steps; firstly, the opening of the insolvency procedure, and then the ordering of the termination of activities. Therefore, the insolvency of the employer does not necessarily require termination of the employment contract. The employee may acquire wages and other monetary rights during the insolvency procedure. The question is the due date of claims which fall under the minimum scope of protection.

Article 3(2) of Directive 80/987, in its original version before amendment by Directive 2002/74, allowed for Member States to choose between three reference dates. The amendments introduced by Directive 2002/74 and maintained by Directive 2008/94 removed this structure. Article 3 § 2 of Directive 2008/94 states that outstanding claims should be related to a "prior to and/or, as applicable, after a given date determined by the Member States". The European Court of Justice held that Member States are free to determine an appropriate date. Therefore, there is no requirement for protection at every stage of the insolvency procedure. Even if the employer's activities continue after the opening of insolvency, the Member States may guarantee employees' claims which are due before the entry of the decision to open insolvency proceedings in the company register.[39]

The third paragraph related to Article 25 of the Appendix states that the claim in question is to be due prior to the insolvency or the termination of employment. Even if the contract of employment continues despite the insolvency, claims should be due prior to the insolvency. Wages which become due after the insolvency occurred are not under the minimum scope of protection. Nevertheless, this does not affect the option of States to introduce laws which guarantee workers' claims due after insolvency.

4 Insolvency

Insolvency is a technical legal term, and its definition varies from one legal system to another. ILO Convention No. 95, as a first step, provides privileged protection in the event of bankruptcy or judicial liquidation of an undertaking. However, in most national systems, both bankruptcy and judicial liquidation signify the legal closure of an enterprise and exclude the option for the rehabilitation of enterprises.[40]

To safeguard employment by rehabilitating insolvent enterprises, ILO Convention No. 173 has extended protection to cases of insolvency. In its Article 1, insolvency is defined as involving proceedings which "have been opened relating to an employer's assets with a view to the collective reimbursement of its creditors", a similar definition given by Article 2 of Directive 80/987/EC.

---

39 ECJ, 18 April 2013, *Meliha Veli Mustafa v. Direktor na fond 'Garantirani vzemania na rabotnitsite i sluzhitelite' kam Natsionalnia osiguritelen institut*, C-247/12, § 43.

40 For the development of procedures from bankruptcy to insolvency cf. Bronstein, "Comparative study", *cit.*, pp. 3–8.

Therefore, instead of bankruptcy or judicial liquidation, a collective procedure is required to grant protection.

The original Directive (80/987/EEC) and its codified version (Directive 2008/94/EC) also define the material scope of protection by referring to collective proceedings.[41] According to Article 2(1) of Directive 2008/94/EC, an employer is to be deemed to be in a state of insolvency when a request has been made for the opening of collective proceedings, involving the partial or total divestment of the employer's assets and the appointment of a liquidator and wherein the competent authority has either decided to open the proceedings, or established that the employer's undertaking or business has been definitively closed down and that available assets are insufficient to warrant the opening of proceedings.

Unlike the Directive as well as Convention No. 173, the revised Charter gives no definition for the term "insolvency". It is stated in the Appendix that "the definition of the term 'insolvency' must be determined by national law and practice" (Article 25 § 2 of Appendix, Revised Charter). Nevertheless, the Committee of Social Rights has adopted a very similar frame with Convention No. 173 and Directive 2008/94 to "insolvency" while assessing whether the protection afforded is adequate and effective.

The protection should firstly be granted in cases wherein a bankruptcy procedure is initiated to resolve the insolvency of the employer. Both debtor and creditor may initiate the bankruptcy procedure by applying to the competent court for an order setting the procedure in motion, regardless of who has made the request for the opening of the collective procedure. It should be noted that the term "insolvency" is broader than the term "bankruptcy".[42]

Following the request, the bankruptcy procedure may be opened or not. Protection is also to be provided in cases where the collective procedure has been requested but not opened yet. The most common case is in situations where the employer's assets are recognised as insufficient to justify the opening of formal insolvency proceedings.[43] The employer may either be subjected to a personal debt repayment programme or enter into voluntary arrangements under insolvency legislation. Hence, the fact that the employer is in a permanent state of inability to pay constitutes insolvency.

As from its first decisions, the Committee consistently underlined not only that the term "insolvency" covers formal insolvency proceedings, but also that

41 Cf. Sargeant, *cit.*, pp. 54–56.

42 Edoardo Ales *et al.*, *cit.*, Art. 25 § 3.

43 ECSR, Conclusions 2003, France; ECSR, Conclusions 2007, Albania; ECSR, Conclusions 2016, Austria.

the protection of workers' claims extends to situations where an enterprise closes down without being able to honour its commitments, even though formal insolvency proceedings are not opened.[44] The similarity to Directive 2002/74/EC is obvious.

Since the aim is to guarantee the outstanding worker claims, the most extended interpretation should be given to the notion of "insolvency". The nature of the procedure may differ in relation to the nature of the debt, whether civil liability or business liability, or the status of the debtor, whether an individual or commercial company. The size of the undertaking may also play a role in determining the procedure.[45] Thus, varying greatly from one State to another, insolvency procedures may only involve business undertakings or commercial companies. However, the protection mechanism should cover all employers' insolvency, regardless of the applicable procedure. Therefore, the Committee questions whether another form of protection exists for those working for employers who fall out of the scope of insolvency regulations, such as State institutions, public enterprises, trade unions, law and notary offices and housing construction co-operatives, as well as individual employers, public officials and judicial and military personnel.[46]

To conclude, the aim of Article 25 is to grant protection in cases wherein the employer is unable to satisfy workers' claims, regardless of the legal insolvency of the employer. In all cases wherein a request has been made for opening a collective procedure, no matter whether the procedure has been opened or not, wherein voluntary arrangement with creditors has been concluded under insolvency legislation or wherein the enterprise has closed down without having met workers' claims, workers should benefit from a guarantee mechanism.

III Guarantee Mechanisms

A *Guarantee Institutions*

ILO Convention No. 173, Directive 2008/94/EC and the revised Social Charter enforce the protection provided to workers' claims by guarantee institutions. Guarantee institutions are usually set up as wage guarantee funds and insolvency insurance schemes. They are organized under social security systems

44 ECSR, Conclusions 2003, Slovenia; ECSR, Conclusions 2003, Sweden; ECSR, Conclusions 2007, Albania; ECSR, Conclusions 2008, Malta; ECSR, Conclusions 2012, Ireland; ECSR, Conclusions 2016, Portugal.

45 Bronstein, "Comparative study", *cit.*, p. 4.

46 ECSR, Conclusions 2008, Belgium; ECSR, Conclusions 2008, Bulgaria.

and are funds that, in principle, are financed by the employer's contributions or public funds. Contributions are, in principle, wage-related.[47]

Article 5 of Directive 2008/94/EC provides that even though States are free to lay down rules for organizing, financing and operating guarantee institutions, these rules should be in conformity with the principles stated therein: the independence of these institutions' assets, financing by public authorities or employers; and independence of institutions' liabilities from the fulfilment of contributions. Unlike Directive 2008/94/EC, the revised Charter sets out no principle in respect to the financing and organization of guarantee institutions.

B *Other Mechanisms*

In the absence of guarantee institutions, States are under the duty to establish alternative mechanisms which effectively guarantee worker claims in cases where employer assets fall short, given that Article 25 of the Charter refers to "any other effective form of procedure". As the Committee underlines, a guarantee institution is not the only mechanism which provides protection in the event of insolvency.[48] A wage guarantee fund, as well as any other kind of mechanism, could satisfy the requirements of Article 25. One group of workers may benefit from guarantee funds, another from other mechanisms which provide equivalent advantages. It is up to the Committee to assess how effective these protection mechanisms are.[49]

The most common example of other mechanisms is the privilege system. The Appendix makes an apparent reference to the privilege system by increasing the secured amount of claims compared to guarantee systems. However, the protection provided under such a system depends on the amount of assets of the employer, the amount of the employer's debts secured *in rem* and the ranking system.[50] The Committee held that a privilege system, as the sole protection mechanism, does not provide sufficient protection within the sense of Article 25, because if the employer has no or not sufficient assets to distribute among creditors, workers will be left without any protection.[51] Thus, the

---

47 ILC, Report III (Part 1B), §§ 346–350.

48 ECSR, Conclusions 2003, Bulgaria.

49 ECSR, Conclusions 2008, Belgium.

50 For shortcomings of the preferential system cf. Bronstein, "The protection of of Workers' Claims", *cit.*, pp. 722–724; Bronstein, "Comparative study", *cit.*, pp. 33–35.

51 ECSR, Conclusions 2003, Bulgaria; ECSR, Conclusions 2005, Bulgaria; ECSR, Conclusions 2012, Malta; ECSR, Statement of interpretation on Article 25, 2012; ECSR, Conclusions 2020, Albania; Edoardo Ales *et al.*, *cit.*, Art. 25 § 9; Karin Lukas, *cit.*, § 25.10.

Committee requires an alternative mechanism which protects workers' rights in these cases.

IV Adequate and Effective Protection

A *The Guaranteed Amount*

The Appendix to the revised Charter states the minimum amounts to be guaranteed; three months or eight weeks of wages depending on the nature of the protection mechanisms. Nevertheless, it does not prevent higher protection to workers. The question is whether the guaranteed amount of wages should be equal to the amount that the worker is receiving. The Appendix lays down the principle that "National laws or regulations may limit the protection of workers' claims to a prescribed amount, which shall be of a socially acceptable level" (Article 25(3)(4) of Appendix, ESC (rev)). Therefore, States have the power to set ceilings for the amount guaranteed, considering a very large range of wage levels. Nevertheless, the Committee questions whether the ceiling is at a socially acceptable level.[52] Likewise, Articles 7(1) and 13(1) of Convention No. 173 enable national regulations to limit protection, as long as the protected amount is not below such level.

Even if there is no specific calculation method, the Committee aims at "suitably balanced social protection".[53] The average monthly wage and minimum wage are the criteria generally referred to. In the case of Estonia, payable amounts can be up to three times the average monthly remuneration of the worker and may not exceed an amount equivalent to three times Estonia's average monthly wage, which is considered to be adequate protection.[54] In the case of Lithuania, protection provided by the guarantee fund is "up to a maximum of three times the average gross monthly wage; monetary compensation for unused annual leave up to a maximum sum equivalent to one month of the minimum wage; severance pay restricted to two months' worth of the minimum wage; compensation for paid periods of inactivity up to a maximum of one month's worth of the minimum wage". This has been considered sufficient.[55]

52 ECSR, Conclusions 2005, Estonia; ECSR, Conclusions 2008; ECSR, Conclusions 2008, Malta; ECSR, Conclusions 2012, Ireland; Karin Lukas, *cit.*, § 25.08.

53 ECSR, Conclusions 2012, Ireland.

54 ECSR, Conclusions 2008, Estonia.

55 ECSR, Conclusions 2008, Lithuania.

B *Duration*

The Committee questions not only the amount but also the normal or average duration of the period from the lodging of a claim until the moment the worker has received the payment.[56] States are to demonstrate efficient protection by establishing an efficient guarantee mechanism. The Committee focuses on actual payment periods rather than on statutory regulations. An average period of 15 days,[57] of 60 days,[58] of 2 months and 24 days,[59] of 116 days,[60] or of 6 weeks[61] is considered reasonable. On the contrary, a period of 12 months[62] or of 11 months[63] is not in conformity with the Charter.

C *Coverage of Protection*

To assure adequate and effective protection of workers' claims, the Committee questions the overall proportion of workers' claims which are not satisfied by guarantee institutions and requests the reasons for refusal to satisfy a claim.[64] On the base of the information that 66 percent of worker claims were granted, the Committee asks the State Party to summarise the main reasons for one third of the claims not being granted.[65] Likewise, in the case of Serbia, where 2.384 claims were satisfied out of 4.885 requested, the effective coverage of less than 50 % was considered low.[66]

Concluding Remarks

The vital importance of wages for workers and their families requires enhanced protection in times of economic difficulties that employers are experiencing. Unlike individual debt enforcement claims, insolvency or bankruptcy procedures involve employers' assets so as to collectively satisfy the claims of creditors, including workers' claims. The shortcomings of privilege systems

---

56 ECSR, Conclusions 2003, Sweden; ECSR, Conclusions 2007, Albania; ECSR, Conclusions 2008, Romania; ECSR, Conclusions 2012, Ireland.

57 ECSR, Conclusions 2008, Estonia.

58 ECSR, Conclusions 2016, Slovak Republic; ECSR, Conclusions 2012, Finland.

59 ECSR, Conclusions 2008, Bulgaria.

60 ECSR, Conclusions 2012, Estonia.

61 ECSR, Conclusions 2008, Norway.

62 ECSR, Conclusions 2012, Lithuania.

63 ECSR, Conclusions 2012, Belgium; ECSR, Conclusions 2016, Portugal.

64 Edoardo Ales *et al.*, *cit.*, Art 25 § 11.

65 ECSR, Conclusions 2005, Slovenia; ECSR, Conclusions 2008, Slovenia.

66 ECSR, Conclusions 2012, Serbia.

reveal the need for a system based on social security principles. Protection of workers' claims in the event of employer insolvency is one of the new rights inserted in the revised Charter. Article 25 of the revised Charter is inspired by ILO Convention No. 173 and EU Directives on employer's insolvency. This new right strengthens the protection provided to workers' claims and places the risk of non-payment by the insolvent employer on the guarantee institution. In spite of its importance, Article 25 is one of the few approved Charter provisions.[67]

Article 25 clearly states its aim to ensure the effective exercise of the right of workers to the protection of their claims in the event of the insolvency of their employer. The Charter requires neither the existence of a specific guarantee institution, nor a specific form of protection. Therefore, States Parties enjoy a margin of appreciation in terms of the institutional structure and form of protection. Nevertheless, the European Committee of Social Rights monitors the effective protection of workers' outstanding claims by scrutinizing national practices. National reports are the main source for this monitoring process. The Committee considers that the absence of information amounts to a breach of the reporting obligation under the Charter.[68] Additionally, should the report not provide all information requested, the Committee concludes that the situation in the concerned State is not in conformity with Article 25.[69] The jurisprudence of the Committee is in line with the comments of the ILO Committee of Experts on the Application of Conventions and Recommendations. To conclude, the Charter provides protection not only in theory, but also in practice.[70]

---

67 Karin Lukas, *cit.*, § 25.12.

68 ECSR, Conclusions 2012, Malta.

69 ECSR, Conclusions 2020, Romania; ECSR, Conclusions 2020, Malta.

70 Edoardo Ales *et al.*, *cit.*, Article 25 § 12.

ARTICLE 26

The Right to Dignity at Work

Güçlü Akyürek, Canan Ünal Adınır and Deniz Ugan Çatalkaya

With a view to ensuring the effective exercise of the right of all workers to protection of their dignity at work, the Parties undertake, in consultation with employers' and workers' organisations:

1 to promote awareness, information and prevention of sexual harassment in the workplace or in relation to work and to take all appropriate measures to protect workers from such conduct;

2 to promote awareness, information, and prevention of recurrent reprehensible or distinctly negative and offensive actions directed against individual workers in the workplace or in relation to work and to take all appropriate measures to protect workers from such conduct.

Introduction

The Revised Charter regulated a new fundamental right: "the right to dignity at work" under Article 26 of Part II, whereas such an article does not exist in the Charter of 1961. This article emphasises the promotion of awareness and prevention of sexual harassment (§ 1) and other types of harassment at work (§ 2), although it does not require that Parties ensure protection against such conduct. In addition, it follows from the Appendix that Parties do not need to enact legislation. Nonetheless, they are required to take "all appropriate measures" to protect workers[1] and, furthermore, among the "rights and principles", it is laid down by § 26 of Part I that "all workers have the right to dignity at

1 European Social Charter (Revised), Explanatory Report No. 97, May 3, European Treaty Series No. 163, p. 11.

 | DOI:10.1163/9789004434158_008

work". The ECSR has also interpreted Article 1 § 2 in a way that protects workers' privacy[2] as a fundamental component of safeguarding workers' rights.

1 Dignity at Work

Article 26, focused on well-being and the worker as an individual, protects dignity at work, a relatively new concept. Yet, dignity is one of the key concepts of the human rights framework and plays a central role in this field,[3] given that it constitutes a commonplace and acts as a threshold for human rights issues, from restrictions on abortion in the United States to dwarf-throwing in France.[4]

Likewise, a large number of international texts mention this concept. Historically, the English Bill of Rights of 1689 refers to "royal dignity" without providing any clear definition. Reaching further back in time, according to Roman Law, "*dignitas*" meant "status", and a person deserved honour and respect due to his/her status.[5] This word derives from Greek "*axia*", which meant "value".[6] In the Middle Ages, "*dignitas*" served to distinguish humans (as "an image of the God") from other creatures.[7] Nevertheless, "dignity" became a "human trait" during the Renaissance.[8] Finally, Article 151 of the German Weimar Constitution of 1919 was one of the first legal instruments to make direct reference to "dignity".[9]

Today, especially international or regional human rights texts make reference to this concept. In the Preamble of the Charter of the United Nations, it can be read: "to reaffirm faith (...) in the dignity and worth of the human person (...)". Likewise, the International Declaration of Human Rights of 1948 makes five references thereto (two times in the Preamble and in Articles 1, 22 and 23); the UN International Covenant on Civil and Political Rights three times (two in the Preamble and Article 10), and the UN International Covenant

2 Matti Mikkola, *Social Human Rights of Europe*, Karelactio, 2010, p. 163.
3 Christopher McCrudden, "Human dignity and Judicial Interpretation of Human Rights", *The European Journal of International Law*, Vol. 19, No. 4, 2008, p. 656.
4 Christopher McCrudden, *cit.*, p. 656.
5 Christopher McCrudden, *cit.*, pp. 656–657.
6 Jacques Fierens, "La dignité humaine comme concept juridique", *Journal des Tribunaux*, No. 6064, 21 septembre 2002, p. 577.
7 Christopher McCrudden, *cit.*, p. 657.
8 Jacques Fierens, *cit.*, pp. 577–578.
9 Jacques Fierens, *cit.*, p. 578.

on Economic, Social and Cultural Rights of 1966 three times as well (same Preamble and Article 10).

Moreover, one of the titles in the Charter of Fundamental Rights of the European Union is "dignity" and it includes human dignity (Article 1), the right to life (Article 2), the right to the integrity of the person (Article 3), prohibition of torture and inhuman or degrading treatment or punishment (Article 4), and prohibition of slavery and forced labour (Article 5). This Charter also underlines in the preamble that "the Union is founded on the indivisible, universal values of human dignity, freedom, equality and solidarity". It points out the connection between working conditions and human dignity in Article 31: "Every worker has the right to working conditions which respect his or her health, safety and dignity".[10] In the Explanation of this article, a reference to Article 26 has been made. It shows that the article of the Revised European Social Charter has been a real "source" of Article 31 of the CFREU and there is a direct and clear connection between dignity at work and "fair and just working conditions".

To further the discussion on the importance of dignity in the workplace, it is important to point out Convention No. 190 (Violence and Harassment Convention, 2019) of the ILO. It makes this connection very clear by placing human dignity at its core (Preamble: "Recognizing the importance of a work culture based on mutual respect and dignity of the human being to prevent violence and harassment") and aiming to prevent such behaviours in the world of work (Preamble: "Recognizing the right of everyone to a world of work free from violence and harassment"). Thereby, it requires ratifying countries, i.e., to define and prohibit violence and harassment in the world of work (Article 7) and to take appropriate measures to prevent them (Article 8), which is directly related to working conditions.[11]

Previously, the European Court of Justice had already started to use the concept of dignity, even before the Charter had full legal status, and the Court even approved the right to dignity as a part of European Union Law in 2001.[12] Accordingly, Recommendation No. 202 of the International Labour

10 Within this framework, the European Commission made a proposal for a Directive to the European Parliament and the Council for "adequate minimum wages in the European Union", which led to the approval of Directive (EU) 2022/2041 of the European Parliament and of the Council of 19 October 2022 on adequate minimum wages in the European Union.

11 For further information, see ILO, Violence and harassment in the world of work, 2021.

12 Jackie Jones, "Human Dignity in the EU Charter of Fundamental Rights and Its Interpretation Before the European Court of Justice", *Liverpool Law Review*, 2012, Vol. 33, pp. 290–291.

Organisation (2012), Social Protection Floors Recommendation, refers twice to dignity (Articles 3(f) and 8(b)), albeit without providing any definition. In this context, the ILO establishes a connection between the right to social security and human dignity by emphasising that the former "is of central importance in guaranteeing" the latter.[13]

In the same way, the United Nations refer several times to dignity in the 2030 Agenda for Sustainable Development, underlining the fact that "the dignity of the human person is fundamental".[14]

Yet, the most famous international human rights text is perhaps the European Convention on Human Rights, or, officially, the Convention for the Protection of Human Rights and Fundamental Freedoms, although it lacks mentions to dignity in the articles and in the Preamble until the Additional Protocol No. 13 in 2002 because of a potential "pragmatism". Nevertheless, the European Court of Human Rights always emphasises its importance in case-law.

In *Tyrer v. United Kingdom* (25 April 1978), one of the first leading cases on this issue, the Court pointed out that the main purpose of Article 3 is to protect the person's dignity and it stressed in § 30 that: "the prohibition contained in Article 3 of the Convention is absolute: no provision is made for exceptions and, under Article 15(2) there can be no derogation from Article 3 (art. 3)".[15]

In *Pretty v. United Kingdom* (29 April 2002) § 65: "The very essence of the Convention is respect for human dignity and human freedom. Without in any way negating the principle of sanctity of life protected under the Convention, the Court considers that it is under Article 8 that notions of the quality of life take on significance. In an era of constant medical advancements combined with longer life expectancies, many people are concerned that they should not be forced to linger on in old age or in states of advanced physical or mental decrepitude which conflict with strongly held ideas of self and personal identity".[16]

In *Bouyid v. Belgium* (28 September 2015) § 89: "The word 'dignity' appears in many international and regional texts and instruments (see paragraphs 45–47 above). Although the Convention does not mention that concept – which nevertheless appears in the Preamble to Protocol No. 13 to the Convention, concerning the abolition of the death penalty in all circumstances – the Court

13 ILO, *Universal Social Protection for Human Dignity, Social Justice and Sustainable Development, International Labour Conference*, 108th Session, 1st ed., Geneva, International Labour Office, 2019, p. 23.

14 https://sdgs.un.org/2030agenda.

15 ECtHR, 25 April 1978, *Tyrer v. United Kingdom*, No. 5856/72, § 30.

16 ECtHR, 29 April 2002, *Pretty v. United Kingdom*, No. 2346/02, § 65.

has emphasised that respect for human dignity forms part of the very essence of the Convention (see, inter alia, Svinarenko and Slyadnev, cited above, § 118), alongside human freedom (see C.R. v. the United Kingdom, 22 November 1995, § 42, Series A no. 335-C, and S.W. v. the United Kingdom, 22 November 1995, § 44, Series A no. 335-B; see also, among other authorities, Pretty v. the United Kingdom, no. 2346/02, § 65, ECHR 2002-III)".[17]

Moreover, "dignity" appears in the Preamble to Protocol No. 13 on the abolition of the death penalty as the second case stated.

As all these texts show that dignity is an inherent value of the human being, that means anyone has dignity, simply for being a human and, furthermore, these texts confirm that this concept is the source of all rights. Because the work relationship between employer and employee is of utmost importance and puts the working individual in a vulnerable position, he or she always faces the risk of interference with his/her private life and personal rights. Thus, the protection of an employee's rights, including dignity, becomes a *conditio sine qua non* of a suitable workplace.[18]

For this reason, "dignity at work" is one of the rights protected by the revised European Social Charter. While this concept is relatively new and in development,[19] the European Social Charter of 1961 does not provide any reference, even if in the *Travaux préparatoires* a great number of references to "dignity" were made. Nevertheless, the revised European Social Charter explicitly protects dignity at work under Article 26. In fact, this concept "guarantees inherent human rights at work".[20] This guarantee is limited to the workplace and activities related to work, according to § 97 of the Explanatory Report to the revised European Social Charter.

Article 26 has the purpose of such a guarantee. Even if neither the article nor its Explanatory Report define the concept of dignity, the latter focuses on "the promotion of awareness and prevention of sexual harassment and victimisation". Thus, this article deals exclusively with two facets of dignity at work: Awareness and prevention of sexual harassment (§ 1) and awareness and

---

17 ECtHR, 28 September 2015, *Bouyid v. Belgium*, No. 23380/09, § 89. The Court also decided that States have positive obligations to prevent violations such as human trafficking (cf. ECtHR, 30 March 2017, *Chowdury v. Greece*, No. 21884/15, § 86).

18 Olivier De Tissot, "Pour une Analyse Juridique du Concept de 'Dignité' du Salarié", *Droit Social*, No. 12, December 1995, pp. 972 ff.; Patrice Adam, "La Dignité du Salarié (Deuxième partie)", *RDT*, 2014, p. 244.

19 Mariann Arany Toth, "The Right to Dignity at Work: Reflections on Article 26 of the Revised European Social Charter", *Comparative Labor Law & Policy Journal*, Vol. 29, 2008, p. 276.

20 Mariann Arany Toth, *cit.*, p. 277.

prevention of negative and offensive actions (§ 2).[21] The Revised Charter also stresses these two forms of "harassment" by avoiding an "unduly wide interpretation" of dignity.[22]

On the other hand, the Appendix emphasises that the Parties do not need to enact legislation relating specifically to harassment as the European Committee of Social Rights repeated it in its Conclusions,[23] despite the ECSR also underlining in the same Conclusions that legal instruments duly interpreted by national authorities can provide an effective protection against these actions. In this context, the ECSR considers consultation procedures between employees' and employers' organisations and official authorities. Moreover, States have to establish national policies and programmes concerning the protection of dignity at work.[24]

As interesting examples, in the United Kingdom, the Protection from Harassment Act 1997 prohibits harassment and not only creates civil remedies but also recognizes new offences. According to the House of Lords, it covers the behaviour of employees.[25] In Germany, there is a special act against discrimination (AGG: *Allgemeines Gleichbehandlungsgesetz* / General Act on Equal Treatment) of 2006. These legal instruments make reference to dignity (Article 3) and provide civil remedies against discrimination to employees. This Act considers harassment as discrimination in some cases.[26]

In France, alongside the offense of sexual harassment (Article 222–33 of the French Penal Code), there is "moral harassment", which constitutes an offense committed by repeated harassment acts which deteriorate the victim's working conditions and causes harm to his/her rights or dignity (Article 222-33-2).

Likewise, the Turkish Penal Code punishes, *inter alia*, anyone who subjugates a person to working conditions which do not conform with human dignity (Article 117 § 2). Furthermore, Equality Code No. 6701 refers to dignity while prohibiting different forms of discrimination such as harassment.

21 Matti Mikkola, *cit.*, pp. 162–163.

22 Karin Lukas, *The Revised European Social Charter*, 2021, p. 304. Cf. https://www.elgaronline.com/view/9781789903638/40_article26.xhtml.

23 For example, ECSR, Conclusions 2005, Moldova.

24 Mariann Arany Toth, *cit.*, p. 297.

25 Majrowski (Respondent) v. Guy's and St Thomas' NHS Trust (Appellants) [2006] UKHL 34.

26 Cf. https://www.gesetze-im-internet.de/englisch_agg/englisch_agg.html#p0057 (Accessed on 9 April 2019).

II Scope

While the revised European Social Charter regulates the right to dignity at work, the term "at work" has not been defined. According to the Explanatory Report of the ESC (rev), the purpose of Article 26 is to guarantee workers the right of dignity "at work" and "in connection with work".[27] By taking a literal interpretation, the extent of protection covers not only the stage of performing work, but the circumstances relating to all rights and duties at work.[28]

On the one hand, the scope *ratione personae* of the ESC (rev) has been defined in the appendix, according to which the Charter includes foreigners "only in so far as they are nationals of other Contracting Parties lawfully resident or working regularly within the territory of the Contracting Party concerned".[29] On the other hand, the personal scope of Article 26 has been determined as "all workers" in wording. Thus, the right to dignity at work applies to workers in both the private and in public sector.[30]

Regarding specific content, Article 26 regulates both sexual and moral harassment. While § 1 deals exclusively with sexual harassment, § 2 covers moral harassment.[31]

III Sexual Harassment

A *Definition*

Sexual harassment is regulated, but not defined in Article 26 § 1 of the ESC (rev). However, it is defined in the Explanatory Report of the ESC (rev) as an "unwanted conduct of a sexual nature, or other conduct based on sex affecting the dignity of workers, including the conduct of superiors and colleagues".[32]

The same perspective is reflected by the ECSR. The Committee defines sexual harassment based upon the concept of "human dignity" and addresses this concept as a breach of equal treatment characterised by the adoption, towards one or more persons, of preferential or retaliatory conduct, or other forms of insistent behaviour, which may undermine their dignity or harm their

27 ESC (rev), Explanatory Report No. 97, p. 11.
28 Mariann Arany Toth, *cit.*, p. 292.
29 ESC (Rev), Ratione Personae Appendix, May 3, 1996, European Treaty Series No. 163, p. 1; ESC (rev), Explanatory Report No. 97, p. 17.
30 Mariann Arany Toth, *cit.*, p. 293.
31 Cf. ESC (rev), Ratione Personae Appendix, p. 5.
32 ESC (rev), Explanatory Report No. 97, p. 11.

career.[33] The ECSR also stresses that sexual harassment is not necessarily a form of discrimination based on gender but always qualifies as a breach of equal treatment.[34]

Besides the revised European Social Charter, the concept of sexual harassment is also mentioned in other regional texts. Especially after 1985, the Community institutions started to deal with the phenomenon of sexual harassment.[35] For instance, in 1999, the European Commission published a study on sexual harassment at the workplace in the European Union to present an overview of all relevant research projects conducted in eleven Member States between 1987 and 1997 and made up 74 surveys and qualitative studies. In this study, it is reported that the lack of a universal definition of what constitutes sexual harassment makes it more difficult to objectively measure and quantify it.[36]

The European Union defines sexual harassment generally by reviewing it based on the scope of the principle of equal treatment and/or prohibition of discrimination. For the first time, the Commission Proposal of 28 November 2000 amending Council Directive 76/207/EEC clearly defined sexual harassment as discrimination based on sex at the workplace. It proposed an amendment, which concerned inserting a new article making it explicit that sexual harassment constitutes discrimination on the ground of sex and defined it as "unwanted conduct related to sex (which) takes place with the purposes or effect of affecting the dignity of a person and/or creating an intimidating, hostile, offensive or disturbing environment, in particular if a person's rejection of, or submission to, such conduct is used as a basis for a decision which affects that person".

Thereafter, Directive 2002/73/EC of the European Parliament and of the Council of 23 September 2002 amended Council Directive 76/207/EEC[37] and explained that sexual harassment is contrary to the principle of equal treatment between women and men (Recital 8). In this Recast Directive, sexual

---

33 ECSR, Conclusions 2005, Moldova; ECSR, Conclusions 2007, Belgium; ECSR, Conclusions 2014, Sweden; ECSR, Conclusions 2014, Georgia; ECSR, Conclusions 2014, Turkey.

34 ECSR, Conclusions 2003, Sweden; ECSR, Conclusions 2003, France.

35 For further information, cf. Commission Proposal for a Directive of the European Parliament and of the Council amending Council Directive 76/207/EEC on the implementation of the principle of equal treatment for men and women as regards access to employment, vocational training and promotion, and working conditions, *OJ C 337 E, 28 November 2000, pp. 0204–0206.*

36 European Commission, *Sexual Harassment at the Workplace in the European Union*, European Communities, 1999, pp. iii, 3, 5, 9, 11.

37 OJ L 269, 5 October 2002, pp. 15–20.

harassment is defined as an offense "where any form of unwanted verbal, non-verbal or physical conduct of a sexual nature occurs, with the purpose or effect of violating the dignity of a person, in particular when creating an intimidating, hostile, degrading, humiliating or offensive environment". Within the meaning of this Directive, sexual harassment is deemed to be discrimination on the grounds of sex and therefore prohibited. Directive 2006/54/EC[38] repealed this Directive, but the new Directive contains the very same definition of sexual harassment.

Furthermore, it is observed in some regional texts that sexual harassment is also associated with human dignity. To a certain extent, EU law also takes into account human dignity being at odds with sexual harassment.[39] According to the *OZ v. European Investment Bank* judgment of the CJEU, sexual harassment is detrimental to human dignity.[40]

A clear exponent of the human dignity approach to sexual harassment is the Autonomous Framework Agreement on Harassment and Violence at Work,[41] which was signed on 26 April 2007 by ETUC, BUSINESSEUROPE UEAPME and CEEP, after approval by the respective decision-making bodies of these organizations.[42] In this agreement, although sexual harassment is not defined, it is described as a form of harassment, and harassment occurs when one or more workers or managers are repeatedly and deliberately abused, threatened, and/or humiliated in circumstances relating to work.

B *Prevention*

Article 26 § 1, through its own wording, entails undertakings to promote "awareness, information and prevention" of sexual harassment in the workplace or in relation to work, in consultation with employers' and workers' organisations.

This provision requires States Parties to take appropriate preventive measures (information, awareness-raising, and prevention campaigns in the workplace or in relation to work) in order to combat sexual harassment. In consultation with social partners, in particular, they should inform workers as to the nature of the behaviour in question and the available remedies.[43] In other

38 OJ L 204, 26 July 2006, pp. 23–36.

39 European Commission, *cit.*, pp. 7, 25.

40 ECJ, 4 April 2019, *OZ v. European Investment Bank*, C-558/17, § 66.

41 Cf. https://www.businesseurope.eu/sites/buseur/files/media/imported/2007-00697-EN.pdf (Accessed on 31 December 2019).

42 European Commission, *Harassment Related to Sex and Sexual Harassment Law in 33 European Countries*, Publication of European Union, 2013, p. 5.

43 ECSR, Conclusions 2018, Latvia; ECSR, Conclusions 2018, Lithuania; ECSR, Conclusions 2014, Slovak Republic; ECSR, Conclusions 2014, The former Yugoslav Republic of

words, the public should be made more aware of the problem of sexual harassment, including efforts to consult employers' and workers' representatives.[44]

The ECSR considered that public education programmes, campaigns, cooperation with NGOs and employers' organisations, and provision of online sources of information on sexual harassment count as awareness-raising measures regarding sexual harassment.[45]

C *Protection*

1 Effective Protection

Article 26 § 1, by its own wording, entails undertakings to take all appropriate measures to protect workers from sexual harassment in the workplace or in relation to work, in consultation with employers' and workers' organisations. This protection must include the right to appeal to an independent body in the event of sexual harassment, the right to obtain suitable compensation, and the right not to be retaliated against for upholding these rights.[46]

Note that in the event of lack of information by the State to the ECSR as to the employer's responsibility for effective protection, the Committee considers that there are no sufficient and effective remedies against sexual harassment in relation to work. Accordingly, it would conclude that the State is not in conformity with Article 26 § 1.[47]

a *Domestic Norms*

Article 26 § 1 requires effective protection to be afforded to workers against sexual harassment by domestic norms.[48] However, as the Appendix emphasises, Article 26 does not require that legislation be enacted by the Parties.[49] This means States have no obligation to enact laws relating specifically to harassment where workers are afforded effective protection against harassment by existing norms, irrespective of whether such norms are general anti-discrimination acts or specific laws against harassment.[50]

Macedonia; ECSR, Conclusions 2014, Lithuania; ECSR, Conclusions 2014, Andorra; ECSR, Conclusions 2014, Italy; ECSR, Conclusions 2014, Netherlands.

44 ECSR, Conclusions 2007, Bulgaria.

45 ECSR, Conclusions 2018, Serbia.

46 ECSR, Conclusions 2014, Azerbaijan; ECSR, Conclusions 2014, Moldova; ECSR, Conclusions 2016, Ukraine; ECSR, Conclusions 2016, Turkey; ECSR, Conclusions 2018, Latvia.

47 ECSR, Conclusion 2018, Lithuania.

48 ECSR, Conclusion 2014, Turkey.

49 ESC (rev), Ratione Personae Appendix, p. 5.

50 ECSR, Conclusions 2014, Georgia; cf. also ECSR, Conclusions 2005, Moldova; ECSR, Conclusions 2014, Turkey; ECSR, Conclusions 2016, Turkey.

In other words, under Article 26 § 1 of the Charter, there is no need for a State's legislation to make express reference to harassment where that State's law encompasses measures making it possible to afford employees effective protection against the various forms of discrimination.[51]

b *Interpretation of Norms by the Domestic Courts*

The effectiveness of legal protection against sexual harassment also depends on how the domestic courts interpret the law.[52] Conclusive information on relevant case law[53] is therefore requested.

c *Burden of Proof*

From the procedural standpoint, effective protection of victims also requires somewhat of a shift in the burden of proof, making it possible for a court to find in favour of the victim on the basis of sufficient *prima facie* evidence and the personal conviction of the judge or judges.[54]

2 Liability of Employer and Remedies

a *The Term "Worker"*

While the personal scope of Article 26 has been determined as "all workers" in its own wording, the meaning of "worker" has been specified with respect to the liability of employers because of sexual harassment.[55]

It is clear that all persons working for an employer irrespective of the legal classification are included to Article 26. In addition, the provision requires employers to be held liable towards persons other than employees and job applicants[56] who might suffer sexual harassment from personnel under their responsibility, or at premises under their responsibility, from persons working for them in a capacity other than as employees such as independent

51 ECSR, Conclusions 2003, Sweden; ECSR, Conclusions 2003, France; ECSR, Conclusions 2005, Moldova; ECSR, Conclusions 2007, Belgium.

52 ECSR, Conclusions 2005, Moldova; ECSR, Conclusions 2007, Slovenia; ECSR, Conclusions 2014, Turkey; ECSR, Conclusions 2016, Turkey.

53 ECSR, Conclusions 2005, Moldova; ECSR, Conclusions 2007, Slovenia; ECSR, Conclusions 2014, Turkey; ECSR, Conclusions 2016, Turkey.

54 ECSR, Conclusions 2003, Sweden; ECSR, Conclusions 2003, France; ECSR, Conclusions 2005, Moldova; ECSR, Conclusions 2007, Belgium; ECSR, Conclusions 2014, Ukraine; ECSR, Conclusions 2014, Turkey; ECSR, Conclusions 2014, The former Yugoslav Republic of Macedonia.

55 Mariann Arany Toth, *cit.*, p. 293.

56 ECSR, Conclusions 2007, Sweden.

contractors, self-employed, etc.,[57] and persons not employed by them such as customers, visitors, clients, guests, etc.[58]

b *Damages*

Victims of sexual harassment must have effective judicial remedies to seek reparation for pecuniary and non-pecuniary damage. These remedies must, in particular, allow for appropriate compensation for the victim's pecuniary and non-pecuniary damage and also act as a deterrent to the employer.[59]

c *Reinstatement*

In addition, the right to reinstatement should be guaranteed to employees unfairly dismissed pressured to resign for reasons related to sexual harassment.[60]

---

57 ECSR, Conclusions 2003, France; ECSR, Conclusions 2003, Bulgaria; ECSR, Conclusions 2003, Italy; ECSR, Conclusions 2005, Moldova; ECSR, Conclusions 2010, Malta; ECSR, Conclusions 2010, Italy; ECSR, Conclusions 2014, Slovak Republic; ECSR, Conclusions 2014, Bulgaria; ECSR, Conclusions 2014, Turkey; ECSR, Conclusions 2014, Ukraine; ECSR, Conclusions 2014, Finland; ECSR, Conclusions 2014, Azerbaijan; ECSR, Conclusions 2014, Montenegro; ECSR, Conclusions 2014, Estonia; ECSR, Conclusions 2014, Sweden; ECSR, Conclusions 2018, Slovak Republic; ECSR, Conclusions 2018, Latvia; ECSR, Conclusions 2018, Ukraine; ECSR, Conclusions 2018, Lithuania; ECSR, Conclusions 2018, Azerbaijan; ECSR, Conclusions 2018, Sweden.

58 ECSR, Conclusions 2003, Italy; ECSR, Conclusions 2005, Moldova; ECSR, Conclusions 2010, Malta; ECSR, Conclusions 2010, Italy; ECSR, Conclusions 2014, Slovak Republic; ECSR, Conclusions 2014, Bulgaria; ECSR, Conclusions 2014, Turkey; ECSR, Conclusions 2014, Ukraine; ECSR, Conclusions 2014, Finland; ECSR, Conclusions 2014, Azerbaijan; ECSR, Conclusions 2014, Montenegro; ECSR, Conclusions 2014, Estonia; ECSR, Conclusions 2014, Sweden; ECSR, Conclusions 2018, Slovak Republic; ECSR, Conclusions 2018, Latvia; ECSR, Conclusions 2018, Ukraine; ECSR, Conclusions 2018, Lithuania; ECSR, Conclusions 2018, Azerbaijan; ECSR, Conclusions 2018, Sweden.

59 ECSR, Conclusions 2007, Bulgaria; ECSR, Conclusions 2010, Georgia; ECSR, Conclusions 2010, Turkey; ECSR, Conclusions 2010, Malta; ECSR, Conclusions 2010, Portugal; ECSR, Conclusions 2010, Andorra; ECSR, Conclusions 2010, Lithuania; ECSR, Conclusions 2014, Ukraine; ECSR, Conclusions 2014, Slovak Republic; ECSR, Conclusions 2014, The former Yugoslav Republic of Macedonia; ECSR, Conclusions 2014, Estonia; ECSR, Conclusions 2014, Georgia; ECSR, Conclusions 2014, Moldova; ECSR, Conclusions 2014, Azerbaijan; ECSR, Conclusions 2014, Netherlands; ECSR, Conclusions 2014, Serbia; ECSR, Conclusions 2014, Lithuania; ECSR, Conclusions 2016, Turkey; ECSR, Conclusions 2016, Ukraine; ECSR, Conclusions 2018, Ukraine; ECSR, Conclusions 2018, Turkey.

60 ECSR, Conclusions 2005, Lithuania; ECSR, Conclusions 2005, Republic of Moldova; ECSR, Conclusions 2010, Portugal; ECSR, Conclusions 2010, Lithuania; ECSR, Conclusions 2014, Ukraine; ECSR, Conclusions 2014, Slovak Republic; ECSR, Conclusions 2014, Montenegro; ECSR, Conclusions 2014, Estonia; ECSR, Conclusions 2014, Portugal; ECSR, Conclusions 2014, Georgia; ECSR, Conclusions 2014, The former Yugoslav Republic of Macedonia; ECSR,

IV Moral Harassment

Article 26 § 2 of the ESC (rev) recognizes the right to protection of human dignity against recurrent reprehensible or distinctly negative and offensive actions directed against individual workers in the workplace or in relation to work. Article 26 § 2 is the first international provision to establish a fundamental right to protection of human dignity against harassment creating a hostile working environment related to a specific characteristic of a person.[61] The Appendix to the Charter clarifies that this second paragraph does not cover sexual harassment.

The link established between harassment and attack on dignity appears judicious if we consider that moral harassment characterizes a process of enslavement, degradation, and objectification of the individual.[62] Harassment, whatever its form, constitutes a direct attack on the dignity of the worker.[63] Thus, it is considered that "the dignity of the human person constitutes the central axis, the pivot on which the protection of the victim of harassment is based".[64] The concept of dignity is therefore considered to be the legal basis for the prohibition of harassment.[65]

Labour law standards were first developed to protect the body of the workers; yet, the transformations of work in "post-industrial" society have brought along new physical and psychological risks in the workplace.[66] It is undeniable that certain modes of human resource management may appear to be the cause of moral harassment.

Conclusions 2014, Moldova; ECSR, Conclusions 2014, Netherlands; ECSR, Conclusions 2014, Serbia; ECSR, Conclusions 2014, Slovenia; ECSR, Conclusions 2016, Turkey; ECSR, Conclusions 2016, Ukraine; ECSR, Conclusions 2018, Ukraine; ECSR, Conclusions 2018, Lithuania; ECSR, Conclusions 2018, Turkey.

61 ECSR, Conclusions 2003, Bulgaria; ECSR, Conclusions 2003, France; ECSR, Conclusions 2005, Lithuania. Cf. Carole Nivard, *La Justiciabilité des Droits Sociaux, Étude de Droit Conventionnel Européen*, Bruxelles, Bruylant, 2012, p. 431; Mariann Arany Toth, *cit.*, pp. 305–306.

62 Patrice Adam, "Répertoire de Droit du Travail, Harcèlement Moral", septembre 2014, § 1 3.

63 Philippe Waquet, *L'Entreprise et les Libertés du Salarié*, Paris, Éditions Liaisons, 2003, p. 165.

64 Antoine Mazeaud, "Harcèlement entre Salariés: Apport de la Loi de Modernisation Sociale", *Droit Social*, 2002, p. 321.

65 Patrice Adam, " La Dignité du Salarié (Deuxième partie)", *cit*, p. 244.

66 Alain Supiot, *Le Droit du Travail*, 4e éd. mise à jour, Paris, Puf, 2009, pp. 117–118.

A *Definition*

It seems appropriate to state from the beginning that there is no uniformly accepted definition of the concept of "moral harassment".

The Explanatory Report of the ESC (rev) outlines that Article 26 § 2 aims at forms of victimising conduct which affect the right to dignity at work (victimisation, defined as bullying), forms other than sexual harassment. According to the Report, the definition of such behaviour has been taken from existing national regulations dealing with this problem and comprises recurrent reprehensible or distinctly negative and offensive acts by superiors and colleagues affecting the dignity of a worker in the workplace or in relation with work.[67] The situation of a worker who, for reasons of hostility on the part of the employer and/or his or her colleagues, is systematically excluded from discussions relating to organising work which his or her colleagues are invited to take part in or not giving a worker an office or withholding duties corresponding to his or her position and functions for similar reasons are given as examples of such victimisation.

According to Leymann, who is considered as the initiator of the term "*mobbing*", "psychological terror or mobbing in working life involves hostile and unethical communication which is directed in a systematic manner by one or more individuals, mainly toward one individual, who, due to mobbing, is pushed into a helpless and defenceless position and held there by means of continuing mobbing activities. These actions occur on a very frequent basis (statistical definition: at least once a week) and over a long period of time (statistical definition: at least six months' duration). Because of the high frequency and long duration of hostile behaviour, this maltreatment results in considerable mental, psychosomatic and social misery".[68]

Although the term "moral harassment" has been identified in the case law of the ECSR,[69] the concept has not been clearly and concretely determined.[70] Nevertheless, it is clear that the forms of victimisation can vary from one State to another, due to the wording of Article 26 § 2, which covers heterogeneous issues that cannot be listed exhaustively.[71] For example, in the Conclusions

67 ESC (rev), Explanatory Report No. 97, p. 11, § 100.

68 Heinz Leymann, *The Mobbing Encyclopaedia*, http://www.leymann.se/English/12100E.HTM.

69 Cf. ECSR, Conclusions 2003, Bulgaria; ECSR, Conclusions 2003, France; ECSR, Conclusions 2005, Lithuania; ECSR, Conclusions 2007, Ireland; ECSR, Conclusions 2010, Italy; ECSR, Conclusions 2016, Georgia; ECSR, Conclusions 2018, Turkey.

70 Mariann Arany Toth, *cit.*, p. 307.

71 Mariann Arany Toth, *cit.*, pp. 306–307.

regarding France, the ECSR considers that the definition provided by Article L. 122–49 of the French Labour Code reflects the behaviour targeted in Article 26 § 2.[72]

Thus, current Article L. 1152–1 of the French Labour Code provides that "No employee should be subject to repeated acts of moral harassment which have as its purpose or effect a deterioration of his conditions of work liable to harm his rights and his dignity, to damage his physical or mental health or compromise his career".[73] In accordance with the requirement of "recurrent reprehensible or distinctly negative and offensive actions" affirmed in Article 26 § 2 of the Charter, the cited provision of the French Labour Code considers that a single fact is not sufficient to characterise moral harassment.[74] Yet, the actions can take place in a short period of time.[75]

Moreover, in two judgments delivered by the French Court of Cassation, it was considered that moral harassment is constituted independently of the intention of its perpetrator[76] and that the management methods implemented by a supervisor, as soon as they appear in the form of repeated acts of moral harassment which have as their purpose or effect a deterioration of his or her conditions of work liable to harm an individual's rights and dignity, damaging his or her physical or mental health or compromising his or her career, can characterise such harassment.[77] However, the possession of a hierarchical power, even if it is likely to facilitate the determination of the existence of moral harassment, is not essential for the characterisation of such behaviour.[78]

Similarly, following the initiatives of the ILO, which is based on the idea that work is a source of personal dignity,[79] Convention 190[80] concerning the elimination of violence and harassment in the world of work was adopted in 2019. For the purpose of this Convention, the term "violence and harassment" in the world of work refers to a range of unacceptable behaviours and practices, or threats thereof, whether a single occurrence or repeated, that aim at, result in or are likely to result in physical, psychological, sexual or economic harm, and

72 ECSR, Conclusions 2003, France.

73 Cf. Philippe Waquet, *cit.*, pp. 166 ff.

74 Gilles Auzero, Dirk Bougard, Emmanuel Dockès, *Droit du Travail*, 32e éd., Paris, Dalloz, 2019, p. 1128.

75 Cour de Cassation, Chambre sociale, 26 May 2010, No. 08–43.152.

76 Cour de Cassation, Chambre sociale, 10 November 2009, No. 08–41.497.

77 Cour de Cassation, Chambre sociale, 10 November 2009, No. 07–45.321.

78 Gilles Auzero, Dirk Bougard, Emmanuel Dockès, *cit.*, p. 1129.

79 Patrice Adam, La Dignité du Salarié (Deuxième partie), *cit*, p. 244.

80 ILO C190, Violence and Harassment Convention, 2019. Cf. https://www.ilo.org/dyn/normlex/en/f?p=NORMLEXPUB: 12100:0::NO::P12100_ILO_CODE:C190.

includes gender-based violence and harassment. Thereby, the term "gender-based violence and harassment" means violence and harassment directed at persons because of their sex or gender or affecting persons of a particular sex or gender disproportionately and includes sexual harassment.

B *Prevention*

According to Article 26 § 2, the Parties undertake, "in consultation with employers' and workers' organisations to promote awareness, information and prevention of recurrent reprehensible or distinctly negative and offensive actions directed against individual workers in the workplace or in relation to work and to take all appropriate measures to protect workers from such conduct". Parties are required to take all necessary preventive and reparatory measures to protect individual workers against recurrent reprehensible or distinctly negative and offensive actions directed against them in the workplace or in relation to their work, since these actions constitute humiliating behaviour.[81] Therefore, States Parties are required to take appropriate preventive measures (information, awareness-raising, and prevention campaigns in the workplace or in relation to work) in order to combat moral harassment.[82]

In particular in situations where harassment is likely to occur, a failure to take any preventative, training or awareness-raising action in such situations may amount to a violation of Article 26 § 2.[83] As part of a complaint by the *Confederazione Generale Italiana del Lavoro* (CGIL) against Italy, the ECSR had the opportunity to render a decision[84] concerning Articles 1, 2, 3, 11 and 26 of the ECS (rev).

In this case, the CGIL alleges in its complaint that Section 9 of Act No. 194/1978, which governs the conscientious objection of medical practitioners and other medical personnel in relation to abortion services, is not applied in practice and, as such, this violates Articles 1, 2, 3, 11 and 26 of the ECS (rev).

Concerning the factual circumstances linked with Article 26, the CGIL alleges that, due to the inadequate application of Section 9 of Act No. 194/1978 and high rates of objecting medical practitioners, the few non-objecting practitioners available are left to perform the entire workload of all requested abortion procedures.[85] This involves, in particular, more and repeated abortion

81 Conclusions 2003, Bulgaria; ECSR, Conclusions 2005, Interpretative statement on Article 26 § 2.

82 ECSR, Conclusions 2018, Ukraine.

83 ECSR, Conclusions 2018, Andorra.

84 ECSR, *Confederazione Generale Italiana del Lavoro* (CGIL) *v. Italy*, complaint No. 91/2013, decision on the merits of 12 October 2015.

85 ECSR, *Confederazione Generale Italiana del Lavoro* (CGIL) *v. Italy*, § 283.

procedures that are often outside the field of training and specialisation of non-objecting medical practitioners. The situation, the CGIL contends, affects the career and dignity of non-objecting physicians and medical personnel, in breach of the right to dignity at work enshrined in Article 26 of the ECS (rev), read alone or in conjunction with the non-discrimination clause in Article E.

As the complainant organisation refers to moral harassment, the ECSR examines this allegation under § 2 of Article 26. The ECSR recalls that, under Article 26 § 2, irrespective of admitted or perceived grounds, harassment creating a hostile working environment characterized by the adoption towards one or more persons of persistent behaviours which may undermine their dignity or harm their career shall be prohibited and repressed in the same way as acts of discrimination. And this independently from the fact that not all harassment behaviours are acts of discrimination, except when presumed by law.[86]

In this case, although it is considered by the Committee that the statements by non-objecting medical practitioners alleging moral harassment to be insufficient to be considered grounds for a violation of the ESC (rev), as they are largely anecdotal, the ECSR observes that the Government does not refute the allegations of moral harassment in any way, for example by referring to preventive and reparatory means taken to protect individual non-objecting workers against such harassment. Besides, considering that there is no indication on the practical application of existing laws by the relevant authorities or courts that would provide the necessary protection in practice, nor of any policy measures, and believing that Article 26 § 2 of the Charter imposes positive obligations on States to take preventative action to ensure moral harassment does not occur in particular in situations where harassment is likely, the Committee finds that the failure of the Government to take any preventative, training or awareness-raising action to ensure the protection of non-objecting medical practitioners amounts to a violation of Article 26 § 2 of the ESC (rev).[87]

As a situation is considered "not in conformity" with the ESC (rev) if the relevant legislation is incompatible with its requirements or if compatible legislation is incorrectly or not fully applied,[88] in this case, the lack of indication

---

86 ECSR, *Confederazione Generale Italiana del Lavoro* (CGIL) *v. Italy*, § 290. Cf. Conclusions 2007, Interpretative statement on Article 26 § 2.

87 ECSR, *Confederazione Generale Italiana del Lavoro* (CGIL) *v. Italy*, §§ 296–297.

88 Régis Brillat, "The European Social Charter", in Gudmundur Alfredsson, Jonas Grimheden, Bertrand G. Ramcharan, Alfred Zayas (eds.), *International Human Rights Monitoring Mechanisms. Essays in Honour of Jakob Th. Möller*, 2nd rev. ed., Leiden Boston, Martinus Nifhoff Publishers, 2009, p. 510.

on the practical application of existing laws which provide the necessary protection seems the reason for Committee's decision.

C *Protection*

The nature of States' obligations is similar to their duties relating to protection against sexual harassment. It follows from the Appendix that Parties do not need to enact legislation; however, with a view to ensuring the effective exercise of the right of all workers to protection of their dignity at work, the Parties undertake to take all appropriate measures to protect workers from moral harassment.[89]

Along these lines, the Committee considers that there is no requirement for a State's legislation to make express reference to harassment where that State's law encompasses measures making it possible to afford employees effective protection against these phenomena.

This protection must include the right to appeal to an independent body in the event of harassment, the right to obtain suitable compensation, and the right not to be retaliated against for upholding these rights.[90] In particular, the Parties should inform workers as to the nature of the behaviour in question and available remedies.[91]

Regarding the responsibility of the employer, it is asked by the Committee whether employers can be held liable towards persons working for them who are not their employees (subcontractors, self-employed persons, etc.) and have suffered psychological harassment on their business premises or from employees under their responsibility. It is also asked whether the liability of employers towards workers (whether they are employees or not) also applies in cases of psychological harassment suffered by persons not working for them (such as customers, visitors, etc.).[92]

Furthermore, from the procedural standpoint, the Committee considers that effective protection of employees may require a shift in the burden of proof to a certain extent, making it possible for a court to find in favour of the victim on the basis of sufficient *prima facie* evidence and the conviction of the judge or judges.[93]

---

89 ESC (rev), Explanatory Report No. 97, p. 11. Cf. Mariann Arany Toth, *cit.*, p. 313.

90 Conclusions 2007, Interpretative statement on Article 26 § 2; Digest of the case law of the ECSR, 2018, p. 211; ECSR, Conclusions 2010, Albania; Conclusions 2016, Turkey.

91 ECSR, *Confederazione Generale Italiana del Lavoro* (CGIL) *v. Italy*, § 291.

92 ECSR, Conclusions 2018, Holland; Conclusions 2018, Ukraine.

93 ECSR, *Confederazione Generale Italiana del Lavoro* (CGIL) *v. Italy*, § 292; Conclusion 2007, Interpretative statement on Article 26 § 2; ECSR, Conclusions 2014, Azerbaijan.

Regarding compensation for financial loss and moral damage, the Committee asks for information on the applicable kinds and amounts of compensation awarded to victims of moral harassment; it also requests examples of case law and awards of damages under civil, administrative, or labour law.[94] The Committee points out that victims of harassment must have effective judicial remedies to seek reparation for pecuniary and non-pecuniary damage. These remedies must, in particular, allow for appropriate compensation for the victim's pecuniary and non-pecuniary damage and act as a deterrent to the employer.[95] In addition, the persons concerned must have the right to be reinstated to their post when unfairly dismissed or pressured to resign for reasons linked to harassment.[96]

However, as a conclusion, it should be noted that the lack of information on moral harassment in State reports concerning the questions raised by the Committee creates an obstacle to reaching well-founded conclusions. Thus, the Committee defers its conclusion and leaves off with reiteration of its questions when a State report does not provide requested information.[97] Moreover, it seems that in some cases, the Committee only considers that the situation in a Member State is not in conformity with Article 26 § 2 after repetitive failure of provision of information.[98]

Concluding Remarks

Article 26, focusing on a key concept of the human rights framework, such as protecting dignity at work, deals exclusively with sexual harassment (§ 1) and recurrent reprehensible or distinctly negative and offensive actions (§ 2). By promoting the awareness and the prevention of these harassments and actions, Article 26 aims to guarantee workers the right to dignity "at work" and "in connection with work". The article abstains from defining these concepts. Thus, the ECSR evaluates them, in consideration of The Explanatory Report and based upon the concept of "human dignity".

---

94 ECSR, Conclusions 2018, Serbia; Conclusions 2018, Malta; Conclusions 2018, Ukraine; Conclusions 2016, Lithuania.

95 ECSR, Conclusions 2018, Malta.

96 ECSR, Conclusions 2018, Serbia; Conclusions 2018, Malta; Conclusions 2018, Ukraine; Conclusions 2018, Sweden.

97 ECSR, Conclusions 2018, Serbia; Conclusions 2018, Turkey; Conclusions 2018, Slovenia.

98 ECSR, Conclusions 2018, Ukraine; ECSR, Conclusions 2018, Malta.

ARTICLE 27

The Right of Workers with Family Responsibilities to Equal Opportunities and Equal Treatment

Giovanni Calvellini

With a view to ensuring the exercise of the right to equality of opportunity and treatment for men and women workers with family responsibilities and between such workers and other workers, the Parties undertake:

1 to take appropriate measures:
   a to enable workers with family responsibilities to enter and remain in employment, as well as to reenter employment after an absence due to those responsibilities, including measures in the field of vocational guidance and training;
   b to take account of their needs in terms of conditions of employment and social security;
   c to develop or promote services, public or private, in particular child daycare services and other childcare arrangements;

2 to provide a possibility for either parent to obtain, during a period after maternity leave, parental leave to take care of a child, the duration and conditions of which should be determined by national legislation, collective agreements or practice;

3 to ensure that family responsibilities shall not, as such, constitute a valid reason for termination of employment.

Introduction

Article 27 recognises the right to equality of opportunity and treatment for men and women workers with family responsibilities and between such workers and other workers, committing States Parties to adopt a series of work-life balance measures to ensure the effective exercise of that right itself. Therefore, this provision can be added to the numerous other provisions of the revised

 | DOI:10.1163/9789004434158_009

Charter characterised by the objectives of protecting the family and guaranteeing gender equality at work and in the labour market. In this perspective, among others, the following may be recalled: Article 4 § 3 on the right of men and women workers to equal pay for work of equal value, Article 8 on the right of employed women to special protection in the case of maternity, Article 16 on the right of the family to social, legal and economic protection, Article 17 on the right of children and young persons to grow up in an environment which encourages the full development of their personality and of their physical and mental capacities, Article 20 on the right to equal opportunities and equal treatment in matters of employment and occupation without discrimination on the grounds of sex, and Article E – taken in conjunction with another relevant provision – on the prohibition of discrimination in recognising the rights provided for by the Charter.

Within this regulatory framework, Article 27 deals specifically with preventing "family responsibilities" from becoming a source of difference in treatment or opportunity between women and men workers or between those who bear such responsibilities and those who do not. In this sense, the commitment required of States Parties concerns the aspects that are traditionally the subject of policies aimed at facilitating reconciliation between work and family life: leave from work, personal care services, flexibility of working conditions, vocational guidance and training for entry, stay or re-entry into the labour market, and protection against dismissal motivated by reasons related to the worker's care duties. Moreover, it is evident that, by promoting interventions in these matters, the revised Charter aims not only to add a piece to the mosaic in the protection of gender equality, but also to facilitate the fulfilment of care tasks within the family and therefore – as anticipated – to offer instruments of protection for the latter. Indeed, as pointed out in the Preambles of ILO Convention No. 156 and Recommendation No. 165 of 1981 on Workers with Family Responsibilities, sources which – by express admission of the Council of Europe[1] – influenced the formulation of Article 27, "the problems of workers with family responsibilities are aspects of wider issues regarding the family and society which should be taken into account in national policies".

The fact that the provision in question was inspired by the aforementioned ILO documents reveals that it was absent from the 1961 Charter. Its introduction in 1996 in the revised Charter can be considered an expression of the growing attention that has been dedicated in Europe to the issue of work-life

1 See Council of Europe, *Explanatory Report to the European Social Charter (Revised)*, Strasbourg, 3 May 1996, § 102.

balance since the 90s of the last century. It is precisely by virtue of this particular interest in the matter that Article 27 has been widely ratified. Only five States Parties – Albania, Andorra, Bosnia-Herzegovina, Hungary, and Serbia – have not yet accepted any of the paragraphs of the provision under consideration. One paragraph has been ratified by three countries – Moldova and Romania (§ 2), and North Macedonia (§ 3) –, while two have been accepted by Bulgaria, Cyprus, and Malta (§§ 2–3), and by Austria, Belgium, and Norway (§§ 1–2).[2]

1 Personal Scope of the Provision

The beneficiaries of the measures provided for in Article 27 are "workers with family responsibilities". Before analysing the content of this provision, it is therefore appropriate to understand what is meant by this expression.

To this end, the *Appendix* to the revised Charter[3] helps by clarifying that the provision in question refers to those workers who have responsibilities towards two classes of individuals: dependent children and other members of their immediate family who clearly need their care or support. This second category therefore includes family members who are not completely self-sufficient, such as elderly or disabled people.

However, for both classes of individuals, a further condition must be met for the guarantees of Article 27 to be able to act: the commitment in the care required from the worker must be such as to restrict his/her possibilities of preparing for, entering, participating in, or advancing in economic activity. Indeed, the reading of Article 1 of the aforementioned ILO Convention No. 156 – the content of which[4] has been taken up in substantially identical terms

2 The current table of provisions accepted by States Parties is available on the European Social Charter web portal: https://www.coe.int/en/web/european-social-charter/provisions-of-the-charter.

3 Council of Europe, *Appendix to the European Social Charter (Revised)*, Strasbourg, 3 May 1996, Article 27.

4 In order to facilitate the reader, the first two paragraphs of Article 1 are reported below: "1. This Convention applies to men and women workers with responsibilities in relation to their dependent children, where such responsibilities restrict their possibilities of preparing for, entering, participating in or advancing in economic activity. 2. The provisions of this Convention shall also be applied to men and women workers with responsibilities in relation to other members of their immediate family who clearly need their care or support, where such responsibilities restrict their possibilities of preparing for, entering, participating in or advancing in economic activity".

for the explanation present in the *Appendix* – confirms that this condition, unlike what some scholars would argue,[5] refers to both dependent children and other members of the worker's immediate family who clearly need his/her care or support. In other words, the provision in question is applicable when the care of dependent children or of a member of the immediate family in need of this can represent an impediment to the full participation of the worker to productive life.

In any case – as the *Appendix* further specifies – the expressions "dependent children" and "other members of their immediate family who clearly need their care or support" acquire the meaning assigned to them by national legislation. It is therefore necessary to look at the latter to concretely define the cases in which a child depends on his or her parent worker, the types of family ties included in the concept of "immediate family" and those needs for care of the worker's family members (other than dependent children) which the recognition of some work-life balance measures aims to protect.

In light of the foregoing, if a State Party were to limit the enforcement of Article 27 only in relation to workers burdened with caring for their children, it would fall into a violation of the Charter. In this regard, the fact that the provision in question devotes more attention to parenthood, to which explicit reference is often made,[6] should not be misleading. This may suggest that, on the whole, "parents of young children are prioritised",[7] but it is sure that, where such a specification is not present, the provision must undoubtedly refer to the more comprehensive category of workers with family responsibilities, as defined in the *Appendix*.

---

5 Isabelle Shömann, "Article 27. The Right of Workers with Family Responsibilities to Equal Opportunities and Equal Treatment", in Niklas Bruun, Klaus Lörcher, Isabelle Schömann and Stefan Clauwaert (eds.), *The European Social Charter and the Employment Relation*, Oxford and Portland, Hart, 2017, p. 458; Eugenia Caracciolo di Torella, "Article 27 RESC. The Right of Workers with Family Responsibilities to Equal Opportunities and Equal Treatment", in Edoardo Ales, Mark Bell, Olaf Deinert and Sophie Robin-Olivier (eds.), *International and European Labour Law. Article-by-Article Commentary*, Baden-Baden, München, Oxford and Portland, Nomos, Beck and Hart, 2018, p. 346.

6 See § 1(c) and § 2.

7 See Eugenia Caracciolo Di Torella, "Article 27 RESC", *cit.*, pp. 346–347. In the same way Isabelle Shömann, *cit.*, p. 458.

II Measures Provided For

The content of Article 27 is divided into three paragraphs. The first one provides for a commitment by States Parties to adopt appropriate measures in favour of workers with family responsibilities to: enable them to enter, remain and re-enter in employment (including measures in the field of vocational guidance and training); take account of their needs in terms of conditions of employment and social security; develop or promote services, public or private, in particular child day care services and other childcare arrangements (A). The second paragraph requires States Parties to guarantee to men and women workers the possibility of enjoying a period of parental leave (B). Finally, the third paragraph states the principle according to which family responsibilities cannot justify the dismissal of the worker (C).

A *The "Appropriate Measures" to Be Taken Pursuant to § 1*

According to Article 27 § 1, States Parties must take appropriate measures in some fields to facilitate participation in working life for those facing care responsibilities within the family. This being said, the *Explanatory Report* clarifies that, in the context of the provision in question, measures that are "suitable to national conditions and possibilities" must be considered "appropriate".[8] This means that States Parties will have a certain margin of discretion that will allow them to adapt the content of the implementing rules of the accepted provisions to the characteristics of their own legal system.

1 Appropriate Measures to Enable Workers with Family Responsibilities to Enter, Remain and Re-enter in Employment (a)

Article 27 § 1(a) was inspired by Article 7 of ILO Convention No. 156 and, in analogy with this, requires States Parties to take appropriate measures aimed at workers with family responsibilities being allowed to have access to work, maintaining employment and being re-integrated into the workforce after a period of absence due to those responsibilities. In short, the provision aims

8 Council of Europe, *Explanatory Report, cit.*, § 104. Articles 4, 5 and 7 of the ILO Convention No. 156, which have contents similar to the three subparagraphs of Article 27 § 1, prescribe States Parties to adopt "measures compatible with national conditions and possibilities". According to Eugenia Caracciolo di Torella, "ILO Convention 156. Workers with Family Responsibilities Convention, 1981 (No. 156)", in Edoardo Ales, Mark Bell, Olaf Deinert and Sophie Robin-Olivier (eds.), *cit.*, p. 1146, the use of these expressions "*de facto* water[s] down [...] the potential impact [of the Convention's provisions]. Seen in this light, they might remain little more than a declaration of intent".

to prevent the latter from having detrimental consequences on the worker's employment opportunities. To this end, national lawmakers are called upon to intervene in the field of vocational guidance and training, but – as seems to be inferred from the wording of Article 27[9] – without limiting themselves to this.

The ECSR, on the other hand, has interpreted the provision as referring almost exclusively to measures that are placed in that field. Indeed, starting from the shareable premise that family responsibilities can lead to difficulties in terms of employment, even exposing people who bear them to the risk of being excluded from the labour market, the ECSR has underlined that, "to be able to return to professional life, [such people] need special assistance in terms of vocational guidance and training".[10]

It is true that it has also been stated, in general, that "under Article 27 § 1, States must develop an overall national policy or strategy to enable persons with family responsibilities to carry out occupational activities in a non-discriminatory manner",[11] but it is undeniable that the attention of the ECSR has been focused in an absolutely prevalent way on placement, information, counselling or training services organised by States.

However, from this last point of view, it should be noted as to how the orientation of the ECSR has developed such that Article 27 does not require that people with family responsibilities be provided with additional services compared to those recognised to the generality of workers. The relevance of the provision is thus reduced by the interpretation given by the monitoring body: on the one hand, as seen, it has been stated that these persons need special assistance in terms of vocational guidance and training; on the other hand, it has been clarified that "if the standard employment services (those available to everyone) are well developed, the lack of extra services for people with family responsibilities cannot be regarded as a human right violation".[12] Actually, interpreted in this way, the operative content of Article 27 § 1(a) is absorbed by that of §§ 3 and 4 of Article 10 on the right to vocational training, with the consequence that the specific needs of protection for people with family responsibilities may not be valued in the organisation of training and employment services.

9 The provision refers to "appropriate measures [...], *including* measures in the field of vocational guidance and training" (emphasis added).

10 ECSR, Conclusions 2003, Sweden. More recently, *inter alia*, ECSR, Conclusions 2019, Belgium; ECSR, Conclusions 2019, Greece.

11 ECSR, Conclusions 2015, Russia; ECSR, Conclusions 2019, Greece.

12 ECSR, Conclusions 2003, Sweden. Later, for instance, ECSR, Conclusions 2015, Latvia; ECSR, Conclusions 2015, Armenia; ECSR, Conclusions 2019, Belgium.

2 Appropriate Measures to Take Account of the Needs of Workers with Family Responsibilities in Terms of Conditions of Employment and Social Security (b)

Article 27 § 1(b) was inspired by Article 4 § b of the ILO Convention No. 156 and, in analogy with this, requires States Parties to adopt appropriate measures to recognise the needs of workers with family responsibilities in terms of working conditions and social security.

The ECSR has specified that enforcing this provision involves, first of all, the adoption of measures concerning the duration and the organisation of working time, as well as the recognition for workers with family responsibilities of the possibility of working part-time and returning subsequently to full-time employment.[13] More generally, the monitoring body has asked States to give account in their reports of all working conditions which "may facilitate a reconciliation of working and private life, such as working from home, flexible working hours or working for a limited period of time".[14]

However, these conclusions, reiterated over the years,[15] did not clarify whether these measures referred to by the ECSR – and, in particular, the possibility of obtaining part-time employment and being subsequently reinstated full-time – should have been considered the subject of a worker's individual right or if, instead, they could also have been left to agreement between the parties, with the consequent necessity for the employer to consent.

The requests for clarification sent by the ECSR to various States Parties regarding whether the national legislation of a right to part-time employment for workers with family responsibilities exists[16] suggested that the monitoring body intended to guarantee the worker the right to decide. In favour of this reconstruction there was also the affirmation – recurrent in the ECSR conclusions – according to which the aforementioned measures of implementation of § 1(b) cannot be left to the discretion of the employer but must be contained in a legally binding instrument (law or collective agreement).[17]

---

13 ECSR, Conclusions 2005, Estonia.

14 ECSR, Conclusions 2011, Lithuania.

15 See, for instance, ECSR, Conclusions 2007, Armenia; ECSR, Conclusions 2011, Georgia; ECSR, Conclusions 2015, Austria; ECSR, Conclusions 2015, Lithuania; ECSR, Conclusions 2019, Belgium; ECSR, Conclusions 2019, Georgia.

16 See, *inter alia*, ECSR, Conclusions 2007, Armenia; ECSR, Conclusions 2007, Italy, in which the monitoring body asked "whether workers with family responsibilities are allowed to work part-time or to return to full-time employment upon their corresponding request or whether this may depend on the employer's discretion and to what extent".

17 ECSR, Conclusions 2011, Estonia; ECSR, Conclusions 2011, Georgia; ECSR, Conclusions 2019, Belgium. Moreover, in the legal systems where collective agreements do not have *erga omnes* effects, it does not suffice that legislation devolves to social partners the duty

Anyway, the issue seems to have been clarified recently, when the ECSR pointed out that, in compliance with the provision in question, "legislation or practice should provide for arrangements entitling workers to take time off from work on grounds of urgent family reasons where sickness or accident make the immediate presence of the worker indispensable", and that "legislation should provide guarantees to grant part-time work to a parent raising a child or nursing a sick family member when requested, and provide for arrangements enabling parents to reduce or cease their professional activity because of the serious illness of a child".[18]

But it must be said that the content of Article 27 § 1(b) has yet to be fully defined. Especially the resulting constraints for the States Parties in terms of length and organisation of working time are uncertain. Under these profiles, the ECSR has been called on three times to assess the situation of some categories of workers (especially managerial staff) for which French law provided for very wide margins of working-time flexibility in favour of the employer (*inter alia*, absence of a maximum weekly limit, applicability of an annual working days system, consideration of on-call time as rest) that clearly might have had a detrimental impact on the possibilities of reconciling professional and family life.[19] However, in all three cases, the monitoring body found that there was no violation of Article 27, motivating the decisions on this point in a "disappointing"[20] manner and therefore avoiding clarification of the preceptive scope of § 1(b).

It is important to underline that all workers with family responsibilities, regardless of whether they are women or men, must be able to benefit from the measures referred to – according to ECSR case law – in the provision under

to establish the measures needed to implement Article 27 (ECSR, Conclusions 2003, Italy).

18 ECSR, Conclusions 2015, Latvia; ECSR, Conclusions 2015, Russia; ECSR, Conclusions 2019, Greece; ECSR, Conclusions 2019, Belgium.

19 ECSR, *Confédération Française de l'Encadrement* (CFE-CGC) *v. France*, complaint No. 9/2000, decision on the merits of 16 November 2001, §§ 51–55; ECSR, *Confédération Française de l'Encadrement* (CFE-CGC) *v. France*, complaint No. 16/2003, decision on the merits of 12 October 2004, §§ 67–72; ECSR, *Confédération Française de l'Encadrement* (CFE-CGC) *v. France*, complaint No. 56/2009, decision on the merits of 23 June 2010, §§ 79–84.

20 This expression has been used in relation to two of the decisions mentioned (the one of 2001 and the other of 2010) by Cathryn Costello, "Article 33 – Family and Professional Life", in Steve Peers, Tamara Hervey, Jeff Kenner and Angela Ward (eds.), *The EU Charter of Fundamental Rights. A Commentary*, Oxford and Portland, Hart, 2014, p. 910, and by Jeff Kenner and Katrina Peake, "Article 33 – Family and Professional Life", in Steve Peers, Tamara Hervey, Jeff Kenner and Angela Ward (eds.), *The EU Charter of Fundamental Rights. A Commentary*, Oxford, Hart, 2021, 2nd ed., p. 961.

consideration. A difference in treatment on grounds of sex would, in fact, constitute discrimination in the recognition of rights provided for in Article 27 § 1, as such prohibited pursuant to Article E.[21]

Regarding the obligation for States Parties to take account of the needs of workers with family responsibilities in terms of social security, the ECSR[22] has stated that social security benefits under the different schemes – and in particular health care – should be recognised for workers during periods of parental / childcare leave. Therefore, from this point of view, the other types of absence due to family responsibilities, such as, for instance, leave to provide care to disabled or elderly adults, do not seem to be taken into consideration.

The ECSR has also required that, for the purposes of accruing the right to a pension and calculating the amount thereof, periods of leave due to family responsibilities are considered. In this case, therefore, there is no differentiation between the various family reasons that justify leave from work. And even when the monitoring body has stated that "crediting periods of childcare leave in pension schemes should be secured equally to both men and women", the specific reference to childcare leave cannot be overestimated. This is for two reasons. Firstly, because, in case of leave due to other family responsibilities, ascribing that right only to female workers would mean promoting the fulfilment of care tasks by women themselves, in contrast to the equal logic that inspires Article 27. Secondly, because an unjustified difference in treatment between men and women in the recognition of the right to credit in pension schemes – for instance – of a period of leave for care of a non-self-sufficient elderly family member would constitute discrimination prohibited by the combined provisions of Article 27 § 1(b) and Article E.

3 Appropriate Measures to Develop or Promote Services, in Particular Childcare Facilities (c)

Article 27 § 1(c) was inspired by Article 5 § b of the ILO Convention No. 156 and, in analogy with this, requires States Parties to adopt appropriate measures to develop or promote care services, whether public or private. However, it must be said that, while the second provision cited provides examples of these services as "childcare and family services and facilities", Article 27 exemplifies with "in particular child day care services and other childcare arrangements". Reading this provision of the revised Charter, it is therefore clear that

21 ECSR, Conclusions 2005, Lithuania.

22 The orientation can be inferred, *inter alia*, from ECSR, Conclusions 2011, Ireland; ECSR, Conclusions 2015, Latvia; ECSR, Conclusions 2019, Greece; ECSR, Conclusions 2019, Belgium.

the individuals to whom it is addressed are not generically workers with family responsibilities, but those who are parents of small children. In this sense, the document of the Council of Europe affirms a right that is symmetrical to that recognised in Article 18 § 3[23] of the UN Convention of 1989 on the Rights of the Child.

Although in the past the ECSR, as part of its assessments on compliance with Article 27 § 1(c), has sometimes requested States Parties to also provide information on available family services and arrangements for other members of the immediate family who clearly need care and support,[24] it has always been steadfast in focusing attention on the organisation of child day care services and facilities,[25] considering the issue "a core element for the reconciliation of professional and family life".[26]

It should also be added that the provision concerned does not allow for distinctions between employed and unemployed parents: the notion of worker within Article 27 includes both parents who work and unemployed parents seeking work. The monitoring body therefore considered the situation in Finland in breach of the revised Charter on the grounds that, where one of the parents was unemployed, child day care services were not available full-time, but only for a maximum of 20 hours weekly.[27] Furthermore, it is significant that it was underlined that national regulation of this type, which introduces a pejorative treatment for unemployed parents without an objective and reasonable justification, "penalises [precisely] those who are in most need of support to be able to enter or re-enter employment".[28]

With a view to facilitating reconciliation of professional and family life for parents, the ECSR has stated that, under the provision in question, affordable, good quality childcare facilities should be made available. Child day care services may be arranged in many ways, but, in any case, they must provide a

23 "States Parties shall take all appropriate measures to ensure that children of working parents have the right to benefit from child-care services and facilities for which they are eligible".

24 ECSR, Conclusions 2005, Sweden; ECSR, Conclusions 2005, Lithuania; ECSR, Conclusions 2005, Norway.

25 According to Council of Europe, *Digest of the Case Law of the European Committee of Social Rights*, Strasbourg, December 2018, p. 214, "the aim of Article 27 § 1(c) is to develop or promote services, in particular child day care services and other childcare arrangements, available and accessible to workers with family responsibilities".

26 ECSR, Conclusions 2011, Turkey; ECSR, Conclusions 2011, Armenia.

27 ECSR, *Central Union for Child Welfare* (CUCW) *v. Finland*, complaint No. 139/2016, decision on the merits of 11 September 2019, §§ 79–96.

28 *Ibid.*, § 95.

sufficient number of places and be affordable and of high standard, the latter being assessed on the basis of the number of children under the age of six enrolled, staff to child ratios, staff qualifications, suitability of the premises and amount of financial contribution parents are asked to make.[29]

Finally, it should be emphasised that it is not clear in ECSR case law as to the relationship between Article 27 § 1(c) and Article 16 on the right of the family to social, legal, and economic protection if a State has ratified both provisions. Indeed, the monitoring body stated, with regard to Article 27, that "where a State has accepted Article 16, childcare arrangements are dealt with under that provision"[30] and, with regard to Article 16, that "where a State Party has accepted Article 27 […] childcare facilities and arrangements are examined under this provision".[31] However, it must be said that, in its Conclusions of 2019, the assessment of the services in question was carried out with reference to Article 16 and, when examining compliance with Article 27, the ECSR restricted itself to observing that, as the State concerned "has accepted Article 16 […], the measures taken to develop and promote child day care facilities are examined under that provision".[32]

B *The Right to Parental Leave in § 2*

According to Article 27 § 2, States Parties undertake to provide the possibility for either parent to obtain parental leave to care for a child, the duration and conditions of which should be determined by national legislations, collective agreements or practice.

Therefore, the provision addresses parents only, to allow them to take care of their children. It does not establish a right to leave from work in order to provide personal care or support to members of the worker's immediate family.

---

29 ECSR, Conclusions 2011, Armenia; ECSR, Conclusions 2015, Armenia; ECSR, Conclusions 2015, Latvia.

30 See Council of Europe, *Digest, cit.*, p. 214, and ECSR, Conclusions 2003, Italy.

31 See Council of Europe, *Digest, cit.*, p. 165, and ECSR, Conclusions 2011, Azerbaijan.

32 See, *inter alia*, ECSR, Conclusions 2019, Greece; ECSR, Conclusions 2019, Portugal. However, the ambiguities have not disappeared: according to ECSR, *CUCW v. Finland, cit.*, § 33, "So far the Committee has considered [the conditions of access to an education and care facility for a child before the compulsory school age] under Article 27 for States that have accepted this provision […] and under Article 16 for States that have not accepted Article 27". Further, as observed by Karin Lukas, *The Revised European Social Charter. An Article-by-Article Commentary*, Cheltenham and Northampton, Edward Elgar, 2021, p. 309, in the cited collective complaint, the ECSR "examined the issue under Article 17 (the right of children and young persons to social, legal and economic protection) as the main assessment standard, as well as under Articles 16 and 27".

With respect to this last necessity, it has been seen that, in any case, the ECSR has extracted minimum (but clearly insufficient) guarantees from § 1(b).

Preliminarily, it must also be noted that the leave referred to in Article 27 § 2 must be kept distinctly separate from maternity leave, the national regulation of which is assessed under Article 8 § 1. Parental leave is a period of absence from work – aimed at both parents being allowed to take care of their children – which the States shall make the subject of an individual right and which comes into play after maternity leave.[33]

In its case law, the ECSR has constantly reiterated the centrality of parental leave for purposes of the reconciliation of professional, private and family life, as well as the importance, with the perspective of promoting equal opportunities and equal treatment between men and women, of conceding it to either parent as a non-transferable individual right in the event of the birth or adoption of a child. In short, it should be an individual entitlement granted separately to all[34] working fathers and mothers. Moreover, it is precisely on this element – and, more specifically, on the necessity to provide an autonomous right to parental leave for the father – that the monitoring body has found over the years a large part of violations of said provision by the States.[35]

These findings show the effort of the ECSR to promote the affirmation of a precise scheme of development for the family-work relationship: the *dual earner / dual carer* scheme, according to which both parents are equally engaged in paid work and equally share family responsibilities. Indeed, the alleged need to provide an individual right to parental leave on a non-transferable basis for the working father and the affirmation according to which, under the provision concerned, "the States Parties are under a positive obligation to encourage the use of parental leave by either parent"[36] must be read in this perspective. The fact that the father should be entitled in an exclusive manner to a part of this specific work-life balance instrument, which, moreover, he must be encouraged to use, obviously responds precisely to the purpose of promoting

33 ECSR, Conclusions 2011, Turkey; ECSR, Conclusions 2015, Georgia; ECSR, Conclusions 2015, Azerbaijan; ECSR, Conclusions 2015, Turkey.

34 The ECSR concluded that the situation in Turkey was not in conformity with Article 27 § 2 on the grounds that fathers, other than civil servants, did not have the right to parental leave (ESCR, Conclusions 2015, Turkey). This means that the monitoring body demands that all categories of employees be entitled to parental leave.

35 See, *inter alia*, ECSR, Conclusions 2011, Turkey; ECSR, Conclusions 2011, Malta; ECSR, Conclusions 2015, Montenegro.

36 ECSR, Conclusions 2015, Statement of interpretation of Article 27 § 2.

the involvement of such parent in the fulfilment of childcare activities.[37] All this in a twofold perspective: that – expressly referred to in Article 27 – of gender equality with regard to opportunities in the labour market and treatment at work, and that – equally important in terms of respect for fundamental human rights – of the child's interest in establishing a strong bond with both parents from early on.

Although – as the examined provision states verbatim – the duration and the conditions of parental leave should be determined by States Parties, the ECSR has pointed out that, as the remuneration during the period of absence "plays a vital role" in the uptake of leave,[38] it must be ensured that an employed parent is adequately compensated for his/her loss of earnings due to time off from work. The ways in which these compensations take place are "within the margin of appreciation of the States Parties and may be either paid leave (continued payment of wages by the employer), a social security benefit, any alternative benefit from public funds or a combination of such compensations"; and, in any case, "regardless of the modalities of payment, the level shall be adequate".[39] Further, it should be highlighted that there are many cases in which the ECSR has found that national legislations violate Article 27 § 2 due to the absence or inadequacy of the compensations system for parental leave.[40]

As some studies have shown,[41] non-transferability and adequate compensation of parental leave are very important factors in ensuring that fathers take advantage of the leave itself and, consequently, participate to a greater extent in the fulfilment of care tasks in the family, with immediate positive effects on female employment. The ECSR, being aware of this, insists on demanding States Parties to adopt those measures in order to promote gender equality through the affirmation of the *dual earner/dual carer* model.

37 According to Cathryn Costello, *cit.*, p. 910, and Jeff Kenner and Katrina Peake, *cit.*, p. 959, "the ECSR has shown an awareness of the importance of encouraging men to take up parental leave".

38 ECSR, Conclusions 2011, Malta; ECSR, Conclusions 2011, Armenia; ECSR, Conclusions 2015, Russia; ECSR, Conclusions 2015, Montenegro.

39 ECSR, Conclusions 2015, Statement of interpretation of Article 27 § 2.

40 See ECSR, Conclusions 2015, Georgia; ECSR, Conclusions 2015, Azerbaijan; ECSR, Conclusions 2015, Turkey; ECSR, Conclusions 2017, Georgia; ECSR, Conclusions 2019, Ukraine; ECSR, Conclusions 2019, Turkey; ECSR, Conclusions 2019, Malta; ECSR, Conclusions 2019, Ireland; ECSR, Conclusions 2019, Georgia; ECSR, Conclusions 2019, Azerbaijan; ECSR, Conclusions 2019, Armenia.

41 See, for instance, Eurofound, *Parental and paternity leave – Uptake by fathers*, Luxembourg, Publications Office of the European Union, 2019.

C *The Protection against Dismissal Motivated by Family Responsibilities in § 3*

Article 27 § 3 was inspired by Article 8 of the ILO Convention No. 156 and, in analogy with this, requires States Parties to ensure that family responsibilities shall not, as such, constitute a valid reason for termination of employment. The provision is also closely related to Article 24 of the revised Charter on the right to protection in cases of termination of employment. This is confirmed in the explanation of Article 24 contained in the *Appendix*,[42] where family responsibilities are expressly indicated among the reasons that cannot justify dismissals.

The ECSR, in examining compliance with Article 27 § 3 of the situations in the States Parties, assesses both the protection against dismissal provided for and the effectiveness of the remedies that the worker can avail himself/herself of in the event being dismissed due to his/her family responsibilities.

Under the first aspect, the monitoring body has specified that the family responsibilities referred to in the provision in question are – according to the explanation present in the *Appendix*,[43] seen above when analysing the personal scope of Article 27 – "obligations in relation to dependent children and also other members of the immediate family who need care and support".[44] Thus, violations of the revised Charter have been found in cases where, although the invalidity of the dismissal for reasons related to parenthood was foreseen, the employee was not protected against dismissal because of family responsibilities towards dependent relatives (other than children) requiring care, such as elderly parents.[45] It should also be added that protection must be granted to all workers with family responsibilities – men and women – and regardless of the occupational size of the company. Indeed, from the latter point of view, delimitation of the scope of the guarantee to workers in companies with more than 30 employees was deemed not in conformity with Article 27 § 3.[46]

With reference to the second aspect mentioned, namely to the effectiveness of the remedies, it has been determined that "workers dismissed on such illegal grounds must be afforded the same level of protection afforded in other cases of discriminatory dismissal under Article 1 § 2 of the Charter".[47] Following this

42 Council of Europe, *Appendix*, *cit.*, Article 24.

43 *Ibid.*, Article 27.

44 ECSR, Conclusions 2003, Sweden; ECSR, Conclusions 2003, Bulgaria; ECSR, Conclusions 2003, France; ECSR, Conclusions 2005, Lithuania.

45 ECSR, Conclusions 2019, Italy.

46 ECSR, Conclusions 2019, Turkey.

47 Council of Europe, *Digest*, *cit.*, p. 215.

approach, the ECSR has stated that national judicial bodies should be able to order the reinstatement of the employee or, in cases when he/she prefers not to continue or re-enter employment, award him/her compensation.[48] The level of the latter – consistent with what the monitoring body has established with regard to the right to adequate compensation of the employee dismissed without valid reason pursuant to Article 24[49] – must be both proportionate to the damage suffered by the unlawfully dismissed worker and sufficiently dissuasive for the employer. Any pre-defined upper limit that prevents the worker from being awarded compensation consistent with these parameters is to be considered contrary to Article 27 § 3. Thus, a ceiling on compensation for pecuniary damage can only be admitted if the victim has the possibility of obtaining the compensation for non-pecuniary damage through other legal avenues (e.g., anti-discrimination legislation).[50] Finally, it is interesting to note that most of the violations of Article 27 § 3 ascertained by the ECSR consist precisely of the failure to comply with the aforementioned parameters of adequacy of the sanction system set up for the case of dismissal motivated by family responsibilities.[51]

III The Other Main International and European Sources in the Matter

Article 27 of the revised Charter is part of a very broad and varied framework of sources that, at international and European levels, deals with work-life balance from the perspective of gender equality and protection of family. In the following subsections, only the (main) instruments which, in terms of content and inspiration, are comparable to the provision under consideration will be taken into account. Therefore, those sources which, albeit relating to the theme of

---

48 ECSR, Conclusions 2011, Finland; ECSR, Conclusions 2011, Armenia; ECSR, Conclusions 2011, Turkey; ECSR, Conclusions 2019, Greece.

49 See, *inter alia*, ECSR, *Finnish Society of Social Rights v. Finland*, complaint No. 106/2014, decision on the merits of 8 September 2016, §§ 45–46; ECSR, *Confederazione Generale Italiana del Lavoro* (CGIL) *v. Italy*, complaint No. 158/2017, decision on the merits of 11 September 2019, §§ 87 and 96.

50 See ECSR, Conclusions 2015, Statement of interpretation on Articles 8 § 2 and 27 § 3, where the monitoring body adds that "the courts competent for awarding compensation for pecuniary and non-pecuniary damage must decide within a reasonable time".

51 ECSR, Conclusions 2005, Estonia; ECSR, Conclusions 2005, Cyprus; ECSR, Conclusions 2007, Finland; ECSR, Conclusions 2007, Ireland; ECSR, Conclusions 2011, Finland; ECSR, Conclusions 2011, Cyprus; ECSR, Conclusions 2011, Armenia; ECSR, Conclusions 2015, Cyprus; ECSR, Conclusions 2015, Armenia; ECSR, Conclusions 2015, Turkey; ECSR, Conclusions 2019, Turkey; ECSR, Conclusions 2019, Finland; ECSR, Conclusions 2019, Italy.

the reconciliation between professional and family life, intervene on different profiles of that matter will not be examined. In addition, it must be specified that, in order not to overly complicate the discussion, the analysis will mostly be limited to the sources in force, without considering those repealed or, in any case, replaced/superseded.

A *UN Sources*

Among the UN sources, two in particular take on prominence in the context of a comment to Article 27 of the revised Charter: the International Covenant on Economic, Social and Cultural Rights (ICESCR), and the Convention on the Elimination of All Forms of Discrimination against Women (CEDAW).

The first, in Article 7,[52] recognises the right to just and favourable conditions of work, implying, among other things, fair wages and equal pay for work of equal value (§ a), equal opportunity for everyone to be promoted in his/her employment to an appropriate higher level (§ c), and rest, leisure and reasonable limitation of working hours and periodic holidays with pay, as well as remuneration for public holidays (§ d).

The Committee on Economic, Social and Cultural Rights (CESCR), in its General Comments on this provision, has stated that States Parties should promote adequate policies for childcare and care of dependent family members[53] and introduce other measures such as training[54] in order to eliminate the obstacles that women and men may encounter in reconciling professional and family responsibilities. Furthermore, it has underlined that "rest and leisure, limitation of working hours and paid periodic holidays help workers to maintain an appropriate balance between professional, family and personal responsibilities"[55] and has highlighted, in this same perspective, the importance of forms of leave from work for family reasons (in particular

52 For a broad comment of Article 7 see Ben Saul, David Kinley and Jacqueline Mowbray, *The International Covenant on Economic, Social and Cultural Rights. Commentary, Cases and Materials*, Oxford, Oxford University Press, 2014, pp. 392 ff.

53 CESCR, *General Comment No. 16, The equal right of men and women to the enjoyment of all economic, social and cultural rights (art. 3 of the International Covenant on Economic, Social and Cultural Rights)*, 2005, § 24.

54 CESCR, *General Comment No. 23, The right to just and favourable conditions of work (article 7 of the International Covenant on Economic, Social and Cultural Rights)*, 2016, § 32.

55 *Ibid.*, § 34.

entitlements to maternity, paternity and parental leave)[56] and of flexible working arrangements.[57]

The CEDAW does not use the gender-neutral approach linked to the concept of worker with family responsibilities, but rather that of the protection of women against discrimination, also with the aim of promoting a social change that goes in the direction of family responsibilities being shared between men and women. Precisely in the awareness of the traditional and stereotyped role of women within the family, Article 11 § 2[58] contemplates, among provisions aimed at ensuring the effective right to work of women without discrimination on the grounds of marriage and maternity, that according to which "States Parties shall take appropriate measures […] to encourage the provision of the necessary supporting social services to enable parents to combine family obligations with work responsibilities and participation in public life, in particular through promoting the establishment and development of a network of child-care facilities". The other measures verbatim indicated in the aforementioned provision – such as the prohibition of dismissal on the grounds of pregnancy and maternity and the guarantee of maternity leave – can be compared to Article 8 of the revised Charter, rather than to Article 27. However, in the context of an analysis of the latter provision, it is also important to point out that the Committee on the Elimination of Discrimination against Women (CEDAW Committee) has constantly required States Parties – on the basis of Article 11 of the CEDAW – to intensify efforts to promote the use of flexible working arrangements, to introduce shared parental leave and to encourage men to participate equally in childcare responsibilities.[59]

56 *Ibid.*, § 44. The necessity of guaranteeing adequate maternity, paternity and parental leave is extracted also from Article 9 on the right to social security, taken in conjunction with Article 3 on the right to equal enjoyment of the rights provided for by the ICESCR. In this respect, see CESCR, *General Comment No. 16*, *cit.*, § 26.

57 CESCR, *General Comment No. 23*, *cit.*, § 46.

58 For a detailed overview of Article 11 see Frances Raday, "Article 11", in Marsha A. Freeman, Christine Chinkin and Beate Rudolf (eds.), *The UN Convention on the Elimination of All Forms of Discrimination against Women. A Commentary*, Oxford, Oxford University Press, 2012, pp. 279 ff.

59 See, for instance, CEDAW Committee, *Concluding Observations*, Japan, 10 March 2016, CEDAW/C/JPN/CO/7–8, § 35; CEDAW Committee, *Concluding Observations*, Ireland, 9 March 2017, CEDAW/C/IRL/CO/6–7, § 41; CEDAW Committee, *Concluding Observations*, Norway, 22 November 2017, CEDAW/C/NOR/CO/9, § 37; CEDAW Committee, *Concluding Observations*, Australia, 25 July 2018, CEDAW/C/AUS/CO/8, § 44; CEDAW Committee, *Concluding Observations*, Austria, 30 July 2019, CEDAW/C/AUT/CO/9, § 33; CEDAW Committee, *Concluding Observations*, Denmark, 9 March 2021, CEDAW/C/DNK/CO/9, § 33.

B ILO *Instruments*

It has already been highlighted several times that the content of Article 27 of the revised Charter was inspired by ILO Convention No. 156.[60] Measures provided for in the former almost entirely overlap to provisions contained in the latter. The notion of workers with family responsibilities valid in the context of the revised Charter, in turn, was taken up in substantially analogous terms from the ILO document. In fact, only the right to parental leave referred to in Article 27 § 2 lacks a confirmation in the cited Convention. However, the possibility for either parent of obtaining leave of absence within a period immediately following maternity leave is provided for by ILO Recommendation No. 165 (in § 22), which also establishes that it should be possible for a worker with family responsibilities to obtain leave in case of the illness of a dependent child or of another member of his/her immediate family who needs care or support (§ 23). More generally, this non-binding instrument specifies the provisions and integrates the contents of the Convention, also with reference to vocational training and employment services, terms and conditions of employment, social security and child and family care facilities.

All this means that "together, [the Convention and the Recommendation] set the main international standards in this area with policies and measures to support workers with family responsibilities".[61] Despite this, it must be said that Convention No. 156 is not among the eight ILO "fundamental" conventions, identified by the Governing Body as they refer to principles and rights at work considered to be fundamental. In any case, the centrality of this source in ILO policies cannot be questioned: suffice it to note, in this regard, that it was selected as one of the subjects of the 2023 General Survey on gender equality and non-discrimination, family responsibilities and maternity protection. After all, as the ILO Committee of Experts on the Application of the Conventions and Recommendations (CEACR) has stated, "implementation of Convention No. 156 is inextricably linked to the implementation of the principle of equality contained in the ILO Constitution, as well as the fundamental right to non-discrimination and equality of opportunity and treatment in employment and occupation set out in the Discrimination (Employment and Occupation) Convention, 1958 (No. 111), and the Equal Remuneration Convention, 1951 (No. 100)".[62]

---

60 For analysis, see Eugenia Caracciolo di Torella, "ILO Convention 156", *cit.*, pp. 1142 ff.

61 *Ibid.*, p. 1143.

62 CEACR, *General Observations*, adopted 2019, published 104th ILC session, Workers with Family Responsibilities Convention, 1981 (No. 156).

The definition as "essential" of the possibility of access to child and family care facilities available free of charge or at a reasonable charge in accordance with the workers' ability to pay should be indicated among the most remarkable profiles of the General Observations of the ILO monitoring body.[63] Furthermore, the latter has welcomed the introduction of measures on working time, working arrangements and leave from work, aimed at facilitating the reconciliation of professional and family responsibilities. It has underlined that the adoption of work arrangements, such as reduction of working time generally, flexible working time, part-time work, working remotely and flexible annual leave, should be voluntary and protected in accordance with other international labour standards.

More generally, it has noted that "providing more autonomy and flexibility to workers can create a positive organizational climate that may also lead to improved performance". Having found that the reasons for men not taking up an equal share of available leave include first and foremost the national, social and employment culture, then fear of retaliation and concerns over loss of income or career development opportunities, the CEACR has welcomed the introduction of encouraging measures such as parental leave to be taken by both parents in turn and increasing leave allowances. It has also highlighted the need for greater efforts by States in recognising flexibility and paid leave for carers of elderly or disabled family members.

As can be seen from these few findings, these are conclusions that partly coincide with those of the ECSR on Article 27, but which, compared to the latter, are far more articulated and expansive.

C *European Convention on Human Rights*

The European Convention on Human Rights (ECHR), as interpreted by the European Court of Human Rights (ECtHR), also has important implications for workers with family responsibilities. Specifically, case law on Article 8 on the right to respect for private and family life,[64] read in conjunction with Article 14 on the prohibition of discrimination in the enjoyment of rights set forth in the ECHR, has great importance for the matter under consideration.

The ECtHR has been firm for years in the belief that, "[although] Article 8 does not include a right to parental leave or impose any positive obligation on

63 *Ibid.*

64 For an extensive analysis of Article 8 of the ECHR see Christoph Grabenwarter, *European Convention on Human Rights. A Commentary*, München, Beck, 2014, pp. 183 ff; William A. Schabas, *The European Convention on Human Rights. A Commentary*, Oxford, Oxford University Press, 2015, pp. 358 ff.

States to provide parental leave allowances[,] by enabling one of the parents to stay at home to look after the children, parental leave and related allowances promote family life and necessarily affect the way in which it is organized. Parental leave and parental allowances therefore come within the scope of Article 8". Consequently, if a State decides to grant parental leave to workers with young children, it must do so in such a way so as not to violate Article 14 of the ECHR.[65]

It is of particular interest for this analysis to note that, in this case law, the ECtHR has referred to Article 27 of the revised Charter,[66] has noted the evolution of society "towards a more equal sharing between men and women of responsibilities for the bringing up of their children",[67] and has underlined that the different treatment of men and women as regards entitlement to parental leave "has the effect of perpetuating gender stereotypes and is disadvantageous both to women's careers and to men's family life".[68]

Starting from the cited premises, the ECtHR has found the non-recognition for male soldiers of parental leave that the law afforded to female soldiers and to civilians men and women,[69] as well as the entitlement to parental leave of policemen only in case of lack of maternal care for children,[70] in breach of the conjunction of the two aforementioned provisions.

This orientation – to be read, moreover, in the light of a rather extensive notion of "family" under Article 8[71] – can have significant reflections on the position of workers with family responsibilities. Indeed, it seems to be possible to consider that not only parental leave, but also allowances, work arrangements, services and any other type of leave connected to the worker's family

65 ECtHR, 22 March 2012, *Markin v. Russia*, No. 30078/06, § 130. In the same sense see ECtHR, 6 July 2021, *Gruba and Others v. Russia*, No. 66180/09 and three others, § 75. See also ECtHR, 31 March 2009, *Weller v. Hungary*, No. 44399/2005, § 29; ECtHR, 2 February 2016, *Di Trizio v. Switzerland*, No. 7186/09, § 61. Previously, ECtHR, 27 March 1998, *Petrovic v. Austria*, No. 2458/92, §§ 25–29, where, however, a distinction on the basis of sex with respect to parental leave allowances was found not to be in violation of the ECHR because at the material time there was no European *consensus* in this field, as the majority of Contracting States did not provide for parental leave or related allowances for fathers. As will be seen, the fact that the majority of European countries have later provided for the possibility of taking parental leave both for fathers and for mothers has led the ECtHR to revise its position on this point.

66 Actually, it happened only in ECtHR, *Markin v. Russia, cit.*, § 55.

67 ECtHR, *Petrovic v. Austria, cit.*, § 40; ECtHR, *Markin v. Russia, cit.*, § 139.

68 ECtHR, *Markin v. Russia, cit.*, § 141.

69 *Ibid.*

70 ECtHR, *Gruba and Others v. Russia, cit.*

71 See recently Jeff Kenner and Katrina Peake, *cit.*, pp. 950–951.

needs constitute forms of implementation of the right to respect for family life protected by the ECHR. If so, when these instruments are adopted by a State (which is not obligated by Article 8 to do so), compliance with Article 14 must be guaranteed.

Proof of what has just been said, namely of the fact that the aforementioned orientation of the ECtHR potentially does not refer only to parental leave, can be found in the case where the exclusion of natural fathers from the entitlement to receive parental allowances (aimed at supporting new-born children and the whole family raising them), when mothers, adoptive parents and guardians were entitled to them, was judged in contrast with Articles 8 and 14 of the ECHR.[72]

D *EU Instruments*

The explanation to Article 33 of the EU Charter of Fundamental Rights (EUCFR) maintains that § 2 draws on, *inter alia*, Article 27 of the revised Charter.[73] That provision of the EU source establishes that, in order to reconcile family and professional life, everyone shall have the right to parental leave following the birth or adoption of a child, in addition to the right to protection from dismissal for a reason connected with maternity and the right to paid maternity leave.[74] These are rights already existing in EU legislative sources, which, in this way, are constitutionalised. However, it is clear that the provision addresses the subject of reconciliation between professional and family life in an excessively delimited way, avoiding touching on burning issues for European social policy, such as, for instance, that of pro-labour flexibility in working conditions. For this reason, even if it could be unfair to speak of "a derisory set of rights",[75] it must at least be admitted that the formulation of Article 33 § 2 is very disappointing.

---

72 ECtHR, *Weller v. Hungary*, *cit.*

73 *Explanations relating to the Charter of Fundamental Rights*, OJ C 303, 14 December 2007, pp. 17–35.

74 For a complete overview of Article 33 see Cathryn Costello, *cit.*, pp. 891 ff; Silvia Borelli, "Article 33 CFREU. Family and Professional Life", in Edoardo Ales, Mark Bell, Olaf Deinert and Sophie Robin-Olivier (eds.), *cit.*, pp. 225 ff; Csilla Kollonay Lehoczky and Barbara Kresal, "Article 33 – Family and Professional Life", in Filip Dorssemont, Klaus Lörcher, Stefan Clauwaert and Mélanie Schmitt (eds.), *The Charter of Fundamental Rights of the European Union and the Employment Relation*, Oxford and Portland, Hart, 2019, pp. 583 ff; Jeff Kenner and Katrina Peake, *cit.*, pp. 943 ff.

75 Cathryn Costello, *cit.*, p. 917. Similarly, Csilla Kollonay Lehoczky and Barbara Kresal, *cit.*, p. 586, affirm that "Article 33 is rather weak and modest in defining the content and the concrete rights in the area of reconciliation of family and professional life".

From the point of view of aiming towards facilitating the work-life balance, the main deficiencies are the absence of any reference to the issue of workers as caregivers of elderly or disabled family members and – as anticipated – the non-recognition of a right to flexible working arrangements for workers with family responsibilities, as well as the fact that "the exigency to redistribute care tasks is quite unclear".[76] As a confirmation of this last assertion, the failure to mention a right to paternity leave and the absence of indications about the non-transferability of parental leave and about the adequacy of the compensation system for this time off from work can be reported.

Furthermore, there is no protection against dismissal motivated by family responsibilities and no commitments to promoting accessible and affordable family care services. It is true that these measures can be derived from other provisions of the EUCFR (Article 30 and Article 34 § 1, respectively), but it must be said that a specific reference to them in Article 33 would have been appropriate to certify their instrumentality with respect to work-life balance.

Despite all this, it must nevertheless be appreciated that the provision in question confers rights that individuals may invoke even in dispute against private persons and that require national courts to disapply any conflicting internal provision.[77] Furthermore, it must be recognised that Article 33 § 2 "has acted as catalyst for development of policies and law at domestic and EU-levels",[78] since it is clear how it played an important role in formulating Principle 9[79] of the non-binding European Pillar of Social Rights,[80] which, in turn, paved the way for the adoption of Directive 2019/1158/EU on work-life balance for parents and carers.

The latter,[81] having replaced Directive 2010/18/EU on the framework agreement on parental leave, is now the main EU source on the matter of

76 Silvia Borelli, *cit.*, p. 226. However, it must be noted that in CJEU, 16 July 2015, *Maïstrellis v. Ypourgos Dikaiosynis, Diafaneias kai Anthropinon Dikaiomaton*, C-222/14, §§ 39–40, Article 33 § 2 of the EUCFR has been recalled as a contextual element that supports an interpretation of Directive 96/34/EC on the framework agreement on parental leave as aimed towards an equal sharing of family responsibilities.

77 See Silvia Borelli, *cit.*, p. 229; Jeff Kenner and Katrina Peake, *cit.*, pp. 981–982.

78 Jeff Kenner and Katrina Peake, *cit.*, p. 983.

79 Under the title "Work-life balance" it is stated that "Parents and people with caring responsibilities have the right to suitable leave, flexible working arrangements and access to care services. Women and men shall have equal access to special leaves of absence in order to fulfil their caring responsibilities and be encouraged to use them in a balanced way".

80 The Pillar was jointly and solemnly proclaimed by European Parliament, Council and Commission at the Gothenburg Social Summit on 17 November 2017.

81 For an overview, see Elisa Chieregato, "Work-Life Balance for All? Assessing the Inclusiveness of EU Directive 2019/1158", *International Journal of Comparative Labour Law,*

reconciliation between professional and family life. By trying to facilitate work-life balance, it wishes to make a contribution to efforts in achieving equality between men and women with regard to labour market opportunities and treatment at work.

The most important news provided by the Directive in this perspective is the introduction of autonomous paternity leave, the doubling of the months of the non-transferable parental leave, the provision for the first time of a carers' leave, the recognition of the guarantee for workers to return to their jobs or to equivalent posts on terms and conditions which are no less favourable to them at the end of paternity, parental and carers' leave, the confirmation of the right to time off from work on grounds of force majeure for urgent family reasons, the introduction of the right to request flexible working arrangements for caring purposes, and the prohibition of dismissal and less favourable treatment of workers on the grounds that they have exercised the rights provided for in the Directive.

It is evident, from this concise list, that the contents of the European source are the most advanced in the framework of European and international instruments aimed at promoting work-life balance. Likewise, it is indisputable that, with these, a further step forward in the process of affirming the *dual earner/dual carer* model of work-family relationships is taken. However, the fact that the measures actually put in place by the EU lawmaker are still lacking must not be ignored. There is a considerable space between the objectives initially pursued (partly reflected in an ambitious original proposal by the Commission)[82] and the mandatory content of the approved document. Non-compulsory paternity leave, restrained duration of the latter and of the carers' leave, no indication of a minimum level of payment/allowance due for the exercising of the right to parental leave, no payment/allowance required for carers' leave, and the provision of a mere right to make a request for flexible working arrangements (and of an employer's obligation to respond and provide reasons in case of refusal) are just some of the weaknesses of a Directive that bears the wounds of a troubled approval process and feels the effect of the well-known difficulties of the EU institutions in carrying out legislative initiatives promoting a significant social progress.

Vol. 36, No. 1, 2020, pp. 59 ff; Karl Riesenhuber, *European Employment Law. A Systematic Exposition*, Cambridge, Intersentia, 2021, 2nd ed., pp. 673 ff.

82 See Eugenia Caracciolo di Torella, "An Emerging Right to Care in the EU: A New Start to Support Work-Life Balance for Parents and Carers", *ERA Forum*, Vol. 18, No. 2, 2017, pp. 187 ff.

Concluding Remarks

Article 27 is undoubtedly one of the most important provisions on which, at the European and international levels, a protection of the need to reconcile professional and family life is being built as a way to protect the family and promote gender equality.

From a simple reading of the provision in question, it is clear that, on the basis of this, work-life balance must not be considered the final goal of protection, but a means for achieving the equality of opportunity and treatment for men and women workers with family responsibilities and between such workers and other workers. This circumstance and, more specifically, the reference to gender equality are of fundamental importance because they bring with them the need to orient work-life balance national policies to the promotion of sharing care tasks within the family and therefore to overcoming gender stereotypes that hinder the equal participation of both women and men in productive and reproductive work. It has been seen that, from this point of view, the ECSR has given precise indications on how the national regulation of parental leave should be articulated to encourage men to make use of this instrument and thus to involve them more in family responsibilities. The monitoring body therefore has taken note of the fact that the achievement of gender equality also passes through the push to abandon the traditional division of tasks in the family between men and women.

If, from this essential point of view, Article 27 is to be appreciated, the lack of attention that this provision dedicates to workers with family members in need of assistance other than children, such as elderly or disabled family members, is indeed questionable.[83] The care of these individuals can impact no less than the care of children on the possibility for the caregiver to be able to participate in the labour market on an equal basis with all other workers, as well as on the promotion of gender equality, since traditionally this type of family responsibilities falls on women. The limited weight of this issue in the provision and in ECSR case law is therefore inexplicable. It cannot be overlooked that this is also paradoxical in the light of the progressive ageing of the population in most of the Council of Europe member countries.

Overall, however, Article 27 must be considered a provision full of interpretative potentialities that the ECSR could enhance better than it has done so far. The lost opportunities to better define the contents of § 1(b) through the decisions on the merits concerning this subparagraph are proofs of that

83 See also Eugenia Caracciolo di Torella, "Article 27 RESC", *cit.*, p. 348.

circumstance. Greater clarity on the commitments that Article 27 requires from States Parties would certainly be welcome, also because this could facilitate an increasing use of the provision by international, European and national bodies (jurisdictional or not) as an argument in support of an interpretation of other sources that goes in the direction of a major protection of workers with family responsibilities.

ARTICLE 28

The Right of Workers' Representatives to Protection in the Undertaking and Facilities to Be Accorded to Them

Septimiu Panainte

With a view to ensuring the effective exercise of the right of workers' representatives to carry out their functions, the Parties undertake to ensure that in the undertaking:

a they enjoy effective protection against acts prejudicial to them, including dismissal, based on their status or activities as workers' representatives within the undertaking;

b they are afforded such facilities as may be appropriate in order to enable them to carry out their functions promptly and efficiently, account being taken of the industrial relations system of the country and the needs, size and capabilities of the undertaking concerned.

Appendix Part II: Articles 28 (and 29)

For the purpose of the application of this article, the term "workers' representatives" means persons who are recognised as such under national legislation or practice.

∴

I General Presentation

A *Context and Rationale*

Ab initio, for the general context, it has to be mentioned that, prior to the revision of the Charter and the inclusion of Article 28, ILO Convention Workers' Representatives Convention, 1971 (No. 135) and its corollary, Workers' Representatives Recommendation, 1971 (No. 143), were adopted. As it is

 | DOI:10.1163/9789004434158_010

explicitly stated in the Explanatory Report to the Revised Charter,[1] Article 28 was inspired by ILO Convention No 135. Also, in the Statement of interpretation of Article 28,[2] the Committee expressly refers, *inter alia*, to the facilities enumerated by Recommendation No. 143.

The provisions of Article 28 are intended to guarantee the right of workers' representatives to protection in the undertaking (subsection a, which corresponds to Article 1 of ILO Convention No. 135) and to certain facilities (subsection b, which is modelled on Article 2 of the same Convention). For the rationale of the text, it was pointed out that Article 28 "has a functional nature".[3] It was introduced, as the text explicitly indicates, in order to ensure an "effective exercise of the right of workers' representatives to carry out their functions".

Even though Article is not part of the "hard core" provisions of the Charter, only a few of the States that have ratified the revised treaty have decided not to be bound by this provision.[4]

B *Relation with Other Provisions of the Charter*

Despite the selective mechanism of ratification, the architecture and content of the Charter reveal an organic relation between its norms. Article 28 assures an indispensable protective background and should be interpreted in the light of the other texts dealing with workers' rights if, by nature, these could be exercised through representatives. Also, this article is meant to guarantee adequate facilities for workers' representatives to carry out functions stipulated in other texts of the Charter. Therefore, systematic interpretation is appropriate and, as a consequence, it can be found in many of the ECSR Conclusions.

A close connection exists between Article 28 and Article 5 – *The right to organise*. It should be emphasised that, as the ECSR stated, Article 28 complements Article 5, which recognises, *inter alia*, a similar right in respect to trade union

---

1 Explanatory Report to the ESC (Rev), ETS 163, § 106, p. 11, available at https://rm.coe.int/16800ccde4.

2 ECSR, Activity Report 2010, pp. 14–15.

3 Andrzej M. Swiatkowski, *Charter of Social Rights of the Council of Europe*, Alphen aan den Rijn, Kluwer Law International, 2007, p. 256.

4 Apart from situations of signatures not followed by ratifications, from 35 States which have ratified the revised Charter, only four have chosen, for different reasons, to remain outside Article 28 (Andorra, Georgia, Hungary and Sweden). One motive for such an option might be that, in some national systems, workers' representatives traditionally receive protection through collective agreements and so only trade union representatives are, in most cases, the main beneficiaries. See Niklas Bruun, *Article 28 –The Right of Workers' Representatives to Protection in the Undertaking and Facilities to be Accorded to Them*, in Niklas Bruun, Klaus Lörcher, Isabelle Schömann, Stefan Clauwaert (eds.), *The European Social Charter and the Employment Relation*, Oxford, Hart Publishing, 2017, p. 468.

representatives.[5] Although, considering the role of trade unions and the need to be largely independent, Article 5 indirectly protects trade union representatives[6] and implies the right to certain facilities,[7] several reasons justified the necessity of a different and explicit provision. Thus, Article 28 specifically aims to guarantee the function of representing workers and, as a consequence, it expressly establishes the necessity of protection and of facilities to be afforded. Yet, unlike Article 5, the purpose of ensuring the effective exercise of the right to carry out functions is universal rather than limited. Article 28 implies a general application to all kinds of representatives (regardless of whether workers are unionised or non-unionised). Moreover, it does not contain a special reference to the police and armed forces, and exceptions or limitations determined by national laws or regulations are not allowed. Accordingly, the contents of compared texts should be understood as autonomous.

Collective bargaining (Article 6 – *The right to bargain collectively*) is a field in which the role of workers' representatives is vital: "joint consultation between workers and employers" and "voluntary negotiations between employers or employers' organisations and workers' organisations", are conducted, almost every time, through representatives.[8]

The effective exercise of the general right of workers to be informed and consulted within the undertaking (Article 21 – *The right to information and consultation*) implies the existence of representatives. In the case of collective redundancies procedures (Article 29 – *The right to information and consultation in collective redundancy procedures*), the right to information and consultation is intended precisely for workers' representatives and not for workers individually.

---

5 ECSR, Conclusions 2003, Bulgaria. For details, see David Harris and John Darcy, *The European Social Charter: The Protection of Economic and Social Rights in Europe*, 2nd. ed., New York, Transnational Publishers, 2001, pp. 278–279.

6 Trade union members must be protected from any harmful consequence that their trade union membership or activities may have on their employment, particularly any form of reprisal or discrimination in the areas of recruitment, dismissal or promotion because they belong to a trade union or engage in trade union activities (ECSR, Conclusions 2010, Republic of Moldova). Prohibiting the election of or appointment of foreign trade union representatives constitutes infringement in breach of Article 5 (ECSR, Conclusions 2010, Georgia; ECSR, Conclusions XX-3, 2014, United Kingdom).

7 For instance, trade union officials must have access to the workplace and union members must be able to hold meetings at work in so far as employers' interests and company requirements permit (ECSR, Conclusions XV-1, 2000, France).

8 These representatives may be workers in enterprises or not. At the branch or sectoral level, quite often the representatives are exclusively on the payroll of the trade union federation.

Distinct fields of activity for workers' representatives are mentioned in Article 22 (*The right to take part in the determination and improvement of the working conditions and working environment*): the protection of health and safety within the undertaking; the organisation of social and socio-cultural services and facilities within the undertaking; and the supervision of the observance of regulations on these matters.

The ECSR resolutions concerning the right to protection of workers in cases of termination of employment, remedies and sanctions (Article 24 – *The right to protection in cases of termination of employment*) reveal minimum standards of protection in the matter of workers' representatives.[9]

Also, the greater risk of violating the right to dignity at work has to be pointed out, especially through actions mentioned in Article 26 section b of the Charter and directed against workers' representatives, in relation to their activities.

Regarding all these connections, even if it appropriates and integrates relevant issues from mentioned texts, Article 28 is still supposed to have content that is autonomous from other articles of the Charter. Thus, the complete effectiveness of regulation is ensured (especially in cases in which some of related texts are not ratified).

II Developments

A *Meaning of the Term "Workers' Representatives"*

According to the Appendix of Article 28, the term "workers' representatives" means persons who are recognised as such under national legislation or practice.[10] Thus, it does not have a substantive definition and an autonomous

9 In the particular case of termination of employment on the ground of trade union activities, ECSR stated, in accordance with its ruling under Article 24 of the Charter, that the compensation must at least correspond to the wage that would have been payable between the date of the dismissal and the date of the court decision or reinstatement. See, for instance, ECSR, Conclusions 2014, Article 28, Slovak Republic.

10 For the purpose of ILO Convention No. 135, the term workers' representatives means "persons who are recognized as such under national law or practice, whether they are: (a) trade union representatives, namely, representatives designated or elected by trade unions or by members of such unions; or (b) elected representatives, namely, representatives who are freely elected by the workers of the undertaking in accordance with provisions of national laws or regulations or of collective agreements and whose functions do not include activities which are recognized as the exclusive prerogative of trade unions in the country concerned" (Article 3 of the Convention which is similar to § 2 of Recommendation No. 143).

content in the sense of the Charter. As such, the specificity of the national systems concretised in a large heterogeneity of models and types of workers' representation is considered and respected. States Parties may therefore set different kinds of workers' representatives, whether trade union representatives or other types of representatives or both. Representation may be exercised, for example, through workers' commissioners, workers' council or workers' representatives on the enterprise's supervisory board.[11]

In the face of such genuine diversity, Article 28 obliges States Parties to ensure protection for all kinds of workers' representatives. Subsequently, it is the role of the Committee to ensure that the rights established in the Social Charter must take a practical and effective, rather than purely theoretical, form.[12] In that light, to ensure that Article 28 is given full effect, the ECSR is entitled to appreciate whether national legislation, conventions or practice recognises workers' representatives in a restrictive manner, which can cause a limited application of the concerned text.

In a vertical approach, the protection envisaged in Article 28 appears justified not only in the period of effective exercise of function by workers' representatives but also for candidates too (even those who are unsuccessful), as for elections or positions stated by law or in collective agreements.[13] Furthermore, it shall be extended for a reasonable amount of time after the effective end of the period of their office.

The horizontal approach implies observing that protection is granted regardless of the field of activity or functions of workers' representatives. This extended protection covers the diversity of workers' representative types, domains and aims: information and consultation, collective bargaining,

---

11 ECSR, Conclusions 2003, Bulgaria. For further details and a comparative analysis across Europe see https://www.worker-participation.eu/National-Industrial-Relations/Across-Europe/Workplace-Representation2.

12 See ECSR, Statement of interpretation on Article 28; ECSR, *International Commission of Jurists v. Portugal*, Complaint No. 1/1998, decision on the merits of 9 September 1999, § 32, and ECSR, *International Movement ATD Fourth World v. France*, Complaint No. 33/2006, decision on the merits of 5 December 2007, § 59. In § 60 of the last cited decision, the ECSR also explained conditions for a situation to be in conformity with the treaty States Parties "must: a. adopt the necessary legal, financial and operational means of ensuring steady progress towards achieving the goals laid down by the Charter; b. maintain meaningful statistics on needs, resources and results; c. undertake regular reviews of the impact of the strategies adopted; d. establish a timetable and not defer indefinitely the deadline for achieving the objectives of each stage; e. pay close attention to the impact of the policies adopted on each of the categories of persons concerned, particularly the most vulnerable".

13 ECSR, Conclusions 2010, Netherlands.

health, safety and working conditions, establishment, organisation and functioning of European Works Councils, participation in institutionalized social dialogue structures, solving individual and collective labour disputes, participative management, etc. Likewise, it is of no legal relevance whether they are elected or designated by unions or other workers/professional associations or if the entity where the workers are represented is in any particular situation: autonomous or not, in the process of transfer of undertakings, in insolvency, belongs to public administration[14] or to private sector etc. Whereas, according to Article 19 of the Charter, migrant workers benefit from treatment not less favourable than that of nationals of the Member State in respect of membership in trade unions, it may be understood that this status cannot have juridical impact for the incidence of Article 28.

A workers' representative does not necessarily have to be an active worker, executing a contract concluded with the employer. The (non)existence of such a contract or the fact of its termination should not essentially influence the position of a representative or the fulfilment of obligations in this capacity (particularly in the case of trade union representatives). It is possible for a representative to be paid by the union (eventually on the background of suspension of the employment contract).

B *Protection of Workers' Representatives (Article 28 Section A)*

1 General Aspects

With regard to workers' general level of protection, any worker is guarded against unfair dismissal and cannot be put into a less favourable position, as far as working conditions are concerned, if she or he complies with the rules. The legislative framework prohibits discrimination in the workplace, including on the ground of trade union affiliation or activity.

In the Charter system, the right of all workers not to have their employment terminated without valid reasons connected with their capacity or conduct or based on the operational requirements of the undertaking, establishment or service, is guaranteed (Article 24a of the Charter). Also, Article 26 refers to the effective exercise of the right to protection of dignity at work and to the necessity of prevention of any recurrent reprehensible or distinctly negative and offensive actions directed against individual workers in the workplace or in relation to work and to take all appropriate measures to defend workers from such conduct (section b). In conclusion, by virtue of Articles 5, 24 and

14 Needed protection of workers' representatives of civil servants caught ECSR attention (see, for example, Conclusions 2022, Latvia).

26 of the Charter, any worker has to be protected against dismissal and any other prejudicial act as far as these are substantiated by her or his trade union affiliation or activity.

At the national level, it is true that, hypothetically, a state law system could comprise strong enough protective measures applicable to workers that would be adequate for effective protection of workers' representatives, as well. In spite of that, observing reality, it seems that it was concluded either that, most frequently, the general defending framework was not satisfactory or that the dedicated protective rules could be improved in terms of clarity and efficiency. Moreover, those situations when workers' representatives have a suspended employment contract or when they are not workers of the employer where they are performing their functions have to be taken into account.

Considering all these aspects, it can be deduced that adding special protective rules through Article 28 means that the general standard of workers' security was not appreciated as sufficient to allow workers' representatives to carry out their functions properly. Indeed, due to the status and activity of workers' representatives, their protection definitely implies a high standard, which most often can be reached by special protective rules.[15] Thus, the main question that must be asked is what exactly does Article 28 imply as specific requirements for an adequate standard of protection?

2 The Consistency and Specificity of Workers' Representatives' Protection

The protection of workers' representatives must be comprehensive and efficient for the unrestricted exercise of functions to be ensured. Therefore, all harmful acts based on the status or activities as representatives should be targeted. Among these acts, dismissal is emphasized in view of its importance and effects, and, as such, it requires special attention.[16] In this context, the ECSR often reiterates that protection should cover the prohibition of dismissal by reason of position or activity as a workers' representative and the defence against detriment in employment other than dismissal.[17]

---

15 From this perspective, it can be observed that § 6 of ILO Recommendation No. 143 (Workers' Representatives) does have a more detailed content than Article 28, section a of ESC. See infra, section *Short overview of ILO standards concerning workers' representatives*.

16 For instance, ECSR decided that the protection granted to workers' representatives is not effective when those could be dismissed without the consent of the Labour Inspectorate for the reason that the "employee no longer enjoys the employer's confidence" (the notion of "employer's confidence" with respect to worker's representatives may be open to abuse). See ECSR, Conclusions 2022, Armenia.

17 For example, ECSR, Conclusions 2022, Finland; ECSR, Conclusions 2022, Portugal.

As a matter of principle, workers' representatives shall not be held accountable or put into a less favourable position, as far as working conditions are concerned, due to their status or activity, if they comply with the law or a collective agreement. Yet, prohibiting discrimination on the ground of trade union membership and penalizing impediments of worker representatives' actions are not enough to conclude that representatives, in particular, are effectively guarded against any prejudicial acts. For example, the ECSR established that a protection materialized in outlawing disciplinary measures against participants of collective bargaining during the period of negotiations, albeit positive, is not satisfactory to decide that the protection against any form of detrimental treatment is sufficient and effective, especially outside the performed collective bargaining activity.[18]

A *sine qua non* protection aims at the stability of the work relationship: the terms and conditions of the employment of representatives have to be secured.[19] Specifically, such representatives cannot be compelled to accept any changes in their contracts that would obstruct or disturb the exercise of their mandate.

Furthermore, the dynamic dimension of the employment relationships of the representatives has to be considered. From this perspective, the Committee recurrently stated that prejudicial acts may entail, for instance, denial of certain benefits, training opportunities, promotions or transfers, discrimination when issuing lay-offs or assigning retirement options, being subjected to shifts cut-down or any other taunts or abuse.[20] Particular attention must be paid to disciplinary proceedings, to reductions in pay, forced or, on the contrary, denied transfer[21] and to selection of a workers' representative for redundancy.[22]

Following the desideratum of practical and effective form of the rights recognised in the Charter, it has been stated that the protection covers the period of time in which a person is entitled to exercise the function as a representative (of the mandate or designation), a *reasonable* period after,[23] and, also, if

18 ECSR, Conclusions 2018 and 2022, Azerbaijan.

19 See ECSR, Conclusions 2003, France.

20 See, for instance, ECSR, Conclusions 2018 and 2022, Armenia; ECSR, Conclusions 2022, Finland.

21 It should be noticed that transfer could also intervene on the ground of transfers of undertakings in the sense of Council Directive 2001/23/EC on the approximation of the laws of the Member States relating to the safeguarding of employees' rights in the event of transfers of undertakings, businesses or parts of undertakings or businesses.

22 See, for example, ECSR, Conclusions 2010, Slovenia.

23 ECSR, Statement of interpretation on Article 28; ECSR, Conclusions 2010, Bulgaria, and, among ECSR last Conclusions (2022), see, for instance, Albania, Armenia, Austria,

pertinent, a period before the mandate, when the person is a candidate for such a position, even in the case of being unsuccessful. For example, the ECSR has concluded that the situation is in conformity with the requirements of Article 28 in countries where the protection is extended after the end of the mandate of workers' representatives for six months,[24] one year[25] or for two years.[26] Conversely, a period of only three months does not meet the condition of being reasonable.[27] Therefore, the protection should extend for at least six months after the end of the mandate (as a general term).[28]

As a protection provided by substantive rules, no worker should suffer a prejudicial act due to her or his trade union affiliation or activity for an indefinite duration (even if states can set a period of limitation for the right to action). Regarding Article 28, it should be understood that only the *special* protective provisions, including corresponding remedies, concerning the workers' representatives and their mandate, may be limited in time.

Moreover, the exercise of function must be secured during the period in which representatives are in service. For instance, the dismissal of a union official should not imply the immediate loss of her or his position. Maintaining the function, especially during the court's procedure, if initiated, may be important and could discourage abuse. However, this is a matter pertaining to the internal autonomy of the union.[29]

Azerbaijan, Bulgaria, Bosnia and Herzegovina, Republic of Moldova, North Macedonia, Malta, Romania, Türkiye.

24 ECSR, Conclusions 2010, Bulgaria; ECSR, Conclusions 2014, Portugal; ECSR, Conclusions 2022, Bosnia and Herzegovina; ECSR, Conclusions 2022, Lithuania.

25 ECSR, Conclusions 2010, Estonia; ECSR, Conclusions 2010, Slovenia; ECSR, Conclusions 2022, Bosnia and Herzegovina; ECSR, Conclusions 2018 and 2022, Serbia.

26 For instance, Portugal determined that "workers elected to collective representation structures, as well as candidates, until two years after the end of respective mandate, cannot be transferred to another place of work without their express consent and without hearing the structure to which they belong" (ECSR, Conclusions 2022).

27 See ECSR, Conclusions 2022, Austria; ECSR, Conclusions 2022, Bosnia and Herzegovina.

28 There are national systems with terms depending on the type of mandate (for instance, between 3 months and 5 years, case of France, see ECSR, Conclusions 2003 and 2022).

29 In the ILO system, regarding Article 2 of ILO Convention No. 87 on freedom of association and protection of the right to organise, the Freedom of Association Committee settled: "A provision depriving dismissed workers of the right to union membership is incompatible with the principles of freedom of association since it deprives the persons concerned of joining the organization of their choice. Such a provision entails the risk of acts of anti-union discrimination being carried out to the extent that the dismissal of trade union activists would prevent them from continuing their trade union activities within their organization". See *ILO. Freedom of Association: Digest of decisions and principles of Freedom of Association Committee of the Governing Body of the ILO*, Geneva, International Labour Office, Fifth (revised) edition, Geneva, 2006, § 268, p. 56.

The national reports communicated over time and the conclusions of the ECSR allow one to identify some specific modalities that have been validated as satisfactory for exigencies imposed by Article 28 in case of dismissal or other prejudicial acts. Thereby, in practice, some conditions were set out, as, for illustration:

- the prior authorisation of an administrative body (for instance, Labour Inspectorate[30] or Ministry of Labour[31]) based on an in-depth investigation to verify the regularity of the internal procedure followed by the employer, the reality of the grounds for prejudicial act invoked, and in particular the absence of discrimination;[32] dismissal without that prior authorisation should be null and void;
- the prior consent of a court and, eventually, with the termination not having any legal effect otherwise;[33]

30 ECSR, Conclusions 2003, France: The workers representatives "cannot be dismissed for reasons connected, even marginally, to their mandate. (…) An employer who seeks to terminate the employment of a worker representative is required to consult the works council. For the termination to take effect, authorisation must be sought from the labour inspectorate, which will investigate to ensure that the grounds alleged are genuine and bear no relation to the worker's mandate. (…) Dismissal of a worker representative without the authorisation of the labour inspectorate is null and void and constitutes an offence for which the employer may be fined". See, also, ECSR, Conclusions 2022, Armenia; ECSR, Conclusions 2022, Bulgaria; ECSR, Conclusions 2022, Lithuania.

31 See ECSR, Conclusions 2022, Bosnia and Herzegovina (the prior approval of the Federation's Ministry of Labour is required for dismissal of trade union representatives only; for members of the Employees' Council, the prior consent of that Council should exist).

32 See, e.g., ECSR, Conclusions 2022, France, regarding investigation of dismissal of staff representatives.

33 ECSR, Conclusions 2010, Netherlands: "The Civil Code provides that an employer may not terminate the employment contract of an employee who is a member of a central works council, group works council, standing committee of these councils or divisional committee of a works council or employee representative body. The Civil Code also stipulates that an employee who has been placed on the candidate list for a works council, central works council, group works council or employee representative body, may not have his or her contract terminated without the prior consent of the district court. The above does not apply to terminations during a probationary period or for a compelling reason." An extensive system is revealed in the ECSR, Conclusions 2022, Austria: "[T]he termination of the employment contract or the dismissal of a workers' representative must be previously approved by a civil court judgment. A termination or dismissal without the court's approval is invalid. According to the report, the court gives its consent to dismissal of a workers' representative only in cases specified in the law. However, in some severe and exceptional cases such as misleading about contract conditions, violent behaviour or severe libel that impedes reasonable cooperation with the employer, the workers' representative may be dismissed without a court decision, but the approval of

- the prior consultation of the representative body in which workers representatives perform their duties;[34]
- the prior consent of the representative body in which workers representatives perform their duties;[35]
- the prior approval of the majority of the employees they represent;[36]
- the employer is required to wait for the relevant court ruling before giving effect to his or her decision.[37]
- enacting a contravention and setting of administrative fines for non-compliance with the *sine qua non condition* of prior consent or authorisation;[38]
- setting an urgent protective procedure making it possible to obtain the immediate reinstatement of a trade union leader who has been wrongfully dismissed;[39]
- the trade union or other professional organizations to benefit from the right to file an administrative complaint or to bring an action before the court concerning prejudicial acts against a workers' representative;[40]
- setting a case of suspension of the employment contract while holding a position of a union leader, as long as the leader is paid by union;[41]
- establishing a relative presumption that the dismissal or other prejudicial act is substantiated by the position or activity of a worker representative.[42]

---

the court should be sought after the dismissal. (...) [A]fter the expiry of the three months period, the decision on the dismissal of a former workers' representative should be notified by the employer to the Works Council. The Works Council may approve, acquiesce or object to the decision within a period of five working days. The employer may only proceed after this period has expired or the Works Council has reacted. Otherwise, the termination will be void".

34 ECSR, Conclusions 2010, Estonia.

35 ECSR, Conclusions 2003 and 2010, Slovenia; ECSR, Conclusions 2022, Latvia.

36 ECSR, Conclusions 2007, Finland.

37 ECSR, Conclusions 2010, Norway: "Employers are required to consult the trade union of which the representative is a member. Trade union representatives and their trade union may appeal to the relevant court against dismissal proceedings. If the trade union and the employer disagree over the dismissal, the employer is required to wait for the relevant court ruling before giving effect to his or her decision".

38 ECSR, Conclusions 2003, France.

39 ECSR, Conclusions 2014, Italy.

40 ECSR, Conclusions 2010, Norway.

41 ECSR, Conclusions 2007, Romania.

42 ECSR, Conclusions 2014, Portugal.

In the light of principle that the rights recognised in the treaty must take a practical and effective form,[43] the Committee evaluates not only the existence of an adequate protective legal framework but also the implementation of this in practice, if the adopted rules are fully applied and efficient.[44]

C *Right to be Afforded Facilities (Article 28 Section B)*

The right to be afforded facilities ensures the effective exercise of the right of workers' representatives to carry out their functions promptly and efficiently. Even in case of an adequate protection, the workers' representatives will not be able to perform their duties without inherent facilities. Thus, a relation of complementarity can be observed between section a and section b of Article 28.

In the light of mentioned purpose, some facilities have been considered appropriate. In the Statement of interpretation of Article 28, the ECSR sets out that: "protected workers must be granted the following facilities: paid time off to represent employees, financial contributions to work councils, the use of premises and materials for works councils, as well as other facilities mentioned by the R143 Recommendation concerning protection and facilities to be afforded to workers representatives within the undertaking adopted by the ILO General Conference of 23 June 1971 (support in terms of benefits and other welfare benefits because of the time off to perform their functions, access for workers representatives or other elected representatives to all premises, where necessary, the access without any delay to the undertaking's management board if necessary, the authorisation to regularly collect subscriptions in the undertaking, the authorisation to post bills or notices in one or several places to be determined with the management board, the authorization to distribute information sheets, factsheets and other documents on general trade unions' activities). The Committee also considers that participation in training courses on economic, social and union issues should not result on a loss of pay. Training costs should not be borne by the workers' representatives".[45]

In addition, it can be observed that, starting in 2010, the ECSR has paid special attention to travelling expenses as a facility under Article 28 section b and has often asked Member States to provide all the necessary information on this matter.[46]

---

43 See note 12 above.

44 See, for instance, ECSR, Conclusions 2018, Serbia.

45 ECSR, Conclusions 2010, Statement of interpretation on Article 28.

46 From country reports it can be concluded that the payment of travel costs is usually subject to the collective agreements and/or company regulations. See, for example, ECSR, Conclusions 2014, Netherlands.

As stated in the text of section b, the facilities system may be established by "account being taken of the industrial relations system of the country and the needs, size and capabilities of the undertaking concerned". In view of these parameters, States Parties benefit from a margin of appreciation in the implementation of the provisions of the Charter and may opt for suitable facilities to be granted and for proper methods of enforcement. Yet, the facilities are primarily engaged with the aim that has to be reached. Therefore, the peculiarity of a national system cannot justify a limited effectiveness of the chosen facilities or ways of enforcement. However, in all cases, the process of evaluation whether facilities are adequate and/or sufficient for the prescribed purpose has to be done holding in high regard the specificity of the industrial relations system of the country and the characteristics of undertakings. The Committee established that it is within the margin of appreciation of the country in implementing Article 28 section b of the Charter if, for instance, the facilities comprising paid time off are subject to conditions and agreement between the parties and, where such an agreement is not reached, minimum facilities are to be provided for by the employer according to the national Labour Code.[47]

D *Remedies and Sanctions*

When carrying out their functions, workers' representatives shall enjoy adequate guarantees to enable them to properly perform the duties which have been assigned to them. Thus, States Parties shall ensure that appropriate administrative and/or judicial procedures are available in the cases of unfair dismissal or other prejudicial acts against workers' representatives and in the event of violation of afforded facilities. The trade union or other professional association to which the representative belongs may benefit from *legitimatio ad causam* and, as a result, may be entitled to initiating such a procedure as well.[48] Especially judicial remedies have to be taken into account.

In cases of unfair dismissal of workers' representatives, two remedies are particularly analysed: reinstatement and the amount of compensation to be received. In the view of ECSR, reinstatement is not a mandatory effect, if and only if, it can be concluded that an effective protection is assured through other remedies.[49] Also, it was pointed out that where a dismissal based on trade

47 ECSR, Conclusions 2014, Slovak Republic.

48 See, for instance, ECSR, Conclusions 2022, Austria: if the Works Council does not approve the dismissal of a workers' representative, it is entitled to file a complaint with the labour court.

49 See, also, Niklas Bruun, *cit.*, p. 474. Under Article 24, ECSR stated that "compensation systems are considered appropriate if they include the following provisions: – reimbursement of financial losses incurred between the date of dismissal and the decision of the

union membership has occurred, there must be adequate reparation provided that is proportionate to the damage suffered by the victim. The compensation must at least correspond to the wage that would have been payable starting from the date of the dismissal up through the date of the court decision or reinstatement. The ECSR considers that fixed upper limits on compensation may result in situations where compensation awarded is not commensurate with the loss suffered even if national courts should examine the labour disputes in short terms and/or non-pecuniary damages could be awarded.[50]

In the case of a judicial procedure, one of the main questions is who should bear the burden of proof? The answers should be assessed in the context of the peculiarity of the national legal systems and of other protective rules regarding workers' representatives.

In their reports on Article 28, States Parties referred especially to the Courts' procedures regarding dismissals. Thus, we should first observe the ECSR conclusions on Article 24, regarding burden of proof in the context of the protection required in all cases of termination of employment, as a minimum standard for the dismissal of a workers' representative. On this issue, it was stated as follows: "the burden of proof should not rest entirely on the complainant, but should be the subject of an appropriate adjustment between employee and employer".[51]

Subsequently, it can be noted that such an adjustment between parties can be identified in cases in which the plaintiff (including a workers' representative) is referring to the principle of equal treatment.[52] In this situation, the

---

appeal body; – the possibility of reinstatement; and/or – compensation of a high enough level to dissuade the employer and make good the damage suffered by the employee" (Digest of the case law of the European Committee of Social Rights, 2018, p. 206, available at https://rm.coe.int/digest-2018-parts-i-ii-iii-iv-en/1680939f80).

50 See ECSR, Conclusions 2018, Montenegro; ECSR, Conclusions 2007, 2010, 2014 and 2022, Bulgaria; ECSR, Conclusions 2022, Finland; ECSR, Conclusions 2022, Slovak Republic.

51 ECSR, Conclusions 2008, Statement of interpretation on Article 24.

52 This approach corresponds to specific rules for EU Member States in situations of alleging discriminations imposed by European Directives regarding this field: Article 19 (1) of Directive 2006/54/EC on the implementation of the principle of equal opportunities and equal treatment of men and women in matters of employment and occupation (recast), JO L 204, 26.7.2006, pp. 23–36; Article 10 (1) of Council Directive 2000/78/EC establishing a general framework for equal treatment in employment and occupation, JO L 303, 02.12.2000 pp. 0016–0022; Article 8 (1) of Council Directive 2000/43/EC implementing the principle of equal treatment between persons irrespective of racial or ethnic origin, JO L 180, 19.07.2000, pp. 0022–0026. More recently, the same algorithm was provided by Article 18 (3) of Directive (EU) 2019/1152 on transparent and predictable working conditions in the European Union, JO L 186, 11.07.2019, pp. 105–121, and Article 12 (3) of Directive

burden of proof will shift to the employer once the worker has established, before a court or other competent authority, facts from which it may be presumed that there has been direct or indirect discrimination. Following this formula, *mutatis mutandis,* a possible general solution can be outlined, no matter whether discrimination was expressly alleged or not: workers' representative should establish, before a court or other competent authority or body, facts from which it may be presumed that there has been a dismissal or another prejudicial act by reason of position or activity or a violation of afforded facilities, and then it is for the employer to prove that the action was exclusively based on other grounds.

A different approach, which implies a higher standard, is that the burden of proof should fall, *ab initio*, on the employer.[53] This rule can be generalized for all situations when a worker claims the protection of her/his rights[54] or it can be enacted for workers' representatives only. In this case, as a procedural issue, the employer must first demonstrate that the act is based on a valid, justified and compelling reason, without any connection with the position or activity of the workers' representative (without excluding the possibility of the plaintiff being active in providing her/his own evidence whenever she/he considers it necessary).

A deterrent effect should result from sanctions that might be applicable in cases of unlawful treatment of workers' representatives as far as these are effective, dissuasive and proportionate in relation to the severity of the breach of the law. In that field, it should be noted that reports of some States Parties reveal different approaches, such as: the application of administrative fines for non-compliance with compulsory condition of prior authorisation/consent for dismissal of a workers' representative[55] or for unfair prejudicial acts against them;[56] criminalisation in the Penal Code of violation of the rights of a workers' representative.[57]

(EU) 2019/1158 on work-life balance for parents and carers and repealing Council Directive 2010/18/EU, JO L 188, 12.07.2019, pp. 79–93.

53 See, for instance, ECSR, Conclusions 2010, Estonia; ECSR, Conclusions 2010, Slovenia. This solution is also mentioned in § 6 (2) (e) of Workers' Representatives Recommendation No. 143.

54 Case in point: Romania. If the burden of proof lies from the beginning with the defendant employer, it does not necessarily mean that a relative presumption has been established that the dismissal, penalty applied or another claimed act is illegal and/or unjustified.

55 ECSR, Conclusions 2003, France.

56 ECSR, Conclusions 2003, Slovenia.

57 ECSR, Conclusions 2007 and 2022, Finland.

III Other Relevant International and European Instruments

A *Short Overview of ILO Standards Concerning Workers' Representatives*

With regard to the general standards established on protection against acts of discrimination and interference, at a general level, Article 1 § 1 of ILO Convention No. 98/1949 on the right to organise and collective bargaining states that "workers shall enjoy adequate protection against acts of anti-union discrimination in respect of their employment".

ILO Convention No. 135/1971 on the protection of workers' representatives in the organizations and the rights to be granted to them supplements the provisions of ILO Convention No. 98/1949. Relating to anti-union discrimination, although ILO Convention No. 98 refers to the protection needed by workers and trade union members, it does not specifically deal with the protection of workers' representatives and the facilities necessary for them.

For the purposes of the Workers' Representatives Convention, the representatives may, in accordance with national law or practice, "be designated or elected by trade unions, or representatives who are freely elected by the workers of the enterprise (although in the latter case, their functions must not include activities which are recognized as the exclusive prerogative of trade unions). The type or types of representatives concerned may be determined through national laws or regulations, collective agreements, arbitration awards or court decisions".[58] Furthermore, the Convention states that the existence of elected representatives should not be "used to undermine the position of the trade unions concerned or their representatives" and, at the same time, that appropriate measures have to be taken to "encourage cooperation on all relevant matters between the elected representatives and the trade unions concerned and their representatives" (Article 5).

Listed in § 6(2) of Workers' Representatives Recommendation No. 143, there are examples of a number of specific measures with a view to affording effective protection against acts deemed to be prejudicial, such as the following:

(a) *detailed and precise definition of the reasons justifying termination of employment of workers' representatives*;
The principle that a worker or, especially, a trade union official should not suffer prejudice by reason of her or his trade union

58 A. Odero (coord.), *International Labour Standards. A Global Approach*, publication of International Labour Office, first edition, Geneva, 2002, available at https://www.ilo.org/sites/default/files/wcmsp5/groups/public/%40ed_norm/%40normes/documents/publication/wcms_087692.pdf, pp. 19–20.

activities "does not necessarily imply that the fact that a person holds a trade union office confers immunity against dismissal irrespective of the circumstances".[59] Yet, on the subject of the specificity of such circumstances, the ILO stated that "the activities of trade union officials should be considered in the context of particular situations which may be especially strained and difficult in cases of labour disputes and strike action".[60] Regarding the justifying reasons, it should be recalled that "acts of anti-trade union discrimination should not be authorized under the pretext of dismissals based on economic necessity".[61]

(b) *a requirement of consultation with, an advisory opinion from, or agreement of an independent body, public or private, or a joint body, before the dismissal of a workers' representative becomes final;*

(c) *a special recourse procedure open to workers' representatives who consider that their employment has been unjustifiably terminated, or that they have been subjected to an unfavourable change in their conditions of employment or to unfair treatment.*

The general standards in the field of prevention of anti-union discrimination impose the enactment of national procedures which should be prompt, impartial and accepted as such by the parties concerned.[62] Moreover, these procedures have to be able to ensure that effective protection against such acts is guaranteed.[63] The text

---

59 See the 2006 *ILO Digest*, § 801; 316th Report, Case No. 1972, § 706; 335th Report, Case No. 2236, § 963. We also note that ILO Freedom of Association Committee has pointed out that: "one way of ensuring the protection of trade union officials is to provide that these officials may not be dismissed, either during their period of office or for a certain time thereafter except, of course, for serious misconduct" (see *ILO Digest*, § 804; 311th Report, Case No. 1934, § 129; 316th Report, Case No. 1972, § 706; 334th Report, Case No. 2046, § 350).

60 See the 2006 *ILO Digest*, § 811; 320th Report, Case No. 2014, § 815; 324th Report, Case No. 2091, § 892.

61 See the 2006 *ILO Digest*, § 795; 304th Report, Case No. 1853, § 299; 332nd Report, Case No. 2187, § 725; 335th Report, Case No. 2303, § 1371.

62 See the 2006 *ILO Digest*, § 817, and, for example, 307th Report, Case No. 1877, § 403; 310th Report, Case No. 1880, § 539; 321st Report, Case No. 1972, § 77; 327th Report, Case No. 1995, § 211; 330th Report, Case No. 2126, § 152; 334th Report, Case No. 2126, § 73; 335th Report, Case No. 2228, § 897; 336th Report, Case No. 2336, § 536; 337th Report, Case No. 2395, § 1200; and 338th Report, Case No. 2402, § 467.

63 See the 2006 *ILO Digest*, § 818, 740 and 742, and, for example, 320th Report, Case No. 2034, § 745; 324th Report, Case No. 2035, § 574; 330th Report, Case No. 2186, § 372; 331st Report, Case No. 2215, § 178; 332nd Report, Case No. 2227, § 608; 333rd Report, Case No. 2186, § 350; 334th Report, Case No. 2222, § 210, and Case No. 2215, § 236; 335th Report, Case No. 2236, § 967; 337th Report, Case No. 2395, § 1200; 338th Report, Case No. 2186, § 53.

above underlines that workers' representatives need a recourse procedure that is special, dedicated and even more exigent than it appears in these ordinary standards.

(d) *in respect of the unjustified termination of employment of workers' representatives, provision for an effective remedy which, unless this is contrary to basic principles of the law of the country concerned, should include the reinstatement of such representatives in their job, with payment of unpaid wages and with maintenance of their acquired rights*;

The Recommendation lists three effects (reinstatement, payment of unpaid wages and maintenance of acquired rights) as cumulative. The Committee on Freedom of Association has stated that "the remedy of reinstatement should be available to those who are victims of anti-union discrimination"[64] and only if reinstatement is not possible for objective reasons should the government "ensure that the workers concerned are paid adequate compensation which would represent a sufficient dissuasive sanction for anti-trade union dismissals".[65] The reason for this compensation is the impossibility of reinstatement and, therefore, it should be added to the amount of unpaid wages, directly determined by wrongful dismissal (without excluding the possibility of being assessed together).

(e) *provision for laying upon the employer, in the case of any alleged discriminatory dismissal or unfavourable change in the conditions of employment of a workers' representative, the burden of proving that such action was justified*;

64 See the 2006 *ILO Digest*, § 837; 306th Report, Case No. 1867, § 67; 316th Report, Case No. 1970, § 555; 327th Report, Case No. 2046, § 433; 330th Report, Case No. 2186, § 374; ECSR, Conclusions 2022, Finland. In the case of trade union leaders and members who have been dismissed due to their legitimate trade union activities, "the application against the enterprises concerned of the corresponding legal sanctions" also has to be ensured (2006 *ILO Digest*, § 839).

65 See the 2006 *ILO Digest*, § 845; 336th Report, Case No. 2380, § 795; 337th Report, Case No. 2371, § 239, Case No. 2262, § 260, and Case No. 2268, § 1104, 1107 and 1109; 338th Report, Case No. 2228, § 195, and Case No. 2399, § 1172. If the post occupied by the worker has been eliminated, she or he "should be reinstated in a comparable post if the dismissal constituted an act of anti-union discrimination" (2006 *ILO Digest*, § 847).

Such a rule is fully justified considering the fact that, especially for representatives, furnishing proof of an act of anti-union discrimination may often be difficult, if not impossible.[66]

(f) *recognition of a priority to be given to workers' representatives with regard to their retention in employment in case of reduction of the workforce.*

According to Recommendation (§ 7), the protection set out in the Convention should also apply "to workers who are candidates, or have been nominated as candidates through such appropriate procedures as may exist, for election or appointment as workers' representatives" and to workers who have ceased to be representatives. At the end of the mandate, the worker can resume work in the undertaking and should benefit from all rights, including those related to the nature of their job, to wages and to seniority.

Recommendation No. 143 has enumerated the most important facilities with the view that granting these should not impair the efficient operation of the undertaking concerned.[67] *Ratione personae*, elected representatives (of workers) should be given similar facilities as trade union representatives.

Regarding necessary time off from work, without loss of pay or social and fringe benefits, it is mentioned that on the amount of time reasonable limits may be set. Furthermore, in the absence of appropriate provisions, a workers' representative "may be required to obtain permission from his immediate supervisor or another appropriate representative of management designated for this purpose before he takes time off from work", provided that such permission is not unreasonably withheld (§ 10(2)). In order to enable workers' representatives to carry out their functions effectively, time off should be granted, *exempli gratia, "for attending trade union meetings, training courses, seminars, congresses and conferences"* (§ 11(1)).

Paragraphs 12 and 17 expressly refer to access needed to workplaces in the undertaking, where such access is necessary to enable workers' representatives, including union representatives who are not employed in the undertaking but whose union has members employed therein, to perform their duties.

66 See the 2006 ILO *Digest*, § 819; 310th Report, Case No. 1867, § 88; 311th Report, Case No. 1934, § 127; 316th Report, Case No. 1970, § 556; 330th Report, Case No. 2186, § 372; 333rd Report, Case No. 2186, § 354; 335th Report, Case No. 2265, § 1348.

67 Article 2 § 3 of ILO Convention No. 135 and § 9 (3) of ILO Recommendation No. 143. Yet, it should be explored whether granting such facilities or whether using them could impair the efficient operation of an undertaking.

Also, workers' representatives should have access to the management of the undertaking and to management representatives empowered to take decisions, as may be necessary for the proper exercise of their functions and without undue delay (§ 13).

In the absence of other arrangements for collecting trade union dues, it is recommended that authorised workers' representatives should have the right to collect such dues regularly on the premises of the undertaking (§ 14).

Union representatives should be allowed to post trade union notices on the premises of the undertaking in places agreed on with the management and to which the workers have easy access and to distribute news sheets, pamphlets, publications, and other documents of the union among the workers of the undertaking. There are two limitations: union notices and documents should relate to normal union activities and their posting and distribution should not prejudice the orderly operation and tidiness of the undertaking (§ 15).

Finally, paragraph 16 of the Recommendation highlights that the management should make available to workers' representatives "such material facilities and information as may be necessary for the exercise of their functions".

The subject of facilities granted to workers' representatives is more technical. Especially considering the decisions of the Freedom of Association Committee, Professor Dorssemont has synthesized the main related issues that have to be taken into account: access to the workplace, use of the undertaking's facilities, free time accorded to workers' representatives, trade union meetings, collection of dues, access to the management, facilities on plantations.[68] He also structured these facilities in four main dimensions:

- *access to the undertaking:* the right to enter the workplace or the premises of the workplace to carry out representation functions can be related with the necessity of contacting workers/union members, monitoring whether working conditions are respected, enforcement of collective agreements, recruitment activities, etc.;[69]
- *facilities related to functioning* ("the temporal axis") *id est* release (paid or unpaid) to enable workers to exercise their functions as representatives; release to participate in training, congresses, social dialogue processes, etc. during working hours outside of the undertaking;[70]

---

68 ILO Report, *Facilities for trade union officials and members to exercise their rights – A comparative review*, by Filip Dorssemont, 2020, p. 15, § 21, available at https://www.ilo.org/wcmsp5/groups/public/---ed_protect/---protrav/---travail/documents/publication/wcms_760829.pdf. In this study, the examined countries are Belgium, Denmark, France, Germany, Italy, Spain and Sweden.

69 *Ibid.*, p. 39, §§ 79–81.

70 *Ibid.*, p. 39, § 82.

- *facilities within the undertaking* ("the spatial axis"): provision of office space and other facilities such as computers, locking filing cabinets, access to internal mailboxes, to email or to photocopying free of charge, etc.;[71]
- *the issue of communication with management and with the constituency* (regarding communication with the constituency following issues were pointed out as relevant: trade union meetings on work premises; collection of union dues; usage of notice boards; the right to post and distribute trade union information; the usage of electronic communication tools).[72]

B *European Convention on Human Rights*

"All human rights are universal, indivisible, interdependent and interrelated",[73] be they civil, political, economic, social or cultural, and one set of rights cannot be enjoyed fully without the other. On the background of extensive debates on the complementarity or connections between ESC and ECHR, some important points of interference[74] can be underlined. In that context, we are particularly interested in the major principles stated in the Court's case law and less so the verdicts themselves.

At a general level, the Convention "safeguards freedom to protect the occupational interests of trade union members by trade union action, the conduct and development of which the Contracting States must both permit and make possible".[75] We have the view that, in principle, whenever the ECtHR finds a

71 *Ibid.*, p. 40, § 84.

72 *Ibid.*, p. 41, § 89. For details related to all four dimensions, see comparative sections of the study: *Access to workplace*, pp. 43–45, *Facilities related to functioning* (*Temporal axe*), pp. 47–52, *Facilities within the Undertaking* (*Spatial Axis*), pp. 53–54, *Communication with management*, pp. 55–56, and *Communication with the Constituency*, pp. 57–59.

73 The Council of Europe reaffirmed this principle on various occasions (*exempli gratia*, Declaration of the Committee of Ministers on the occasion of the 50th Anniversary of the Universal Declaration of Human Rights, adopted on 10 December 1998; Declaration of the Committee of Ministers on the 50th anniversary of the European Social Charter, adopted on 12 October 2011). Following this credo, the Charter of Fundamental Rights of the European Union pursued a comprehensive and integrated approach to human rights.

74 About the ECHR's "genuine social dimension", see Filip Dorssemont, Klaus Lörcher, *The European Convention on Human Rights and the Employment Relation* (*ECSR, Conclusions*), in Filip Dorssemont, Klaus Lörcher, Isabelle Schömann (eds), *The European Convention on Human Rights and the Employment Relation*, Oxford, Hart Publishing, 2013, pp. 417–430.

75 ECtHR (Second Section), 2 July 2002, App. nos. 30668/96, 30671/96 and 30678/96, *Wilson, National Union of Journalists and others v. The United Kingdom*, § 42; ECtHR (Fifth Section), 30 July 2009, App. no. 67336/01, *Danilenkov and others v. Russia*, § 121.

violation of a right with respect to the quality of being a trade union member, the reasoning applies to trade union representatives as well. But there are also some decisions in which the Court has examined the rights of the trade union officials acting in this capacity. Considering all types of workers' representatives, Article 10 (Freedom of expression), Article 11 (Freedom of assembly and association) and Article 14 (Prohibition of discrimination) from the ECHR have a special relevance.

Obviously, freedom of expression is a cardinal right for workers' representatives that have to be able to perform their duties promptly and efficiently. As a general principle, the Court stated that "the members of a trade union must be able to express to their employer their demands by which they seek to improve the situation of workers in their company. A trade union that does not have the possibility of expressing its ideas freely in this connection would indeed be deprived of an essential means of action. Consequently, for the purpose of guaranteeing the meaningful and effective nature of trade union rights, the national authorities must ensure that disproportionate penalties do not dissuade trade union representatives from seeking to express and defend their members' interests (see Palomo Sánchez and Others, cited above, § 56). Furthermore, there is little scope for restrictions on debates on matters of public interest (see Wingrove v. the United Kingdom, 25 November 1996, § 58, Reports of Judgments and Decisions 1996-V; Ceylan v. Turkey [GC], No. 23556/94, § 34, ECHR 1999-IV)".[76] For example, in the case Vellutini and Michel v. France (a violation of Article 10) the Court found that the interference with the applicants' right to freedom of expression, in their capacity as trade union officials (President and General Secretary of the municipal police officers' union) and in connection with the professional situation of one of the union's members, had not been necessary in a democratic society.[77]

76 ECtHR (Second Section), 9 October 2012, App. No. 29723/11, *Szima v. Hungary*, § 28. In this case, the ECtHR found no violation of Article 10 read in the light of Article 11 of the Convention considering, *inter alia*, Article 11 paragraph 2 and the special situation of being a member of the police. In the view of the same particular case (members of the police and trade union representatives) in the case *Trade Union of the Police in the Slovak Republic and others v. Slovakia* the Court found that there was no violation of Article 11 of the Convention, read in the light of Article 10 (ECtHR (Third Section), 25 September 2012, App. No. 11828/08).

77 ECtHR (Fifth Section), 6 October 2011, App. No. 32820/09, *Vellutini and Michel v. France*: "Court found that the impugned remarks had been made in the context of a debate of general interest, a situation in which the Convention did not generally allow for restrictions on freedom of expression. (...) In their capacity as representatives of a trade union, Mr Vellutini and Mr Michel had nevertheless been obliged to ensure that their remarks fell within the limits of the right to freedom of expression, namely by giving

Inherently, trade unions will always fall within the scope of Article 11 of the ECHR and "the Contracting States enjoy a wide margin of appreciation as to how trade union freedom may be secured".[78] In certain cases, the Court appreciated that some particular treatments of trade union members signify a violation of Article 11.[79]

It was previously affirmed that: "It seems clear that at least trade union representatives are protected under Article 11, because acts against trade union activists might also be regarded as a violation of Article 11. Especially when trade union representatives are defending workers interests in conflict situations, dismissals or reprisals against trade unionists might ensue".[80] In the case of Sanchez Navajas v. Spain, the applicant, in his capacity as a trade-union representative (elected by the council employees), asked for a facility and the request was turned down. The Court's decision has a special significance. Recalling that Article 11 ECHR does not secure any particular treatment of trade union members by the State, the Court "nevertheless considers that it may infer from Article 11 of the Convention, read in the light of Article 28 of the European Social Charter (Revised), that workers' representatives should as a rule, and within certain limits, enjoy appropriate facilities to enable them to perform their trade union functions rapidly and effectively".[81]

Thinking about the needed protection of worker's representatives, in the sense of Article 28 section a of the Charter, we appreciate that Article 14 (regarding prohibition of discrimination) is particularly significant. Fundamentally,

consideration to the interest of the "protection of the reputation and rights of others"" (§ 37).

78 See, for instance, *Wilson, National Union of Journalists and others v. The United Kingdom*, cited above, § 44 and cited cases.

79 For instance: "by permitting employers to use financial incentives to induce employees to surrender important union rights, the respondent State has failed in its positive obligation to secure the enjoyment of the rights under Article 11 of the Convention" (*Wilson, National Union of Journalists and others v. The United Kingdom*, cited above, § 48). Also, in case *Tek Gıda İş Sendikası v. Turkey*, the Court unanimously ruled that allowing the employer, after carrying out wrongful large-scale dismissals, to freely choose between reinstating dismissed employees and paying compensations to them equivalent to one year's wages constituted a disproportionate restriction of the freedom of association (ECtHR (Second Section), 4 April 2017, App. no. 35009/05).

80 Niklas Bruun, *cit.*, p. 475.

81 ECtHR (Fourth Section), 21 June 2001, App. No. 57442/00, *Sanchez Navajas v. Spain*, § 2. In this case the Court declared the application inadmissible. In other relevant cases concerning union officials' activities, it was decided a violation of Article 11 of the ECHR. See, for instance: ECtHR (Third Section), 21 April 2009, App. No. 68959/01, *Enerji Yapi-Yol Sen v. Turkey*; ECtHR (Second Section), 27 September 2011, App. No. 1305/05, *Şişman and others v. Turkey*.

any prejudicial act against them based on their position and/or activity represent an act of discrimination prohibited by Article 14 ECHR. In the case of Danilenkov and others v. Russia, the Court assessed that: "The wording of Article 11 explicitly refers to the right of "everybody", and this provision obviously includes a right not to be discriminated against for choosing to avail oneself of the right to be protected by a trade union, given also that Article 14 forms an integral part of each of the Articles laying down rights and freedoms whatever their nature (see National Union of Belgian Police, cited above, § 44). Thus, the totality of the measures implemented to safeguard the guarantees of Article 11 should include protection against discrimination on the ground of trade union membership which, according to the Freedom of Association Committee, constitutes one of the most serious violations of freedom of association, capable of jeopardising the very existence of a trade union".[82]

C *EU Directives and Charter of Fundamental Rights*

Neither the EU Directives, nor the Charter of Fundamental Rights of the European Union contain substantive and detailed rules dedicated to the special protection of workers' representatives or to the facilities they need.

As EU Directives follow specific objectives, the fragmented regulation of protection to workers' representatives and facilities provided for their duties is understandable. However, in regards to protection, Article 7 (*Protection of employees' representatives*) of Directive 2002/14/EC which establishes a general framework for informing and consulting employees in the European Community[83] and Article 10 (*Role and protection of employees' representatives*) of Directive 2009/38/EC on the establishment of a European Works Council or a procedure in Community-scale undertakings and Community-scale groups of undertakings for the purposes of informing and consulting employees (Recast)[84] can be mentioned.

---

82 ECtHR (Fifth Section), 30 July 2009, App. No. 67336/01, § 123. The Court declared a violation of Article 14 of the Convention taken together with Article 11.

83 JO L 080, 23.03.2002, pp. 29–34. Article 7 stipulates: "Member States shall ensure that employees' representatives, when carrying out their functions, enjoy adequate protection and guarantees to enable them to perform properly the duties which have been assigned to them".

84 JO L 122, 16.5.2009, pp. 28–44. Article 10 (3) state that "Members of special negotiating bodies, members of European Works Councils and employees' representatives exercising their functions under the procedure referred to in Article 6(3) shall, in the exercise of their functions, enjoy protection and guarantees similar to those provided for employees' representatives by the national legislation and/or practice in force in their country of employment".

For the purpose of Directive 2009/38/EC – to improve the right to information and to consultation of employees, some facilities can be identified: the right to information – Article 4 (4); right of workers' representatives of a European Works Council to communicate with their constituency – Article 10 (2); the right to training without loss of pay – Article 10 (4).[85] Other examples of facilities can be found in Article 2 of Directive 98/59/EC on the approximation of the laws of Member States relating to collective redundancies[86] (the right of workers' representatives to call on the services of experts or their right to make proposals in the context of collective redundancy procedures) and in Article 7 (Information of workers) of Directive 89/654/EEC concerning the minimum safety and health requirements for the workplace[87] ("workers and/or their representatives shall be informed of all measures to be taken concerning safety and health at the workplace").

The Charter of Fundamental Rights of the European Union is a very important instrument which expresses, among others, the principle that all human rights are interdependent and inseparable. Despite this cohesive approach, social rights are summarized rather (mainly in Chapter IV – *Solidarity*) than satisfactorily regulated. One explanation could be that the ESC was already an EU Treaty in force and a reference point for the field of social rights at the moment the EU Charter of Fundamental Rights was drafted (1999–2000).[88] Still, this treaty contains general rules with indirect relevance for protection and facilities of workers' representatives in Article 27 (Workers' right to information and consultation within the undertaking) and Article 30 (Protection in the event of unjustified dismissal).

Concluding Remarks

The importance of Article 28 derives from its functional nature and its essentiality for the appropriate exercise of social rights, stipulated either in the ESC or in the national systems. Almost all States Parties have ratified Article 28 of the

85 For details, see ILO Report, *Facilities for trade union officials ..., cit. supra*, pp. 37–38, §§ 73–77.

86 JO L 225, 12.08.1998, pp. 16–21.

87 JO L 393, 30.12.1989, pp. 1–12. Article 7 was not affected by successive amendments.

88 See, for details, Olivier de Schutter, *The European Social Charter in the Context of Implementation of the EU Charter of Fundamental Rights*, study for AFCO Committee, European Parliament, Directorate General for Internal Policies Policy Department C: Citizens' Rights and Constitutional Affairs, 2016, pp. 5 ff., available at https://www.europarl.europa.eu/RegData/etudes/STUD/2016/536488/IPOL_STU(2016)536488_EN.pdf.

revised Charter. Nevertheless, only in 2022 did the ECSR state that the situation is not in conformity with Article 28 in thirteen States.[89]

The commentary underlines on a general level that ensuring an effective exercise of the right of all kind of workers' representatives to carry out their functions means guaranteeing, at a certain level, viable use of different rights established in the Charter (especially the right to organise, but also some other important rights: to bargain collectively, to information and consultation, to take part in the determination and improvement of the working conditions and working environment, to dignity at work, to information and consultation in collective redundancy procedures, etc.).

We considered two main dynamic, multidimensional and interdependent perspectives. First, the evolution of the ECSR statements reveals minimal standards of compliance, adapted to social and legal realities. The analyses by the ECSR are polyvalent, mainly focusing on types of workers' representatives, protection against dismissal and, distinctly, against other prejudicial acts, needed facilities to carry out their functions, public sector and private sector, available remedies and sanctions, and, more recently, covid-19 situation and effects. The Committee pays special attention to administrative and/or judicial procedures available in the cases of unfair dismissal of workers' representatives and to specific remedies in that situation: reinstatement and the amount of compensation to be received.

The second perspective refers to the evolution (or involution) of national legislation, conventions, and practice, which must be constantly examined. Fundamentally, any analytical survey must take into account two essential aspects: the specificity of every national system, and, concurrently, that the rights established in the Social Charter must take a practical and effective form. Therefore, national rules must be appropriate and satisfactory. National reports disclose different valuable solutions. Thus, a process of legal acculturation cannot be excluded.

Finally, it must be emphasized that workers' representatives are facing significant changes due to globalization and to the digitalization of employment relations. Under these circumstances, their role and duties seem to be more difficult to be accomplished. That being so, their protection and the needed facilities are and will be topical.

---

89 See https://hudoc.esc.coe.int.

ARTICLE 29

The Right to Information and Consultation in Collective Redundancy Procedures

Giuseppe Antonio Recchia

With a view to ensuring the effective exercise of the right of workers to be informed and consulted in situations of collective redundancies, the Parties undertake to ensure that employers shall inform and consult workers' representatives, in good time prior to such collective redundancies, on ways and means of avoiding collective redundancies or limiting their occurrence and mitigating their consequences, for example by recourse to accompanying social measures aimed, in particular, at aid for the redeployment or retraining of the workers concerned.

Introduction

Article 29, concerning the right of workers' representatives to be informed and consulted in collective redundancy procedures, was introduced and included in Part I of the 1996 Revised European Social Charter as one of the provisions – such as Article 24, on the right to protection in cases of termination of employment, or Article 26, on the right to dignity at work – aimed at taking account "both of developments in social and economic rights as reflected in other international instruments and in the legislation of Member States and also of social problems not covered by the other international instruments in force".[1] Thus, it helped in broadening the scope of the Charter, since it had been drawn up in 1961, and in protecting fundamental rights beyond the traditional catalogue recognized by the European Convention of Human Rights.

1 Council of Europe, Explanatory Report of the European Charter Revised, 12, Strasbourg, 3 May 1996, § 7.

 | DOI:10.1163/9789004434158_011

In particular, the drafting of the Article took inspiration from Directive 92/56/EEC, amending Directive 75/129/EEC on the approximation of the laws of the Member States relating to collective redundancies, as well as ILO Convention No. 158 of 1982, on termination of employment: both sources are expressly referenced in the Explanatory Report of the European Charter (Revised).[2] Nonetheless, while the International and European sources already in force were set to enshrine detailed rules on the quantitative and qualitative scope of collective dismissals and the procedures of notification and consultation with workers' representatives, the European Social Charter's reformers set in Article 29 a clear, albeit concise, recognition of the importance of information and consultation as a means of avoiding collective redundancies or, at least, mitigating their consequences.

1 The Context

A *Article 29 in the Context of the European Social Charter* (*Revised*)

The 1996 Revised Charter dedicated two new provisions to the right to information and consultation, which partially overlap. Article 21 – replicating, word by word, Article 2 of the 1988 Additional Protocol to the Charter[3] – widely strengthens workers' voice in their relationship with employers, conferring a right to appropriate and comprehensible information on the economic and financial situation of the undertaking that workers are employed by and a right to an in-good-time consultation on substantial decisions affecting workers' interests.[4] Article 29 confers a new explicit right for workers' representatives to be informed and consulted in good time by employers planning collective redundancies; furthermore, it implies an obligation for Contracting Parties not only to establish such information and consultation procedures through legislation and/or collective agreements, but also to design accompanying social measures to facilitate, in particular, workers' redeployment or

2 Council of Europe, Explanatory Report of the European Charter Revised, 12, Strasbourg, 3 May 1996, § 109.

3 Additional Protocol of 1988 extending the social and economic rights of the 1961 Charter (CETS No. 128).

4 As such, it would be echoed only a few years later in Article 27 of the European Charter of Fundamental Rights ("Workers or their representatives must, at the appropriate levels, be guaranteed information and consultation in good time in the cases and under the conditions provided for by Community law and national laws and practices").

retraining.[5] To this purpose, Article 29 has been described as a *lex specialis*, compared to Article 21's *structural* principle of workers' involvement, since it addresses "events dramatically affecting the economic and financial situation of undertakings".[6]

The choice of a specific protection related to collective redundancies should not come as a surprise. By the mid-1990s it was evident, on the one hand, how much the European Community secondary legislation had already impacted on the economic and social consequences of downsizing decisions, by imposing information and consultation procedures with workers' representatives to take place before the process commencing and with a view to reaching agreements avoiding, limiting, or mitigating the effects of mass dismissals and lay-offs. It is sufficient to be borne in mind that the first Directive on collective redundancies was adopted due to the outrage sparked by the 1973 AKZO restructuring, in which the Dutch-German multinational had dismissed some 5,000 employees (due to the oil crisis) with the simple strategy of choosing workers in countries where it was cheapest to do so.[7] The explanatory statement accompanying the Directive proposal spoke clearly of the need of "tackling disparities in conditions of competition" between European companies, since such disparities were "less justifiable socially" when workers had to face similar restructuring processes,[8] and the subsequent development of the EU legislation brought forward, if not the expected harmonisation of national collective dismissal regulations, at least a clear focus on the information and consultation rights of those workers affected by collective redundancies.[9]

5 Council of Europe (1996), Explanatory Report of the European Charter Revised, 12, Strasbourg, 3 May 1996, § 110, clearly stating that "it is understood that recourse to social measures in this context is not solely the responsibility of the employer".

6 Bruno Veneziani, "Article 29. The Right to Information and Consultation in Collective Redundancy Procedures", in Niklas Bruun *et al.* (eds.), *The European Social Charter and the Employment Relation*, Oxford, Hart, 2017, p. 479. According to Matti Mikkola, *Social Human Rights*, Karelactio, 2010, p. 221, Article 29 can be linked to Article 22 ESC, as they both "oblige the employer to consult with employees on the working conditions of the employees in a broad meaning".

7 Jari Hellsten, *On Social and Economic Factors in the Developing European Labour Law, Reasoning on Collective Redundancies, Transfer of Undertakings and Converse Pyramids*, Stockholm, Elanders Gotab, 2005, p. 14.

8 Commission of the European Communities: Proposal for a Council Directive on the harmonisation of the legislation of the Member States relating to redundancies, COM(72) 1400, 8 November 1972, pp. 1–2.

9 Nicola Countouris *et al.*, *Report on Collective Dismissals: A Comparative and Contextual Analysis of the Law on Collective Redundancies in 13 European Countries*, Geneva, ILO, 2016, pp. 115–116. A similar remark (and subtle criticism) is made by Montse SOLE, "Employees' Right to Information and Consultation: A Risky Right?", in *Sui Generis. Festschrift in*

On the other hand, once the post-war boom had become a memory, and so too the idea of constant economic growth and prosperity, it became quite evident how collective redundancies would become a standard and structural facet for the functioning of any firm, not only when facing economic downturns or restructuring processes, but also when organisational changes would be pursued to cope with the dynamics of competitive market economies or even simply to increase profit margins and financial viability.[10] To this purpose, it appeared necessary for law-makers to confront such transformations and their adverse impact on the workforce in a way that could balance the different (business, workers, public) interests involved: the revised European Social Charter thus offers a crucial provision strongly oriented towards the protection of the workers affected, by functionally connecting the participatory democracy model of workers' representatives involved in information and consultation procedures with the expected outcome of "avoiding collective redundancies or limiting their occurrence and mitigating their consequences". The scope of Article 29 could have been even broader, as the Committee of Independent Experts proposed to also add a further goal of "*…limiting the number of workers made redundant*", yet such inclusion was dropped in the final text.[11]

Nonetheless, the widely available, although mainly procedural, protection enshrined in Article 29 has been cast aside by the more detailed and legally binding EU Directives and will likely be forgotten. Apart from the authoritative interpretation given by the European Committee of Social Rights (ECSR) through the Statements of Interpretations and the Conclusions on the State Parties reports with regard to the conformity of national regulations,[12] no

---

Honour of Professor Stein Evju, University of Oslo, 2016, p. 613: "the most recent EU initiatives on employees' information and consultation are aimed at simplification, reduction of regulatory costs and consolidation of legislation on one hand and, on the other, to enhance employees' – as well as other stakeholders' – involvement in restructuring processes. These developments cannot be dissociated from the new European economic governance and are geared at the protection of employment as a competitive factor. In this context employees' interests come to be a tool to reach economic objectives".

10 A more in-depth analysis is offered in Göran Therborn *et al.*, "The 1970s and 1980s as a Turning Point in European History?", *Journal of Modern European History*, Vol. 9, No. 1, 2011, pp. 8–26.

11 Council of Europe, Committee of Ministers, Opinion of the Committee of Independent Experts, CM(95)53, 13 April 1995. See Karin Lukas, *The Revised European Social Charter – An Article-by-Article Commentary*, Camberley, Edward Elgar Publishing, 2021, p. 319, concluding that "Article 29 is mainly a procedural and fairly clear-cut article" (p. 321).

12 Council of Europe, Digest of the case law of the European Committee of Social Rights, Strasbourg, 2018, presenting the interpretation that the European Committee of Social Rights has made of the different articles of the European Social Charter (available https://rm.coe.int/digest-2018-parts-i-ii-iii-iv-en/1680939f80).

relevant case law can be registered when it comes to collective complaints: at the time of writing, apart from two pending complaints,[13] the very few cases alleging a violation of the Charter's provision have been declared inadmissible.[14]

Finally, it has to be noted that a few States, even when ratifying the Revised Charter, have not accepted Article 29 (Andorra, Armenia, Austria, Bosnia and Herzegovina, Hungary, and Norway) and others have so far ratified only the 1961 European Social Charter, which does not include the right to information and consultation in collective redundancy procedures (Croatia, Czech Republic, Denmark, Iceland, Luxembourg, Poland, and the United Kingdom).

B *Article 29 and the International Sources*

At the international level, collective dismissals are covered by many sources which can help interpret Article 29. As already mentioned, the Explanatory Report refers explicitly to two, ILO Convention no. 158 of 1982 ("Termination of Employment Convention"), and European Community Directive 92/56 of 1992 amending Directive 75/129 on the approximation of the laws of Member States relating to collective redundancies.

ILO Convention No. 158, although not referring directly to collective redundancies, addresses in Part III employment termination "for economic, technological, structural or similar reasons" in which the number of workers whose termination of employment is contemplated in laws and regulations is at least a specified number or percentage of the workforce (Article 14). The provisions of Articles 13 and 14 revolve, firstly, around the need to inform and consult with workers' representatives, and, secondly, around a notification duty to public authorities. The Convention is supplemented by ILO Recommendation No. 166. As of 2022, however, the Convention has been ratified by only 36 of 187 ILO Member States.

At the European level, Council Directive 92/56 and 75/129 on the approximation of the laws of Member States relating to collective redundancies have been replaced by Council Directive 98/59/EC of 20 July 1998. The Directive aims to protect workers in balance with company rights (preamble 2) and to

---

13 ECSR, *Syndicat CFDT de la métallurgie de la Meuse v. France*, complaint No. 182/2019; ECSR, *Syndicat CFDT général des transports et de l'environnement de l'Aube v. France*, complaint no. 181/2019.

14 ECSR, *Syndicat CGT FORD Blanquefort v. France*, complaint No. 184/2019, decision on admissibility 13 May 2020; ECSR, *Syndicat CGT YTO France v. France*, complaint No. 183/2019, decision on admissibility 13 May 2020; ECSR, *ATTAC ry, Globaali sosiaalityö ry and Maan ystävät ry v. Finland*, complaint No. 163/2018, decision on admissibility and on immediate measures, 22 January 2019.

ensure a level playing field of protective standards across the European Union (preamble 3). The provisions are therefore not aimed at restricting the freedom of undertakings to organise their activities, but at establishing instead strong procedural measures as a means to protect workers. More specifically, the Directive requires Member States to oblige employers contemplating collective redundancies to inform and consult employee representatives in good time with a view to reaching an agreement. Besides the obligation to dialogue with the workforce, it also provides for public authorities to be notified of any projected collective redundancies and requires that redundancies cannot take effect earlier than 30 days after such notification.

The information and consultation procedure with workers' representatives suggests, at the European level, a unitary model which is also reprised in the Directives on transfer of undertaking (Directive 2001/23/EC) and in the general framework for informing and consulting employees (Directive 2002/14/EC) and has its foundation in Article 27 of the European Charter of Fundamental Rights.[15] Furthermore, it is worth noting that the 2017 European Pillar of Social Rights includes a principle on the importance of social dialogue and the involvement of workers, with specific reference to collective redundancies.[16]

II The Content

A *The Notion of Collective Redundancies and the Grounds for Dismissals*

Article 29 does not provide for a definition of "collective redundancies". While the Explanatory Report to the Revised European Social Charter simply refers to EU Directives 92/56/EEC and 75/129/EEC and ILO Convention No. 158 of

15 In April 2015, the Commission started first phase consultation with the prospect of consolidating the EU Directives on the informing and consulting of workers, underlining two aspects which would support extending EU information and consultation rights to public administration, namely massive restructuring – resulting in redundancies and changes in working conditions – and increasing the role of a private employment contract in the public sector in the Member States (European Commission, Consultation Document, "First phase consultation of Social Partners under Article 154 TFEU on a consolidation of the EU Directives on information and consultation of workers", C(2015) 2303 final, Brussels, 10.4.2015). However, the less than positive feedback of some employers' organisations dissuaded launching the second-phase consultations. On the topic, Sylvaine Laulom, "Better Regulation and the Social Acquisition: Is the REFIT Fit for Purpose?", *European Labour Law Journal*, Vol. 9, No. 1, 2018, pp. 7–23.

16 European Commission, Communication of 26 April 2017 establishing a European Pillar of Social Rights, COM(2017) 250 final, principle n. 8.

1982 as points of reference, the Committee of Independent Experts (ECSR) has eventually explained that the collective redundancies referred in the provision are "redundancies affecting several workers within a period of time set by law and decided for reasons which have nothing to do with individual workers, but correspond to a reduction or change in the firm's activity".[17]

Even with such clarification, the scope of the notion ends up being devolved to each national legal system, both in relation to the *subjective* requirements (*i.e.*, the number of workers likely to be affected by the redundancy, the period over which the dismissals are intended to be carried out), as well as the *objective* requirements (*i.e.*, the reasons and grounds for the redundancy). The absence of a clear definition of such thresholds, as well as the haziness of calling for a relation between the lay-offs and "a reduction or change in the firm's activity" – an expression which, as has been rightly noted, refers only to the unilateral employer's decision, based on the most diverse of circumstances, and even purely discretionary choices[18] – would lead to limited effectiveness of the Charter, if national laws and practices were not interpreted in line with the *ratio* of Article 29 and taking also into consideration the EU secondary law and ILO Convention No. 158.[19]

To this purpose, when assessing the scope of collective redundancies in domestic law, the ECSR requires for the national definition not to be "restrictive"[20] and has often asked States to clarify whether there are any exceptions for certain categories of workers or enterprises as to the procedures applied in the case of collective redundancies.[21] The aim – consistent with Article 1 § 2 of

---

17 ECSR, Conclusions 2003, Statement of Interpretation on Article 29.

18 Bruno Veneziani, *op. cit.*, p. 480.

19 For the latter, see ILO, Tripartite Meeting of Experts to Examine the Termination of Employment Convention and Recommendation (Geneva, 18–21 April 2011), available at https://www.ilo.org/global/standards/subjects-covered-by-international-labour-standards/employment-security/WCMS_165186/lang--en/index.htm.

20 ECSR, Conclusions 2014, Azerbaijan: in this case, Article 63 of the Azerbaijan Labour Code defined collective redundancy as the termination of employment of more than 50% of all employees in an enterprise with 100–500 employees, 40% in an enterprise of 500–1000 employees and 30% in an enterprise with more than 1000 employees at the same time or at separate times within three months. The Committee considered such definition of redundancies as restrictive and also asked the actual coverage of employees concerned, *i.e.*, the percentage of employees working in enterprises with more than 100 employees in proportion to all employees.

21 An example is in ECSR, Conclusions 2007, Belgium: according to the information available to the Committee, certain categories of employees (port employees, ship repair employees as well as employees in the construction industry and employees working in the sea fishing industry) were excluded from the scope of the provisions regulating

the Charter, which considers the right to (general) information and consultation of Article 21 to be effective if applied to the great majority of the workers concerned – is to ensure a wide protection of those affected by the redundancy process.[22]

Hence, national reports submitted to the Committee indicate how over the years law-makers have mostly modelled their regulation on the scheme offered by Directive 98/59/EC of 20 July 1998, and especially on the option enshrined in Article 1(a)(i), according to which a redundancy is considered to be collective when calculated as a net number or a percentage of the total workforce:[23] the actual regulations may vary between merely reproducing such a threshold[24] and extending its scope,[25] but generally appear to be in conformity with Article 29. The ECSR has deferred its conclusions only when the information provided has appeared (initially) to be insufficient.[26]

---

collective redundancies, prompting the Committee to ask what rules, if any, were applicable to these workers.

22 ECSR, Conclusions 2014, Russian Federation. As the national report stated that a definition of collective redundancies had been taken up by industry-specific or territorial agreements, the Committee asked whether a definition of collective redundancies could still be found in the national law and, if not, whether all workers were "covered by social partnership agreements". Similarly, in ECSR, Conclusions 2014, Cyprus, the Committee noted a wide range of exclusions from the Collective Redundancies Law (establishments that employ 20 or fewer persons, workers employed by the public sector, semi-governmental organisations, local authorities or legal entities covered by public law) and adjourned its conclusion, requesting more information on the average number of employees not covered by the legal provisions.

23 As Article 1(a)(i) of Directive 98/59/EC provides, a redundancy is collective when, over a period of 30 days, the number of redundancies is at least 10 workers in establishments normally employing more than 20 and less than 100 workers; alternatively, at least 10% of the number of workers in establishments normally employing at least 100 but less than 300 workers, or at least 30 workers in establishments normally employing 300 workers or more.

24 ECSR, Conclusions 2010, Albania; ECSR, Conclusions 2010, Malta; ECSR, Conclusions 2014, Montenegro; ECSR, Conclusions 2010, Romania; ECSR, Conclusions 2014, Turkey.

25 ECSR, Conclusions 2014, Portugal, where Article 359(1) of the revised Labour Code defines collective redundancies as a result of termination of employment by the employer, simultaneously or successively within a three-month period of either at least two employees if the employer has less than 50 employees; or at least five employees if the employer has 50 or more employees; ECSR, Conclusions 2014, France, whose Loi 2013–504 "strengthens the job security" as redundancies are considered collective when executed by the employer due to economic reasons, affecting at least two employees within a period of 30 days.

26 ECSR, Conclusions 2010, Georgia; in the following assessment (ECSR, Conclusions 2014, Georgia) a more precise definition of collective redundancy was offered, although the Committee concluded for the non-conformity with Article 29, on the ground that the Georgian legislation did not effectively guarantee the right of workers to be consulted.

Nevertheless, some grey areas still exist. For example, Article 29 does not specify *categories* of workers which are included or may be excluded from the scope of protection: the subjective exclusions provided in the Appendix (workers having a contract or employment relationship with a total duration not exceeding one month and/or with a working week not exceeding eight hours; casual and/or specific nature employment relationships) are linked explicitly to the individual right of information on conditions of work. However, as the ILO and EU sources identify exceptions to the general rule of protection,[27] and the actual scope of the definition of collective redundancies is left by the Charter to national legislators (and courts), the ECSR appears to have acknowledged national provisions, seldom questioning their extent and impact;[28] an exception is the assessment of the Turkish report, when the Committee noted that provisions regulating collective redundancies did not apply "in the case of seasonal and 'campaign' work" and requested more information on the category of campaign workers and whether there were any other categories not falling under the scope of rules governing collective redundancy procedures.[29] Another problematic implementation may rise from the way domestic thresholds are calculated, in relation to the number/type of workers employed and to the site in which they are employed, as a narrow interpretation would allow companies to escape the information and consultation procedures.[30] The latter criterion has found a specific reference only in the EU secondary legislation, which mentions the term "establishment", while the ECSR has not offered any significant remarks when the national reports refer to "undertaking",[31]

27 According to Article 2 of Directive 98/59/EC, fixed term contracts, public sector workers, and crews of seagoing vessels are excluded from the scope of its protection; similarly, Article 2 of ILO Convention no. 158 offers the chance to national legislations to exclude specific categories (workers engaged under a contract of employment for a specified period of time or a specified task; workers serving a period of probation or a qualifying period of employment, determined in advance and of reasonable duration; workers engaged on a casual basis for a short period), provided that they are subject to special arrangements which are as a whole at least equivalent to that afforded under the Convention. The exclusions have been interpreted very strictly: *e.g.*, the European Court of Justice has stated the illegitimacy of the Italian legislation on collective dismissals (Law no. 223/1991) with reference to the exclusion of executives from the procedure (CJEU, 13 February 2014, *Commission v. Italy*, C-596/12).

28 ECSR, Conclusions 2010, Belgium.

29 ECSR, Conclusions 2014, Turkey.

30 The risk was specifically addressed in European case law: CJEU, 17 January 1996, *Rockfon A/S v. Specialarbejderforbundet I Danmark*, C-449/1993; CJEU, 30 April 2015, *USDAW and another v. WW Realisation 1 Ltd*, C-80/14, CJEU, 13 May 2015, *Cañas v. Nexea Gestión Documental SA and another*, C-392/13.

31 ECSR, Conclusions 2003, France.

"enterprise",[32] an all-encompassing "employer",[33] and even a benchmark for "employees working in the same geographical area".[34]

It must be remarked how the objective requirements of the definition of collective redundancies, *i.e.*, the reasons or grounds for dismissals, are also not addressed in the Revised Charter, preferring instead a quantitative notion of the redundancies as "collective", inasmuch as more than a single worker is involved. However, in the 2003 Statement of interpretation, the ECSR inferred a substantive feature in the notion, explaining that the reasons for a collective redundancy "correspond to a reduction or change in the firm's activity", thus devolving to each national legal system the task of defining the scope of the operational transformation or reduction affecting the workforce. The expression "reduction or change in the firm's activity" is subtly different and less precise than the one used in Article 13 of ILO Convention No. 158, which speaks of "economic, technological, structural or similar reasons",[35] but must be read together with the Committee's preceding *caveat* that such reasons "have nothing to do with individual workers".[36]

Consequently, the ECSR interpretation appears in line with the notion of "dismissals effected by an employer for one or more reasons not related to the individual workers concerned" enshrined in Article 1(1)(a) of Directive 98/59/EC. Furthermore, the European Court of Justice has long adopted a broad concept of collective redundancies, faulting national legislation when they are defined by a limited range of economic grounds, and not by any reason not related to the individual workers concerned;[37] in more recent rulings, the Court has even gone so far as to consider as dismissal for the purposes of the directive when "an employer – unilaterally and to the detriment of the employee – makes significant changes to essential elements of his employment contract for reasons not related to the individual employee concerned", eventually leading to a termination of the employment relationship, precisely

32 ECSR, Conclusions 2007, Belgium.

33 ECSR, Conclusions 2007, Lithuania.

34 ECSR, Conclusions 2014, Netherlands.

35 According to the ILO's Committee of Experts on the Application of Conventions and Recommendations (CEACR), the reasons of an economic, technological, structural or similar nature are "related to operational requirements of undertakings, establishments or services and could also be defined in negative terms as those necessitated by economic, technological, structural or similar requirements which are not connected with the capacity or conduct of the workers" (CEACR, General Survey – Protection against unjustified dismissal, 1995, § 98).

36 ECSR, Conclusions 2003, Statement of Interpretation on Article 29.

37 CJEU, 12 October 2004, *Commission v. Portugal*, C-55/02, § 62.

because, by not opting for this broad interpretation, it "would alter the scope of the directive and thus [...] deprive it of its full effect".[38] The same observation should be applied to Article 29: although lacking a definitive list of reasons that may be invoked for collective redundancies, giving domestic labour legislation wide room for manoeuvre, the goal to afford greater protection for workers implies that the legal grounds for collective redundancies should not be narrowed down. As collective dismissals may take place for a wide number of economic and organisational reasons, including the insolvency or the shutting down of the business, allowing different termination procedures may result in a lowering of protection for affected workers. Hence, the Committee has accepted a wide range of phrases from national reports, such as "economic circumstances, or technological or organisational changes, that make it necessary to reduce the workforce",[39] "technological, economic and restructuring changes",[40] "reduction or transformation of business activity",[41] "business reasons",[42] "financial or production related grounds".[43]

B *The Parties Involved in the Collective Redundancy Procedures*

As for the actors entitled to collective redundancy procedures, Article 29 refers exclusively, at least *prima facie*, to employers and workers' representatives. They are called to foster the necessary dialogue for the employer's economic decisions not to fall arbitrarily on workers, but as the result of a dynamic process and exchange of views that enables workers' representatives to express opinions based on the information provided and to affect the scope and the social consequences of the proposed redundancies. As a matter of fact, as will be said shortly, the participation envisaged by the Social Charter opens also, albeit implicitly, to a tripartite dialogue by means of a public intervention, either in the form of a possible direct involvement of the public authorities in the consultation procedure,[44] or through their strategic role in governing

38 CJEU, 11 November 2015, *Christian Pujante Rivera v. Gestora Clubs Dir SL and Fondo de Garantía Salarial*, C-422/14, §§ 54–55; CJEU, 21 September 2017, *Małgorzata Ciupa and Others v. II Szpital Miejski im. L. Rydygiera w Łodzi obecnie Szpital Ginekologiczno-Położniczy im dr L. Rydygiera Sp. z o.o. w Łodzi*, C-429/16, §§ 32–38.

39 ECSR, Conclusions 2018, Georgia.

40 ECSR, Conclusions 2014, Montenegro.

41 ECSR, Conclusions 2003, Italy.

42 ECSR, Conclusions 2014, The former Yugoslav Republic of Macedonia (now, North Macedonia).

43 ECSR, Conclusions 2007, Finland.

44 Nicola Countouris *et al.*, *op. cit.*, p. 45, noticing how the form for submitting reports refers to "possibilities of intervention by the public authorities" "in case of default by the employer" implying that the authorities are expected to play a secondary, posteriori

social measures and mitigating the impact of collective dismissals, *e.g.*, supporting workers in the labour market through, among others, unemployment benefits, retraining, and redeployment.[45]

1 Workers' Representatives

The Appendix to the Revised Social Charter expressly states that, for the purpose of the application of Article 29, "the term 'workers' representatives' means persons who are recognized as such under national legislation or practice".[46] The provision therefore devolves the task of recognizing the relevant bodies to the national discipline and practice and is worded in the same way as ILO Convention No. 158 (Article 13(3), which additionally demands for the domestic regulation to be in conformity with the Workers' Representatives Convention No. 135 of 1971) and in the EU Directives on collective redundancies (Article 1(b) Directive 98/59/EC).

Furthermore, all these sources address the right to information and consultation laid down in the case of collective redundancies as an entitlement intended for workers' representatives and not for workers individually; for the Social Charter in particular, this represents a departure from Article 21, where the (general) right to information and consultation within the undertaking belongs to "workers *or* their representatives".

The different formula needs to be briefly addressed. The issue is not whether participatory rights are individual or collective – beyond Article 29, the general regulatory framework suggests a *dual* nature of the right[47] – but rather why the Revised Charter, not unlike the other supranational and international sources mentioned, identifies solely collective forms of worker representation as the right-holders of the information and consultation rights in the case of collective redundancies.

The question has found an answer, albeit from the EU secondary legislation perspective, in the notorious *Mono Car Styling* case: on the one hand, the teleological interpretation of Directive 98/59 prompted the Court of Justice to consider workers' representatives as "best placed to achieve the objective

---

role at some point in the redundancy procedure in the event of default by the employer. However, as already mentioned, there is not, as yet, any case law on this subject.

45 ECSR, Conclusions 2003, Statement of Interpretation on Article 29. This perspective is reprised in the evaluation of national reports. See, among others, ECSR, Conclusions 2003, Romania; ECSR, Conclusions 2005, Lithuania.

46 Appendix to the European Social Charter (Revised), 3 May 1996, Article 28 and 29.

47 On the topic, Sára Hungler, *The Dual Nature of Employee Involvement*, Paris, L'Harmattan, 2020, especially pp. 27 ff.

which the directive seeks to attain"; on the other hand, the Court remarked how the right to information and consultation thereby provided "is intended to benefit workers as a collective group and is therefore collective in nature".[48]

The same reasoning can be applied to Article 29: the topics at stake and the purposes to which the social dialogue is called for (*i.e.*, formulating constructive proposals to avoid collective redundancies, limit their occurrence or mitigate their negative consequences, collaborating and making comments to the competent authorities) can be effectively guaranteed only through an adequate representation of the workers involved. What is relevant in collective redundancies is the social dimension of the phenomenon. It cannot be argued that from a juridical (and sociological) point of view, the employer's powers and prerogatives appear more meaningful and impactful when directed to reduce the company personnel rather than to suppress a single job.

Ultimately, the interest that the rights set in Article 29 serve is of an entire group and not of a single worker whose job is potentially at risk. Nonetheless, such a perspective is not incompatible with the protection still to be individually awarded to those affected by the consequences of the managerial decision: the *individual* scope of protection is in any case guaranteed in the right of individual employees to contest the lawfulness of their dismissal, as recognized in Article 24.[49]

As a consequence, although the States Parties are free to decide how the workers' representatives who have to be informed and consulted are to be appointed,[50] the ECSR's most recent Statement of interpretation on Article 29 has acknowledged the need for employees to be represented by persons "acting on behalf of all workers employed in the workplace" and "who may be potentially subject to collective redundancies",[51] namely

- either bodies already operating, such as trade unions or workers' councils (in other words, representatives designated or elected by trade unions or freely elected by the workers)
- or *ad hoc* representatives appointed to take part in this information and consultation process.[52]

48 CJEU, 16 July 2009, *Mono Car Styling SA v. Dervis Odemis and Others*, C-12/08, §§ 42 and 50.
49 Conclusions 2014, Statement of Interpretation on Article 29.
50 ECSR, Conclusions 2003, Sweden.
51 ECSR, Conclusions 2014, Statement of Interpretation on Article 29.
52 ECSR, Conclusions 2005, Lithuania ("Under Article 130.4 of the Labour Code an employer who plans to dismiss employees for financial reasons or due to restructuring must consult the workers' representatives. According to Article 19 of the Labour Code these are trade unions. If there is no trade union representation within the enterprise and if a general meeting of the staff has not delegated the duty of representing employees to their sectoral

Even if, in theory, both ways guarantee a collective form of workers' representation, the chance of *ad hoc* representatives likely to act as efficiently as trade union representatives or workers' councils is far from certain. Besides, another question is whether the implementation of Article 29 demands the national labour legislation to provide for some kind of mechanism in case workers have not established the required representative bodies. As rightly pointed out, "not establishing the respective bodies should not fall on the Member State, which obviously cannot force employees to organize themselves",[53] but domestic legislation can surely ensure that rules on worker representation are adequate to attain the goal of effective protection in information and consultation procedures.

The purpose of granting effectiveness to the workers' participatory procedure has therefore prompted the Committee to explicitly demand that national law-makers should ensure that employees may appoint representatives even when they are not otherwise represented, as well as to assess the effectiveness of the protection enshrined in domestic legislation: such is the case of Sweden, where the Co-Determination Act provides for an obligation to inform and negotiate on redundancies only with employee organisations; were it not for the high rate of unionization in Sweden (at least, at the time of the Committee's conclusion), such regulation might have been considered not in conformity with Article 29.[54]

In any case, workers' representatives should not suffer any negative consequences from their activity.[55]

2 The Public Authorities

As already mentioned, Article 29 does not lay down a specific involvement of public authorities in collective redundancies procedures; however, the Explanatory Report to the European Social Charter clearly admits that the "social measures" mentioned as a means of mitigating the consequences of collective redundancies are "not solely the responsibility of the employer".[56]

---

union, the employees are represented by the works council, whose members are elected by secret ballot at a general meeting of the staff").

53 Elisabeth Brameshuber, "Information and Consultation Rights", in Beryl Ter Haar, Attila Kun (eds.), *EU Collective Labour Law*, Cheltenham, Edward Elgar, 2021, p. 248.

54 ECSR, Conclusions 2003, Sweden.

55 Council of Europe, Digest of the case law of the European Committee of Social Rights, Strasbourg, 2018, p. 219.

56 Council of Europe, Explanatory Report of the European Charter Revised, 12, Strasbourg, 3 May 1996, § 110.

The lack of an express reference in this respect differs consistently from ILO Convention No. 158, wherein Article 14(1) requires the employer to notify, in accordance with national law and practice, the competent authority as early as possible, giving relevant information, including a written statement of the reasons for the terminations, the number and categories of workers likely to be affected and the period over which the terminations are intended to be carried out and, from the more detailed framework of the EU Directives on collective redundancies, specifying not only the duty of a written notification of any projected collective redundancies to the competent public authority but also a specific timing between the notification and the effect of redundancy during which the latter can 'seek solutions to the problems raised by the projected collective redundancies' (Article 4(2), Directive 98/59/EC). These requirements are clearly inspired by the idea that the collective dismissal's social and economic impact hits a larger community than merely the group of those workers affected by the employer's decision, and public power can play an important role *during* and *after* the procedure. For example, ILO Recommendation No. 166 details the role of public authority in both the consultation process ("where appropriate, the competent authority should assist the parties"),[57] and in promoting suitable measures for the placement of workers in alternative employment or their training and retraining.[58]

In the 2014 Statement of Interpretation on Article 29, the ECSR recognized the importance of public intervention in assisting and mediating the social dialogue and later in mitigating the impact of dismissals by stressing that "employers should be required to cooperate with administrative authorities or public agencies which are responsible for the policy counteracting unemployment, by for example notifying them about planned collective redundancies and/or cooperating with them in relation to retraining employees who are made redundant or providing them with other forms of assistance with a view to obtaining a new job".[59]

National provisions appear to have all implemented the obligation to inform (usually, in writing) a competent public authority – often the labour inspectorate or a public employment service – although the actual involvement varies from a simple notification[60] and the power to delay the date of the dismissals upon request[61] to actively participating in negotiation meetings,

57 ILO, Recommendation no. 166, 1982, § 19(1).
58 ILO, Recommendation no. 166, 1982, § 25.
59 ECSR, Conclusions 2014, Statement of Interpretation on Article 29.
60 ECSR, Conclusions 2018, Georgia.
61 ECSR, Conclusions 2018, Russian Federation.

promoting compliance with the substantive and procedural rules,[62] helping determine useful solutions for the redeployment of excess staff[63] and even refusing to grant the employer permission to dismiss in case of violations of the procedure.[64] As has been noted, the extent and the nature in which public authorities are specifically involved before and after collective dismissals are closely related as the support in developing social measures has an additional significance when the notification has a purely administrative function.[65] However, given the wording of Article 29, the Committee has so far stopped short of assessing the effectiveness of the public power involvement, preferring instead to address the overall level of protection granted by the information and consultation procedure and the preventive measures and sanctions established in the national legislation.

C *Procedural Requirements: Information and Consultation*

The core of the protection enshrined in Article 29 is represented by the recognition of a two-step procedure – information and consultation with workers' representatives, established as workers' representatives' rights and, accordingly, as employer's duties[66] – with a view to avoiding collective redundancies or limiting their occurrence and mitigating their consequences.

Although the provision's choice of words may not seem to enforce the idea of necessarily reaching an agreement (unlike what is set in Article 2 § 1 of Directive 1992/56/EEC and confirmed in Directive 1998/59/EC),[67] the "finalization" of the workers' involvement model[68] has been rightfully interpreted as implying "a process" to be set in motion, entailing "sufficient dialogue between the employer and the workers' representatives on ways of avoiding redundancies or limiting their number and mitigating their effects".[69] In other words, not

62 ECSR, Conclusions 2014, Portugal.

63 ECSR, Conclusions 2010, Italy; ECSR, Conclusions 2018, Turkey.

64 ECSR, Conclusions 2018, Netherlands.

65 Mariya Aleksynska, Angelika Muller, *The Regulation of Collective Dismissals: Economic Rationale and Legal Practice*, ILO Working Paper, no. 4, 2020, p. 24.

66 For a theoretical framework, Edoardo Ales, "Information and Consultation within the Undertaking: Employees Right or Employers' Duty? Looking for Effectiveness in Europe", in Jens M. Schubert (Hrsg.), *Sozialer Dialog in der Krise – Social Dialogue in Crisis?*, Baden-Baden, Nomos, 2009, pp. 195–212. As the Author notes, whereas information and consultation are rights that must be guaranteed to employees, they rather represent a duty to provide such rights for an employer, and at their core, they require the employer to be active in delivering information and consultation.

67 See, in particular, CJEU 27 January 2005, *Irmtraud Junk v. Wolfgang Kühnel*, C-188/03, § 43.

68 Bruno Veneziani, *op. cit.*, p. 484.

69 ECSR, Conclusions 2003, Statement of Interpretation on Article 29.

only may the participatory process not be limited to a simple duty to "inform unilaterally",[70] but it can also be effective if only taking into account the workers' interests as well as the employer's economic and organisational freedom. Information and consultation are, for all intents and purposes, an immediate counterweight to entrepreneurial freedom and prerogatives.

As such, the ECSR has remarked how Article 29 is directed – on the one hand – towards ensuring that workers are made aware of reasons and scale of planned redundancies, and – on the other hand – at securing that the position of workers is taken into account when their employer is planning collective redundancies, in particular as regards the scope, mode and manner of such redundancies and the extent to which their consequences can be avoided, limited and/or mitigated.[71]

This stance is also present in Article 13 of ILO Convention No. 158, whose consultation procedure has been noted as providing "an opportunity for an exchange of views and the establishment of a dialogue which can only be beneficial for both the workers and employer, by protecting employment as far as possible and hence ensuring harmonious labour relations and a social climate which is propitious to the continuation of the employer's activities"[72] as well as in the EU secondary legislation (Article 2 § 3 of 1992 and 1998 Directives on collective redundancies refers to the information and consultation's purpose as "to enable workers' representatives to make constructive proposals") and its Court of Justice interpretation.[73]

Article 29 stresses that the information and consultation procedure must take place "in good time prior to the process of collective redundancy" and while the expression is not accompanied by a more definite time frame (for example, *'no later than xx days before the first of the dismissals takes effect'*), the 2018 Council of Europe's Digest of case law of the ECSR sets the start of the

70 ECSR, Conclusions 2014 and 2018, Georgia. It has to be noted that in 2020 the Georgian Labour Code was amended with regard to collective redundancies, setting a clear obligation for the employer to start consultations with trade union or workers' representatives, within a reasonable time, as well as to send a written notification to the relevant ministries, including the Ministry of Labour, Health and Social Affairs, and to the employees whose employment contracts are to be terminated, at least 45 calendar days prior to the mass dismissal. The employer is also obliged to send copy of the notification sent to the Ministry to the trade union (or to the workers' representative). Nonetheless, ECSR, Conclusions 2022, Georgia confirms the non-conformity assessment "on the ground that domestic law makes no provisions for sanctions in case of non-compliance by the employer with their obligations in procedures of collective redundancies".

71 ECSR, Conclusions 2014, Statement of Interpretation on Article 29.

72 CEACR, General Survey – Protection against unjustified dismissal, 1995, § 283.

73 CJEU, 27 January 2005, *Irmtraud Junk v. Wolfgang Kühnel*, C-188/03, §§ 42–45.

workers' representatives involvement "as soon as the employer *contemplates* making collective redundancies".[74] It should be noted how such an explanation echoes the wording of Article 2(1) of the EU Directive 98/59/EC, which clearly refers to the employer "contemplating" collective redundancies.

As a result, the issue is whether such reference places the rise of the information and consultation rights at the moment when the employer's strategic or commercial decision, *e.g.*, on restructuring or closing a plan, inevitably leading to redundancies, is taken, even if a concrete proposal as to the number of redundancies and the affected employees has not yet been formed. It is not a punctilious matter, a way to ascertain *ex post* a violation of an obligation of good faith in the compliance of the employer's duty, but it is a question of how to preserve the chance for the consultation process to influence the managerial determination and its social consequences before any irrevocable decision is taken. Or, as the ECSR, puts it, for the sake of the "effectiveness and integrity of protection rights", which is why when the Committee assesses national reports finding that no provision would prevent redundancies from being put into effect before the obligation to inform and consult has been fulfilled, domestic legislation is regarded as being "not in conformity" with Article 29.[75] In the most recent evaluation of national legislation implementing the Charter's labour rights, the Committee issued two negative conclusions precisely on these aspects, stating that Georgia and Azerbaijan were not in conformity with Article 29, the former for not guaranteeing workers' representatives a timely consultation on collective redundancies, the latter for not demonstrating the establishment of measures preventing redundancies from being put into effect before the obligation to inform and consult has been fulfilled.[76] A similar non-conformity conclusion due to a lack of information on preventive measures aiming at ensuring that the redundancies are not put into effect before the consultation requirement is met was put forward in 2022 regarding North Macedonia and Serbia.

1 Information

The first step of the participatory procedure is therefore the obligation for the employer to inform workers' representatives, its scope directly influenced by the goal of assuring an effective protection of the workers involved.

---

74 Council of Europe, Digest of the case law of the European Committee of Social Rights, Strasbourg, 2018, p. 219.

75 ECSR, Conclusions 2014, Sweden.

76 On both decisions, see Andrzej Marian Świątkowski, *Labour Law: Council of Europe*, 4th ed., Zuidpoolsingel, Wolters Kluwer, 2021, p. 244.

According to the Committee,

a) employers should be required to provide employees' representatives with "all the relevant information necessary";[77] a (non-exhaustive) list including
   - the reasons for the proposed redundancies,
   - the criteria for determining which employees are to be made redundant,[78]
   - the proposed order and scheduling of such redundancies,
   - the amount of any cash benefits or other forms of compensation,
   - the scope and content of any planned social measures which are designed to mitigate the consequences of this process.

   This range of items should be considered as a minimum guidance (remarking how this is the information to be provided "*in particular*") without limiting the States from imposing a richer and more detailed regulation;[79]
b) the information about planned collective redundancies should be given not only prior to the commencement of the consultation process, but also "sufficiently far in advance" of the consultation itself, "so as to enable employees and their representatives to become familiar with the key aspects of the planned redundancies";[80]

77 ECSR, Conclusions 2014, Statement of Interpretation on Article 29.

78 In its Conclusions, the ECSR does not specify that such criteria should also comply with the principle of non-discrimination enshrined in Article E, but, as the ILO CEACR highlights, "it is important to ensure that certain protected workers, such as workers' representatives, are not dismissed in an arbitrary manner on the pretext of a collective termination of employment" (CEACR, General Survey – Protection against unjustified dismissal, 1995, § 335). Many national provisions address this point: see, for example, ECSR, Conclusions 2014, Montenegro.

79 A case in point can be found in the evaluation of the Netherlands collective dismissals regulation, where Section 4, subsections 1 and 2, of the Collective Redundancy (Notification) Act, employers must communicate various documents to trade unions, namely the reasons for the collective redundancies planned; the number of employees they plan to make redundant, broken down according to occupation/position, age and gender, together with the number of people usually employed; the method for calculating any redundancy payment; the dates on which it is planned to terminate employment contracts; the criteria for redundancy and information on the order in which redundancies will take place (ECSR, Conclusions 2018, Netherlands).

80 ECSR, Conclusions 2014, Statement of Interpretation on Article 29.

c) the duty to inform does not end with the trigger of the dialogue with workers' representatives but remains throughout the entire duration of the consultation process:[81] in other words, as the right of employees' representatives is to be provided with all relevant information, the dialogue can be fostered only if the communication channel stays open and supplied with all the (new) information regarding the enterprise's situation and the entrepreneurial choices gradually taken.

Article 29 and the Committee's interpretation make no mention of the way the information should be provided; however, the combined influence of EU secondary legislation, as the EU Directives on collective redundancies specify the information to be notified in writing, and of ILO Convention No. 158, wherein Article 14(1) obliges the employer to notify a written statement of the reasons for the terminations, the number and categories of workers likely to be affected and the period over which the terminations are intended to be carried out, has impacted on lawmakers generally imposing that relevant information should be given in writing.[82]

2 Consultation

The fair compliance with the duty to information gives way to the second step of the procedure enshrined in Article 29. Consultation between the employer and the workers' representatives is to be conducted, once again, "*in good time*" prior to the redundancies. The loose time reference – similar to the one used in ILO Convention No. 158 ("as early as possible") – has led the ECSR to clarify that it should occur "within a time period that is sufficient to ensure that employees' representatives have an opportunity to present suitable proposals with a view to avoiding, limiting or mitigating the effect of the proposed redundancies".[83]

As a result, the Committee concludes that national legislations are in conformity with Article 29 if a timeline of the different steps of the entire procedure is offered, even if the timing may vary.[84] On the contrary, a conclusion

81 *Ibid.*

82 See, among others, ECSR, Conclusions 2010, Albania; ECSR, Conclusions 2010, Malta.

83 ECSR, Conclusions 2014, Statement of Interpretation on Article 29.

84 See, for example, ECSR, Conclusions 2007, Bulgaria, where the employer is obliged to provide the information at least 30 days prior to the proposed dismissals, allowing for a task force (composed of National Employment Agency unit, the employer, employee representatives as well as representatives from the local municipality) to be formed; ECSR, Conclusions 2010, Portugal, where the minimum prior notice is 60 days prior to the planned date for termination of the work contract and 10 days after the initial notification to the workers' representative organisation, the employer has the duty to provide

of non-compliance has been handed down when, although the domestic legislation stipulates the obligation of the employer to notify public authorities about collective redundancies and the right for a trade union to submit to the same bodies the proposals on the postponement or suspension of the arrangements related to such collective redundancies, there appears no guarantee of the right of workers and their representatives to be consulted in good time before the redundancies take place.[85]

The scope and the objectives of the consultation process are broadly defined in the Charter provision, as the halt ("avoiding collective redundancies"), the modification ("limiting their occurrence") and the curbing ("mitigating their consequences") of the effects of the entrepreneurial decision are all mentioned. Article 29 offers a few examples of possible means to mitigate the consequences of the redundancies, citing "social measures aimed, in particular, at aid for redeployment or retraining of the workers concerned", but steers clear of explaining how the participatory procedure could succeed in avoiding or limiting the proposed redundancies. To this purpose, an exemplary list can be found in ILO Recommendation No. 166, referring to restriction of hiring, spreading the workforce reduction over a certain period of time, internal transfers, training and retraining, voluntary early retirement with appropriate income protection, restriction of overtime and reduction of normal hours of work (with the chance for partial compensation for loss of wages).[86]

The strategic importance of the dialogue between the employer and the workers' representatives has been regularly highlighted by the ECSR in its Conclusions on national reports, drawing attention to the fact that the consultation procedure covers both

- the redundancies themselves, including the ways and means of avoiding them or limiting their occurrence,
- and support measures, such as social measures to facilitate the redeployment or retraining of the workers concerned and the redundancy package.

---

information and to negotiate with the purpose of reaching an agreement on the extent and effects of the measures the employer envisages to take and other measures designed to reduce the number of workers who are to be made redundant.; ECSR, Conclusions 2010, Ukraine, and ECSR, Conclusions 2018, Moldova, where the information and consultation procedure can cover up to three months. For an overview of the different domestic rules throughout Europe, Roberto Cosio *et al.* (eds.), *Collective Dismissal in the European Union: A Comparative Analysis*, Alphen aan den Rijn, Wolters Kluwer, 2017.

85 ECSR, Conclusions 2014, 2018 and 2022, Georgia.

86 ILO, Recommendation no. 166, 1982, § 22.

The latter especially underlines the social dimension of the Charter, where the procedural principles are functional not only to avert or minimize terminations, but also to mitigate their adverse effects. Although the wording of Article 29 does not differ from the ILO Convention or the EU Directives, it is in the ECSR's interpretation that the obligation of consultation towards the negotiation of what could be intended as a *social plan*[87] becomes as relevant as addressing the extent of the envisaged lay-offs.[88]

As the Committee points out, it represents part of this process that employers should be also required to cooperate with administrative authorities or public agencies which are responsible for the policy counteracting unemployment, by notifying them about planned collective redundancies and cooperating with them in relation to retraining employees who are made redundant or providing them with other forms of assistance with a view to obtaining a new job:[89] among these, counselling, recruitment incentives and support, labour market advice and reintegration services have been mentioned.[90] Furthermore, many national reports suggest an active role of the public authority participating in the consultation meetings, by promoting compliance with the substantive and procedural rules as well as the reconciliation of the parties' interests.[91]

D *Enforcement*

The finalistic approach of the procedural requirements of Article 29 renders the topic of its enforcement crucial. Notwithstanding the silence of the Charter, the ECSR has repeatedly stated that "consultation rights must be accompanied by guarantees that they can be exercised in practice"[92] and, while the lawfulness of the individual dismissals pertains to the scope of Article 24 (the right

87 ECSR, Conclusions 2018, Netherlands; ECSR, Conclusions 2003, France.

88 ECSR, Conclusions 2005, Lithuania, where the Committee concluded for the non-conformity as the social dialogue envisaged in the domestic legislation did not cover "proposed social measures, criteria for dismissals and the order of dismissals". See also ECSR, Conclusions 2022, Greece, where the Committee, noting that "the presentation of a social plan is not an obligation for the employer who is simply free to bring it or not to the attention of the workers", defers its conclusion, asking for an explanation "on how and following which procedure measures to mitigate the effects of redundancy are taken in the practice, *in particular in the absence of a social plan presented by the employer*".

89 ECSR, Conclusions 2014, Statement of Interpretation on Article 29.

90 ECSR, Conclusions 2018, Turkey; ECSR, Conclusions 2014, Finland; ECSR, Conclusions 2014, Serbia.

91 ECSR, Conclusions 2014, Portugal; ECSR, Conclusions 2010, Italy.

92 Council of Europe, Digest of the case law of the European Committee of Social Rights, Strasbourg, 2018, p. 220.

to protection in cases of termination of employment), the domestic legislation should still provide for

- the recourse to administrative or judicial proceedings *before* the redundancies are put into effect, if the employer fails to fulfil the obligation to inform and consult;[93]
- effective sanctions *after* the event in case of procedural violation, *i.e.*, sufficiently deterrent for employers.[94]

The logical outcome for the compliance with such precepts would be that Member States should not permit dismissals to take place until the information and consultation phases has been completed[95] and a sanction of nullity of managerial decisions adopted in light of the breach of the essential content of the right to workers' participation in collective redundancy procedures. However, when moving from the recognized principles of adequacy and effectiveness to the domestic regulations, it is quite evident how the quality of methods of effective enforcement is interpreted by the State legislators in a quite varied way.

The diverse range of sanctions adopted to address failures to comply with Article 29 requirements includes injunctions to fulfil the obligation,[96] fines,[97] compensation orders,[98] reinstatement orders,[99] and refusals by government bodies to authorize a collective dismissal.[100] The Committee defers its conclusion when national reports do not provide information on the sanctions and preventive measures enshrined,[101] but it must be remarked how a repeated

93 ECSR, Conclusions 2003, Statement of Interpretation on Article 29. Similarly, Article 6 of Directive 98/59/EC stipulates that "Member States shall ensure that judicial and/or administrative procedures for the enforcement of obligations under this Directive are available to the workers' representatives and/or workers".

94 ECSR, Conclusions 2003, Statement of Interpretation on Article 29; ECSR, Conclusions 2010, Turkey.

95 ECSR, Conclusions 2007, Sweden ("The Committee notes that there is no right for employee representatives/trade unions to seek an order requiring an employer to inform and consult his/her employees prior to redundancies taking place. Therefore, the Committee concludes that the situation is not in conformity with the Revised Charter").

96 ECSR, Conclusions 2018, Netherlands.

97 ECSR, Conclusions 2007, Ireland; ECSR, Conclusions 2007, Malta; ECSR, Conclusions 2018, Moldova.

98 ECSR, Conclusions 2014, Finland.

99 ECSR, Conclusions 2010, Romania.

100 ECSR, Conclusions 2003, France.

101 ECSR, Conclusions 2018, Montenegro.

failure in providing such information may lead to assuming a void in the legislation and, therefore, a situation not in conformity with Article 29.[102]

The remedial perspective may prove to be the Achille's heel of the Charter provision. On the one hand, the absence in Article 29 of explicit remedies concerning the violation of the procedural aspects of collective dismissals has left room, in the light of the 2008 economic crisis, for States Parties' regulatory changes, often decreasing the standards of protection,[103] whose merits the ECSR has limited ability to enter and evaluate. On the other hand, the *quality* of pre-emptive measures and sanctions has direct and profound repercussions on the overall effectiveness of the right to information and consultation, to the point that any modification in terms of sanctions can alter the right's implementation:[104] the explicit reference to a *different* level of protection, the one enshrined in Article 24 for the employee to contest the lawfulness of the dismissal,[105] determines a split between the individual (and substantive) and the

102 ECSR, Conclusions 2018, Azerbaijan. The Committee had repeatedly asked what preventive measures existed to ensure that redundancies did not take effect before employers' obligation to inform the workers' representatives had been fulfilled, and the absence of a clear reply had determined in 2010 and 2014 the adjournment; but in 2018, "given the repeated failure to provide the information requested", the Committee found that it had not been established "that there are measures that would prevent redundancies from being put into effect before the obligation to inform and consult has been fulfilled". The non-conformity declaration has been confirmed in ECSR, Conclusions 2022, Azerbaijan. Similarly, when addressing the North Macedonia and Serbia national regulation, the Committee has gone from simply taking note of the absence of information with regard to preventive measures and therefore deferring its conclusions (ECSR, Conclusions 2018, North Macedonia; ECSR, Conclusions 2018, Serbia) to a non-conformity conclusion in the light of the national reports' ongoing failure to answer (ECSR, Conclusions 2022, North Macedonia; ECSR, Conclusions 2022, Serbia).

103 For an overview, Angelika Muller, "Employment Protection Legislation Tested by the Economic Crisis. A Global Review of the Regulation of Collective Dismissals for Economic Reasons", *Dialogue in Brief*, no. 3, Geneva, ILO, 2011.

104 The Italian labour reforms of the last ten years can prove this point. As Law no. 223/1991 on collective redundancies introduced the information and consultation procedure with workers' representatives and the active involvement of public authority, any (substantive or procedural) breach was subject to the sanctioning consequences of Article 18 of Workers' Statute, *i.e.*, the reinstatement of the worker unfairly dismissed. In 2012, a first reform distinguished between the violation of the selection criteria, sanctioned with the so-called diminished reinstatement, and the procedural violations, which instead gave title only to compensation (with the exception of the complete lack of the triggering of the information and consultation procedure, entailing a full reinstatement). Lastly, the so-called Jobs Act reform of 2015 abolished the chance for reinstatement in economic dismissals for any workers employed after March 2015 and established a compensation-only protection (of varying amounts).

105 ECSR, Conclusions 2003, Statement of Interpretation on Article 29.

collective (and procedural) dimension of protection, at the risk of losing the rationale and the importance of a constructive social dialogue.[106]

Concluding Remarks

The fundamental social right to inform and consult workers' representatives in collective redundancy procedures enshrined in Article 29 of the Revised European Social Charter and the attention given by the ECSR to its practice appear to have positively impacted the regulatory framework especially in those State Parties not subject to the implementation of the EU Directives. However, the topic of collective redundancies and lay-offs has become increasingly pressing since the 2008/09 economic crisis and more recently due to the Covid-19 sanitary and economic crisis. As noted by the ECSR in the 2021 Statement on Covid-19, the crisis "cannot be an excuse for not respecting the important role of social dialogue in finding solutions to the problems caused by the COVID-19 that also affect the workers".[107] As companies make use of redundancies in significant numbers as a common strategy to respond to market and organisational pressures,[108] some issues are likely to hinder the participatory model envisaged in the Charter.

---

106 The gap between the individual and collective protection and sanctioning system is regrettably imbibed also in CJEU case law, as the Court states that "Directive 98/59, like the earlier Directive 75/129 which it replaced, therefore provides for only a partial harmonisation of the rules for the protection of workers in the event of collective redundancies, that is to say, harmonisation of the procedure to be followed when such redundancies are to be effected" (CJEU, 21 December 2016, *AGET Iraklis*, C-201/15, § 28; CJEU, 10 December 2009, *Ovido Rodríguez Mayor and Others v. Herencia yacente de Rafael de las Heras Dávila and Others*, C-323/08, § 51) and therefore the methods of protection to be granted to a worker subject to an unlawful collective dismissal deriving from a violation *e.g.*, of the selection criteria are manifestly unrelated to the notification and consultation obligations deriving from Directive 98/59 (CJEU, 4 June 2020, *Tj v. Srl Balga*, C-32/20).

107 ECSR, Statement on COVID-19 and social rights, 24 March 2021, p. 5. In the form for the 2017–2020 supervisory cycle on labour rights leading to the 2022 Conclusions, the ECSR expressly requested information about the situation in practice as regards the right to information and consultation in collective redundancy procedures during the pandemic, and about any changes introduced in law modifying or reducing its scope during the COVID-19 crisis.

108 A good indication of the trend is offered by the Eurofund's European Monitoring Centre on Change, whose database also provides information on large-scale restructuring events (*i.e.*, involving more than 100 jobs) reported in the principal national media in each EU Member State since 2002; to date, more than 30,000 restructuring events have been recorded. The database is available at https://www.eurofound.europa.eu/observatories/emcc/erm/factsheets.

A first point is in the concept of *worker* and the personal scope of application of the provision. As the Charter does not seem to distinguish between standard and non-standard workers, between private and public sector or between smaller and bigger companies, Article 29 clashes with some of the subjective limitations set in other international sources and particularly in the EU Directives on collective redundancies. Furthermore, all sources seem to equate workers with employees, as the protective pattern is closely linked to the relationship with the employer. It could be argued, though, that restructuring processes do not affect *only* employees, and that a social right to an effective and constructive involvement when work contracts are at risk of being terminated should be more widely interpreted as benefitting all workers, regardless of their contractual arrangement or employment status. The corollary of this stand would appear in rethinking the forms of collective representation and workers solidarity and their legal recognition, a topic broader than what Article 29 provides for but whose implications seem unescapable nowadays.[109]

A second factor is in the topical difficulty of identifying *who* is obliged to trigger the social dialogue, as the term used in Article 29 ("*employer*") can hide the level at which the economic and organisational decision is taken. Some progress has been made in the context of transnational companies with the adoption of EU Directive No. 2009/38/EC on the establishment of the European Works Council (EWC), offering particular attention to transnational collective dismissals (i.e., concerning the Community-scale undertaking or Community-scale group of undertakings as a whole, or at least two undertakings or establishments situated in two different Member States), and providing the EWC with the right to information and consultation on the situation and probable trend of employment, investments, and substantial changes concerning organisation, introduction of new working methods or production processes, transfers of production, mergers, cut-backs or closures of undertakings, establishments or important parts thereof, and collective redundancies.

109 On the subject, Manfred Weiss, "Challenges for Workers' Participation", in Tindara Addabbo *et al.* (eds.), *The Collective Dimensions of Employment Relations*, London, Palgrave Macmillan, 2021, pp. 15–28; from the standpoint of the EU Charter of Fundamental Rights, Bruno Veneziani, "Article 27 – Worker's Right to Information and Consultation within the Undertaking", in Filip Dorssemont *et al.* (eds.), *The Charter of Fundamental Rights of the European Union and the Employment Relation*, Oxford, Hart, 2019, especially pp. 461–462 and Filip Dorssemont, "Article 27 – Workers' Right to Information and Consultation within the Undertaking", in Steve Peers *et al.* (eds.), *The EU Charter of Fundamental Rights. A Commentary*, Oxford, Hart, 2021, pp. 779–799.

Such advancement can help and remedy the notion that an undertaking controlling the employer, and able to take decisions which are binding on the latter, does not still have the status of employer,[110] but it falls short of covering all the possible layouts of decision-making centres in a globalized economy and affecting the information imbalance, which is ultimately an imbalance of power between the company and the workers' representatives.[111] One example will suffice to illustrate this. In the summer of 2021, the automotive and aerospace components multinational GKN announced the closure of a factory in Florence and the dismissal of over 400 workers, following similar dismantling in the United Kingdom and Germany. The choice was prompted by the owner of the MNE, an equity fund, whose aim was simply to boost profits and pay better dividends to its shareholders. Strong public disapproval eventually led to a change in legislation,[112] introducing stricter procedural constraints for lay-offs related to company closures, applying to companies with more than 250 employees and closing a plant, department or office located in Italy and dismissing at least 50 employees, and obliging the development of a social plan.[113]

This, in turn, leads to the third and most important aspect. Article 29's procedural requirements, like all other European law sources which provide for a recognition of the information and consultation rights of workers' representatives, face the risk of being lessened to bureaucratic formalities. Nevertheless, the social dialogue envisaged in Article 29 is not a mere interference with the employer's economic freedom, but it is the guarantee that workers' interests can intervene *in advance* on the entrepreneurial decision, thus giving all parties involved the chance to negotiate their respective interests and seek a compromise and a solution to the conflict.[114] Understanding the function of the right to information and consultation goes beyond the idea of the need of a

---

110 CJEU, 10 September 2009, *Akavan Erityisalojen Keskusliitto AEK ry and Others v. Fujitsu Siemens Computers Oy*, C-44/08.

111 Romuald Jagodzinski (ed.), *Variations on a Theme? The Implementation of the EWC Recast Directive*, Brussels, ETUI, 2015. On the shortcomings of the Directive, the European Parliament has already brought forward some proposals for its revision in the resolution of 2 February 2023 with recommendations to the Commission on Revision of European Works Councils Directive (2019/2183(INL); as a result, the Commission put forward a proposal to revise the EWC Directive on 24 January 2024 (COM(2024) 14 final).

112 Article 1, subsections 224–238, of Law 30 December 2021, No. 234.

113 Matteo Corti, "Il coinvolgimento dei lavoratori preso sul serio: Il caso GKN", *Diritto delle relazioni industriali*, Nol. 32, No. 1, 2022, pp. 265–271.

114 Mario Giovanni Garofalo, Pasquale Chieco, "Licenziamenti collettivi e diritto europeo", in *I licenziamenti per riduzione di personale in Europa*, Bari, Cacucci, 2001, p. 6.

(theoretical) balance between economic freedom and social rights and moves towards the goal of the Revised European Social Charter and the interpretation of the ECSR: should the principle of effectiveness of the Charter's rights finally be embraced by all State Parties and by EU institutions, then the right to information and consultation would be less frail.

ARTICLE 30

The Right to Protection against Poverty and Social Exclusion

Carole Nivard

With a view to ensuring the effective exercise of the right to protection against poverty and social exclusion, the Parties undertake:

- a to take measures within the framework of an overall and co-ordinated approach to promote the effective access of persons who live or risk living in a situation of social exclusion or poverty, as well as their families, to, in particular, employment, housing, training, education, culture and social and medical assistance;
- b to review these measures with a view to their adaptation if necessary.

∵

Article 30 enshrines one of the most original rights in the Revised Social Charter. No other human rights treaty contains a specific right to combat poverty and social exclusion. It is therefore particularly interesting to recall how such a right could be included in the Revised Charter and to define the social phenomena it aims to address (I). Next, a look at the beneficiaries protected by this provision allows for a reflection on the nature of this right (II). Finally, the content of the obligations that this Article requires of States Parties makes it possible to specify how this right is concretised (III).

I General Presentation

A *Origin*

While a right to combat poverty was not enshrined until the revision of the European Social Charter ("the Charter" hereafter), the issue had already been discussed when the first 1961 Social Charter was drafted. Indeed, on the one hand, the eradication of poverty and deprivation was, of course, central to the idea of such a Charter. In its Memorandum calling for a European Social Charter, the General Secretariat considered that it would serve the objectives of a "progressive social development" and a "continuous improvement

 | DOI:10.1163/9789004434158_012

of the standard of living of all members of society".[1] On the other hand, the same Memorandum suggested that the work should focus on "Adequate food, clothing and housing for everyone", drawing inspiration from the work being done at the time on the International Covenant on Economic, Social and Cultural Rights (ICESCR).[2] Indeed, within the United Nations, negotiations had already begun with a view to adopting such treaties, giving concrete form to the Universal Declaration of Human Rights ("UDHR"). In line with Article 25 of the UDHR, these negotiations led, among other things, to the drafting of Article 11 § 1 of the ICESCR of 16 December 1966, which states that "The States Parties to the present Covenant recognise the right of everyone to an adequate standard of living for himself and his family, including adequate food, clothing and housing, and to the continuous improvement of living conditions".

Moreover, the draft Charter proposed in 1955 by the Parliamentary Assembly of the Council of Europe ("PACE") contained an article enshrining "a right to a decent living". It also had the advantage of specifying States' obligations in a concrete manner by asking them to adopt "whatever measures may be required in order to: (a) keep the market adequately supplied with basic necessities at prices within the reach of all; (b) promote a policy of town planning and rural habitation such as will provide adequate numbers of moderately priced dwellings complying with satisfactory standards of comfort and hygiene".[3] The link between poverty and inadequate housing was thus already well perceived by the members of the Social Affairs Committee in charge of this project, and this was to resurface at the time of the "relaunch" of the Charter in the 1990s. However, the draft Charter finally adopted by the national delegates does not recognise any right to decent living conditions, food or housing. This can be explained considering how the governmental committee responsible for

1 Memorandum by the Secretariat-General concerning the activities which the Council of Europe could properly carry out in the social sphere, 11 May 1953, Doc 140, SG SC (53) 1.

2 *Ibid.*, § 29.

3 Social, Health and Family Affairs Committee, Draft Recommendation on Draft European Social Charter and European Economic and Social Council, Doc. 403 of 26 October 1955 ("Article 10. Everyone has the right to a decent living, and, in particular, to adequate food, clothing and housing. Besides the measures referred to in Articles 1[right to work], 2 [right to fair and stable conditions of work] and 11 [right to social security] of this Part of the Charter, the High Contracting Parties undertake to secure the fulfilment of this right by whatever measures may be required in order to: (a) keep the market adequately supplied with basic necessities at prices within the reach of all; (b) promote a policy of town planning and rural habitation such as will provide adequate numbers of moderate priced dwellings complying with satisfactory standards of comfort and hygiene").

drawing up a draft at the request of the Committee of Ministers proceeded by requesting governments to list the social rights already guaranteed in their legal systems and those they would like to see recognised. Such rights were at the time rarely recognised in the national constitutions of the Member States, and still remain "second category" constitutional rights nowadays.[4] Moreover, in the minds of European decision-makers at the time, it was obvious that the problem of poverty would naturally disappear thanks to the economic development of European States and the fight against unemployment.[5]

From the end of the 1970s onwards, a combination of economic and social factors led to phenomena of massive and lasting unemployment, as well as increasing precariousness and social exclusion in European countries, even though these were among the richest and most developed in the world. The issue of poverty was thus reappearing in the work of the Council of Europe, linked to the identification of the emerging phenomenon of social exclusion.[6] In this context, on the occasion of the re-launch of Charter system, proposals were made to include a right in this area among the new rights intended to enrich the Charter. One of them, made by Judge Valticos, underlined that such a provision might include "the right to protection from poverty, by including: co-ordinated arrangements relating to social, medical and material assistance; the right to decent housing and facilitated access, free from discrimination, to appropriate employment with a fair wage; special programmes of education and training; the right to a guaranteed minimum income for all residents; their measures for the social reintegration of persons excluded on account of their poverty".[7]

---

4 Jean-Claude Oderzo, "Le droit au logement dans les Constitutions des États membres", *Revue internationale de droit comparé*, Vol. 53, No. 4, 2001. pp. 913–926. For instance, in France the Preamble of the 1946 Constitution states that "10. La Nation assure à l'individu et à la famille les conditions nécessaires à leur développement. 11. Elle garantit à tous, notamment à l'enfant, à la mère et aux vieux travailleurs, la protection de la santé, la sécurité matérielle, le repos et les loisirs. Tout être humain qui, en raison de son âge, de son état physique ou mental, de la situation économique, se trouve dans l'incapacité de travailler a le droit d'obtenir de la collectivité des moyens convenables d'existence".

5 Council of Europe, Collected edition of the "Travaux préparatoires", Vol. 2 (1955), p. 216.

6 PACE, *Report on severe poverty and social exclusion: towards guaranteed minimum level of resources* (*Rapporteur: Mrs Havik, Sweden, Social Democrat*), of 7 April 1992, Doc. 6592.

7 Judge Valticos at the 7th International Colloquy on the European Convention on Human Rights (30 May-2 June 1990), doc. H/Coll (90) 13, p.6, quoted in Doreen Collins, Anna Gillett, Patrick Hennessy and Philippa Watson, "International Organizations and European Social Policy", *Journal of European Social Policy*, Vol. 2, No. 2, May 1992, pp. 125–134 and in Secretariat, "Memorandum and Bibliography", in Council of Europe, *Towards greater social justice in Europe: the challenge of marginalisation and poverty* (*Strasbourg, 3–5 December 1991*), Coll. Pov (92) 10 /A, 4.

During the *Travaux préparatoires*, the CHARTE-REL Committee decided to discuss the addition of provisions on protection against social exclusion, particularly in relation to poverty, housing and education and culture. In order to overcome the divergent points of view, particularly with regard to the recognition of a right to a minimum income, the Belgian delegate was asked to prepare a draft article.[8] Eventually, a provision devoted exclusively to protection against poverty and social exclusion (Article 30) and a separate provision on the right to housing (Article 31) were presented and adopted.[9] However, this new provision has been met with some restraint by some States Parties. Indeed, only 19 States Parties have accepted Article 30 out of the 35 States that have ratified the Revised Social Charter.

B *Recognition by the Revised Charter*

The recognition of a human right to be protected from poverty and social exclusion is highly original and progressive. Indeed, poverty is still widely perceived as an inescapable social phenomenon or an economic situation for which individuals are responsible. Although unfortunate, it would not be the State's fault. In any case, if it is States' responsibility to organise a social assistance policy, a person in such a situation could not claim a right to be protected from it. This explains why some members of the CHARTE-REL Committee had considered that this question was out of the Charter's scope,[10] i.e., out of the scope of human rights.

Others argued that there was no point in adding a new provision when such protection was implicit in Articles 13 (Right to social assistance) and 14 (Right to benefit from social services). It is interesting to note that the use of the terms "poor" and "poverty" (*indigents* and *indigence* in French) had been deliberately avoided in the drafting of Article 13 of the 1961 Charter in favour of the terms "person who is without adequate resources" and "want".[11] The aim was

8 This act of voluntariness on the part of the Belgian delegate was perhaps justified by the fact that at that time a proposal had been made since 1988 to insert an article on social rights in the forthcoming Belgian Constitution of 1994. This proposal resulted in Article 23 being inserted in the Constitution according to which "Everyone has the right to lead a life in keeping with human dignity. To this end, the laws [...] guarantee economic, social and cultural rights, taking into account corresponding obligations, and determine the conditions for exercising them. These rights include among others: [...] 3° the right to decent accommodation".

9 Final activity report of the Committee on the European Social Charter (CHARTE-REL), 19 October 1994, CHARTE/REL (94) 23, pp. 37–39.

10 *Ibid.*, pp. 37–38.

11 ECSR, Conclusions I (1967), Statement of interpretation, Article 13 ("An attempt was made, when the Charter was drafted, to break away from the old idea of assistance, which was bound up with the dispensing of charity. The expressions in the Charter reflect a

precisely to mark a shift from the old perception of social assistance as charity. It is therefore stimulating to note the recent return of the term "poverty" in the 1990s, albeit with a renewed understanding.

Article 30 thus marks an adherence to the idea that poverty is *per se* a violation of human rights.[12] It was therefore appropriate to formally recognise such a right so that the "rights of the poor" would no longer be "poor rights".[13] In its first conclusions on Article 30, the European Committee of Social Rights ("ECSR" or "Committee" hereafter) justified such a recognition by considering that "living in a situation of poverty and social exclusion violates the dignity of human beings".[14] However, this Article does not enshrine a right to minimum resources, as the drafters considered that such a right was already provided for by Article 13 of the Revised Charter.[15]

The Revised Social Charter remains, so far, the only treaty to enshrine such a right in a dedicated provision. The European Union also formalised an equivalent protection in Article 34 § 3 of the EU Charter of Fundamental Rights, which states that "In order to combat social exclusion and poverty, the Union recognises and respects the right to social and housing assistance so as to ensure a decent existence for all those who lack sufficient resources, in accordance with the rules laid down by Community law and national laws and practices" as it is inspired by the rights laid out in the Revised Charter.[16]

C *Definition of Notions*

The situation of poverty can be classically defined as a lack of material means or resources. The European Committee of Social Rights has thus considered that "by poverty it is meant deprivation due to the lack of resources".[17] Nevertheless, the determination of the nature and level of means necessary to escape poverty is very relative, depending on the living places and times. It

---

new concept of assistance – the use of the words 'person without adequate resources', for instance, instead of 'the poor' and 'want' instead of 'poverty'").

12 Diane Roman, *Le droit public face à la pauvreté*, Paris, LGDJ, 2002, 494 p.

13 Paul-Henry Imbert, "Droits des pauvres, pauvre(s) droit(s)? Réflexions sur les droits économiques, sociaux et culturels", *Revue de droit public*, 1989, pp. 739–754.

14 ECSR, Conclusions 2003 Statement of Interpretation on Article 30, all countries.

15 Explanatory Report, § 115 ("It must be noted that the Article does not expressly mention the guarantee of minimum resources. The reason is that such protection is already provided for by Article 13 of the Revised Charter and covered by this Article where reference is made in paragraph a to 'effective access to […] social assistance'").

16 The Explanations relating to the EU Charter of Fundamental Rights specify that "Paragraph 3 draws on Article 13 of the European Social Charter and Articles 30 and 31 of the revised Social Charter" (OJ C 303, 14.12.2007).

17 ECSR, Conclusions 2005, Statement of Interpretation on Article 30, all countries.

is therefore relevant to adopt a more global definition that takes into account people's living environment. Thus, in a decision on the fight against poverty in the European Economic Community, the Council of Ministers designated the poor as "persons, families and groups of persons whose resources (material, cultural and social) are so limited as to exclude them from the minimum acceptable way of life in the Member States in which they live".[18] This definition has the advantage of clarifying that the limited resources of these persons have the effect of excluding them from full participation in the society to which they belong.

The notion of "social exclusion" arose from French sociological studies between the 1970's and 1990's.[19] In particular, it emerged into the public eye with the publication of René Lenoir's book *Les exclus*[20] and the work of Joseph Wresinski.[21] Subsequently, it gave rise to the development of the opposite concept of "social inclusion",[22] which has since been widely taken up and displayed as an objective pursued by international and national anti-poverty organisations.[23] Thus, poverty and exclusion are intimately linked and feed off each other. As early as in its Recommendation 893 (1980), *Poverty in Europe*,[24] the Parliamentary Assembly of the Council of Europe emphasised "that the situation of these sectors of the population is characterised not only by material difficulties but also by social exclusion, lack of participation in civic, political and cultural life, and difficulties in fitting into the educational system".

Despite this consubstantial link between the two phenomena, Article 30 of the Revised Social Charter refers to both terms. Should the two concepts be distinguished under the Charter? In this respect, the definitions provided in

---

18 Council, Decision of 19 December 1984 on specific Community action to combat poverty, (85/8/EEC).

19 Cf. the pioneering Jules Klanfer, *L'exclusion sociale. Étude de la marginalité dans les sociétés occidentales*, Bureau des Recherches sociales, Paris, 1965 and the later work of Robert Castel, *Les métamorphoses de la question sociale*, Paris, Fayard, 1995 and Serge Paugam, *La disqualification sociale: essai sur la nouvelle pauvreté*, Paris, PUF, 1991.

20 René Lenoir, *Les exclus*, Paris, Seuil, 1976.

21 Père Joseph Wresinski, "Grande pauvreté et précarité économique et sociale", Rapport au Conseil économique et social présenté le 10 février 1987, Paris, Journal officiel de la République française 1987, p. 14.

22 Niklas Luhmann, *Social Systems*, Stanford University Press, 1984, 2nd ed., 1996, 684 p.

23 For instance, promoting social inclusion is one of the goals of the World Bank https://www.worldbank.org/en/topic/social-inclusion. Social Inclusion is one of the social objectives of EU Member States' cooperation since the Lisbon European Council of March 2000 that launched the so-called "Strategy of Lisbon" and strategies for Social Agendas since then.

24 Adopted on 24 April 1980.

the Explanatory Report give some clues but without determining all the contours of these notions. In consequence, they need to be supplemented by the interpretative work of the ECSR.

The Explanatory Report states that "The term 'poverty' in this context covers persons who find themselves in various situations ranging from severe poverty, which may have been perpetuated for several generations, to temporary situations entailing a risk of poverty". These indications do not allow for concretely determining a situation qualifying as "poverty" or "risk of poverty". The ECSR specified it in its jurisprudence, indicating that "the main indicator used to measure poverty is the relative poverty rate (this corresponds to the percentage of people living under the poverty threshold, which is set at 60% of the equivalised median income).[25] The at-risk-of-poverty rate before and after social transfers (from Eurostat, the statistical office of the European Union) is also used as a comparative value to assess national situations".[26] The "60% of the equivalised median income" threshold is mainly used by Eurostat.[27] It is interesting to note that another threshold, 50% of the equivalised median income, is used by the Committee for monitoring other provisions of the Charter, mainly Article 12 § 1 (Right to social security), Article 13 § 1 (Right to social assistance) and Article 8 § 1 (Minimum rate of maternity benefit paid). These thresholds, formulated in relation to the median income in the country, have the advantage of determining poverty in relative terms. Poverty is not absolute but dependent on the environment and the standard of living in the country of residence. In fact, poverty affects dignity and freedom in that "adequate resources are an essential element to enable people to become self-sufficient".[28]

In regard to social exclusion, the Explanatory Report indicates that "The term 'social exclusion' refers to persons who find themselves in a position of extreme poverty through an accumulation of disadvantages, who suffer from degrading situations or events or from exclusion, whose rights to benefit may have expired a long time ago or for reasons of concurring circumstances. Social

25 Equivalised median income is defined as the household's total disposable income divided by its "equivalent size", to take account of the size and composition of the household, and is attributed to each household member.

26 ECSR, Conclusions 2013, Statement of Interpretation on Article 30.

27 It corresponds to the "At-risk-of poverty rate" which is the first primary indicator of the 18 common statistical indicators on poverty and social exclusion established by the European Council of Laeken in 2001, the so-called "Laeken indicators".

28 ECSR, Conclusions 2013, Statement of Interpretation on Article 30; ECSR, *European Committee for Home-Based Priority Action for the Child and the Family (EUROCEF) v. France*, complaint No. 82/2012, decision on admissibility and the merits of 19 March 2013, § 57.

exclusion also strikes or risks to strike persons who without being poor are denied access to certain rights or services as a result of long periods of illness, the breakdown of their families, violence, release from prison or marginal behaviour as a result for example of alcoholism or drug addiction".

The ECSR's practice does not shed light on a precise definition of "social exclusion". It refers mainly to national indicators, although more recently it seems to favour the European AROPE indicator (see *infra*). The ECSR seems nevertheless to adopt a broader perception than the Explanatory Report, less based on the extreme character of poverty but more on the lack of access to civil and social rights.

In its 2013 Statement of Interpretation of Article 30, the Committee sums up its current jurisprudence affirming that "the scope of Article 30 is relating both to protection against poverty (understood as involving situations of social precarity) and protection against social exclusion (understood as involving obstacles to inclusion and citizen participation)". However, this consideration is not definitive since poverty and exclusion are "multidimensional (…) phenomena", as the Committee itself has acknowledged.[29]

II Beneficiaries

A *A Vulnerable Group?*

If people experiencing poverty or exclusion are covered by a specific provision, it is because the drafters of the Revised Social Charter considered that they presented a form of vulnerability requiring special protection.[30] Moreover, in other human rights protection systems, people in situations of economic and social insecurity are classified as vulnerable groups, even in the absence of recognition of a specific right.[31] In its jurisprudence, the ECSR regularly designates

29 ECSR, Conclusions 2003, Statement of Interpretation on Article 30.

30 Carole Nivard, "Valeur systématisante de la vulnérabilité dans la jurisprudence du Comité européen des droits sociaux", in Caroline Boiteux-Picheral (ed.), *La vulnérabilité en droit européen des droits de l'homme. Conception(s) et fonction(s)*, Limal, Anthémis, 2019, pp. 101–118.

31 Corina Heri, *Responsive Human Rights. Vulnerability, Ill-treatment and the ECtHR*, London, Hart Publishing, 2021; Alexandra Timmer, "A Quiet Revolution: Vulnerability in the European Court of Human Rights", in Martha Albertson Fineman, Anna Grear, *Vulnerability. Reflections on a New Ethical Foundation for Law and Politics*, London, Routledge, 2013; Samantha Besson, "La vulnérabilité et la structure des droits de l'homme: L'exemple de la jurisprudence de la Cour européenne des droits de l'homme", in Laurence Burgorgue-Larsen (ed.), *La vulnérabilité saisie par les juges en Europe*, Éditions Pedone, 2014, pp. 59–85. Rosmerlin Estupiñan-Silva, "La vulnérabilité saisie par la Cour

poor people as vulnerable categories requiring special attention in the implementation of certain public policies. This is particularly the case for measures taken in crises. According to the Committee, when States adopt emergency measures in these exceptional circumstances, whether in times of economic[32] or health crises, they must ensure that they do not significantly burden vulnerable groups and that these groups actually benefit from these measures. In the latter case, the Committee recently stated that "healthcare in a pandemic must be effective and affordable to everyone, and that groups at particularly high risk, such as (...) persons living in poverty (...) must be adequately protected by the healthcare measures put in place".[33] However, these interpretations relate to the application of the Charter as a whole or to articles other than Article 30 of the Charter.

Indeed, findings and decisions under Article 30 never refer to the beneficiaries of the right as a "vulnerable group". On the contrary, the case law on Article 30 designates within these beneficiaries particularly vulnerable groups that should receive special attention or policy. For example, travellers,[34] migrant Roma,[35] highly dependent persons with

---

interaméricaine", in *La vulnérabilité saisie par les juges en Europe, cit.*, pp. 89–115; Marie Rota, "La vulnérabilité dans la jurisprudence de la Cour européenne et de la Cour interaméricaine des droits de l'homme", *Cahiers de la recherche sur les droits fondamentaux*, 2020, pp. 39–46.

32 "[A]lthough the overall standard of living of the population was affected by the reforms, care had been taken to ensure that the burden of these reforms did not weigh too heavily on the economically most vulnerable households" (Conclusions XIV-1, Article 12 Finland) ; ECSR, *Federation of employed pensioners of Greece (IKA-ETAM) v. Greece*, complaint No. 76/2012, decision on the merits of 7 December 2012, § 79 "Even taking into account the particular context in Greece created by the economic crisis and the fact that the Government was required to take urgent decisions, the Committee furthermore considers that the Government has not conducted the minimum level of research and analysis into the effects of such far-reaching measures that is necessary to assess in a meaningful manner their full impact on vulnerable groups in society" and § 81 "In general, the Committee thus concludes that the Government has not established, as is required by Article 12 § 3, that efforts have been made to maintain a sufficient level of protection for the benefit of the most vulnerable members of society, even though the effects of the adopted measures risk bringing about a large scale pauperisation of a significant segment of the population".

33 ECSR, Statement of interpretation on the right to protection of health in times of pandemic, 21 April 2020.

34 ECSR, *International Federation of Human Rights (FIDH) v. Belgium*, complaint No. 62/2010, decision on the merits of 21 March 2010, § 204.

35 ECSR, *Médecins du Monde – International v. France*, complaint No. 67/2011, decision on the merits of 11 September 2012, § 107.

disabilities,[36] homeless persons,[37] unaccompanied foreign minors,[38] etc., have been designated as such. The jurisprudential concretisation of the right thus reveals a sub-categorisation within the vulnerable category of people experiencing poverty.[39] Indeed, among the poor, some meet certain characteristics that make them more particularly subject to the risk of poverty. This has allowed some authors[40] to classify Article 30 of the Charter as a horizontal rather than a sectoral provision for the protection of vulnerable people. It is intended to benefit all persons in a situation of poverty or exclusion and not groups specifically vulnerable because of a particular characteristic (age, sex, nationality, disability, etc.). It is interesting to note how the sub-categorisation makes visible phenomena of "intersectionality", in the sense that it highlights the fact that certain categories of people are at increased risk of impoverishment because of certain characteristics. However, the Committee does not attempt to identify multiple vulnerabilities in a systematic way, in particular by cross-referencing the protections guaranteed by the various Charter rights. The Committee only draws from this a requirement to target these groups in national policies relating to poverty and social exclusion, in other words, "where necessary specifically target the most vulnerable groups and regions".[41] Such targeting may require the adoption of specific positive measures when Article 30 is combined with the principle of non-discrimination (see *infra* C 2).

B *Applicability to Foreigners*

Article 30 has a cross-cutting scope in the sense that it is addressed to any individual, regardless of age, employment status, gender, etc., who finds himself

36 ECSR, *International Federation of Human Rights (FIDH) v. Belgium*, complaint No. 75/2011, decision on the merits of 18 March 2013, § 197.

37 ECSR, *European Federation of National Organisations working with the Homeless (FEANTSA) v. the Netherlands*, complaint No. 86/2012, decision on the merits of 2 July 2014, § 229.

38 ECSR, *European Committee for Home-Based Priority Action for the Child and the Family (EUROCEF) v. France*, complaint No. 114/2015, decision on the merits of 24 January 2018, § 56.

39 Cf. Alexandre Palanco, "Les variations autour des formes de vulnérabilité reconnues en droit européen des droits de l'homme", in Caroline Boiteux-Picheral (ed.), *La vulnérabilité en droit européen des droits de l'homme. Conception(s) et fonction(s)*, Limal, Anthémis, 2019, pp. 33–61.

40 Katarzyna Dunaj and Johanna Ryzka, "The Protection of Vulnerable People in the Charter System", in Anesc, Stefano Angeleri and Carole Nivard (eds.), *The European Social Charter: A Commentary. Volume 1, Cross-Cutting Themes*, Leiden, Brill/Nijhoff, 2022, pp. 319–348.

41 ECSR, Conclusions 2003, Statement of Interpretation, Article 30.

or herself in a situation of poverty or social exclusion, either temporarily or permanently. Nevertheless, as with most Charter rights, the limited personal scope determined by the Appendix is applicable to the right to protection against poverty and social exclusion. Thus, its protection includes "foreigners only in so far as they are nationals of other Parties lawfully resident or working regularly within the territory of the Party concerned".

The question arises, however, as to whether the Committee's broad interpretation of the scope *ratione personae* in relation to the dignity of persons[42] applies to Article 30. Indeed, the link was immediately made between "living in a situation of poverty and social exclusion" and "the dignity of human beings".[43] However, when the issue clearly arose before the ECSR in the context of a collective complaint, it clearly rejected such an extension with regard to the benefit of Article 30. Indeed, in the case of *DCI v. Belgium*,[44] the claimants invoked the violation of Article 30 of the Charter with regard to foreign minors unlawfully present on the territory. The Committee noted that Article 30 "essentially requires States Parties to adopt an overall and co-ordinated approach consisting of measures to promote access to social rights" and therefore does not form part of the Charter's "provisions whose fundamental purpose is closely related to the requirement to secure the most fundamental human rights and to safeguard the persons covered by the provisions in question from serious threats to the enjoyment of those rights".[45] This interpretation was reiterated in the *FEANTSA v. Netherlands* decision[46] but prompted a dissenting opinion from one of its members, and not the least eminent, Luis Jimena Quesada, reflecting a lack of unanimity among the Committee members. The President of the Committee at the time considered that, given "the very close link between the effectiveness of the right recognised by Article 30 of the Charter and the enjoyment of the rights recognised by Articles 13 § 1 and § 4 and 31 § 2", which were applicable and violated in the case in point, as well as the requirement of a

42 Cf. Csilla Kollona-Lehoczky, "The Methods for Interpretating the European Social Charter", in *The European Social Charter: A Commentary. Volume 1, Cross-cutting Themes, cit.*, pp. 241–248 and 257–258; Bige Açimuz and Olgun Akbulut, "The Values Underlying the European Social Charter", in *The European Social Charter: A Commentary. Volume 1, Cross-cutting Themes, cit.*, pp. 283–284.

43 ECSR, Conclusions 2003, Statement of Interpretation, Article 30.

44 ECSR, *Defence for Children International (DCI) v. Belgium*, complaint No. 69/2011, decision on the merits of 23 October 2012.

45 *Ibid.*, §§ 144–145.

46 ECSR, *European Federation of National Organisations working with the Homeless (FEANTSA) v. the Netherlands*, complaint No. 86/2012, decision on the merits of 2 July 2014, § 211.

teleological interpretation of the Charter based on a human rights approach, it should have been possible to recognise the violation of Article 30 in this case.[47]

It seems that for the time being, the applicability of Article 30 remains confined to the literal terms of the Appendix, which reflects the Committee's desire to limit its extensive case law very strictly. So far, the Committee agreed to apply the Charter to all foreigners when an exclusion "from the protection afforded by the Charter would have seriously detrimental consequences for their fundamental rights (such as the right to life, to the preservation of human dignity, to psychological and physical integrity and health)".[48] Concerning the vulnerable group of migrant children, the ECSR considered that these children "come within the personal scope of Articles 7 § 10, 11, 13, 16 (right to shelter), 17 §§ 1 and 2 and 31 § 2 of the Charter".[49] It is true that one may wonder about the value of the applicability of Article 30 in addition to the protection already granted by the Committee's case law. Indeed, the State's obligation to implement an overall and coordinated approach in the fight against poverty does not seem to be adapted to the emergency assistance to destitute foreigners that this case law imposes. In fact, the extreme deprivation of the persons concerned is read in the light of other articles of the Charter: Article 11 in the case of emergency medical aid, Article 13 in the case of emergency social assistance and Article 31 in the case of emergency shelter. Moreover, the Committee is increasingly pronouncing immediate measures when people find themselves exposed to conditions of deprivation that undermine their dignity.[50]

---

47 Partly dissenting opinion of Luis JIMENA QUESADA on *FEANTSA v. the Netherlands*, complaint No. 86/2012, *cit.*,

48 ECSR, *Defence for Children International (DCI) v. Belgium*, complaint n° 69/2011, decision on the merits of 23 October 2012, § 35; ECSR, *International Commission of Jurists (ICJ) and European Council for Refugees and Exiles (ECRE) v. Greece*, complaint No. 173/2018, decision on the merits of 26 January 2021, § 76. So far, the Committee only admitted the "entitlement to medical assistance to foreign nationals" under Article 13 of the Charter (ECSR, *International Federation of Human Rights Leagues v. France*, complaint No. 14/2003, decision on the merits of 8 September 2004, § 35).

49 "in so far as excluding them from the protection afforded by these rights would have seriously detrimental consequences for their fundamental rights to life, health, physical and psychological integrity and to the preservation of their human dignity" (ECSR, *International Commission of Jurists (ICJ) and European Council for Refugees and Exiles (ECRE) v. Greece*, complaint No. 173/2018, decision on the merits of 26 January 2021, § 86).

50 ECSR, *Defence for Children International (DCI) and Others v. Spain*, complaint n° 206/2022, decision on admissibility and immediate measures of 19 October 2022 (electricity and heating for slum dwellers); ECSR, *European Roma Rights Centre v. Belgium*, complaint No. 195/2020, decision on admissibility and immediate measures of 29 June 2021 (Roma evicted without housing solution); ECSR, *European Federation of National Organisations*

III Content

As Article 30 of the Charter is one of the new rights added by the Revised Social Charter and has no equivalent in other human rights protection systems, the obligations it imposes on States Parties need to be clarified through interpretation. The Committee's jurisprudence is thus under construction and is being refined in practice. It should be recognised that Article 30 is "a complex and multifaceted standard".[51] The Committee clarifies what is meant by the obligation of an "overall and coordinated approach" (A). Moreover, it considers that the fight against exclusion goes beyond the framework of social rights by also requiring that the people concerned be given access to civil and political rights and thus their participation in society (B). Interesting assessments have also been adopted with regard to the discrimination of certain vulnerable groups (C). However, there is still a certain vagueness about the relationship between Article 30 and other related provisions of the Charter, which raises the question of the autonomy of Article 30 in relation to them (D).

A *Overall and Coordinated Approach*

Under Article 30, the Parties undertake to respect two distinctive obligations: firstly, "to take measures within the framework of an overall and coordinated approach to promote the effective access of persons who live or risk living in a situation of social exclusion or poverty, as well as their families, to, in particular, employment, housing, training, education, culture and social and medical assistance", secondly, "to review these measures with a view to their adaptation if necessary".

This formulation appears rather broad. It undertakes to follow global and coherent policies encompassing all the manifestations and difficulties of poverty and social exclusion. Moreover, it requires that these policies be adapted in order to assure their effectiveness and pertinence. This formulation seems thus adequate to cover the multidimensional character of these phenomena. On the other hand, the provision might seem insufficiently precise as to the measures expected. In fact, the *Travaux préparatoires* on this article clearly reflect the desire of the majority of States to avoid defining precise obligations or obligations of result. The Belgian delegate thus indicated that his

---

working with the Homeless (FEANTSA) *v. the Netherlands*, complaint No. 86/2012, decision on immediate measures of 1 July 2013 (shelter and basic needs).

51 Karin Lukas, "Article 30", in *The Revised European Social Charter. An Article-by-Article Commentary*, Cheltenham, UK, Northampton, USA, Edward Elgar Publishing, 2021, p. 322.

proposal "could be an instrument of stimulation for national authorities".[52] Furthermore, during the last negotiations on the drafting of the article, it was decided to replace the term "programme" with "approach",[53] which marks further flexibility in the obligations required from States. Moreover, with regard to reviewing the measures, the Explanatory Report of the Revised Charter adds that it "is of a general character and each Party shall decide how it should be organised, depending on national conditions".[54] A certain margin of appreciation is therefore left to the States Parties, although it is specified that the review may "include consultations with the social partners and various other organisations, including organisations representing persons who find themselves in a situation of poverty or social exclusion".

Since its first conclusions in 2003, the Committee clarified what it meant by an "overall and coordinated approach". In its opinion, it "shall consist of an analytical framework, as well as of a set of priorities and measures to prevent and remove obstacles to access to fundamental social rights. Monitoring mechanisms should be put in place, involving all relevant actors, including civil society and persons affected by exclusion and poverty. Policies should moreover be linked and integrated in a consistent way, that is in a manner reaching beyond a sectorial or a targeted group approach".[55] The national policies should aim at guaranteeing these vulnerable persons and their families effective access to all social rights. The Article points to some of these rights: access to employment, housing, training, education, culture, and social and medical assistance. But the Committee immediately specifies "that this list does not exhaust the areas in which measures must be taken to address the multidimensional poverty and exclusion phenomena", meaning that measures could be expected in other areas.

---

52 Final activity report of the Committee on the European Social Charter (CHARTE-REL), 19 October 1994, CHARTE/REL (94) 23, p. 37.

53 *Ibid.*, p. 38.

54 "117. The review of mechanisms under paragraph b of the Article is of a general character and each Party shall decide how it should be organised, depending on national conditions. This review may, in order for the measures mentioned in the provision to be effective, include consultations with the social partners and various other organisations, including organisations representing persons who find themselves in a situation of poverty or social exclusion".

55 ECSR, Conclusions 2003, Statement of Interpretation on Article 30, all countries; ECSR, *International Movement ATD Fourth World v. France*, complaint No. 33/2006, decision on the merits of 5 December 2007, § 134; ECSR, *European Committee for Home-Based Priority Action for the Child and the Family (EUROCEF) v. France*, complaint No. 114/2015, decision on the merits of 24 January 2018, § 182.

The analysis of the ECSR's jurisprudence allows for identifying some precise obligations that arise from Article 30. Thus, when reviewing the national reports, the Committee verifies information in three areas. In a first item, entitled "Measuring poverty and social exclusion", "States Parties must provide detailed information on how they measure poverty and social exclusion. The main indicator used by the Committee to measure poverty is the relative poverty rate. This corresponds to the percentage of people living under the poverty threshold, which is set at 60% of the equivalised median income".[56] This permits the Committee to evaluate the level of poverty in the country and its evolution from one monitoring cycle to another. This level is taken into account in the appreciation of the conformity to the Charter, i.e., a high level involving the adoption of significant measures and an increasing level that may be evidence of policy ineffectiveness. Indeed, according to the ECSR, "the measures should be adequate in their quality and quantity to the nature and extent of poverty and social exclusion in the country concerned".[57] The assessment of exclusion is more complex to carry out. The Committee asked States Parties to specify which indicators are used to evaluate this phenomenon but did not provide any guidance. It seems that since its 2021 conclusions,[58] the Committee accepts the use of the AROPE indicator (used by Eurostat), i.e., the rate of persons "at-risk-of-poverty-or-social-exclusion", measured through three headline indicators: At-risk-of-poverty-rate (AROP), Severe material and social deprivation rate (SMSD), Persons living in a household with very low work intensity (0–59). The measure of AROPE for minors (from 0 to 17) adds four more indicators: impact of social transfers (other than pensions) on poverty reduction, disability employment gap, housing cost overburden rate, children aged less than 3 years in formal childcare and self-reported unmet need for medical care. The AROPE indicator is interesting because it considers not only financial criteria, but also effective access to some social benefits and services. Moreover, Eurostat provides statistics for other European countries outside the EU Member States, which makes the indicator all the more relevant.

The second item monitored in the ECSR's conclusions is the existence of an overall and coordinated "Approach to combating poverty and social exclusion". As seen *supra*, the Committee stated that it consists of "an analytical framework, a set of priorities and corresponding measures to prevent and remove

56 ECSR, Conclusions 2017, Article 30, Andorra, Estonia and Latvia.

57 ECSR, Conclusions 2003, Statement of Interpretation on Article 30, all countries.

58 ECSR, Conclusions 2021, Article 30, Estonia, Latvia, Netherlands, Norway, Serbia, Slovak Republic, Slovenia, Sweden and Turkey.

obstacles to access to social rights".[59] The States Parties have to demonstrate that some mechanisms of coordination exist between the stakeholders of the different relevant policies "embedding the fight against poverty and social exclusion in all strands of policy and moving beyond a purely sectoral or target group approach".[60]

Concerning the measures expected, they "should strengthen entitlement to social rights, their monitoring and enforcement, improve the procedures and management of benefits and services, improve information about social rights and related benefits and services, combat psychological and socio-cultural obstacles to accessing rights and where necessary specifically target the most vulnerable groups and regions".[61]

As a comprehensive approach is expected, the removal of one protective measure for the poorest persons does not, in itself, call into question the existence of a sufficient overall approach as they continue to benefit from other guarantees.[62] The ECSR requires nevertheless that the implementation of Article 30 be carried out effectively, as the aim of the Charter "is to protect rights not merely theoretically, but also in fact".[63]

Thus, among the concrete obligations of States Parties, they must allocate sufficient resources to the fight against poverty. These resources must also increase "as long as poverty and social exclusion persist".[64] Furthermore, they must be proportionate to the extent of the situation on their territory. This is because a high poverty rate "calls for extraordinary measures"[65] and therefore implies major budgetary efforts.

Moreover, an overall and coordinated approach presupposes the collection of statistics to evaluate the real situation of poverty and to measure the effects of national measures. That is why "the State's failure to collect reliable data and statistics" leads to a lack of compliance with Article 30.[66]

---

59 ECSR, Conclusions 2003, Statement of Interpretation on Article 30, all countries.

60 Digest of the case law of the European Committee of Social Rights, 2022, p. 197; Statement on Covid-19 and Social Rights adopted on 24 March 2021.

61 ECSR, Conclusions 2003, Statement of Interpretation on Article 30, all countries.

62 ECSR, *European Committee for Home-Based Priority Action for the Child and the Family (EUROCEF) v. France*, complaint No. 82/2012, decision on admissibility and the merits of 19 March 2013, §§ 59–60.

63 ECSR, *International Commission of Jurists v. Portugal*, complaint No. 1/1999, decision on the merits of 9 September 1999, § 32.

64 ECSR, Conclusions 2003, Statement of Interpretation on Article 30, all countries.

65 ECSR, Conclusions 2017, Article 30, Latvia.

66 ECSR, *International Federation of Human Rights (FIDH) v. Belgium*, complaint No. 75/2011, decision on the merits of 18 March 2013, § 197.

The Committee also emphasised the importance of the involvement of representatives of civil society as well as persons affected by poverty and exclusion when defining the measures[67] and in the monitoring mechanisms created to evaluate them.[68]

Finally, in its conclusions, the ECSR assesses a third item, "Monitoring and evaluation", where States must report the existence of monitoring and evaluation mechanisms, their effectiveness, their sufficient funding and the participation of all stakeholders, including the persons in a situation of poverty or exclusion.

Concerning times of economic crises, the ECSR transposed its jurisprudence relating to other Articles of the Charter to Article 30.[69] In particular, it considers that "the economic crisis should not have as a consequence the reduction of the protection of the rights recognised by the Charter. Hence, the governments are bound to take all necessary steps to ensure that the rights of the Charter are effectively guaranteed at a period of time when beneficiaries need the protection most".[70] Therefore, even when facing economic difficulties, States Parties must not adopt regressive measures that lead to an overall reduction of protection of entire groups of persons and hence must evaluate the effects of their policies on vulnerable groups as persons in a situation of poverty or social exclusion.[71] This interpretation also applies to sanitary crises. In its "Statement on Covid-19 and Social Rights", the ECSR asserted that "States Parties to the European Social Charter must take all measures necessary, including through the redistribution of resources, to combat the virus and to secure the rights of their populations, including those of the most socially vulnerable groups".[72] Specifically, they should ensure that precarious and low-paid workers still enjoy all labour rights and that social and medical assistance reach effectively "the poorest and most vulnerable groups".[73] To that end, the ECSR asked States Parties to indicate in their national reports for 2020 the

67 ECSR, Conclusions 2017, Finland, Article 30; Conclusions 2013, Statement of Interpretation on Article 30, all countries.

68 ECSR, *European Roma Rights Centre* (*ERRC*) *v. France*, complaint No. 51/2008, decision on the merits of 19 October 2009, § 93.

69 ECSR, Conclusions 2013, Statement of Interpretation on Article 30, all countries.

70 ECSR, General Introduction to Conclusions XIX-2 (2009) on the repercussions of the economic crisis on social rights; *ECSR, GENOP-DEI and ADEDY v. Greece*, Complaint No. 65/2011, decision on the merits of 23 May 2012, § 16.

71 ECSR, *IKA-ETAM v. Greece*, complaint No. 76/2012, decision on the merits of 7 December 2012, § 79; ECSR, Conclusions XX-2 (2013), Spain, Article 11–1.

72 Statement adopted on 24 March 2021.

73 *Ibid.*

measures taken to ensure that no person falls below the poverty threshold during or after the Covid-19 crisis and the impact of these measures. But, as this information falls outside the period of reference, they will be assessed in the next report cycle.[74]

B *Access to Civil Rights and Citizen Participation*

In its decision *European Roma Rights Centre (ERRC) v. France*, the ECSR adopted an extensive interpretation of Article 30 protection including access to civil and political rights. Indeed, it considered "that the reference to the social rights enshrined in Article 30 should not be understood too narrowly. In fact, the fight against social exclusion is one area where the notion of the indivisibility of fundamental rights takes a special importance. In this regard, the right to vote, as with other rights relating to civic and citizen participation, constitutes a necessary dimension in social integration and inclusion and is thus covered by Article 30".[75] In the case in point, the Committee stated that the conditions laid down by French law for individuals without fixed domicile or residence exercising the right to vote are particularly unfavourable to Travellers and therefore discriminatory. Indeed, travellers "may only be added to the electoral roll after three years of uninterrupted attachment to the same municipality" while other persons without attached municipality can vote in the municipality "where the welfare provider with whom they have been enrolled for at least 6 months is located".[76] Moreover, the quota limit of 3% of the municipal electorate that can benefit from these specific attachments affects travellers in practice and thus, "is a possible cause of marginalisation and social exclusion".[77]

In its decision *COHRE v. Italy*,[78] the Committee developed its jurisprudence. Firstly, it applied its interpretation to a discriminatory situation in fact, noting that "the segregation and poverty situation affecting most of the Roma and Sinti population in Italy (…) is linked to a civil marginalisation due to the

---

74 ECSR, Conclusions 2021, Article 30, Andorra, Estonia, Latvia, Netherlands, Norway, Serbia, Slovak Republic, Slovenia, Sweden, Turkey and Ukraine.

75 ECSR, *European Roma Rights Centre (ERRC) v. France*, complaint No. 51/2008, decision on the merits of 19 October 2009.

76 *Ibid.*, § 101. This violation is reiterated in ECSR, *European Roma and Travellers Forum (ERTF) v. France*, complaint No. 64/2011, decision on the merits of 24 January 2012 as the law has not changed and that there is no proof that the Travellers can benefit from the application of the ordinary law.

77 *Ibid.*, § 104.

78 ECSR, *Centre on Housing Rights and Evictions (COHRE) v. Italy*, complaint No. 58/2009, decision on the merits of 25 June 2010.

failure of the authorities to address the Roma and Sinti's lack of identification documents. In fact, substandard living conditions in segregated camps imply likewise a lack of means to obtain residency and citizenship in order to exercise civil and political participation".[79] Secondly, the Committee specified that "Under Article 30, States have the positive obligation to encourage citizen participation in order to overcome obstacles deriving from the lack of representation of Roma and Sinti in the general culture, media or the different levels of government, so that these groups perceive that there are real incentives or opportunities for engagement to counter the lack of representation".[80] In consequence, citizen participation concerns not only the access to the right to vote but also the right to a dialogue and consultations with the authorities, the right to defend one's interests and concerns and to participate to the decision-making processes.[81]

C *Non-discrimination*

1 Transposition of Non-discrimination Case Law in Relation to Particularly Poor Vulnerable Groups

The Committee assessed various complaints invoking discriminatory treatments against groups suffering particular vulnerability. For instance, some complaints concerned the lack of sufficient and adequate housing offered to travellers or Roma and Sinti population and the forced evictions from sites where they were actually required to set up illegally. The ECSR concluded that there were violations of Article E in conjunction with Article 31 (Right to housing) but also in conjunction with Article 30. In these cases, the Committee transposed its jurisprudence relative to Article E and the principle of non-discrimination.[82] It condemned situations of direct discrimination when, for instance, national law provides for a different regime for Travellers than for the rest of the population, as seen *supra* concerning the conditions to access to the right to vote.[83] It also condemns measures that directly target these vulnerable groups in evicting them from camps or their being placed in isolated areas lacking minimal accommodations, which also constitutes direct discrimination.[84]

---

79 *Ibid.*, § 103.

80 *Ibid.*, § 104.

81 *Ibid.*, § 108–109.

82 Digest of the case law of the European Committee of Social Rights, 2018, pp. 231 ff.

83 ECSR, *European Roma Rights Centre* (*ERRC*) *v. France*, complaint No. 51/2008, decision on the merits of 19 October 2009; ECSR, *European Roma and Travellers Forum* (*ERTF*) *v. France*, complaint No. 64/2011, decision on the merits of 24 January 2012.

84 ECSR, *Centre on Housing Rights and Evictions* (*COHRE*) *v. Italy*, complaint No. 58/2009, decision on the merits of 25 June 2010, § 109.

Moreover, it condemned substantive discrimination when national authorities failed to adopt specific measures taking into account their specific vulnerability. In other terms, "the prohibition of discrimination, means treating equals equally and unequals unequally".[85] In consequence, the ECSR considered that "indirect discrimination may arise by failing to take due and positive account of all relevant differences or by failing to take adequate steps to ensure that the rights and collective advantages that are open to all are genuinely accessible by and to all".[86] For example, ensuring civil and political participation of the Roma and Sinti population, "not only requires strategies for empowerment from public authorities but also respect for ethnic identity and cultural choices". Thus, States Parties must adopt positive and specific measures to be in conformity with their obligations under the Charter.[87]

The case-law relative to the principle of non-discrimination is sometimes rather subtle due to the complexity of the question of equality in addition to the generality of the obligation under Article 30 which can be complied with despite the persistence of poverty among certain vulnerable groups. In the decision *FIDH v. Belgium*, No. 75/2011, the ECSR concluded that there was no violation of Article E taken in conjunction with Article 30, whereas it found a breach of Article 30 because of the State's failure to collect reliable data and statistics in respect of highly dependent persons with disabilities. Its conclusion arose from its choice to compare the situation of these persons not with the rest of the population but with other persons with disabilities. The Committee considered thus that this situation "constitutes a general and structural policy weakness regarding the collection of statistics on all persons with disabilities and does not specifically disadvantage highly dependent adults with disabilities".[88] Yet, there does seem to be a situation of discrimination, but one affecting the vulnerable group of persons with disabilities, compared to other persons.

Under the reporting mechanism, the ECSR does not monitor the principle of non-discrimination in terms of enjoying the right to protection against poverty

85 ECSR, *International Association Autism-Europe v. France*, complaint No. 13/2002, decision on the merits of 4 November 2003, § 52.

86 *Ibid.*

87 Cf. also ECSR, *European Roma Rights Centre (ERRC) v. Portugal*, complaint No. 61/2010, decision on the merits of 30 June 2011, § 71; ECSR, *International Federation of Human Rights (FIDH) v. Belgium*, complaint No. 62/2010, decision on the merits of 21 March 2010, §§ 204–205; ECSR, *Médecins du Monde – International v. France*, complaint No. 67/2011, decision on the merits of 11 September 2012, §§ 106–108.

88 ECSR, *International Federation of Human Rights (FIDH) v. Belgium*, complaint No. 75/2011, decision on the merits of 18 March 2013, § 218.

and social exclusion. However, States Parties are expected to take measures to strengthen the access to social rights of persons in those situations of poverty or social exclusion and "where necessary specifically target the most vulnerable groups and regions".[89] In consequence, the ECSR reviews the existence of specific measures and policies when it identifies specific groups suffering poverty or particularly at risk, even if it has never yet found a violation of Article 30 on the sole reason of the lack of these measures.

2 The Issue of Discrimination because of Poverty and Exclusion

It is worth noting that there is no precision in the practice of the Committee as to the question of discrimination on the grounds of being a poor or an excluded person. Nevertheless, Article 30 appears as the perfect disposition to enshrine this guarantee. This gap in the Charter's protection is even more surprising considering that the ECSR affirms that its interpretation of Article 30 is inspired by the United Nations' "Guiding principles on extreme poverty and human rights",[90] which explicitly developed this obligation. According to these principles, "Discrimination is both a cause and a consequence of poverty".[91] Thus, "All forms of legislative or administrative discrimination, direct or indirect, on grounds of economic situation or other grounds associated with poverty must be identified and eliminated".[92] In addition, "Equality and non-discrimination are immediate and cross-cutting obligations that must underlie all measures taken by all relevant stakeholders in relation to persons living in poverty" and that oblige States "to take special and positive measures to reduce or eliminate conditions that cause or help to perpetuate discrimination".[93]

In this regard, the collective complaint *EUROCEF v. France*, No. 82/2012 could have given the ECSR the opportunity to comment on this point. It concerned a French law that permits the suspension of family allowances in the event of truancy. When considering the allegation of the discriminatory character of this law due to its specific impact on the lower classes, the ECSR rejected

89 ECSR, Conclusions 2003, Statement of Interpretation on Article 30, all countries.

90 Cf. ECSR, Conclusions 2013, Statement of interpretation on Article 30; ECSR, *Defence for Children International (DCI) v. Belgium*, complaint No. 69/2011, decision on the merits of 23 October 2012, § 81; ECSR, *International Federation for Human Rights (FIDH) v. Ireland*, complaint No. 110/2014, decision on the merits of 12 May 2017, § 167.

91 Guiding principles on extreme poverty and human rights, submitted by the Special Rapporteur on extreme poverty and human rights, Magdalena Sepúlveda Carmona, Adopted by the General Assembly on 18th July 2012 and by the United Nations Human Rights Council on 27 September 2012, A/HRC/21/39, § 18.

92 *Ibid.*, § 19.

93 *Ibid.*, § 20.

it by holding that "taking into account its assessment [of no violation] under Article 30", "no separate issue arose" under the area of Article E in conjunction with Article 30.[94] To our point of view, this conclusion is not relevant insofar as the question of whether such a suspension challenges a comprehensive and coordinated approach to the fight against poverty is not the same as the question of whether it places an additional burden on people experiencing poverty without legitimate justification. A pending complaint,[95] related to a power outage in certain areas of a Madrid shanty town that has lasted for over two years, could be an opportunity for the Committee to change its jurisprudence. Indeed, the slow and insufficient reaction of the public authorities could be explained by the precariousness of the slum dwellers.

It is true that this type of discrimination is rarely invoked because few national laws explicitly condemn it, and even when they do, they actually sanction it.[96] In 2016,[97] France took such a step, unprecedented in Europe, by adding among the grounds of discrimination which may give rise to a criminal sanction[98] or employer sanctions under labour law[99] "the particular vulnerability resulting from their economic situation, apparent or known to the perpetrator".[100] The effectiveness of this prohibition has been discussed by experts, alleging in particular that economic status is not an intrinsic characteristic but a temporary situation, and therefore that would lead to a distortion of the principle of non-discrimination, suggesting that it could be an effective tool in the fight against poverty.[101] The advocates of this recognition consider that this is a step forward in the protection of poor and excluded persons who, because

---

94 ECSR, *European Committee for Home-Based Priority Action for the Child and the Family (EUROCEF) v. France*, complaint No. 82/2012, decision on admissibility and the merits of 19 March 2013, § 66.

95 ECSR, *Defence for Children International (DCI) and Others v. Spain*, complaint n° 206/2022, decision on admissibility and immediate measures of 19 October 2022.

96 Cf. the development and call to prohibit discrimination on the ground on socio-economic status in the Report "Tackling discrimination based on social origin", Doc. 15499, 11 April 2022 at the origin of PACE Resolution (2022), *Tackling discrimination based on social origin*, adopted on 26 April 2022.

97 Law 2016–832 *visant à lutter contre la discrimination à raison de la précarité*, of 24 June 2016.

98 Article 225 § 1 of the French Criminal Code.

99 Article L. 1132–1 of the French Labour Code.

100 Our translation of "la particulière vulnérabilité résultant de leur situation économique, apparente ou connue de son auteur".

101 Cf. The more reserved opinion of the Défenseur des droits, Avis n° 2015–15 du 9 juin 2015 sur la Proposition de loi n° 378 visant à lutter contre la discrimination à raison de la précarité sociale ; Gwenaële Calvès, "La discrimination à raison de la précarité sociale: progrès ou confusion?", *Revue de droit du travail*, 2016, p. 526.

of their stigmatisation, may have their access to social rights restricted.[102] Transposed to Article 30, this would require a demonstration of discrimination in the global and coordinated approach (or lack thereof) pursued by the State. This could be the case when the authorities' behaviour and choices in this area reflect denigration or depreciatory stereotypes against the most disadvantaged.

D *The Issue of Article 30's Autonomy*

The right to protection against poverty and social exclusion aims to protect people against a multi-dimensional phenomenon which concerns many State policies and regulations. This is reflected in Article 30 § 1, which lists, in a non-exhaustive manner, the rights to which access must be promoted by the States for the persons concerned: employment, housing, training, culture and social and medical assistance. However, many of these rights are formally recognised in other provisions. Article 30 must therefore be read in conjunction with these provisions, whose guarantees partly overlap with its own. However, this raises the question of the relationship between these guarantees and therefore, the autonomy of Article 30 in relation to them. In practical terms, does a finding of non-compliance with one of these provisions in relation to precarious persons automatically entail a violation of Article 30, and vice versa? Although this difficulty was anticipated by the drafters of the Charter, the case law of the ECSR initially seemed to hold that the assessment of compliance with Article 30 was dependent on compliance with other provisions of the Charter (1). Subsequently, the Committee clarified the nature of the relationship between this provision and the others, confirming the autonomy of Article 30. Since then, recent practice has been stabilising, despite some uncertainty (2).

1 Initial Period: Clear Statement but No Clear Practice

The necessary overlap between Article 30 and certain provisions of the Revised Social Charter had been anticipated by the drafters of the Charter. Some national delegates had argued that there was no need for such a provision, considering that the fight against poverty was already implicitly included in other articles, such as Article 1 (Right to employment) and Article 13 (Right to social assistance). Therefore, the drafters were careful to specify in the Explanatory report of the Charter that "The purpose of the Article is not to

---

102 Cf. Commission nationale consultative des droits de l'homme, Avis sur les discriminations fondées sur la précarité sociale (Assemblée plénière du 26 septembre 2013); Diane Roman, "La discrimination à raison de la précarité sociale: progrès ou confusion?", *Revue de droit du travail*, 2016, p. 526.

repeat the juridical aspects of the protection covered by other Articles of the Revised Charter although Parties may naturally refer to information given in respect of other provisions when reporting under this provision".[103] Article 30 therefore guarantees an autonomous right, distinct from the other rights in the Charter, even though certain measures adopted by States to implement another social right may also be relevant to demonstrate their action to combat poverty and social exclusion.

However, the first decision's ruling on the grounds of violation of Article 30 in the context of the collective complaints' procedure may have raised doubts as to its autonomy. Thus, in the decision *ATD Quart monde v. France*[104] of 2007, the Committee referred to its conclusion in respect of Article 31 that "the policy in respect of housing for the poorest is insufficient" to conclude that "Therefore, it finds a lack of a co-ordinated approach to promote the effective access of persons who live or risk living in a situation of extreme poverty to housing".[105] Thus, the failure to respect the right to housing of the poor, in and of itself, leads to a violation of Article 30. In the same vein, in its decision *ERRC v. Portugal*, the ECSR held that there is a violation of Article E taken in conjunction with Article 30 because of "the inability and unwillingness of central authorities to correctly oversee/coordinate the implementation of housing programmes at the local level taking into consideration the specific situation of Roma",[106] which is materially the same reason why it found a violation of Article E in conjunction with Article 31 § 2. The Committee adopted a similar conclusion in 2012, concerning the effective access to housing of migrant Roma in France.[107] It should be admitted that the guarantee of Article 31 § 2, which commits States Parties "to prevent and reduce homelessness with a view to its gradual elimination", overlaps with that of Article 30. Homeless persons are *a priori* in a situation of poverty and undoubtedly excluded from society. However, the absence of any additional consideration when assessing compliance with Article 30 could have suggested a total lack of autonomy for Article 30.

---

103 "113. The purpose of the Article is not to repeat the juridical aspects of the protection covered by other Articles of the Revised Charter although Parties may naturally refer to information given in respect of other provisions when reporting under this provision".

104 ECSR, *International Movement ATD Fourth World v. France*, complaint No. 33/2006, decision on the merits of 5 December 2007.

105 *Ibid.*, § 169.

106 ECSR, *European Roma Rights Centre (ERRC) v. Portugal*, complaint No. 61/2010, decision on the merits of 30 June 2011, § 71.

107 ECSR, *Médecins du Monde – International v. France*, complaint No. 67/2011, decision on the merits of 11 September 2012.

2 Since 2013: Clarified Principles but Subtle Application

This unsatisfactory situation has certainly been identified by the Committee, which in its 2013 Conclusions devotes several paragraphs to the issue of autonomy.

Thus, the Committee started by recalling the crucial principles guiding its interpretation, namely the effectiveness of human rights[108] and the human rights approach. Concerning the latter principle, it specified that it "has been recently reaffirmed by the Guiding Principles on extreme poverty and human rights (submitted by the Special Rapporteur on extreme poverty and human rights, Magdalena Sepúlveda Carmona and adopted by the United Nations Human Rights Council on 27 September 2012)". According to these Guiding Principles, "A human rights approach respects the dignity and autonomy of persons living in poverty and empowers them to meaningfully and effectively participate in public life, including in the design of public policy, and to hold duty bearers accountable".[109]

Interpreting Article 30 in the light of these two crucial principles, the Committee specifies that it "has interpreted the scope of Article 30 as relating both to protection against poverty (understood as involving situations of social precarity) and protection against social exclusion (understood as involving obstacles to inclusion and citizen participation), in an autonomous manner or in combination with other connecting provisions of the Charter".[110] Indeed, it states that poverty "can arise *inter alia* from the failure of States Parties to fulfil the obligation 'to ensure that all individuals have the right of access to health care and that the health system must be accessible to the entire population' (*DCI v. Belgium*, Complaint No. 69/2011, decision on the merits of 23 October 2012, par. 100; violation of Article 11); to provide a minimum income to persons in need (*ERRC v. Bulgaria*, Complaint No. 48/2008, decision on the merits of 18 February 2009; violation of Article 13), or to adopt a co-ordinated approach to promoting effective access to housing for persons who live or risk living in a situation of social exclusion (*International Movement ATD Fourth World v. France*, Complaint No. 33/2006, decision on the merits of 5 December 2007, paras.

---

108 "the aim and purpose of the Charter, being a human rights protection instrument, is to protect rights not merely theoretically, but also in fact (*International Commission of Jurists v. Portugal*, Complaint No. 1/1999, decision on the merits of 9 September 1999, para. 32)".

109 Guiding principles on extreme poverty and human rights, submitted by the Special Rapporteur on extreme poverty and human rights, Magdalena Sepúlveda Carmona, Adopted by the General Assembly on 18 July 2012 and by the United Nations Human Rights Council on 27 September 2012, A/HRC/21/39, § 7.

110 ECSR, Conclusions 2013, Statement of interpretation on Article 30.

169–170; violation of Articles 30 and 31)". Also, in its opinion, "In this context, by reaffirming this human rights approach, the Committee emphasizes the very close link between the effectiveness of the right recognized by Article 30 of the Charter and the enjoyment of the rights recognized by other provisions, such as the right to work (Article 1), access to health care (Article 11), social security allowances (Article 12), social and medical assistance (Article 13), the benefit from social welfare services (Article 14), the rights of persons with disabilities (Article 15), the social, legal and economic protection of the family (Article 16), as well as of children and young persons (Article 17), right to equal opportunities and equal treatment in employment and occupation without sex discrimination (Article 20), the rights of the elderly (Article 23) and the right to housing (Article 31), without forgetting the important impact of the non-discrimination clause (Article E), which obviously includes non-discrimination on grounds of poverty".[111] The Committee therefore acknowledges the interrelationship between Article 30 and many other provisions of the Charter. However, aware of the difficulties of coherence in the interpretation and monitoring of the Charter that these provisions may entail, it provides clarification as to how to take into account any assessments of compliance or non-compliance with them when assessing compliance with Article 30.

The Committee concludes in the same Statement of interpretation that "Consequently, together with the indicators mentioned above, when assessing the respect of Article 30, the Committee also takes into consideration the national measures or practices which fall within the scope of other substantive provisions of the Charter in the framework of both monitoring systems (the reporting procedure and the collective complaint procedure). This approach does not mean that a conclusion of non-conformity or a decision of violation of one or several of these provisions automatically or necessarily leads to a violation of Article 30 (*EUROCEF v. France*, Complaint No. 82/2012, decision on the merits of 19 March 2013, para. 59); however, such a conclusion or decision may, depending on the circumstances, be relevant in assessing conformity with Article 30. Indeed, the conclusion reached by the Committee on the existence of one or several violations of these provisions should not be conceived as an exception which confirms the existence of a generally satisfactory overall and co-ordinated approach, but rather as a substantial weakness affecting an essential pillar (or several) of the fundamental obligations of States Parties contained in Article 30 in relation to protection against poverty and social exclusion".[112]

---

111 *Ibid.*

112 *Ibid.*

The infringement of other provisions of the Charter whose guarantees overlap with those of Article 30 does not therefore automatically lead to a violation of the latter. It is, however, an element to be considered in monitoring compliance with this article as an indication of a weakness in the policy to combat poverty. The decisions adopted following the 2013 Statement of Interpretation seem to apply this *modus operandi*. Thus, in 2014, in a decision *FEANTSA v. the Netherlands*,[113] the ECSR had to assess a claim regarding the failure of Dutch legislation and municipalities' practice of providing sufficient shelter to homeless people. It started by reaffirming the autonomy of Article 30 with respect to the right to housing despite evident links, recalling "that a policy with respect to housing does not as such satisfy the requirements of Article 30, but the States Parties must promote an effective access to housing by those living or who risk living in social exclusion or poverty".[114] Nevertheless, the ECSR concluded that there was a violation of Article 30 taking into account the previous findings of violation of the other Charter Articles invoked. Indeed, "The Committee considers that in light of the findings made under Articles 31 § 2, 13 §§ 1 and 4, as well as 19 § 4, it follows that the legislation and policy concerning the access to emergency shelter have brought about a situation where homeless persons in need of shelter are not offered shelter regardless of genuine need". Furthermore, "the Committee finds that the coordination between the responsible authorities is currently insufficient for the purposes of Article 30".[115] Thus, it seems that violations of other Articles are indeed considered in assessing compliance with Article 30, but as an additional indication of failure. The Committee uses here a sort of "*faisceau d'indices*" technique ("bundle of evidence").

Later on, the autonomy of Article 30 was particularly illustrated by the *ERRC v. Ireland*,[116] decision in which the Committee considered that the specific measures taken by the State in relation to travellers' accommodation were part of a comprehensive and coordinated approach, despite the previous finding of a violation of Article 16 due to the inadequacy of accommodation solutions for travellers and the insufficiency of their legal protection in case of eviction. This dissociation of guarantees was however criticised by one of the Committee members, Petros Stangos, in a dissenting opinion. In his view,

---

113 ECSR, *European Federation of National Organisations working with the Homeless* (*FEANTSA*) *v. the Netherlands*, complaint No. 86/2012, decision on the merits of 2 July 2014.

114 *Ibid.*, § 225.

115 *Ibid.*, §§ 229–230.

116 ECSR, *European Roma Rights Centre* (*ERRC*) *v. Ireland*, complaint No. 100/2013, decision on the merits of 1 December 2015.

such an interpretation does not respect the spirit of the 2013 Statement of Interpretation, the "practical purpose [of which] is to ensure that a national measure or practice which is suspected of posing a major risk of social exclusion or poverty and has been examined under another substantive provision will be examined again under Article 30. To some degree, the national measure or practice concerned should be routinely 'reread' or 're-examined' by the Committee under Article 30 in conjunction with the other substantive provision of the Charter". In this case, however, it considered that the Committee has not decided on the same concrete measures and practices under Article 30 as under Article 16.

Despite this, the Committee confirmed again the autonomy of the requirements of Article 30 by finding compliance with this article notwithstanding the violation of Article 16 due to the inadequacy of the social housing stock in Ireland.[117] It considers that "the Government has adopted several measures to improve the situation of those living in social housing in the most deprived areas" and "considers therefore that there are elements indicating efforts by Ireland towards a coordinated approach to protect persons from poverty and combat social exclusion in general". Moreover, "the complaint does not provide information on the possible obstacles for people living in local authority housing to access fundamental social rights other than adequate family housing (…), or on lack of measures or coordinated approach on the part of the Government to overcome such obstacles".[118] In a subsequent decision *EUROCEF v. France*, complaint No. 114/2015, the Committee follows the same reasoning, stating that if "the situation of certain minors could expose them to poverty and social exclusion (…) there are elements indicating efforts by France towards a coordinated approach to protect" them.[119] It seems thus that the sole violation of other Articles is not sufficient to conclude on violation of Article 30 if it is not accompanied by further evidence of a broader lack of an overall and coordinated policy. However, it appears that the members of the Committee are not unanimous in their interpretation of Article 30, as in this case, compliance with Article 30 was not voted by five of its members. As Petros Stangos explains in his dissenting opinion, the violations of Articles 7 § 10, 11 § 1, 13 § 1, 17 §§ 1 and 2 and 31 § 2 prove "that this particularly

---

117 ECSR, *International Federation for Human Rights* (*FIDH*) *v. Ireland*, complaint No. 110/2014, decision on the merits of 12 May 2017.

118 *Ibid.*, §§ 168–169.

119 ECSR, *European Committee for Home-Based Priority Action for the Child and the Family* (*EUROCEF*) *v. France*, complaint No. 114/2015, decision on the merits of 24 January 2018, § 185.

vulnerable group residing on French territory is still exposed to poverty and social exclusion".[120]

The practice of the Committee is therefore clearly not stabilised as to the extent to which the violation(s) of the Articles in relation to Article 30 do or do not reflect the absence of an overall and coordinated approach. In particular, some decisions appear to require some sort of minimum result obligation (Article 30 is violated when some individuals are excluded from protection), while other articles require States to provide only an obligation of means. Nor does an analysis of the conclusions adopted under the reporting procedure provide definitive clarification. Indeed, in accordance with the 2013 Statement of Interpretation and from the 2017 conclusions onwards,[121] the violation of one or more other Article(s) is one of the elements taken into consideration to assess the absence of an overall or coordinated approach, even if it does not in itself lead to a finding of non-compliance. The first ad hoc report on the cost-of-living crisis should contribute to further clarify the normative content of Article 30.[122]

Concluding Remarks

The problems of poverty and social exclusion are particularly complex to understand as multidimensional phenomena. Article 30 and the Committee's case law on the subject are therefore particularly stimulating because of their evolving nature as these phenomena change and are better understood. The unprecedented nature of this right within European and international human rights law makes the monitoring of the Committee's interpretations all the more valuable and worthwhile. Despite the fact that case law on this matter is still under construction, certain clarifications regarding the obligations expected of States Parties have been identified. On the one hand, States must justify the existence of a global and coordinated approach of their public policies affecting the fight against poverty and exclusion, as well as the allocation of sufficient resources for its effectiveness. They must also adopt a cross-cutting vision of the obstacles to the enjoyment of human rights by the persons concerned who also suffer from violations of their civil and political

120 Dissenting opinion of Petros Stangos on *EUROCEF v. France*, complaint No. 114/2015, *cit.*

121 ECSR, Conclusions 2017, Article 30, Belgium, Ireland, Italy, Latvia, Serbia, Slovak Republic, Turkey and Ukraine; Conclusions 2021, Article 30, Estonia, Latvia, Serbia, Turkey, and Ukraine.

122 See Questions to State Partie on an ad hoc report on the cost-of-living crisis.

rights. In addition, they must ensure that no group is discriminated against, either because of stigmatisation or because their specificity is not taken into account. The multidimensional nature of poverty and exclusion leads to multiple interactions with other Charter rights, raising the question of the autonomy of Article 30 in relation to the infringements of these rights. However, the Committee's interpretative practice helps to clarify this point.

ARTICLE 31

The Right to Housing

Silvio Troilo

With a view to ensuring the effective exercise of the right to housing, the Parties undertake to take measures designed:

1. to promote access to housing of an adequate standard;
2. to prevent and reduce homelessness with a view to its gradual elimination;
3. to make the price of housing accessible to those without adequate resources.

∴

Introduction

The right to housing – a broad expression referring to a set of more specific rights related to adequate housing and living conditions – is a crucial social one, closely connected to other important civil, economic, and social freedoms. It may be defined as "the right to live somewhere in security, peace and dignity"[1] and secures inclusion and integration of individuals into society by contributing to overcoming socio-economic inequalities.[2]

Housing-related rights are now considered an integral part of economic, social and cultural rights within many human rights instruments adopted by the United Nations, the Council of Europe, the European Union, besides inter-American and African organizations. Nevertheless, on the Old Continent, a specific and autonomous right to housing is only expressly provided for in the

---

1 Council of Europe, "Recommendation of the Commissioner for Human Rights on the Implementation of the Right to Housing", CommDH(2009)5, p. 3, available at https://www.refworld.org/docid/4a49f6062.html.

2 ECSR, *European Roma Rights Centre (ERRC) v. Italy*, complaint No. 27/2004, decision on the merits of 7 December 2005, "Scope of Article 31" after § 18.

 | DOI:10.1163/9789004434158_013

revised European Social Charter, which is therefore of peculiar importance and represents a pioneering instrument in this regard.

On a national level, in Europe, several constitutions refer to housing or housing rights. However, only a few countries recognize (some of) these rights as individual justiciable ones,[3] while in others a principle is enshrined, which has then to be realized through appropriate laws and resources.[4] Furthermore, most national constitutions do not contemplate housing adequacy as a subject of rights in relations between private individuals and public authorities.

The right to housing is, instead, guaranteed at international and national levels mostly as a part of other rights, for instance to an adequate standard of living, respect for private and family life, etc.

According to the practice of major international organizations operating in this field,[5] the most problematic situations can be traced back, apart from the consequences of natural disasters, to three types of facts: expropriations and evictions, especially when perpetrated on a large scale; discrimination in access to housing against particularly vulnerable categories of people (such as ethnic minorities, women, immigrants); the housing condition of individuals in poverty, often related to the increase in urban settlements as a result of the movement of people to cities, with the creation of entire neighbourhoods of inadequate, unhealthy housing or those lacking essential services.

---

3 Mainly in the constitutional charters of Belgium (Article 23 § 3 No. 3), Portugal (Article 65), and Spain (Article 47), where in any cases specific access to decent housing has to be considered "a constitutional objective to be achieved progressively" rather than a real right (in this sense, for example, the Belgian Constitutional Court). But also in France (where §§ 10–11 of the preamble to the 1946 constitution, referred to in the current one, expressly stipulate only that the State guarantees the individual and the family the conditions necessary for their development and material security) and Italy (where only the State's commitment to facilitate access to home ownership is expressly stated in Article 47) this right is considered implicitly provided for in their respective constitutions – within limits similar to those mentioned above – according to the rulings of their constitutional courts (Conseil constitutionnel français, 19 Janvier 1995, déc. No. 94–359 DC; Corte costituzionale italiana, sent. 7 Aprile 1988, No. 404 and sent. 9 Marzo 2020, No. 44).

4 See, in particular, the constitutions of Finland (Article 19 § 4), Greece (Article 21 § 4), the Netherlands (Article 22 § 2), Poland (Article 75), Sweden (Cap. I, Article 2 § 2), Switzerland (Article 41 § 1 (e)), Turkey (Article 57).

5 See, in particular, the Report of the United Nations Special Rapporteur on Adequate Housing Miloon Kothari of 13 February 2008 (UN Doc. A/HRC/7/16). See also the Statement on Adequate Housing on World Habitat Day of 1 October 2007, by the same Special Rapporteur, available on the website of the United Nations High Commissioner for Human Rights www.ohchr.org. Cf., among others, Francesco Bestagno, "Gli obblighi internazionali in materia di abitazione adeguata", in Francesco Bestagno (ed.), *I diritti economici, sociali e culturali. Promozione e tutela nella comunità internazionale*, Milano, Vita e Pensiero, 2009, pp. 87–88.

I Relevant International Standards

A *The United Nations' Instruments*

Within the framework of the United Nations, in addition to a reference in Article 25 of the Universal Declaration of Human Rights of 1948, the right under consideration is guaranteed by the two International Covenants of 1966, under the profile of the prohibition of "arbitrary or unlawful interference with his or her privacy, family, home or correspondence" (Article 17 ICCPR) and the profile of "the right of everyone to an adequate standard of living for himself and his family, including adequate food, clothing and housing, and to the continuous improvement of living conditions" (Article 11 ICESCR).[6]

These instruments do not prescribe the nature of housing systems to be adopted by ratifying States, but require recognizing, respecting and protecting housing rights to meet "minimum core" obligations, to ensure non-discrimination and direct legislative measures, appropriate policies, and the maximum of available resources toward a progressive realization of these rights.[7]

Further relevant United Nations instruments include international conventions dedicated to specific categories of individuals which, in particular, enshrine the prohibition of discrimination in access to and enjoyment of adequate housing. In addition to racial discrimination, forbidden by the relevant general convention,[8] other treaties, promoted especially by the United Nations, identify refugees,[9] women,[10] children,[11] migrant

6 Article 11 ICESCR adds that "The States Parties will take appropriate steps to ensure the realization of this right, recognizing to this effect the essential importance of international co-operation based on free consent".

7 Cf. Padraic Kenna, "International Instruments on Housing Rights", *Journal of Legal Affairs and Dispute Resolution in Engineering and Construction*, Vol. 2, No. 1, 2010, p. 12. See also: Philip Alston and Gerald Quinn, "The Nature and Scope of States Parties Obligations under International Covenant on Economic, Social and Cultural Rights", *Human Rights Quarterly*, Vol. 9, No. 2, 1987, pp. 156–229; Manisuli Ssenyonjo, *Economic, Social and Cultural Rights in International Law*, 2nd ed., London, Hart Publishing/Bloomsbury, 2016, pp. 78–156.

8 See Article 5 (e)(iii) of the International Convention on the Elimination of All Forms of Racial Discrimination of 21 December 1965.

9 See Article 21 of the Convention Relating to the Status of Refugees of 28 July 1951, devoted to the right of refugees to the most favourable treatment possible with respect to housing.

10 See Article 14 § 2 (h) of the Convention on the Elimination of All Forms of Discrimination against Women of 18 December 1979, which includes housing as part of the right to benefit from decent living conditions.

11 See Article 27 of the Convention on the Rights of the Child of 20 November 1989, which provides for housing as one of the conditions necessary for a sufficient standard of living to enable the child to develop.

workers,[12] persons with disabilities[13] and elderly people[14] as in need of specific housing protection. Provisions relating to the right to adequate housing are also found in conventions promoted by the International Labour Organization (ILO),[15] as well as in declarations or recommendations of the ILO itself and other international organizations.[16]

B *The United Nations' Comments*

There have been many attempts to clarify the contents of international housing rights, including the concepts of "minimum core obligations" and progressive realization of rights according to available resources,[17] even through indicators and benchmarks.[18]

---

12 See Article 43 § 1 (d) of the International Convention on the Protection of the Rights of All Migrant Workers and Members of Their Families of 18 December 1990, which provides for equal treatment in access to housing and the possibility of protection against excessive rents.

13 The Convention on the Rights of Persons with Disabilities of 13 December 2006 devotes several provisions to the non-discriminatory access of such persons to "reasonable accommodation". See also Committee on ESCR, general comment No. 5, on persons with disabilities (UN Doc. E/1995/22), and general comment No. 14, on the right to the highest attainable standard of health (UN Doc. E/C.12/2000/4).

14 See Committee on ESCR, general comment No. 6, on the economic, social, and cultural rights of older persons (UN Doc. E/1996/22).

15 See, in particular, ILO Recommendation No. 115 concerning workers' housing (1961); ILO Convention No. 117 concerning basic aims and standards of social policy (1962); ILO Convention No. 161 concerning occupational health services (1985); and ILO Domestic Workers Convention No. 189 (2011).

16 See, in particular: UN Agenda 2030 for Sustainable Development (2015), according to which States have to ensure "by 2030, […] access for all to adequate, safe and affordable housing and basic services and upgrade slums" (Goal No. 11.1); Instanbul Declaration on Human Settlements (1996); Geneva UN Charter on Sustainable Housing (2015); World Health Organisation, "Housing and Health Guidelines" (2018).

17 See the Report of the Special Rapporteur on Adequate Housing to the UN Commission on Human Rights, 3 March 2005 (UN Doc. E/CN.4/2005/48). See also the conclusions and reports of the Committee on ESCR at http://www.ohchr.org/en/treaty-bodies/cescr. Cf.: Padraic Kenna, *cit.*, p. 13; Dipak K. Gupta, Albert J. Jongman and Alex P. Schmid, "Creating a Composite Index for Assessing Country Performance in the Field of Human Rights: Proposal for a New Methodology", *Human Rights Quarterly*, Vol. 16, No. 1, 1994, pp. 131–162.

18 See: Report of Secretary General on indicators and benchmarks (UN Doc. E/EN4/2000/47); UN General Assembly, "Report of the Seminar on appropriate indicators to measure achievements in the progressive realization of economic, social and cultural rights", Geneva, January 25–29, 1993 (UN Doc. A/CONF.157/PC/73); United Nations Human Settlements Programme, "Urban Indicators Guidelines. Monitoring the Habitat Agenda and the Millennium Development Goals", available at http://www.urbanagendaplatform.org. See also Scott Leckie, "Another Step towards Indivisibility: Identifying the Key Features

At the United Nations level, the Committee on Economic, Social and Cultural Rights has devoted considerable effort to the study of this right, compared to the others under the ICESCR, with the publication of general comment No. 4 (1991), dedicated to the right to housing in general, as well as general comment No. 7 (1997), on the phenomenon of forced evictions.[19] In addition, the Committee has intervened in a number of concrete cases over the years under the Optional Protocol to the ICESCR, on the basis of complaints by those concerned, further specifying States' obligations.[20] At the same time, the

---

of Violations of Economic, Social and Cultural Rights", *Human Rights Quarterly*, Vol. 20, No. 1, 1998, pp. 81–99; Maria Green, "What We Talk about When We Talk about Indicators: Current Approaches to Human Rights Measurement", *Human Rights Quarterly*, Vol. 23, No. 4, 2001, pp. 1063–1097.

19 See Committee on ESCR, general comment No. 4, "The right to adequate housing (Article 11 (1) of the Covenant)", 13 December 1991 (UN Doc. E/C.12/1991/4) and general comment No. 7, "The right to adequate housing (Article 11 (1) of the Covenant): forced evictions", 20 May 1997 (UN Doc. E/C.12/1997/4).

20 For a broad overview of obligations imposed by Article 11 ICESCR, arising "from the interpretation of the State Party's obligations under article 2 (1) of the Covenant, read in conjunction with article 11, and in accordance with the requirements of article 4" (as pointed out in the Views adopted on 5 March 2020 in the case *Gómez-Limón Pardo v. Spain*, E/C.12/67/D/52/2018, § 9.4), see, in particular, the Views adopted on 23 November 2021 in the case *Lorne J. Walters v. Belgium* (E/C.12/70/D/61/2018): "in order for an eviction to be justifiable" in light of the right to adequate housing, "it must meet a number of requirements. Firstly, the possibility of eviction must be determined by law. Secondly, it must promote the general welfare in a democratic society. Thirdly, it must be proportionate to the aim pursued. Fourthly, it must be necessary, in that, where there are several means reasonably capable of achieving the legitimate aim of the limitation, the one that is the least restrictive must be selected. Lastly, the benefits of the limitation in promoting the general welfare must outweigh the impact of the limitation on the enjoyment of the right. [...] This inevitably involves making a distinction between properties belonging to individuals who need them as a home or to provide vital income and properties belonging to financial institutions or other entities" (§ 9.3; see also the Views adopted on 11 October 2019 in the case *López Albán v. Spain*, E/C.12/66/D/37/2018, § 11.5). In addition, "the State Party has a duty to take reasonable measures to provide alternative housing to persons who are left homeless as a result of eviction, irrespective of whether the eviction is initiated by its authorities or by private entities such as the owner of the property" (§ 10.1; see also the Views adopted on 20 June 2017 in the case *Ben Djazia and Bellili v. Spain*, E/C.12/61/D/5/2015, § 15.2). Furthermore, "in accordance with the principle of affordability, tenants should be protected by appropriate means against unreasonable rent levels or rent increases and against any undesirable effects that such legislation may have on vulnerable groups, such as older persons" (§ 11.4). Finally, to avoid a disproportionate impact of legislation, albeit compatible in the abstract with the Covenant, on the right to adequate housing of certain groups in vulnerable situations, States Parties "must [first] establish a mechanism to monitor the impact of the application of the legal framework on the most vulnerable and marginalized groups in order to introduce the necessary adjustments [...].

Commission on Human Rights (now replaced by the Human Rights Council) has appointed a Special Rapporteur to deal exclusively with "adequate housing as a component of the right to an adequate standard of living", who liaises with national governments, conducts site visits, receives individual complaints and submits very detailed annual reports.[21]

The reconstruction of the law and related international obligations undertaken mainly by the Committee on ESCR, although it covers only Article 11 of the ICESCR per se, has stood as a point of reference for the interpretation of the other international instruments on the right to housing, such as the European Social Charter and further conventional provisions.[22]

The aforementioned comments outline a conception of housing not as a mere shelter, or as "a roof over one's head", but as a place where every person must have the opportunity to live stably and with dignity.[23] In summary, the essential factors for the right to be considered realized are identified in the satisfaction of minimum housing needs, consisting of access to housing that meets the requirements of habitability, not excessive cost, with the availability of essential infrastructure and services, adequate with respect to cultural traditions, and with regard to which the domestic system provides protection at the legal level.[24]

Second, the policy must include mechanisms and flexibility to ensure that the application of the legal framework does not have a disproportionate impact in certain cases" (§ 12.3).

21 These reports, drafted by successive Rapporteurs, can be found at https://www.ohchr.org/fr/special-procedures/sr-housing/annual-thematic-reports-special-rapporteur-adequate-housing. See also the Guidelines for the Implementation of the Right to Adequate Housing of 26 December 2019, by the same Special Rapporteur (UN Doc. A/HRC/43/43).

22 About the influence on the European Social Charter's interpretation, see the decision of the European Committee of Social Rights in the case *European Federation of National Organisations Working with the Homeless* (FEANTSA) *v. France*, complaint No. 39/2006, decision on the merits of 7 December 2007, § 65, which refers to general comments No. 4 and No. 7 and the Reports of the Special Rapporteur, Miloon Kothari. In general, on the relevance of the principles expressed by the ICESCR and Committee on ESCR as an interpretative reference point for other covenant provisions on housing rights, see Scott Leckie, "The Human Right to Adequate Housing", in Asbiørn Aide, Catarina Krause and Allan Rosas (eds.), *Economic, Social and Cultural Rights*, 2nd ed., Martinus Nijhoff Publishers, Dordrecht-Boston-London, 2002, p. 153.

23 See Committee on ESCR, general comment No. 4, *cit.*, § 7. It should be noted that the preparatory work of the ICESCR shows that the expression "adequate housing" was preferred to the expression "dwelling consistent with human dignity" because it was considered more far-reaching: cf. Matthew Craven, *The International Covenant on Economic, Social and Cultural Rights. A Perspective on its Development*, Oxford, Clarendon Press, 1995, p. 290.

24 See Committee on ESCR, general comment No. 4, *cit.*, § 8.

C The European Convention on Human Rights

In the context of the Council of Europe, although the right to housing is not specifically enshrined in the European Convention on Human Rights (ECHR), Article 8 of this instrument guarantees the protection of private and family life and home, and Protocol No. 1 to the ECHR the protection of possessions, of which the Strasbourg Court has given a broad interpretation, including, in some cases, the right to housing.[25] In particular, the Court has recognized a wide meaning to the notion of "home", excluding only situations where putting a particular place within the scope of home would mean to interpret Article 8 § 1 beyond its objective.[26] This complies with the conviction that the European Convention is a living instrument which has to be read in light of present-day conditions.

So, while there is no duty under the ECHR for a universal State housing provision,[27] certain positive obligations have been found by the Court under

---

25 If Article 8 ECHR and Article 1 of Protocol No. 1 happen to be among the most frequently invoked provisions before the Court, also Article 3 (prohibition of torture or inhuman or degrading treatment or punishment), Article 6 (right to fair trial) and Article 14 (prohibition of discrimination) have sometimes been interpreted by the Strasbourg Court in the context of housing. See the Court's case law analysis on the official website https://www.ks.echr.coe.int/en/web/echr-ks/ and, among others, Francesco Bestagno, *cit.*, pp. 112–116; Arturs Kucs, Zane Sedlova and Liene Pierhurovica, "The Right to Housing: International, European and National Perspectives", *Cuadernos Constitucionales de la Cátedra Fadrique Furió Ceriol*, No. 64/65, 2008, pp. 105–106.

26 According to the Strasbourg Court, "home" is an autonomous concept, which does not depend on classification under domestic law, and it is a wide term, given that the French equivalent "domicile" has a broader connotation: see ECtHR, 24 November 1986, *Gillow v. the United Kingdom*, No. 9063/80, § 46; ECtHR, 16 December 1992, *Niemietz v. Germany*, No. 13710/88, § 30; Antoine Buyse, "Strings Attached: the Concept of 'Home' in the Case Law of the European Court of Human Rights", *European Human Rights Law Review*, Vol. 6, No. 3, 2006, pp. 294–307; Arturs Kucs, Zane Sedlova and Liene Pierhurovica, *cit.*, pp. 106–108.

27 "It is important to recall that Article 8 does not in terms recognise a right to be provided with a home. Nor does any of the jurisprudence of the Court acknowledge such a right. While it is clearly desirable that every human being have a place where he or she can live in dignity and which he or she can call home, there are unfortunately in the Contracting States many persons who have no home. Whether the State provides funds to enable everyone to have a home is a matter for political not judicial decision" (ECtHR, 18 January 2001, *Chapman v. the United Kingdom*, No. 27238/95, § 99). Even recently the Strasbourg Court reiterated that Article 8 "does not recognise, as such, a right to be provided with a home [...] nor does it confer a right to live in a particular location [...] or guarantee the right to have one's housing problems solved by the authorities, as the scope of any positive obligation to house the homeless is limited" (ECtHR, 31 March 2022, *Faulkner v. Ireland and McDonagh v. Ireland*, Nos. 30391/18 and 30416/18, § 98).

Article 8,[28] particularly in relation to protection against smells and nuisance from a waste treatment plant,[29] toxic emissions emanating from a chemical factory,[30] environmental pollution from a steel plant,[31] and noise from bars and nightclubs.[32]

In *Marzari v. Italy* and other cases,[33] the obligation for public authorities to provide housing assistance to an individual suffering from a severe disability was recognized in the abstract, because of the impact of the relevant refusal on his private life. Respect for domicile may also imply the adoption by public authorities of measures to secure such a right even in the sphere of relations between individuals, for instance by preventing others from entering and interfering with the applicant's home.[34]

In a line of case law concerning the situation of the Roma,[35] the Strasbourg Court has recognized the positive obligation on the contracting States, under Article 8 ECHR, to facilitate the lifestyle of gypsies, which involves travelling around and settling in different places: indeed, as members of a minority in a vulnerable position, they must be given a special consideration for their needs and their different way of life both in the relevant regulatory framework and in reaching decisions in particular cases.[36] Moreover, due attention must be

28 On which cf., among others, Padraic Kenna, "Housing Rights: Positive Duties and Enforceable Rights at the European Court of Human Rights", *European Human Rights Law Review*, Vol. 8, No. 2, 2008, pp. 193–208. On the influence of the Court's interpretative convergences and judicial dialogue with the European Committee of Social Rights in the recognition of these positive obligations, see Christina Deliyanni-Dimitrakou, "The European Social Charter and the European Convention on Human Rights", in ANESC, *The European Social Charter: A Commentary*, Vol. 1, Leiden, Brill, 2022, pp. 361–364.

29 ECtHR, 9 December 1994, *López Ostra v. Spain*, No. 16798/90.

30 ECtHR, 19 February 1998, *Guerra and Others v. Italy*, No. 14967/89.

31 ECtHR, final 30 November 2005, *Fadeyeva v. Russia*, No. 55723/00.

32 ECtHR, final 16 February 2005, *Moreno Gomez v. Spain*, No. 4143/02.

33 ECtHR, dec. 4 May 1999, *Marzari v. Italy*, No. 36448/97; ECtHR, dec. 13 May 2000, *Maggiolini v. Italy*, No. 35800/97. See also ECtHR, 24 February 1998, *Botta v. Italy*, No. 36448/97, §§ 33–34 (with specific regard to architectural barriers in public buildings).

34 ECtHR, final 10 November 2004, *Surugiu v. Romania*, No. 48995/99, § 59, and references therein.

35 In particular ECtHR, *Chapman v. the United Kingdom*; ECtHR, final 27 August 2004, *Connors v. the United Kingdom*, No. 66746/01; ECtHR, dec. 7 February 2006, *Codona v. the United Kingdom*, No. 485/05.

36 ECtHR, 29 September 1996, *Buckley v. the United Kingdom*, No. 20348/92, § 80; ECtHR, *Connors v. the United Kingdom*, § 84; ECtHR, final 7 September 2020, *Hudorovič and Others v. Slovenia*, Nos. 24816/14 and 25140/14, §§ 142 and 147; ECtHR, *Faulkner v. Ireland and McDonagh v. Ireland*, § 97. In this regard Article 16 of the European Social Charter contains similar obligations, as pointed out by the European Committee of Social Rights (see,

paid to the consequences of their removal from their home and the risk of their becoming homeless. The Court pointed out that "numerous international instruments, some of which have been adopted within the Council of Europe, emphasise the necessity, in the event of the forced eviction of Roma and travellers, of providing them with alternative housing, except in cases of *force majeure*".[37] And it sometimes added that "this same finding led the European Committee for Social Rights to conclude, [for instance] in complaint No. 51/2008 (*European Roma Rights Centre v. France*), that there had been a violation of Article 31 § 1 of the revised Charter".[38]

This, however, without going so far as to recognize, on the part of individual signatory States, a positive obligation to provide housing for those who do not have it or who are in conditions of economic and/or social hardship.[39]

If anything, obligations of means would flow from the Convention, in the sense that States would have to make efforts to address the housing problem for those most in need and to assist them in finding solutions in order to protect their right to private and family life and home.[40]

for example, ECSR, *European Roma Rights Centre* (*ERRC*) *v. Greece*, complaint No. 15/2003, decision on the merits of 8 December 2004, § 25).

37 In particular ECtHR, 17 October 2013, *Winterstein and Others v. France*, No. 27013/07, § 159.

38 *Ibid.*, § 165; see also ECtHR, 24 April 2012, *Jordanova and Others v. Bulgaria*, No. 25446/06, §§ 73–74, recalling a Committee ruling on the violation of Article 16 ESC with regard to family housing.

39 Furthermore, the Court has found it legitimate for States to put criteria in place according to which social housing can be allocated, when the available supply is insufficient to satisfy demand, provided that such criteria are not arbitrary, discriminatory, or out of proportion (see, among others, ECtHR, final 27 December 2011, *Bah v. the United Kingdom*, No. 56328/07, § 49).

40 In this regard see, among others, Francesco Bestagno, *cit.*, pp. 116–122 and 124–127; Françoise Tulkens and Sebastien Van Drooghenbroeck, "Le droit au logement dans la Convention européenne des droits de l'homme. Bilan et perspectives", in Nicolas Bernard and Charles Mertens (eds.), *Le logement dans sa multidimensionnalité: une grande cause régionale*, Namur, Ministère de la Région wallonne, collection Etudes et documents, 2005, pp. 311–325; Nicolas Bernard and Françoise Tulkens, "Le 'droit au logement' dans la Convention européenne des droits de l'homme: une illustration de l'idée 'ostienne' d'intérêt", in Yves Cartuyvels *et al.* (eds.), *Le droit malgré tout*, Bruxelles, Presses de l'Université Saint-Louis, 2018, pp. 441–461. However, within the Court of Human Rights there is no lack of minority positions calling for recourse to the guidance contained in the case law of the European Committee of Social Rights, "which is the competent body on questions of the right to housing and discrimination in access to housing": cf., in particular, §§ 27–28 of the dissenting opinion of Judge Pinto de Albuquerque, joined by Judge Vehabović, to ECtHR, 6 November 2017, *Garib v. the Netherlands*, No. 43494/09.

D *The European Union Law*

The right to housing is also considered at the European Union level.[41] Actually, neither the founding Treaties nor the Charter of Fundamental Rights include a specific right to housing,[42] but Article 34 § 3 of the Charter, on social security and social assistance, states: "In order to combat social exclusion and poverty, the Union recognizes and respects the right to social and housing assistance so as to ensure a decent existence for all those who lack sufficient resources, in accordance with the rules laid down by Community law and national laws and practices".

This is a rather general provision and relates to a *principle*, that in the Nice Charter – by contrast to a *right* – does not create any directly enforceable right but may impact on the law-making process in the European Union and member countries, providing a foundation on which more precise rights can be based. Moreover, this paragraph can only be invoked in the context of EU social inclusion policies, based on Article 153 TFEU, and, as it refers to the laws and practices of the Member States, it cannot impose standards on them, unless the national legislation concerned is intended to implement Union law.[43]

In addition, it is not entirely clear what is covered by the expression "housing assistance": the term seems to have to be restricted as to include the assistance (financial, social, legal, etc.) needed to access a dwelling, whereby each Member State is free to define the level of protection of the right to housing it deems most appropriate.[44]

But this provision could take on particular importance if read in light of the regulation of the right to housing contained in the European Social Charter, which defines an essential core of that right.[45] After all, the preamble to the Nice

41 On EU developments in the consideration of social rights in general see Giuseppe Palmisano, *L'Europa dei diritti sociali*, Bologna, Il Mulino, 2022, pp. 264–273.

42 On the other hand, many European policies set out in the Treaties, notably on social and environmental issues and the functioning of the single market, affect the quantity, quality and availability of housing in the Union. For a brief overview, before and after the Lisbon Treaty, see Arturs Kucs, Zane Sedlova and Liene Pierhurovica, *cit.*, pp. 115–118.

43 Cf. CJEU, 15 January 2014, *Association de médiation sociale v. Union locale des syndicats CGT and Others*, C-176/12 (referring to Article 27 of the Charter, but transposable to other provisions).

44 In this sense cf., for example, Arturs Kucs, Zane Sedlova and Liene Pierhurovica, *cit.*, p. 117.

45 Cf., among others, Olivier De Schutter and Natalie Boccadoro, "Le droit au logement dans l'Union européenne", *Cridho Working Paper series*, No. 2, 2005, available at https://cridho.uclouvain.be/documents/Working.Papers/CridhoWPs022005.PDF; Nicolas Bernard, "Les ressources – préjudicielles notamment – qu'offre l'article 34, paragraphe 3, de la Charte des droits fondamentaux de l'Union européenne (droit à une aide au logement)", *Revue Trimestrielle des Droits de l'Homme*, No. 97, 2014, pp. 81–125; Lucia Serena Rossi, "Member States' obligations in relation to housing rights – views of the CJEU", in

Charter contains an explicit reference to "rights derived […] from the Social Charters adopted by the Council of Europe". Moreover, in the EU Charter's explanation of Article 34 – drafted and then updated under the responsibility of the European Convention's Praesidium – it is stated that paragraph 3 is inspired by, *inter alia*, Article 31 of the revised European Social Charter.

Article 34 § 3 was invoked successfully before the Court of Justice in the case *Kamberaj* and the case *Land Oberösterreich* (*Aide au logement*):[46] the Court held that it was incompatible with EU law for legislation to treat long-term residents less favourably than European citizens with regard to housing allowances, stressing that Member States must be regarded as bound by that provision when they implement Union law.

The supreme judicial body also emphasized Article 7 of the Nice Charter, which states that "Everyone has the right to respect for his or her private and family life, home and communications": the Court of Justice held, in the case *Kušionová*,[47] that the right to accommodation is a fundamental one, guaranteed under the aforementioned Article 7 of the Charter.

In general, the Court has adopted a far from passive role in policing unfair terms to prevent that people be evicted from their homes in financial crises.[48]

Noria Derdek and Padraic Kenna (eds.), *The European and International Contribution to the Right to Housing: Standards, Litigation and Advocacy*, Brussels, Abbé Pierre Foundation – FEANTSA – University of Galway, 2023, pp. 23–28, https://www.housingrightswatch.org/resource/european-and-international-contribution-right-housing-standards-litigation-and-advocacy. On the role of the Social Charter in EU law and practice see Giuseppe Palmisano, *cit.*, pp. 239–263; on conflicts and tensions between the two systems see Marco Rocca, "The European Social Charter and the European Union", in ANESC, *cit.*, pp. 390–398.

46 CJEU [GC], 24 April 2012, *Kamberaj v. Istituto per l'Edilizia Sociale della Provincia autonoma di Bolzano (IPES) and Others*, C-571/10; CJEU, 10 June 2021, *Land Oberösterreich v. KV*, C-94/20.

47 CJEU, 10 September 2014, *Monika Kušionová v. SMART Capital a.s.*, C-34/13.

48 In this regard see Jacobien W. Rutgers, "The Right to Housing (Article 7 of the Charter) and Unfair Terms in General Conditions", in Hugh Collins (ed.), *European Contract Law and the Charter of Fundamental Rights*, Cambridge, CUP, 2017, pp. 125–138; Joan Solanes Mullor, "The Right to Housing and the Protection of Family Life and Vulnerable Groups: European Judicial Activism", in Maribel Gonzales Pascual and Aida Torres Perez, *The Right to Family Life in the European Union*, London, Routledge, 2017, pp. 214–231.

II The European Social Charter

A *The Charter and Housing*

1 The Charter's Provisions on Housing

In contrast to other continental covenants, the right to housing is expressly provided for in Article 31 of the revised European Social Charter, which is the only legally binding European instrument that contains a provision specifically and exclusively addressing this right.

Beyond Article 31, housing is also considered under Article 16 in the context of securing the right of families to social, legal, and economic protection. To do this, families must be guaranteed an adequate supply of dwellings, their needs must be taken into account in the definition and implementation of housing policies, and existing dwellings must be of an adequate standard and include essential services, as stated by the European Committee of Social Rights.[49]

In addition, the revised Social Charter recognizes housing rights specifically to persons with disabilities (Article 15),[50] children and young persons (Article 17),[51] migrant workers (Article 19),[52] and elderly people (Article 23).[53]

---

49 See, for example, ECSR, *European Roma Rights Centre (ERRC) v. Bulgaria*, complaint No. 31/2005, decision on the merits of 18 October 2006, § 9.

50 The needs of disabled persons must be taken into account in housing policies, including the construction of an adequate supply of public, social or private suitable dwellings. Further, financial assistance should be provided for the adaptation of existing housing (among others, ECSR, Conclusions 2003, Italy, p. 299). In any case, all newly constructed or renovated public buildings, facilities and buildings open to the public and cultural and leisure activities should be physically accessible.

51 The Committee emphasized the importance of the interests of children. Therefore, "children placed in institutions are entitled to the highest degree of satisfaction of their emotional needs and physical well being as well as to a special protection and assistance. [...] A unit in a child welfare institution should be of such a size as to resemble home environment and should not therefore accommodate more than 10 children" (ECSR, Conclusions 2005, Moldova, p. 474).

52 The Committee reiterated the need to eliminate all legal and *de facto* discrimination concerning access to public and private housing to home-buying migrant workers (ECSR, Conclusions IV (2002), Norway, p. 121), including access to subsidized dwellings or housing aids, such as loans or other allowances (ECSR, Conclusions III (2002), Italy, p. 92).

53 The Committee highlighted the significance of housing rights for elderly people and specified that the supply of adequate dwellings for them must be sufficient. Housing law and policy must take account of the special needs of this group. Policies should help elderly persons to remain in their own homes for as long as possible through the provision of sheltered/supported housing and assistance for the adaptation of homes (ECSR, Conclusions 2003, Slovenia, p. 530).

Moreover, Article 30, enshrining the right to protection against poverty and social exclusion, includes the duty of States to promote effective access to, *inter alia*, housing.[54] In particular, contracting Parties have to adopt positive measures for groups generally recognized as excluded or disadvantaged, such as Roma, to ensure that they are able to access housing, which in turn will have an impact on enjoyment of other rights such as education, employment and health.[55]

2 The History of Article 31

Reference to housing had already been included in the drafts of the Charter of 1961. Especially in two 1956 drafts, it was considered part of the right to a high standard of health or part of the right to a decent living and the rights of the family to social and economic protection.[56] However, housing was introduced as the subject of a specific right only in the revised Charter, except for family housing, which had been enshrined in original Article 16, and the equal treatment of migrants with regard to housing as well, provided for in Article 19 § 4 (c) of 1961. Indeed, the ad hoc 'Charte-Rel' Committee on the revision of the European Social Charter, set up by the Committee of Ministers of the Council of Europe and composed of experts appointed by each Member State,[57]

---

54 The Committee pointed out that housing is a critical policy area in fighting poverty and social exclusion (for example, ECSR, Conclusions 2003, France on Article 30, Italy on Article 30).

55 See, among others, ECSR, *European Roma Rights Centre (ERRC) v. Portugal*, complaint No. 61/2010, decision on the merits of 30 June 2011, § 65. On the line of case law about Roma's housing rights see Jessie Hohmann, *The Right to Housing: Law, Concepts, Possibilities*, Oxford, Hart Publishing, 2013, pp. 60–66; Giuseppe Palmisano, *cit.*, pp. 219–226.

56 The first draft (Council of Europe, Parliamentary Assembly, European Social Charter and European Economic and Social Council, Report by Social, Health and Family Affairs Committee, Doc. 488, 14 April 1956), which was rejected and not referred to the Committee of Ministers, dealt with the two provisions respectively in Articles 10 and 11. In addition, it stated the right to a decent living in Article 8, including adequate food, clothing and housing, and promoted a policy of town planning and rural habitation to provide adequate numbers of moderately priced dwellings complying with satisfactory standards of comfort and hygiene. The second draft of the same year (Council of Europe, Parliamentary Assembly, Establishment of a European Convention on Social and Economic Rights, Report by the Committee on Economic Affairs and Development, Doc. 536, 27 September 1956), accepted and submitted for consideration to the Committee of Ministers, repeated the first two provisions under Article I (former Article 10) and Article J (former Article 11).

57 Whose meetings were also attended in a non-voting capacity by representatives of the Parliamentary Assembly, the International Labour Organization, the European Trade Union Confederation (ETUC) and the Union of Industrial and Employers' Confederations of Europe (UNICE). On this body and its work see, in brief, Stefano Angeleri and Róisín Dunbar, "The Reform of the European Social Charter", in ANESC, *cit.*, pp. 41–42.

decided – albeit by a narrow majority – to include a general right to housing in the Charter, in the context of improving its substantive content.[58]

Article 31 ESC (rev) requires States Parties to take measures "in so far as possible"[59] to promote access to housing of an adequate standard, to make the price of housing accessible to people without adequate resources, and to prevent and reduce, to the point of elimination, homelessness.

It cannot be interpreted as imposing obligations of results, but, as "the rights recognised in the Social Charter must take a practical and effective, rather than purely theoretical, form",[60] States Parties have positive obligations of conduct. To this end, they are required not only to take legal measures, but also to introduce the necessary operational procedures and make sufficient resources available, in order to give full effect to this right.[61]

---

58 First, at its 5th meeting (May 1992), the Charte-Rel Committee held a preliminary general discussion on improvement of the substantive content of the Charter and agreed that developments in social rights, as reflected in other international instruments and in the legislation of the Member States, should be taken into account, but even social problems not dealt with in other instruments should be considered. Then, at its 7th meeting (January 1993), the Committee examined the report of a working party it had mandated to examine all the proposals for improving the substantive content of the Charter: the proposals, including the one on housing, were examined in thematic groups suggested by the working party (Group I, as regards protection against social exclusion, where divergence of views emerged on the right to housing). Finally, at its 11th meeting (26–29 April 1994), after reconfirming the wish to include a right to protection against poverty and social exclusion in the Charter, the Charte-Rel Committee decided, by a narrow majority vote (8 for, 7 against, and 5 abstentions), to consider the inclusion of a right to housing in the Charter and asked the Finnish delegate to present his draft proposal at the Committee's next meeting.

At its 12th meeting, the Committee, after examining the Finnish proposal, adopted the first paragraph of the future Article 31 ESC (rev) with 12 votes in favour, 7 votes against, and 6 abstentions. The Committee then agreed on the text of § 2 and § 3 of the article and decided to clarify in the explanatory report that "adequate standard" especially referred to an acceptable standard with regard to health. That report should also have clarified that for a definition of the words "without adequate resources" reference was made to Article 13. Two Belgian proposals to include a fourth and a fifth paragraph to the provision, concerning the acquisition of a fixed abode, for the purpose of establishing where certain social rights are to be exercised, and the notification of the implementation of an eviction, were, however, rejected (cf. Council of Europe, Committee on the European Social Charter (Charte-Rel), *Final Activity Report*, 19 October 1994, pp. 2–3 and 37–39).

59 Council of Europe, *Explanatory Report to the European Social Charter (Revised)*, Strasbourg, 3 May 1996, § 118, available at https://rm.coe.int/16800ccde4.

60 ECSR, *European Federation of National Organisations Working with the Homeless (FEANTSA) v. France*, § 53 (et seq.).

61 Among others, ECSR, *International Association Autism-Europe v. France*, complaint No. 13/2002, decision on the merits of 4 November 2003, § 53. Cf. Karin Lukas, *The Revised European Social Charter*, Cheltenham UK-Northampton USA, Edward Elgar, 2021, p. 330.

3 The Personal Scope

With regard to the personal scope of Article 31, the basic right to shelter must be accorded to all individuals, even though § 1 of the Appendix to the Charter limits the entitlement to almost all the rights enshrined in the Social Charter to citizens of the Member State under consideration and to "nationals of the other Parties lawfully resident or working regularly within the territory of the Party concerned". Indeed, the European Committee of Social Rights has specified that "the restriction of the personal scope included in the Appendix should not be read in such a way as to deprive foreigners coming within the category of unlawfully present migrants of the protection of the most basic rights enshrined in the Charter or to impair their fundamental rights such as the right to life or to physical integrity or the right to human dignity".[62] Such an interpretation certainly cannot apply to "all the provisions of the Charter, but solely [to] those provisions whose fundamental purpose is closely linked to the requirement to secure the most fundamental human rights and to safeguard the persons concerned by the provision in question from serious threats to the enjoyment of those rights". These include the right to housing, at least in the form of protection against homelessness.[63]

4 Actual Implementation

Despite its fundamental importance, Article 31 is the least accepted of the Social Charter's provisions: only 11 States Parties have adhered to it in its entirety (Finland, France, Greece, Italy, Netherlands, Norway, Portugal, Slovenia, Spain,

62 Therefore, "the Committee indeed considers that, beyond the letter of paragraph 1 of the Appendix, the restriction on personal scope contained therein should be interpreted – as is generally the case for any provision of an international treaty – in light of the object and purpose of the treaty concerned and in harmony with other relevant and applicable rules of international law (Vienna Convention on the Law of Treaties, 23 May 1969, Article 31, paragraphs 1 and 3), including first and foremost the peremptory norms of general international law (*jus cogens*), which take precedence over all other international norms and from which no derogation is permitted (Vienna Convention on the Law of Treaties, 23 May 1969, Article 53)" (ECSR, *Defence for Children International* (DCI) *v. Belgium*, complaint No. 69/2011, decision on the merits of 23 October 2012, §§ 28–29; see also, among others, ECSR, *International Federation of Human Rights Leagues* (FIDH) *v. France*, complaint No. 14/2003, decision on the merits of 8 September 2004, §§ 30–31; ECSR, *Conference of European Churches* (CEC) *v. the Netherlands*, complaint No. 90/2013, decision on the merits of 1 July 2014, § 66). Cf. Giuseppe Palmisano, *cit.*, pp. 70–76.

63 ECSR, *Defence for Children International* (DCI) *v. Belgium*, § 36; ECSR, *Conference of European Churches* (CEC) *v. the Netherlands*, §§ 71 and 129; ECSR, *European Federation of National Organisations Working with tbe Homeless* (FEANTSA) *v. the Netherlands*, complaint No. 86/2012, decision on the merits of 2 July 2014, §§ 58–61. Cf. Karin Lukas, *cit.*, pp. 335–336.

Sweden, and Turkey), and a further 4 States have accepted it partially (Andorra, Lithuania and Ukraine for paragraphs 1 and 2, and Latvia only for paragraph 1).

In any case, regardless of adherence to specific provisions under Part II of the Charter, all signatory countries have accepted, under Part I, "as the aim of their policy, to be pursued by all appropriate means both national and international in character, the attainment of conditions in which [all of] the following rights and principles may be effectively realised: [...] 31. Everyone has the right to housing".

Accordingly, the recusal of Article 31 limits the scope of monitoring of Member States' compliance with this provision, but it does not lessen their responsibility for promoting and upholding this fundamental right. Moreover, the European Committee of Social Rights can examine aspects of the right to housing under the other mentioned provisions: Article 30 on poverty and social exclusion, Article 16 concerning the family (which is accepted by most States Parties), and the rules regarding vulnerable people, such as persons with disabilities (Article 15), children (Article 17), migrant workers (Article 19) and elderly people (Article 23).

The fact remains that the scope of these articles with respect to housing is more limited and, in addition, the Committee's far-reaching interpretation is not uncontroversial.[64]

B *Article 31 § 1*

1 States' Obligations

As mentioned above, Article 31 § 1, while not imposing obligations of results, places positive duties of conduct on States Parties to promote access to housing of an adequate standard.

According to the case law of the European Committee of Social Rights, this means that each country has to:[65]

(a) adopt the necessary legal, financial and operational means of ensuring steady progress towards achieving the goals laid down by the Charter;

64 Cf. Council of Europe, "The right to housing under the European Social Charter", pp. 1–2, available at https://www.ohchr.org/sites/default/files/Documents/Issues/Housing/COVID19/UN_Entities/Coucil_of_Europe_Right2Housing.docx.

65 See, among others, ECSR, *International Association Autism-Europe v. France*, § 53; ECSR, *European Federation of National Organisations Working with the Homeless (FEANTSA) v. France*, § 55; ECSR, *International Movement ATD Fourth World v. France*, complaint No. 33/2006, decision on the merits of 5 December 2007, §§ 58–60. Cf. Nico Moons, *The Right to Housing in Law and Society*, New York, Routledge, 2018, pp. 120–123.

(b) maintain meaningful statistics on needs, resources and results;
(c) undertake regular reviews of the impact of the strategies adopted;
(d) establish a timetable and not indefinitely defer the deadline for achieving the objectives of each stage;
(e) pay close attention to the impact of the adopted policies on each of the categories of persons concerned, particularly the most vulnerable.

However, following the jurisprudence of the European Court of Human Rights, the Committee of Social Rights acknowledges a margin of appreciation of the States in determining the steps to be taken to ensure compliance with the Charter,[66] in particular as regards "the balance to be struck between the general interest and the interest of a specific group and the choices which must be made in terms of priorities and resources".[67] Furthermore, when the achievement of one of the rights in question is exceptionally complex and particularly expensive to resolve, a State Party has to take measures that allow it to achieve the objectives of the Charter "within a reasonable time, with measurable progress and to an extent consistent with the maximum use of available resources".[68]

2 Adequate Housing

The main element of the right to housing envisaged under Article 31 § 1 is *adequacy*.

The term "adequate standard" is specified by the Explanatory Report to the revised Charter, recalling the 1956 draft text, as "acceptable standard concerning health requirements", which is to be defined by the competent authorities of each country.[69]

The European Committee of Social Rights has specified and broadened the notion of adequacy, which has to be set in national law on the basis of the following criteria:[70]

66 In this regard see Giovanni Cavaggion, "The Implementation of the European Social Charter by National Authorities", in ANESC, *cit.*, pp. 153–156; Carole Nivard, *La justiciabilité des droits sociaux. Etude de droit conventionnel européen*, Bruxelles, Bruylant, 2012, pp. 340–343.

67 ECSR, *European Roma Rights Centre (ERRC) v. Bulgaria*, § 35 (et seq.).

68 Among others, ECSR, *International Association Autism-Europe v. France*, § 53; ECSR, *International Federation for Human Rights (FIDH) v. Ireland*, complaint No. 110/2014, decision on the merits of 12 May 2017, § 109.

69 Council of Europe, *Explanatory Report cit.*, §§ 118–119.

70 See, among others, ECSR, Conclusions 2003, France, p. 221; ECSR, *European Roma Rights Centre (ERRC) v. Greece*, § 24; ECSR, *International Commission of Jurists (ICJ) and European*

(a) safety from a sanitary and health point of view: a dwelling must protect its inhabitants from harsh weather conditions or other threats to health and must possess all basic amenities (such as water, heating, electricity, waste disposal, sanitation facilities, etc.); in addition, it must be structurally secure to ensure the physical safety of occupants, and its specific dangers (for example, the presence of lead or asbestos materials) must be under control;[71]
(b) not over-crowding: the size of a dwelling has to be suitable in light of the number of persons in residence and the composition of the household;
(c) guarantee of the security of tenure, i.e., protection from forced eviction and other threats.[72]

Moreover, adequate housing must be in a location which allows access to public services, employment, health-care services, schools and other social facilities. Therefore, "States should be vigilant when implementing housing policies so as to prevent spatial or social segregation of ethnic minorities or immigrants".[73] The European Committee emphasizes that living in segregated settings means that there will be inadequate access to schooling, fewer opportunities for employment, and more difficult access to medical facilities. Likewise, inadequate standards of housing easily lead to poor health and higher incidences of diseases.[74]

In its case law, the Committee explicated a new aspect of adequate housing, namely cultural adequacy, which must be taken into account to avoid a violation of the principle of non-discrimination as well. The Committee therefore held that social housing offered to Roma should be, as far as possible, "culturally suited" to them. Consequently, attention must be paid to re-housing

---

Council for Refugees and Exiles (ECRE) *v. Greece*, complaint No. 173/2018, decision on the merits of 26 January 2021, § 115. For comparison, see general comment No. 4 of the UN Committee on Economic, Social and Cultural Rights, *cit.*, where the criteria for adequate housing were developed. These criteria include: (a) legal security of tenure; (b) availability of services, materials, facilities, and infrastructure; (c) affordability; (d) habitability; (e) accessibility; (f) location; and (g) cultural adequacy. On them see, among others, Jessie Hohmann, *cit.*, pp. 20–29, and, more concisely, Monika Smusz-Kulesza, "The Right to Housing in the Light of the European Social Charter", *Nieruchomości@*, Vol. 1, No. 1, 2023, pp. 126–127.

71 See, for example, ECSR, *European Roma Rights Centre* (ERRC) *v. Portugal*, § 37.

72 See, among others, ECSR, Conclusions 2005, Lithuania, p. 406.

73 ECSR, *European Roma Rights Centre* (ERRC) *v. Portugal*, § 41.

74 Cf. Dovilė Gailiūtė, "Right to Housing in the Jurisprudence of the European Committee of Social Rights", *Socialinių mokslų studijos/Societal Studies*, Vol. 4, No. 4, 2012, pp. 1611–1612.

Roma families in apartment blocks, which often prevents family and casual gatherings, given that their means of existence as a community and bonds of solidarity are broken. Moreover, Roma are not infrequently faced with hostile attitudes of their new neighbours.[75]

Adequacy standards shall be applied to both dwellings available for rent as well as to those occupied by their owners, and not only to new constructions but also gradually to the existing housing stock in the case of its renovation.[76]

Moreover, the requirements of adequate housing should be applied to caravans and stopping places for the Travellers as well. In the view of the Committee of Social Rights, "any place in which a family resides legally or illegally, whether a building or a movable piece of property such as a caravan, must be regarded as housing within the meaning of the Charter. By extension, [...] the site on which the caravan is installed must also be considered to form part of the dwelling".[77]

The Committee stated that the feature which undoubtedly makes nomadic families completely different is their caravan lifestyle. This situation calls for differentiated treatment for such families and tailored measures to improve their housing conditions.[78] This means that public sites for Travellers must be properly fitted out with the aforementioned basic amenities necessary for a decent life, such as water, electricity, sanitation facilities, etc., and must be structurally secure, not overcrowded, and with secure tenure supported by law.[79]

Finally, it should be emphasized that the temporary supply of shelter cannot be considered sufficient to ensure compliance with Article 31 § 1, whereby individuals should be provided with adequate housing within a reasonable period of time.[80]

---

75 See, among others, again ECSR, *European Roma Rights Centre* (ERRC) *v. Portugal*, §§ 49–50. Cf. Giuseppe Palmisano, *cit.*, pp. 221–223.

76 See, for example, ECSR, Conclusions 2003, France, p. 221, Italy, p. 342, Slovenia, p. 554, and Sweden, p. 650.

77 ECSR, *International Federation of Human Rights* (FIDH) *v. Belgium*, complaint No. 62/2010, decision on the merits of 21 March 2012, §§ 73–74. Also according to Recommendation Rec(2004)14 of the Committee of Ministers to Member States on the movement and encampment of Travellers in Europe, adopted on 1 December 2004, the site where a caravan is installed must be considered to form part of the dwelling.

78 See, for example, again ECSR, *International Federation of Human Rights* (FIDH) *v. Belgium*, § 141.

79 Among others, ECSR, *European Roma Rights Centre* (ERRC) *v. France*, complaint No. 51/2008, decision on the merits of 19 October 2009, § 46.

80 See, for example, ECSR, *European Roma Rights Centre* (ERRC) *v. Italy*, § 35; ECSR, *Conference of European Churches* (CEC) *v. the Netherlands*, § 140.

3 Implementation of the Provision

In light of Article 31 § 1 ESC (rev), it is incumbent on public authorities to ensure that dwellings are adequate through various appropriate measures, such as an inventory of the housing stock, injunctions against owners who disregard housing rights, urban development regulation, and maintenance obligations for landlords. Public authorities must also limit the interruption of essential services such as water, electricity, and telephone.[81]

The effectiveness of the right to adequate housing also requires its legal protection through appropriate procedural safeguards (assessed under subsequent § 2 of Article 31). Tenants must therefore have access to affordable and impartial judicial or extra-judicial remedies,[82] and any appeals procedure must be effective, as well as the means of redress.[83]

Even if, under national law, local or regional authorities are responsible for exercising a particular function, nonetheless, States Parties to the Charter are ultimately responsible for ensuring that such duties are properly exercised. Thus, national governments bear the responsibility for housing policy implementation, involving at least supervision and regulation of local action: to this end, they must be able to show that both local or regional authorities and central authorities have taken practical steps to ensure that action on the ground is effective.[84]

At the level of practical implementation of this legislation, the European Committee of Social Rights had to note the persistent lack of follow-up by States after its decisions on collective complaints. The Committee therefore had to reiterate its findings in several pronouncements, pointing out that, in many countries, a number of dwellings are substandard and not equipped with suitable amenities, lacking reliable access to water or electricity or being unsafe or unhealthy.[85]

In particular, despite certain progress achieved by some States in ameliorating the living conditions of Roma, the Committee found insufficient

---

81 Among others, ECSR, Conclusions 2003, France, p. 224.

82 *Ibid.*

83 See, in particular, ECSR, *European Federation of National Organisations Working with the Homeless* (*FEANTSA*) *v. France*, § 78, where the Committee noted "the inefficacy of means of redress, which most often result in a compensatory payment or reduction in rent".

84 For example, ECSR, *European Roma Rights Centre* (*ERRC*) *v. Italy*, § 26; ECSR, *European Federation of National Organisations Working with the Homeless* (*FEANTSA*) *v. France*, § 79.

85 Cf., for instance, the reminder in the 2011 report (ECSR, *Activity Report 2011*, p. 22, available, like all other reports, at https://www.coe.int/en/web/european-social-charter/activity-reports), as well as what was highlighted in the latest reviews of national reports on Article 31 (ECSR, *Activity Report 2019*, pp. 36–37; ECSR, *Activity Report* 2023, pp. 39–40).

improvement in elimination of substandard housing conditions for a large number of them and held that there were violations of the right to housing in cases where a significant number of Roma continued to live in conditions failing to meet minimal standards.[86] Although the Committee recognizes that the effective implementation of the right in question may require time, it also finds that, given the urgency of the housing situation of Roma families, a time frame should not be too long.[87]

C *Article 31 § 2*

1 Preventing Homelessness

Paragraph 2 of Article 31 requires States Parties "to prevent and reduce homelessness, with a view to its gradual elimination". Homeless persons are individuals who legally do not have adequate housing at their disposal in the meaning of paragraph 1.[88]

Ratifying countries must try to prevent people in vulnerable situations from becoming homeless. This includes a housing policy for disadvantaged groups to ensure their access to social housing.[89]

National authorities enjoy a wide margin of discretion in housing policies, but they have to take into account the fundamental rights of individuals, especially of persons in vulnerable situations, balancing the general interest against them when it comes to housing.[90]

2 Forced Evictions

Homelessness can also be caused by forced eviction. This is "the deprivation of housing which a person occupied due to insolvency or wrongful occupation".[91]

86 See, among others, ECSR, *European Federation of National Organisations Working with the Homeless (FEANTSA) v. France*, § 78; ECSR, *International Centre for the Legal Protection of Human Rights (INTERIGHTS) v. Greece*, complaint No. 49/2008, decision on the merits of 11 December 2009, §§ 38–39; ECSR, *Centre on Housing Rights and Evictions (COHRE) v. Italy*, complaint No. 58/2009, decision on the merits of 25 June 2010, §§ 55 and 57.

87 For instance, the period of six years was acknowledged sufficient to realize significant improvements: see ECSR, *European Roma Rights Centre (ERRC) v. Bulgaria*, § 39.

88 See, for example, ECSR, Conclusions 2003, France, p. 225 and Italy, p. 345; ECSR, *Conference of European Churches (CEC) v. the Netherlands*, § 135.

89 Among others, ECSR, *European Roma Rights Centre (ERRC) v. Italy*, § 45.

90 For example, ECSR, *European Roma Rights Centre (ERRC) v. Bulgaria*, § 54; ECSR, *International Federation of Human Rights (FIDH) v. Belgium*, § 133.

91 Among others, ECSR, Conclusions 2003, Sweden, p. 653.

The European Committee of Social Rights has pointed out that States have to put procedures in place to limit the risk of evictions[92] and to ensure that, when these do occur, evictions are:[93]

- carried out under conditions which respect the dignity of the persons concerned;
- governed by rules of procedure sufficiently protective of the individuals' rights;
- accompanied by proposals or possibilities for alternative accommodation.

Indeed, even when an eviction is justified by public interest, authorities have to adopt measures to re-house or financially assist the persons concerned to find new adequate housing.[94]

To comply with the Charter, legal protection for persons threatened by eviction must be prescribed by law and include:[95]

(a) an obligation to consult the affected parties in order to find alternative solutions to eviction;
(b) an obligation to fix a reasonable notice period before eviction;
(c) a prohibition to carry out evictions at night or during winter;
(d) accessibility to legal remedies and legal aid to claim them;
(e) a compensation for illegal evictions.

As highlighted by the Committee, "illegal occupation of a site or dwelling may justify the eviction of the illegal occupants. However, the criteria of illegal occupation must not be unduly wide, the eviction should take place in accordance with the applicable rules of procedure, and these should be sufficiently protective of the rights of the persons concerned".[96]

---

92 See, for example, ECSR, *European Federation of National Organisations Working with the Homeless (FEANTSA) v. France*, § 85; ECSR, Conclusions 2015, Ukraine, p. 1260.

93 See, among others, ECSR, Conclusions 2003, France, p. 225; ECSR, *European Roma Rights Centre (ERRC) v. Italy*, § 41; ECSR, *International Federation of Human Rights (FIDH) v. Belgium*, § 163.

94 For instance, ECSR, *International Movement ATD Fourth World v. France*, § 78.

95 *Ibid.*; cf. Dovilė Gailiūtė, *cit.*, p. 1613. Of course, the destruction of dwellings or forced evacuation of villages particularly violate the right to housing: in such situations, States must provide effective remedies to the victims (ECSR, Conclusions XIII-1, Turkey, pp. 258–259) and must take measures in order to re-house families in decent accommodation or to provide financial assistance (ECSR, Conclusions XIII-3, Turkey, pp. 381–385).

96 ECSR, *European Roma Rights Centre (ERRC) v. Bulgaria*, § 51.

Also in case of unlawfully residing persons and migrants in an irregular situation, eviction is permissible and no alternative accommodation may be required to States.[97] However, the eviction of such persons from shelter should be banned if it would place them "in a situation of extreme helplessness which is contrary to the respect for their human dignity".[98] And, "since the right to shelter is closely connected to the right to life and is crucial for the respect of every person's human dignity", States Parties are still required to provide adequate shelter to children and adults unlawfully present in their territory for as long as they are in their jurisdiction, until they are deported or repatriated.[99] Sufficient places must therefore be provided in emergency shelters, where conditions are such as to enable living in human dignity.[100]

As mentioned above, the caravan and the site on which it is installed form part of a Traveller family's home. Therefore, all entries onto that site for the purposes of an eviction have to be regarded as an entry into the occupant's home and must comply with the rules concerning eviction from a home.[101] The Committee has held that "urging Traveller families to leave sites on which they have settled – even illegally – and then, even though there are not enough legal sites, evicting them if they refuse to comply without proposing a suitable long-term alternative accommodation, adds to the failure to respect these families' right to housing".[102]

---

97 Among others, ECSR, *European Federation of National Organisations Working with tbe Homeless* (*FEANTSA*) *v. the Netherlands*, §§ 60 and 110.

98 See, for example, ECSR, *Defence for Children International* (*DCI*) *v. the Netherlands*, complaint No. 47/2008, decision on the merits of 20 October 2009,§ 63.

99 *Ibid.*, §§ 47 and 64; see also ECSR, *European Federation of National Organisations Working with the Homeless* (*FEANTSA*) *v. the Netherlands*, § 61; ECSR, *Conference of European Churches* (*CEC*) *v. the Netherlands*, §§ 128–129; ECSR, *International Commission of Jurists* (*ICJ*) *and European Council for Refugees and Exiles* (*ECRE*) *v. Greece*, § 117.

100 Among others, ECSR, *European Federation of National Organisations Working with the Homeless* (*FEANTSA*) *v. France*, § 106. In particular, shelters must meet health, safety and hygiene standards and be equipped with basic necessities such as access to water, heating and sufficient lighting. Another basic requirement is the security of the immediate surroundings (ECSR, *Defence for Children International* (*DCI*) *v. the Netherlands*, § 62; ECSR, *Conference of European Churches* (*CEC*) *v. the Netherlands*, § 138).

101 See, for example, ECSR, *International Federation of Human Rights* (*FIDH*) *v. Belgium*, § 162.

102 *Ibid.*, § 165. Therefore, "when confronted with Roma or Traveller settlements of undefined legal status, public authorities should make every effort to seek solutions acceptable for all parties, in order to avoid situations in which Roma and Travellers are in danger of being excluded from access to services and amenities to which they are entitled as citizens of the state where they live" (ECSR, *International Movement ATD Fourth World v. France*, § 150). However, this was not the case in Italy in 2008–2009 and, even more so, in France in the summer of 2010, when authorities evicted Roma of Romanian and Bulgarian origin. In the ensuing collective complaints, the Committee pointed out that, apart from

D *Article 31 § 3*

The third paragraph of Article 31 requires States Parties to take measures "to make the price of housing accessible to those without adequate resources".

This implies a sufficient supply of affordable dwellings for persons with limited resources. Housing is affordable if the household can manage to pay initial costs (deposit, advance rent), current rent, and/or other housing-related costs (for example utility, maintenance and management charges) on a long-term basis, while still being able to maintain a minimum standard of living, according to the standards defined by the society in which the household is located.[103]

The European Committee of Social Rights, in its case law, made the obligations of the signatory States in this regard clear.[104]

Firstly, they are required to implement comprehensive housing benefit systems for at least the low-income and disadvantaged sections of the population. Such systems must grant individual rights, which all qualifying household members can enjoy in practice and against the denial of which legal remedies are available.[105]

Secondly, Member States have to adopt appropriate measures to encourage the construction of dwellings, in particular social housing, to which disadvantaged groups must have access,[106] without direct or indirect discrimination (in particular in respect of Roma or Travellers, and including equal access for

---

the breach of the aforementioned requirements for the procedure of evictions, adopted measures were incompatible with human dignity and specifically aimed at vulnerable groups, and the active role of the public authorities in framing and implementing this discriminatory approach to security constituted "an aggravated violation of human rights from the standpoint of Article 31 § 2 of the Revised Charter" (ECSR, *Centre on Housing Rights and Evictions* (COHRE) *v. France*, complaint No. 63/2010, decision on the merits of 28 June 2011, §§ 47 and 53–55; similarly ECSR, *Centre on Housing Rights and Evictions* (COHRE) *v. Italy*, §§ 73–76).

103 See, for example, ECSR, Conclusions 2003, Sweden, p. 655; ECSR, *International Movement ATD Fourth World v. France*, § 94. States Parties must provide data in order to show that the affordability ratio of the poorest housing applicants is compatible with their level of income (ECSR, *European Federation of National Organisations Working with the Homeless* (FEANTSA) *v. Slovenia*, complaint No. 53/2008, decision on the merits of 8 September 2009, § 72).

104 The Committee came to conclusions of non-conformity with the provisions on affordable housing, when it found a significant shortage of social housing in a country, or the lack of equal treatment of foreigners in respect to social housing and access to housing benefits, or an excessive waiting period for allocation of non-profit rental housing (for example, see ECSR, Conclusions 2015, Slovenia, p. 1056, and Turkey, p. 1218; cf. Dovilė Gailiūtė, *cit.*, p. 1615).

105 Among others, ECSR, Conclusions 2003, Sweden, p. 655.

106 *Ibid.*, p. 655; ECSR, *International Movement ATD Fourth World v. France*, §§ 95, 98 and 100.

nationals of other Parties to the Charter lawfully residing or regularly working in their territory).[107]

Moreover, signatory countries should adopt measures to ensure that waiting periods for the allocation of housing are not excessive. If so, effective judicial and extra-judicial remedies must be available.[108]

Concluding Remarks

The right to housing is essential for a decent life and as a safeguard against poverty and social exclusion.

On the other hand, it is a complex right that requires many resources to implement.[109] It can hardly be realized without a functioning housing market, without sufficient rental housing stock, and without criteria giving priority to persons and families in vulnerable situations.[110] A further challenge is the obligation to prevent and phase out homelessness, which entails the provision and realization of the right to shelter for everyone as a basic requirement of human dignity.[111]

Given the complexities and the demands placed on the right to housing, there are several aspects on which the European Committee of Social Rights has developed extensive case law: this body has not been content with either a piecemeal approach or a mere assessment of the means made available by States, but has gone so far as to give meaning to the Charter as a whole and to

---

107 See, for example, ECSR, *European Roma Rights Centre (ERRC) v. Italy*, §§ 36–37 and 45–46; ECSR, *International Movement ATD Fourth World v. France*, §§ 148–149 and 154. Discrimination may also arise by failing to take due and positive account of all relevant differences or by failing to take adequate steps to ensure that the rights and collective advantages open to all are truly accessible to every person (ECSR, *International Association Autism-Europe v. France*, § 52; ECSR, *Centre on Housing Rights and Evictions (COHRE) v. Italy*, § 35).

108 See, among others, ECSR, *International Movement ATD Fourth World v. France*, especially § 131, where in § 129 it was held that an average waiting time of 2 years and 4 months for allocation of social housing was too long.

109 For an overview and analysis of the housing situation in European States see the reports of the Housing Europe Observatory, available at https://www.housingeurope.eu/section-135/housing-observatory: the latest ones, to date, are *The state of Housing in Europe 2021* and *The state of Housing in Europe 2023*.

110 Cf. Matti Mikkola, "Housing as a Human Right in Europe", *European Journal of Social Security*, Vol. 10, No. 3, 2008, p. 292.

111 Cf. Karin Lukas, *cit.*, pp. 337–338.

verify the effectiveness of the results obtained on the basis of a dense list of obligations deemed essential for the fulfilment of the right in question.[112]

Unfortunately, so far, a low degree of compliance with this right has emerged on the part of the relatively few States Parties that have accepted Article 31 of the revised Charter, so much so a general lack of political commitment to its realization (and more generally to the realization of the rights under the Social Charter) has been denounced.[113]

Indeed, the most recent review, under the reporting system of the Charter, of the right to housing under Articles 16 and 31 ESC (rev) by the European Committee of Social Rights in 2019–2023 has come to the conclusion that just two countries, Finland and Sweden, in full conformity with Article 31, while another one, Andorra, is compliant only with paragraph 1, and all others are in non-conformity (or, as far as § 3, in two cases – Greece and Turkey – are unable to provide sufficient information).[114] Even so, it should be pointed out that in the parallel examination, in 2019, 2020 and 2023, of the national simplified reports dealing with the follow-up given to decisions of collective complaints, the Committee noted that several violations found in the past had been fully or partially brought into conformity with the Charter.[115]

---

112 On this approach of the Committee see among others: Giovanni Guiglia, "Il diritto all'abitazione nella Carta Sociale Europea: a proposito di una recente condanna dell'Italia da parte del Comitato Europeo dei Diritti Sociali", *Rivista AIC*, Vol. 2, No. 3, 2011, pp. 4–5; Jessie Hohmann, *cit.*, pp. 52–53. In particular, it has been emphasized that the Committee's decision of the complaint *FEANTSA v. France* of 5 December 2007 was a "groundbreaking" pronouncement in its attention to outcomes and in defining housing rights "in a tangible and quantifiable way" (Padraic Kenna and Marc Uhry, "FEANTSA v. France: Collective Complaint on Housing Rights at Council of Europe", *Housing and ESC Rights Law Quarterly*, Vol. 5, No. 3, 2008, pp. 1–3).

113 See, for instance, Jessie Hohmann, *cit.*, pp. 66–67 and 92–93; Nico Moons, *cit.*, p. 129, who, while considering it "exaggerated to say that lodging a collective complaint before the ECSR is useless", notes that the "flaws inherent in the ECSR system have led to a sense of indifference among all relevant parties, to which we can also add the media".

114 See ECSR, *Activity Report 2019*, pp. 36–37. Most of the non-conformities concern: with respect to § 1, substandard housing conditions of Roma and Travellers (France, Greece, Italy, Latvia, Portugal, Turkey and Ukraine); with reference to § 2, insufficient legal protection for persons threatened with eviction (Andorra, France, Greece, Lithuania, Portugal, Turkey and Ukraine) or for evictions of Roma (France, Greece and Italy); with respect to § 3, the shortage of social housing (France and Portugal) or the access of Roma and Travellers to social housing or housing assistance (France and Italy). Other non-compliances are related to more general problems, such as substandard housing for a large number of dwellings (France), insufficient measures to prevent and reduce homelessness in general (France, Italy and Turkey) and unsatisfactory protection of the right to shelter (Lithuania, Portugal, Turkey and Ukraine). Cf. *ibid.*; Monika Smusz-Kulesza, *cit.*, pp. 137–138.

115 See ECSR, *Activity Report 2020*, pp. 31–45 (reporting the closure of the follow-up to the decisions of five cases concerning France, one of which only partially related to Article

In the end, European States recognize the right to housing in principle but "consider that its implementation implies the adoption of a public policy which must be a matter for their sovereign decision-making in economic and social matters" and "do not wish to be constrained in their choices by supranational obligations".[116]

In any case, "housing is not simply a commodity, but a human right. It should move to the top of the political agenda in Europe".[117] The right to housing is indeed the logical and necessary prerequisite not only for adequate protection from poverty and social exclusion, whether for individuals or families, but also more generally for the effective guarantee of many other social and even civil and political rights.

Therefore, a serious commitment by European countries in this field is needed: first of all, further States among the signatories of the revised Charter are required to accept Article 31, since this alone elevates housing to a position of paramount importance, as is necessary. Furthermore, housing rights need to be integrated not merely into national policies and laws, but also into the regulation frameworks of all elements of housing systems. Indeed, to effectively guarantee the right to housing, it is necessary for States to regulate the housing market and to impose certain constraints on private owners. But this can only be the result of clear political will.[118]

---

31), *Activity Report 2019*, pp. 20–24 (reporting the closure of the follow-up to the decisions of two cases concerning the Netherlands, one case concerning Slovenia, and one case concerning Croatia on family housing under Article 16) and *Activity Report 2023*, p. 22 (reporting full or partial restoration of compliance with the Charter in respect of 16 decisions concerning Finland, France, Greece, Ireland, Italy and Portugal).

116 As Carole Nivard well points out in her "Conclusion", summarising the reflections of the contributors to the recent volume edited by Noria Derdek and Padraic Kenna (eds.), *cit.*, p. 126.

117 As emphasized by the Commissioner for Human Rights of the Council of Europe Dunja Mijatovic, *The right to affordable housing: Europe's neglected duty*, 23 January 2020, available at https://www.coe.int/fr/web/commissioner/blog/-/asset_publisher/xZ32OPEoxOkq/content/id/57979683?_com_liferay_asset_publisher_web_portlet_AssetPublisherPortlet_INSTANCE_xZ32OPEoxOkq_languageId=en_GB#p_com_liferay_asset_publisher_web_portlet_AssetPublisherPortlet_INSTANCE_xZ32OPEoxOkq.

118 Cf. Padraic Kenna, "International Instruments" *cit.*, p. 16; Dunja Mijatovic, *cit.* On the possibilities, even for social transformation, and the potential of the right to housing see also Jessie Hohmann, *cit.*, pp. 231–250; Nico Moons, *cit.*, pp. 215–234. Finally, see Nicolas Bernard and Koldo Casla, "Lessons from strategic human rights litigation: From climate change to adequate housing", in Noria Derdek and Padraic Kenna (eds.), *cit.*, pp. 51–60, on the innovative perspective of transposing recent successes in strategic climate litigation to housing rights, in order to hold States accountable for their responsibilities and commitments by condemning their inaction.

Selected Bibliography

Adam P., "La Dignité du Salarié (Deuxième partie)", *RDT*, 2014, No. 4, pp. 244–254.

Adam P., *Répertoire de Droit du Travail, Harcèlement Moral*, septembre 2014.

Aleksynska M. and Muller A., *The Regulation of Collective Dismissals: Economic Rationale and Legal Practice*, ILO Working Paper, No. 4, 2020.

Ales E., "Information and Consultation within the Undertaking: Employees Right or Employers' Duty? Looking for Effectiveness in Europe", in Schubert J.M. (Hrsg.), *Sozialer Dialog in der Krise – Social Dialogue in Crisis?*, Baden-Baden, Nomos, 2009, pp. 195–212.

Ales E., Bell M., Deinert O., Robin-Olivier S., *International and European Labour Law, A Commentary*, Baden-Baden, Beck/Hart/Nomos, 2018.

Alston P. and Quinn G., "The Nature and Scope of States Parties Obligations under International Covenant on Economic, Social and Cultural Rights", *Human Rights Quarterly*, Vol. 9, No. 2, 1987, pp. 156–229.

ANESC, Angeleri S. and Nivard C. (eds.), *The European Social Charter: A Commentary. Vol. 1 – Cross-Cutting Themes*, Leiden, Brill/Nijhoff, 2022.

Angeleri S. and Dunbar R., "The Reform of the European Social Charter", in ANESC, *The European Social Charter: A Commentary*, Vol. 1, Leiden, Brill, 2022, pp. 38–61.

Auer P. and Grazier B., *The Future of Work, Employment and Social Protection. The Dynamics of Change and the Protection of the Workers*, ILO, 2002.

Auzero G., Bougard D. and Dockès E., *Droit du Travail*, 32e ed., Paris, Dalloz, 2019.

Barbosa M. M., *Maiores Acompanhados – Primeiras Notas depois da Aprovação da Lei n.º 49/2018*, Lisboa, Gestlegal, 2018.

Bernard N. and Casla K., "Lessons from Strategic Human Rights Litigation: From Climate Change to Adequate Housing", in Derdek N. and Kenna P. (eds.), *The European and International Contribution to the Right to Housing: Standards, Litigation and Advocacy*, Brussels, Abbé Pierre Foundation – FEANTSA – University of Galway, 2023, pp. 51–60.

Bernard N., "Les Ressources – Préjudicielles Notamment – Qu'offre l'Article 34, Paragraphe 3, de la Charte des Droits Fondamentaux de l'Union Européenne (Droit a une Aide au Logement)", *Revue Trimestrielle des Droits de l'Homme*, No. 97, 2014, pp. 81–125.

Bernard N. and Tulkens F., "Le 'Droit au Logement' dans la Convention Européenne des Droits de L'Homme: Une Illustration de l'Idée 'Ostienne' d'Intérêt", in Cartuyvels Y. *et al.* (eds.), *Le Droit Malgré Tout*, Bruxelles, Presses de l'Université Saint-Louis, 2018, pp. 441–461.

Bestagno F., "Gli Obblighi Internazionali in Materia di Abitazione Adeguata", in Bestagno F. (ed.), *I Diritti Economici, Sociali e Culturali. Promozione e Tutela nella Comunità Internazionale*, Milano, Vita e Pensiero, 2009, pp. 87–127.

Boiteux-Picheral C. (ed), *La Vulnérabilité en Droit Européen des Droits de L'Homme. Conception(s) et Fonction(s)*, Limal, Anthémis, 2019.

Borelli S., "Article 33 CFREU. Family and Professional Life", in Ales E., Bell M., Deinert O. and Robin-Olivier S. (eds.), *International and European Labour Law. Article-by-Article Commentary*, Baden-Baden, München, Oxford and Portland, Nomos, Beck and Hart, 2018, pp. 225–234.

Brameshuber E., "Information and Consultation Rights", in Ter Haar B. and Kun A. (eds.), *EU Collective Labour Law*, Cheltenham, Edward Elgar, 2021, pp. 239–254.

Brandl B. and Meuer T., "Domestic Abuse in Later Life", *Elder Law Journal*, No. 8, 2001, pp. 297–322.

Brillat R., "The European Social Charter" in Alfredsson G., Grimheden J., Ramcharan B. G. and Zayas A. (eds.), *International Human Rights Monitoring Mechanisms. Essays in Honour of Jakob Th. Möller*, 2nd rev. edition, Leiden Boston, Martinus Nifhoff Publishers, 2009, pp. 503–513.

Brillat R., "La Carta Sociale Europea e il Sistema di Tutela dei Diritti Sociali nelle Fonti Europee", in *La Carta Sociale Europea e La Tutela dei Diritti Sociali, Atti del Convegno del 18 Gennaio 2013 Università degli Studi di Milano*, Edizione Scientifiche Italiane, 2013, pp. 17–38.

Bronstein A. S., "Comparative Study", in Yemin E. and Bronstein A. S. (eds.), *The Protection of Workers' Claims in the Event of Employer's Insolvency*, Geneva, International Labour Office, 1991 (Labour-Management Relations Series No. 76), pp. 13–32.

Bronstein A. S., "The Protection of Workers' Claims in the Event of the Insolvency of their Employer", *ILR*, Vol. 126, No. 6, November-December 1987, pp. 722–724.

Bruun N., "Article 22: The Right to Take Part in the Determination and Improvement of the Working Conditions and Working Environment", in Bruun N., Lörcher K., Schömann I. and Clauwaert S. (eds.), *The European Social Charter and the Employment Relation*, Bloomsbury, London, 2017, pp. 404–411.

Bruun N., Lörcher K., Schömann I. and Clauwaert S. (eds), *The European Social Charter and the Employment Relation*, Oxford, Hart Publishing, 2017.

Burgorgue-Larsen L. (ed.), *La Vulnérabilité Saisie par les Juges en Europe*, Paris, Éditions Pedone, 2014.

Butler R., *Why Survive? Being Old in America*, New York, Harper and Row, 1975.

Buyse A., "Strings Attached: The Concept of 'Home' in the Case Law of the European Court of Human Rights", *European Human Rights Law Review*, Vol. 6, No. 3, 2006, pp. 294–307.

Calves G. and Roman D., "La Discrimination a Raison de la Précarité Sociale: Progrès ou Confusion?", *Revue de Droit du Travail*, 2016, pp. 526–531.

Caracciolo di Torella E., "An Emerging Right to Care in the EU: A 'New Start to Support Work-Life Balance for Parents and Carers'", *ERA Forum*, Vol. 18, No. 2, 2017, pp. 187–198.

Caracciolo di Torella E., "Article 27 RESC. The Right of Workers with Family Responsibilities to Equal Opportunities and Equal Treatment", in Ales E., Bell M., Deinert O. and Robin-Olivier S. (eds.), *International and European Labour Law. Article-by-Article Commentary*, Baden-Baden, München, Oxford and Portland, Nomos, Beck and Hart, 2018, pp. 346–348.

Caracciolo di Torella E., "ILO Convention 156. Workers with Family Responsibilities Convention, 1981 (No. 156)", in Ales E., Bell M., Deinert O. and Robin-Olivier S. (eds.), *International and European Labour Law. Article-by-Article Commentary*, Baden-Baden, München, Oxford and Portland, Nomos, Beck and Hart, 2018, pp. 1142–1149.

Casey N., "The European Social Charter and the Revised European Social Charter", in *Fundamental Social Rights. Current European Legal Protection and the Challenge of the EU Charter on Fundamental Rights*, European Commission, 2000, pp. 55–77.

Cavaggion G., "The Implementation of the European Social Charter by National Authorities", in ANESC, *The European Social Charter: A Commentary*, Vol. 1, Leiden, Brill, 2022, pp. 136–176.

Chieregato E., "Work-Life Balance for All? Assessing the Inclusiveness of EU Directive 2019/1158", *International Journal of Comparative Labour Law*, Vol. 36, No. 1, 2020, pp. 59–80.

Collins H., "An Emerging Human Right to Protection against Unjustified Dismissal", *Industrial Law Journal*, Vol. 50, Issue 1, March 2021, pp. 36–69.

Cooter R. and Ulen T., *Law and Economics*, Pearson/Addison Wesley, 2008.

Corti M., "Il Coinvolgimento dei Lavoratori Preso sul Serio: Il Caso GKN", *Diritto delle Relazioni Industriali*, Vol. 32, No. 1, 2022, pp. 265–271.

Cosio R. *et al.* (eds.), *Collective Dismissal in the European Union: A Comparative Analysis*, Alphen aan den Rijn, Wolters Kluwer, 2017.

Costello C., "Article 33 – Family and Professional Life", in Peers S., Hervey T., Kenner J. and Ward A. (eds.), *The EU Charter of Fundamental Rights. A Commentary*, Oxford and Portland, Hart, 2014, pp. 891 ff.

Countouris N. et al., *Report on Collective Dismissals: A Comparative and Contextual Analysis of the Law on Collective Redundancies in 13 European Countries*, Geneva, ILO, 2016.

Craven M., *The International Covenant on Economic, Social and Cultural Rights. A Perspective on its Development*, Oxford, Clarendon Press, 1995.

D'Amico M., "La Carta Sociale Europea e la Tutela dei Diritti Sociali", in *La Carta Sociale Europea e la Tutela dei Diritti Sociali, Atti del Convegno del 18 Gennaio 2013, Università degli Studi di Milano*, Napoli, Edizioni Scientifiche Italiane, 2013, pp. 9–16.

D'Ascola S., "Anche il Comitato Europeo dei Diritti Sociali Boccia le Tutele Crescenti", LABOR – Il Lavoro nel Diritto, 06/03/2020.

De Schutter O. and Boccadoro N., "Le Droit au Logement dans l'Union Européenne", *Cridho Working Paper Series*, No. 2, 2005, https://cridho.uclouvain.be/documents/Working.Papers/CridhoWP022005.PDF.

De Schutter O., *The European Social Charter in the Context of Implementation of the EU Charter of Fundamental Rights*, study for AFCO Committee, European Parliament, Directorate General for Internal Policies Policy Department C: Citizens' Rights and Constitutional Affairs, 2016, available at https://www.europarl.europa.eu/RegData/etudes/STUD/2016/536488/IPOL_STU(2016)536488_EN.pdf.

Deakin S. and Wilkinson F., "Labour Law and Economic Theory: A Reappraisal", Centre for Business Research – University of Cambridge, 1998.

Deliyanni-Dimitrakou C., "The European Social Charter and the European Convention on Human Rights", in ANESC, *The European Social Charter: A Commentary*, Vol. 1, Leiden, Brill, 2022, pp. 351–374.

Derdek N. and Kenna P. (eds.), *The European and International Contribution to the Right to Housing: Standards, Litigation and Advocacy*, Brussels, Abbé Pierre Foundation – FEANTSA – University of Galway, 2023.

Doron I., "Older Europeans and the European Court of Justice", *Age and Ageing*, Vol. 42, No. 5, September 2013, pp. 604–608.

Dorssemont F. and Rocca M., "Article 6 ESC: The Right to Bargain Collectively", in Bruun N., Loercher K., Schoemann I. and Clauwaert S., *The European Social Charter and the Employment Relation*, Oxford, Hart Publishing, 2017, pp. 249–306.

Dorssemont F., "Article 27 – Workers' Right to Information and Consultation within the Undertaking", in Peers S. *et al.* (eds.), *The EU Charter of Fundamental Rights. A Commentary*, Oxford, Hart, 2021, pp. 779–799.

Dorssemont F., "The Right to Information and Consultation in Article 27 of the Charter of Fundamental Rights of the European Union: Less Than a Right and Less Than a Principle, Just an Ordinary Provision Lacking Direct Effect?", *Maastricht Journal of European and Comparative Law*, 2014, pp. 704–722.

Dorssemont F., Lörcher K. and Schömann I. (eds.), *The European Convention on Human Rights and the Employment Relation*, Oxford, Hart Publishing, 2013.

Faria P. R., "A Proteção Social das Pessoas Idosas na Carta Social Europeia Revista, no Código Europeu da Segurança Social e no Direito Português", *Revista de los Derechos Sociales, Lex Social Monográfico*, No. 1, 2017, pp. 302–322.

Faria P. R., *Os Crimes Praticados contra Idosos*, 3rd Edition, Porto, Edições Universidade Católica, 2019.

Fierens J., "La Dignité Humaine comme Concept Juridique", *Journal des Tribunaux*, No. 6064, 21 septembre 2002, pp. 577–582.

Gailiūtė D., "Right to Housing in the Jurisprudence of the European Committee of Social Rights", *Socialinių Mokslų Studijos/Societal Studies*, Vol. 4, No. 4, 2012, pp. 1605–1622.

Garofalo M.G. and Chieco P., "Licenziamenti Collettivi e Diritto Europeo", in *I Licenziamenti per Riduzione di Personale in Europa*, Bari, Cacucci, 2001, pp. 1–37.

Gomes J. V., *Direito do Trabalho – Relações Individuais*, Coimbra, Coimbra Editora, 2007.

Grabenwarter C., *European Convention on Human Rights. A Commentary*, München, Beck, 2014.

Green M., "What We Talk about When We Talk about Indicators: Current Approaches to Human Rights Measurement", *Human Rights Quarterly*, Vol. 23, No. 4, 2001, pp. 1063–1097.

Guiglia G., "Il Diritto all'Abitazione nella Carta Sociale Europea: A Proposito di una Recente Condanna dell'Italia da parte del Comitato Europeo dei Diritti Sociali", *Rivista AIC*, Vol. 2, No. 3, 2011, pp. 1–16.

Gupta D. K., Jongman A. J. and Schmid A. P., "Creating a Composite Index for Assessing Country Performance in the Field of Human Rights: Proposal for a New Methodology", *Human Rights Quarterly*, Vol. 16, No. 1, 1994, pp. 131–162.

Harris D. and Darcy J., *The European Social Charter: The Protection of Economic and Social Rights in Europe*, 2nd edition, New York, Transnational Publishers Inc., Ardsley/New York, 2001.

Hellsten J., *On Social and Economic Factors in the Developing European Labour Law, Reasoning on Collective Redundancies, Transfer of Undertakings and Converse Pyramids*, Stockholm, Elanders Gotab, 2005.

Herring J., *Older People in Law and Society*, Oxford, OUP, 2009.

Hohmann J., *The Right to Housing: Law, Concepts, Possibilities*, Oxford, Hart Publishing, 2013.

Hungler S., *The Dual Nature of Employee Involvement*, Paris, L'Harmattan, 2020.

Ichino P., "I Giuslavoristi e la Scienza Economica: Istruzioni per l'Uso", CSDLE Massimo D'Antona 2005.

Ichino P., *Lezioni di Diritto del Lavoro. Un Approccio di Labour Law and Economics*, Padova, Cedam, 2008.

ILO, *International Labour Standards. A Global Approach*, Odero A. (eds.), International Labour Office, Geneva, 2002.

Imbert P.-H., "Droits des Pauvres, Pauvre(s) Droit(s)? Réflexions sur les Droits Economiques, Sociaux et Culturels", *Revue de Droit Public*, No. 1, 1989, pp. 739–754.

Jacqmain J., "La Négociation Collective dans les Services Publics et la Charte Sociale Européenne", *Chroniques de Droit Social*, No. 7, 2006, pp. 369–370.

Jagodzinski R. (ed.), *Variations on a Theme? The Implementation of the EWC Recast Directive*, Brussels, ETUI, 2015.

Jaspers T., "Article 22 The Right to Take Part in the Determination and Improvement of the Working Conditions and Working Environment", in Ales E., Bell M., Deinert O., and Robin-Olivier S. (eds.), *International and European Labour Law. Article-by-Article Commentary*, Nomos/Beck/Hart, Baden-Baden/München/Oxford, 2018, pp. 330–336.

Jimena Quesada L., "El Derecho a la Protección contra la Pobreza y la Exclusión Social como Paradigma del Respeto de la Dignidad Humana. La Inserción del Ingreso Mínimo Vital en el Marco de la Evolución de los Estándares Internacionales", *Lex Social: Revista de Derechos Sociales*, 2020, 10(2), pp. 361–423. https://doi.org/10.46661/lexsocial.5073.

Jones J., "Human Dignity in the EU Charter of Fundamental Rights and its Interpretation before the European Court of Justice", *Liverpool Law Review*, 2012, pp. 281–300.

Kenna P. and Uhry M., "FEANTSA v. France: Collective Complaint on Housing Rights at Council of Europe", *Housing and ESC Rights Law Quarterly*, Vol. 5, No. 3, 2008, pp. 1–4.

Kenna P., "Housing Rights: Positive Duties and Enforceable Rights at the European Court of Human Rights", *European Human Rights Law Review*, Vol. 8, No. 2, 2008, pp. 193–208.

Kenna P., "International Instruments on Housing Rights", *Journal of Legal Affairs and Dispute Resolution in Engineering and Construction*, Vol. 2, No. 1, 2010, pp. 11–20.

Kenner J. and Peake K., "Article 33 – Family and Professional Life", in Peers S., Hervey T., Kenner J. and Ward A. (eds.), *The EU Charter of Fundamental Rights. A Commentary*, 2nd ed., Oxford, Hart, 2021, pp. 943–984.

Kenner J., "Protection in the Event of Unjustified Dismissal", in Peers S. *et al.* (eds.), *The EU Charter of Fundamental Rights: A Commentary*, Oxford, Hart, 2021, pp. 837–873.

Kollonay Lehoczky C. and Kresal B., "Article 33 – Family and Professional Life", in Dorssemont F., Lörcher K., Clauwaert S. and Schmitt M. (eds.), *The Charter of Fundamental Rights of the European Union and the Employment Relation*, Oxford and Portland, Hart, 2019, pp. 583–605.

Kollonay Lehoczky C., "The Fundamental Right of Workers to Information and Consultation Under the European Social Charter", in Dorssemont F. and Blanke T. (eds.), *The Recast of the European Works Council Directive*, Antwerpen, Intersentia, 2010, pp. 3–29.

Kollonay-Lehoczky C., "The Right to Equal Opportunities and Equal Treatment in Matters of Employment and Occupation Without Discrimination on the Grounds of Sex", in Bruun N., Lörcher K., Schömann I. and Clauwaert S. (eds.), *The European Social Charter and the Employment Relation*, Oxford, Hart Publishing, 2017, pp. 358–380.

Kotsoni M., "Placing Gender Equality in the Workplace at the Forefront of Social Rights in Europe: Equal Pay and Equal Opportunities Under the Scrutiny of the European Committee of Social Rights", *Strasbourg Observers*, 5 October 2020, available at https://strasbourgobservers.com/2020/10/05/placing-gender-equality-in-the-workplace-at-the-forefront-of-social-rights-in-europe-equal-pay-and-equal-opportunities-under-the-scrutiny-of-the-european-committee-of-social-rights/.

Kowal P. and Dowd J. E., *Definition of an Older Person. Proposed Working Definition of an Older Person in Africa for the MDS Project*, World Health Organization, 2001.

Kresal B., "Gender Pay Gap and Under-Representation of Women in Decision-Making Positions: UWE Decisions of the European Committee of Social Rights", *ERA Forum*, No. 22, 2021, pp. 311–325.

Kucs A., Sedlova Z. and Pierhurovica L., "The Right to Housing: International, European and National Perspectives", *Cuadernos Constitucionales de la Cátedra Fadrique Furió Ceriol*, No. 64/65, 2008, pp. 101–123.

Laulom S., "Better Regulation and the Social Acquisition: Is the REFIT Fit for Purpose?", *European Labour Law Journal*, Vol. 9, No. 1, 2018, pp. 7–23.

Leckie S., "Another Step towards Indivisibility: Identifying the Key Features of Violations of Economic, Social and Cultural Rights", *Human Rights Quarterly*, Vol. 20, No. 1, 1998, pp. 81–99.

Leckie S., "The Human Right to Adequate Housing", in Aide A., Krause C. and Rosas A. (eds.), *Economic, Social and Cultural Rights*, 2nd edition, Dordrecht-Boston-London, Martinus Nijhoff Publishers, 2002, pp. 149–168.

Lenoir R., *Les Exclus*, Paris, Seuil, 1976.

Leymann H., *The Mobbing Encyclopaedia*, http://www.leymann.se/English/12100E.HTM.

Luhmann N., *Social Systems*, Stanford University Press, 1984, reed. 1996.

Lukas K., *The Revised European Social Charter – An Article-by-Article Commentary*, Cheltenham/Northampton, Edward Elgar Publishing, 2021.

Márquez Prieto A., "Derecho a Participar en la Determinación y en la Mejora de las Condiciones de Trabajo y del Entorno de Trabajo. Artículo 22 de la Carta Social Europea", in Monereo Atienza C. and Monereo Pérez J. L. (coord.), *La Garantía Multinivel de los Derechos Fundamentales en el Consejo de Europa: El Convenio Europeo de Derechos Humanos y la Carta Social Europea*, 2017, pp. 809–819.

Mazeaud A., "Harcèlement entre Salariés: Apport de la Loi de Modernisation Sociale", *Droit Social*, No. 3, 2002, pp. 321–324.

McCrudden C., "Human Dignity and Judicial Interpretation of Human Rights", *The European Journal of International Law*, Vol. 19, No. 4, 2008, pp. 655–724.

McGaughey E., "Behavioural Economics and Labour Law", King's College, 2015, pp. 1–36.

Mijatovic D., *The Right to Affordable Housing: Europe's Neglected Duty*, 23 January 2020, https://www.coe.int/fr/web/commissioner/blog/-/asset_publisher/xZ32OPEoxOkq/content/id/57979683?_com_liferay_asset_publisher_web_portlet_AssetPublisherPortlet_INSTANCE_xZ32OPEoxOkq_languageId=en_GB#p_com_liferay_asset_publisher_web_portlet_AssetPublisherPortlet_INSTANCE_xZ32OPEoxOkq.

Mikkola M., "Housing as a Human Right in Europe", *European Journal of Social Security*, Vol. 10, No. 3, 2008, pp. 249–294.

Mikkola M., *Social Human Rights*, Helsinki, Karelactio, 2010.

Mikolajczyc B., "The Council of Europe's Approach Towards Ageism", in *Contemporary Perspectives on Ageing*, Ayalon, Liat/Tesch Römer, Clemens, Springer Verlag, 2013, Vol. 19, pp. 321–339.

Monteiro A. P., "Das Incapacidades ao Maior Acompanhado – Breve Apresentação da Lei n.º 49/2018", in *O Novo Regime do Maior Acompanhado*, Lisboa, Centro de Estudos Judiciários, 2019, pp. 33–38.

Moons N., *The Right to Housing in Law and Society*, New York, Routledge, 2018.

Mückenberger U. and Lühr H.-H., "Dokumentation zum Rationalisierungsschutz", *Kritische Justiz*, No. 13, 1980, pp. 84–102.

Muller A., "Employment Protection Legislation Tested by the Economic Crisis. A Global Review of the Regulation of Collective Dismissals for Economic Reasons", *Dialogue in Brief*, No. 3, Geneva, ILO, 2011.

Nivard C., "Conclusion", in Derdek N. and Kenna P. (eds.), *The European and International Contribution to the Right to Housing: Standards, Litigation and Advocacy*, Brussels, Abbé Pierre Foundation – FEANTSA – University of Galway, 2023, pp. 123–136.

Nivard C., *La Justiciabilité des Droits Sociaux. Etude de Droit Conventionnel Européen*, Bruxelles, Bruylant, 2012.

Orimo H., Ito H., Suzuki T., Araki A., Hosoi Y., Sawabe M., "Reviewing the Definition of 'Elderly'", *Geriatrics and Gerontology International*, Vol. 6, No. 3, February 2005, pp. 149–156.

Palmisano G., *L'Europa dei Diritti Sociali*, Bologna, Il Mulino, 2022.

Payne B., *Crime & Elder Abuse, an Integrated Perspective*, 3rd edition, Illinois, Charles C. Thomas Publisher Ltd., 2011.

Perrone F., "La Forza Vincolante delle Decisioni del Comitato Europeo dei Diritti Sociali: Riflessioni Critiche alla Luce della Decisione CGIL c. Italia dell'11 Febbraio 2020 sul Jobs Act sulle Tutele Crescenti", *Lavoro Diritti Europa*, 2020, pp. 1–12.

Raday F., "Article 11", in Freeman M.A., Chinkin C. and Rudolf B. (eds.), *The UN Convention on the Elimination of All Forms of Discrimination against Women. A Commentary*, Oxford, Oxford University Press, 2012, pp. 279–310.

Riesenhuber K., *European Employment Law. A Systematic Exposition*, 2nd ed., Cambridge, Intersentia, 2021.

Rocca M., "The European Social Charter and the European Union", in ANESC, *The European Social Charter: A Commentary*, Vol. 1, Leiden, Brill, 2022, pp. 375–401.

Rodriguez-Pinzon D. and Martin C., "The International Human Rights Status of Elderly Persons", *American University International Law Review*, No. 18, 2003, pp. 915–1008.

Roman D., *Le Droit Public face à la Pauvreté*, Paris, LGDJ, 2002.

Rossi L.S., "Member States' Obligations in Relation to Housing Rights – Views of the CJEU", in Derdek N. and Kenna P. (eds.), *The European and International Contribution to the Right to Housing: Standards, Litigation and Advocacy*, Brussels, Abbé Pierre Foundation – FEANTSA – University of Galway, 2023, pp. 23–28.

Rutgers J.W., "The Right to Housing (Article 7 of the Charter) and Unfair Terms in General Conditions", in Collins H. (ed.), *European Contract Law and the Charter of Fundamental Rights*, Cambridge, CUP, 2017, pp. 125–138.

Salcedo Beltrán C., "Las Indemnizaciones por Despido Injustificado y el Art. 24 de la Carta Social Europea Revisada: No Hay Dos Condenas (Finlandia e Italia) sin Tres (Francia)", *Lex Social*, Vol. 12, No. 1, 2022, pp. 625–631.

Sargeant M., "Protecting Employees with Insolvent Employers", *ILJ*, Vol. 32, No. 1, March 2003, pp. 53–59.

Saul B., Kinley D. and Mowbray J., *The International Covenant on Economic, Social and Cultural Rights. Commentary, Cases and Materials*, Oxford, Oxford University Press, 2014.

Schabas WA, *The European Convention on Human Rights. A Commentary*, Oxford, Oxford University Press, 2015.

Schmitt M., "The Right to Protection in Cases of Termination of Employment", in Bruun N. *et al.* (eds.), *The European Social Charter and the Employment Relation*, Oxford and Portland, Hart Publishing, 2017, pp. 412–438.

Schwab S., "Law-and-Economics Approaches to Labour and Employment Law", *International Journal of Comparative Labour Law and Industrial Relations*, Vol. 33, Issue 1, 2017, pp. 115–144.

Sepúlveda Carmona M., "Guiding Principles on Extreme Poverty and Human Rights", submitted by the Special Rapporteur on extreme poverty and human rights, adopted by the General Assembly on 18 July 2012 and by the United Nations Human Rights Council on 27 September 2012, A/HRC/21/39.

Schömann I., "Article 27. The Right of Workers with Family Responsibilities to Equal Opportunities and Equal Treatment", in Bruun N., Lörcher K., Schömann I and Clauwaert S. (eds.), *The European Social Charter and the Employment Relation*, Oxford and Portland, Hart, 2017, pp. 454–466.

Smusz-Kulesza M., "The Right to Housing in the Light of the European Social Charter", *Nieruchomości@*, Vol. 1, No. 1, 2023, pp. 123–142.

Solanes Mullor J., "The Right to Housing and the Protection of Family Life and Vulnerable Groups: European Judicial Activism", in Gonzales Pascual M. and Torres Perez A. (eds.), *The Right to Family Life in the European Union*, London, Routledge, 2017, pp. 214–231.

Sole M., "Employees' Right to Information and Consultation: A Risky Right?", in *Sui Generis. Festschrift in Honour of Professor Stein Evju*, University of Oslo, 2016, pp. 613–623.

Spanier B., Doron I. and Milman-Sivan F., "Older Persons' Use of the European Court of Human Rights", *Journal of Cross-Cultural Gerontology*, No. 28, 2013, pp. 407–420.

Spanier B., Doron I., "The European Social Charter and the Rights of Older Persons", in *Ageing, Ageism, and the Law: European Perspectives on the Rights of Older Persons*, Cheltenham, Edward Elgar Publishing, 2018, pp. 146–173.

Ssenyonjo M., *Economic, Social and Cultural Rights in International Law*, 2nd edition, London, Hart Publishing/Bloomsbury, 2016.

Straziuso E., "La Carta Sociale del Consiglio d'Europa e l'Organo di Controllo: Il Comitato Europeo dei Diritti Sociali. Nuovi Sviluppi e Prospettive di Tutela" (Gruppo di Pisa, 2012), available at: http://www.gruppodipisa.it/wp-content/uploads/2012/09/StraziusoDEF.pdf.

Supiot A., *Le Droit du Travail*, 4e éd. mise à jour, Paris, Puf, 2009.

Swiatkowski A. M., *Charter of Social Rights of the Council of Europe*, Alphen aan den Rijn, Kluwer Law International, 2007.

Świątkowski A.M., *Labour Law: Council of Europe*, 4th edition, Zuidpoolsingel, Wolters Kluwer, 2021.

Therborn G. *et al.*, "The 1970s and 1980s as a Turning Point in European History?", *Journal of Modern European History*, Vol. 9, No. 1, 2011, pp. 8–26.

Tissot O., "Pour une Analyse Juridique du Concept de 'Dignité' du Salarié", *Droit Social*, No. 12, 1995, pp. 972–977.

Toth M. A., "The Right to Dignity at Work: Reflections on Article 26 of the Revised European Social Charter", *Comparative Labor Law and Policy*, Vol. 29, 2008, pp. 275–316.

Tulkens F. and Van Drooghenbroeck S., "Le Droit au Logement dans la Convention Européenne des Droits de L'Homme. Bilan et Perspectives", in Bernard N. and Mertens C. (eds.), *Le Logement dans sa Multidimensionnalité: une Grande Cause Régionale*, Namur, Ministère de la Région Wallonne, collection Études et Documents, 2005, pp. 311–325.

Vandamme F., "The Revision of the European Social Charter", *ILR*, Vol. 133, No. 5–6, 1994, pp. 635–655.

Vandenberghe A. S., "Employment Contracts", in *Labour and Employment Law and Economics*, Cheltenham, Edward Elgar Publishing, 2009, pp. 61–95.

Veneziani B., "Article 27 – Worker's Right to Information and Consultation within the Undertaking", in Dorssemont F. *et al.* (eds.), *The Charter of Fundamental Rights of the European Union and the Employment Relation*, Oxford, Hart, 2019, pp. 429–463.

Veneziani B., "Article 29. The Right to Information and Consultation in Collective Redundancy Procedures", in Bruun N. *et al.* (eds.), *The European Social Charter and the Employment Relation*, Oxford, Hart, 2017, pp. 477–492.

Viscomi A., "Labour, Law and Economics", *Hungarian Labour Law E-Journal*, Vol. 67, 2015, pp. 67–82.

Waquet P., *L'Entreprise et les Libertés du Salarié*, Paris, Éditions Liaisons, 2003.

Weiss M., "Challenges for Workers' Participation", in Addabbo T. *et al.* (eds.), *The Collective Dimensions of Employment Relations*, London, Palgrave Macmillan, 2021, pp. 15–28.

Wresinski J., "Grande Pauvreté et Précarité Economique et Sociale", Rapport au Conseil Economique et Social, Paris, *Journal officiel*, 1987.

www.ingramcontent.com/pod-product-compliance
Lightning Source LLC
LaVergne TN
LVHW020653300926
849161LV00004B/931